Competition and Efficiency in a Unified European Banking Market

Competition and Efficiency in a Unified European Banking Market

Jacob A. Bikker

Senior economist, Section Banking and Supervisory Strategies
De Nederlandsche Bank
Amsterdam, the Netherlands

Edward Elgar
Cheltenham, UK • Northampton, MA, USA

Published by
Edward Elgar Publishing Limited
Glensanda House
Montpellier Parade
Cheltenham
Glos GL50 1UA
UK

Edward Elgar Publishing, Inc.
136 West Street
Suite 202
Northampton
Massachusetts 01060
USA

A catalogue record for this book
is available from the British Library

Library of Congress Cataloguing in Publication Data

Bikker, Jacob A., 1952-
Competition and efficiency in a unified European banking market / Jacob A. Bikker.
p. cm.
Includes bibliographical references and index.
1. Banks and banking—Europe. 2. Competition—Europe. I. Title.

HG2974.B55 2004
332.1'094—dc22

2003049446

ISBN 1 84376 110 6

Printed and bound in Great Britain by MPG Books Ltd, Bodmin, Cornwall

Contents

Figures

Tables

Preface

This book embodies the results of several years of research on competition, concentration, efficiency and performance in the European banking market. It measures unobservable variables such as competition and efficiency, using different approaches. It seeks to explain the various characteristics of the banking industry in the European Union and where possible to interrelate them. Comparison across European countries and with countries outside Europe is central in all investigated areas. All chapters are written as self-contained sections, so that they can be read separately.

Most chapters are based on articles which have been published in refereed academic journals.[1] They are used in rewritten form in this book with kind permission of the editors of the respective journals. Chapters 2–7 are based on, respectively, Bikker and Wesseling (2003a, b), Bikker and Haaf (2002a, b), Bikker (2002a, 2003) and Bikker and Hu (2002) and were published in *Maandschrift Economie, DNB Occasional Papers* (in Dutch and English, respectively), *Economic & Financial Modelling, Journal of Banking & Finance, Kredit und Kapital* (twice) and *Banca Nazionale del Lavoro Quarterly Review.* Furthermore, some sections draw on Bikker and Groeneveld (2000) and Bikker (2001), published in *Kredit und Kapital* and *Cahiers Economiques de Bruxelles*, respectively. Earlier versions of most of these articles have come out as DNB Staff Reports, a refereed series published by the Nederlandsche Bank.[2]

First drafts have been presented at academic conferences, such as the Annual meetings of the American 'Western Economic Association International' in 1998 in Lake Tahoe (Bikker and Groeneveld, 2000), in 1999 in San Diego (Bikker, 2001), in 2000 in Vancouver (Bikker and Haaf, 2002b) and in 2001 in San Francisco (Bikker, 2002a), the 'Workshop on empirical research on banking supervision and structure' of the Basel Committee on Banking Supervision in June 1999 in Amsterdam (Bikker, 2001), the conference 'Financial Structure, Bank Behaviour and Monetary Policy in the EU' in 2000 at the University of Groningen, the Netherlands (Bikker and Haaf, 2002b), various national research seminars in the Netherlands (such as

'NAKE'), and at other meetings such as in 17 June 2002 at the Bank of Finland in Helsinki. Furthermore, almost all draft articles have been discussed also in the 'Research group on Financial Stability' and departmental colloquiums at the Nederlandsche Bank.

I owe a debt of gratitude to the editors for permission of reuse of the articles, to my co-authors Hans Groeneveld, Katharina Haaf, Haixia Hu and Sandra Wesseling for the pleasant and fruitful cooperation, to unknown referees for the journals and the DNB Staff Reports as well as to participants of the conferences and meetings mentioned above for their stimulating and useful remarks. Special acknowledgement for research assistance is due to Miriam Holman-Rijken (Chapters 2–6) and Danny van den Kommer (Chapters 2 and 7). I am grateful to my employer, the Nederlandsche Bank, for the opportunity to convert earlier papers into this book, and to Job Swank, Klaas Knot and Maarten Gelderman, successive heads of the 'Section Banking and Supervisory Strategies' of the Directorate Supervision, for their stimulating guidance and valuable comment. I am appreciative of René Kurpershoek for his help to correct and improve my English. Finally, I am obliged to Anne-Marie Runderkamp, who has assisted in transforming the original text into the format of the publisher and to Herman Eijhusen who has solved many mysteries of 'Word'. All remaining errors are mine.

Jacob A. Bikker [3]

NOTES

1. Or written for this book and thereafter submitted for publication elsewhere, such as Chapter 2.
2. Bikker and Groeneveld (2000), Bikker (2001), Bikker and Haaf (2002b), Bikker and Hu (2002) and Bikker (2002a) appeared in DNB Staff Reports numbers 26 (1998), 42 (1999), 68 (2001), 86 and 87 (2002), respectively.
3. Section Banking and Supervisory Strategies, Directorate Supervision, De Nederlandsche Bank, POBox 98, NL-1000 AB Amsterdam, the Netherlands. Email address: j.a.bikker@dnb.nl; Fax: 00 31 20 524 3669; Tel.: 00 31 20 524 2352. The views expressed in this book are those of the author and not necessarily those of the Nederlandsche Bank.

For Ineke

1. Introduction to market structure, competition and efficiency

1.1 MARKET STRUCTURE AND CONDUCT

In the current era, market structure and competition in the European financial system are major economic and policy issues. Liberalization and harmonization in the European Union (EU), culminating in the Second Banking Co-ordination Directive as part of the single European market project in 1992[1] and the establishment of Economic and Monetary Union (EMU) in 1999, have dramatically changed the financial environment in Europe in the past decade and are expected to bring further changes in the near future.[2] The creation of large and transparent euro capital markets further enhanced competition in the European banking industry and stimulated disintermediation and securitization. The comparative advantages of domestic banks on the domestic markets for bonds and equity in the field of underwriting and trading activities have diminished since the euro has replaced national currencies. For similar reasons, fund management is no longer the preserve of local financial institutions. These contributions to international integration, together with national deregulation and entry of new types of competitors, have boosted competition between banks in the countries involved and will continue to do so in the years to come. All these developments contribute to further consolidation and rationalization in the European banking sectors.[3]

Moreover, EMU will also further increase the pressure for ongoing harmonization of regulation across EU countries, cutting down remaining obstacles to cross-border competition. The Financial Service Action Plan of the EU (released in late 2002 and to be implemented in 2005) seeks to finalize the integration of the EU financial markets. Especially regarding the retail markets, more progress in terms of harmonization is needed in order to establish a fully integrated market. Examples of impediments are diverging regulation for consumer protection and varying implementation of regulation across countries, and high cross-border costs of payments and asset transactions (European Commission, 2002).

The upcoming new Basel Accord on capital requirements, a new regulatory regime for banks (expected to be released in mid 2004 and to enter into force by end 2006), is another new development which will affect competition, consolidation and efficiency in the banking industry. The effect on competition is extremely difficult to predict. The Basel II framework will closely parallel perceptions of riskiness among banks. This may increase competition in some areas, as banks will be better aware of their risks and price them more accurately, instead of relying on, for example, cross-subsidizing in a more loose sense. It may also reduce competition, as all banks face similar conditions and need certain minimum profit margins, instead of aiming at higher market shares. An opposite effect is the reinforcement in Basel II of supervisory discretion which may lead to a deterioration of the level playing field across countries and cripple foreign competition. Basel II may also affect the position of nonregulated financial firms, such as investment banks and pension funds, which are exempt from capital requirements. The new Accord will bring a certain alignment between capital requirement for regulated firms and capital hold by (at least part of the) nonregulated firms, capital levels often being determined by economic capital models or similar advanced risk measurement techniques.[4] This will improve the level playing field and hence increase fair competition. Transparency will encourage competition and improve efficiency. Market participants will be better informed regarding the real risk of banks and this will affect their funding cost, so that the underlying risks are better priced.

While individual banks may face higher or lower capital requirements, affecting their competitive positions, this may not necessarily affect overall competition, as these effects may cancel each other out. Competitive conditions for smaller banks will be less favourable, as they find it more difficult and expensive to meet the many requirements of the more advanced approaches, such as data collection and storage requirements, model building and organizational requirements. The capital requirements under the 'simple' standardized approach are higher than those imposed by the more advanced approaches. Ongoing consolidation is likely, as the most advanced – and most effective capital-saving – techniques are accessible to only the most sophisticated banks.

The great changes brought about by European economic and financial integration have also put the spotlight on the differences between individual EU countries, especially as regards the starting positions of their banking sectors. For instance, Vives (1991) observed that some EU countries had relatively highly concentrated banking sectors, whereas others faced excess capacity. He asserted that, as a consequence, significant differences in competitive conditions and efficiency existed in banking markets across the

EU countries. The question arises how these country-specific positions have evolved over time.

There are many reasons why market conditions in the banking industry deserve particular attention. To begin with, competition and efficiency developments may have powerful effects on social welfare. Among economic players, it is especially small- and medium-sized firms and consumers that are dependent on banks and have the greatest interest in fair market conditions, that is to say a broad supply of bank services and low prices. High competition and high efficiency may favour that interest. It has long been recognized that well-developed financial markets are essential to economic development (for an overview, see Guzman, 2000). More recently, this has been demonstrated empirically by King and Levine (1993), among others. For instance, further financial integration within the EU, as mentioned above, would lower capital cost, make for a more efficient allocation of capital, and is estimated to result in an increase of gross domestic product (gdp) by 0.8 per cent (European Commission, 2002). Secondly, the soundness and stability of the financial sector may in various ways be influenced by the degree of competition and concentration. Safeguarding the health of the financial system has become one of the key objectives of financial authorities, such as central banks and bank supervisors. Thirdly, inefficient banks are easy takeover prey. In countries where banks are less efficient, large-scale consolidation and rationalization of the banking industry will be unavoidable and even necessary in order to improve the national banking system's soundness and survival prospects.

Finally, Kashyap and Stein (1997) and Cecchetti (1999) argue that the banking system's concentration and health are essential to the analysis of the effectiveness of monetary policy. These authors illustrate that within EMU there are substantial differences in banking structure, which are likely to accentuate the differential impact of monetary policy across EMU members. Countries with high concentration, having higher market power and higher efficiency, will be affected less strongly by the credit channel than countries with smaller banks. After all, smaller banks have weaker balance sheet structures and poorer ability to raise reasonably priced external funds, and are therefore more likely to reduce lending in the event of monetary contraction. The way large colluding banks affect the transmission of monetary policy depends on the structure of the market (Lensink and Sterken, 2002).

Using various theoretical frameworks, this book will test empirically the validity of these qualitative and quantitative notions about market structure, competition and efficiency in the European banking industry. Furthermore, it seeks to reveal different starting positions across the EU countries and the changes therein, in order to assess the current situation.

1.1.1 Market Structure

Market structure is a broad concept, covering many aspects of banking environment and behaviour. This book will focus mainly on measurable characteristics such as numbers of banks and size distributions, which also determine concentration, and on unobservable qualities such as types of markets in terms of competitive behaviour, such as monopoly, perfect collusion, oligopoly, monopolistic competition or perfect competition, on the one hand, and the degree of competition and efficiency, on the other. With respect to these distinguished market features, the question arises how the 'natural' market structure of the banking sector may be characterized. A long-standing view in the literature is that this largely depends on the existence of scale or scope efficiencies or, more precisely, the multiproduct cost subadditivity in banking (Baumol, 1977, among others). Numerous empirical studies have been devoted to this topic (for instance, Berger et al., 1993, and Molyneux et al., 1996). Most studies reach the conclusion that the market conditions prevailing in banking sectors can best be characterized as naturally oligopolistic. This means that – in the long term – there is room for only a few banks. In this context, a highly concentrated banking sector would be the logical outcome of market forces. A countervailing power leading to continuation of the existence of at least some smaller banks or to the entry of new ones, might be ongoing specialization and the servicing of niche markets, a process that is supported by new technologies such as the Internet.

Concentration and capacity in the European banking markets have been investigated in a number of studies (see Baltensperger and Dermine, 1990; Caminal et al., 1990; Molyneux and Forbes, 1995; Group of Ten, 2001). Commonly, the share of assets (or loans or deposits) of the three, five or ten largest banks in a country's total bank assets (loans or deposits) is used to proxy concentration levels in banking markets. Alternative yardsticks of concentration and capacity are the numbers of banks and of branches. Without exception, these articles reveal a striking feature of European banking markets. In line with the theory referred to above, a handful of large banks tends to emerge over time in almost every country, whether through government encouragement (foreseeing the need for larger and more viable banks) or through pure market mechanisms.

Once the level of concentration in banking markets has been identified, the question arises as to what its consequences are for bank behaviour. The theoretical literature suggests that the nature of the link between market structure and market conduct is ambiguous. In certain circumstances, a highly concentrated banking sector can impair competition. The maintained assumption in that case is then that concentration translates into greater market power, translating into collusive behaviour and excess profits for financial institutions (Gual and Neven, 1992). This is in line with the traditional structure–conduct–performance (SCP) paradigm (Bos, 2002,

Chapter 2). The SCP paradigm states that increased concentration fosters collusion and anti-competitive practices. Yet we should acknowledge that some market segments are presumably somewhat more competitive than others. For example, it is difficult for banks to acquire and exercise substantial power in the market for large corporate loans, because many foreign banks compete for that business. Indeed, Neven and Röller (1995) found a higher degree of collusion in the retail segment of seven European countries than in their wholesale markets. This stresses the need to investigate separate submarkets.

This line of reasoning in the SCP paradigm is challenged, however, by two other theoretical strands. The *contestability theory* stresses that a concentrated banking industry may nevertheless behave competitively, if the hurdles to be surmounted by potential entrants to the market are low (Baumol, 1982, Baumol et al., 1982). This theory asserts that the threat of potential entry forces banks with large market shares to price their products competitively under certain conditions. In a perfectly contestable market, there are no entry barriers, neither economic nor legal, so that entry is absolutely free. Other conditions are that exit is completely costless and that demands for bank industry outputs are highly price-elastic. Costless exit implies that a firm considering to enter a new market expects to recover fixed costs, for example, through the sale of assets, if it might later decide to withdraw. These entry and exit features and highly price-elastic demands imply that a contestable market can be effectively competitive, even if it has only a small number of active players. If the proponents of the contestability theory are correct, widely expressed concerns about the domination of a country's financial system by a single type of financial intermediaries may be valid only to the extent that financial markets are not contestable (Nathan and Neave, 1989).

The second theory challenging the SCP model is the *efficiency hypothesis.* This theory states that if a bank enjoys a higher degree of efficiency than its competitors, it can choose between two opposite strategies. The first is to maximize profits by maintaining the present levels of prices and firm size. In this case, the better qualities or market conditions of a bank are employed to increase shareholder value. The second strategy is to maximize profits by reducing prices and expanding firm size. Under the second option, the most efficient banks will gain market share at the cost of less efficient banks. In that case, bank efficiency will be the driving force behind the process of market concentration. Hence, concentration does not have to lead to abuse of market power and higher profits as assumed in the SCP paradigm, but may go hand in hand with lower prices as in the case of high(er) competition. The contestability and the efficiency hypotheses suggest that the competitive environment of banks does not necessarily suffer from market concentration.

For European countries, one of the crucial assumptions underlying the contestability hypothesis, that is free entry and exit, was definitely not satisfied until the late 1980s. Government intervention in most of the banking systems in Europe was fairly extensive up to the mid-1980s. Banks were also legally restricted in their activities both within their national markets and across borders. Some countries applied capital restrictions or erected high obstacles to the establishment of branches by foreign banks (Bisignano, 1992). This tight regulatory environment was relaxed considerably with the adoption of the Second Banking Co-ordination Directive of 1992 as part of the single European market project. These changes make clear that, from the beginning of the nineties, most or all the conditions posed by the contestable hypothesis have been fulfilled, so that this theory can be considered as possibly valid for the European banking sectors.

Chapter 4.4 of this book investigates the link between market structure and competition, testing implicitly the validity of either the structure–conduct part of the SCP paradigm, or one of the alternative theories, the contestability or efficiency paradigm for the European banking industry. For this purpose, the market structure is measured in terms of the number of banks and in terms of one of the various concentration indices, while our proxy of competition is the competitive nature of banking markets as assessed using the Panzar–Rosse approach, to be introduced later. Theoretical and practical characteristics of the various concentration indices, under consideration for the concentration–competition relationship are surveyed in Chapter 3.

1.1.2 Market Conduct

Surprisingly, empirical investigations of market conduct and competition in the EU banking industry are fairly scarce. One obvious reason is that competition cannot be observed directly. This is why competition and other unobservables in the banking industry, such as inefficiency, are often proxied by simple ratios, as discussed in Section 1.2 below. Another reason is that a fully ideal and convincing theoretical measurement framework is lacking. Nevertheless, approaches by Bresnahan (1982, 1989) and, in particular, Panzar and Rosse (1987) are fairly useful and therefore will be discussed below.[5] These methods were first applied to banks in the USA, Canada and Japan, but in later years investigations were published for both single countries and small groups of countries in Europe.[6] The largest number of countries investigated by one study was five. Hence a convincing and truly multicountry study for Europe has so far been lacking.

Panzar and Rosse

The major part of this book tries to fill this gap and extends previous studies on market structure and competition in European banking in several respects. The two approaches mentioned above are applied to examine the overall market conditions in which banks of the EU Member States operate. The first approach, a slightly amended version of the Panzar–Rosse (P–R) methodology, will be applied to all OECD countries, which allows a comparison of Europe with the rest of the world. Panzar and Rosse constructed a so-called *H*-statistic, which creates the possibility to make a quantitative assessment of the competitive nature of banking markets and the market power of banks. The *H*-statistic is calculated from a reduced-form revenue equation and measures the sum of elasticities of a bank's total revenue with respect to the bank's input prices. The testable hypotheses are: the banking industry is characterized by monopoly for $H \leq 0$, monopolistic competition or oligopoly for $0 < H < 1$ and perfect competition for $H = 1$. Furthermore, *H* increases with the competitiveness of the banking industry. In order to have such measure of competition, Chapter 4 applies this framework to the EU as a whole as well as to each separate national banking sector.

In contrast to the original P–R framework, we explicitly account for possible gradual changes in the market structure over time by introducing a time–curve model, which allows for a pooled cross-section and time–series analysis. Apart from a better model fit, this amended model also yields information about the effects which the liberalization and deregulation of international capital markets have had, over time, on the competitiveness of European banking markets.

H reflects the structure and conduct of the market in which the bank operates, which is not necessarily identical to the competitive situation prevailing in the country where the bank is located. Large universal banks with sizeable foreign activities are obviously confronted by other competitive forces than small regional banks.[7] We apply the P–R approach to three size classes, small banks that operate mostly on a local scale, large banks which compete more than others at the international level, and medium-sized banks which occupy an intermediate position.[8] Particularly, retail banking is assumed to be concentrated mostly in small banks, while corporate banking is primarily the domain of large banks. This allows us to investigate the effect of size (large versus small) of markets on competition and thereby to acquire some information about the effect of nature (wholesale versus retail or international versus local). Although what we would be really interested in are direct estimates from wholesale and retail markets, this is at least a step in the right direction.

Bresnahan

The second approach used in this book is that of Bresnahan (1982, 1989), who developed an equilibrium model for volumes and prices based on demand and supply equations and profit maximization. In this model prices are assumed to have a mark-up, whose size is dependent on the price elasticity of demand. The degree to which this mark-up is exploited (λ) can be estimated. Under perfect collusion or monopoly, this profit margin is utilised fully ($\lambda = 1$), whereas under perfect competition it cannot be used at all ($\lambda = 0$). Intermediate λs correspond to other oligopoly concepts. An advantage of the Bresnahan approach is that, owing both to its nature and to its data requirements – and unlike the P–R approach – it allows the investigation of submarkets. Chapter 5 applies Bresnahan's model to two submarkets, deposits and loans, in nine EU countries. In comparing market power for so many countries, this survey is unique in this body of literature. The deposit market reflects banks' competitive conditions with respect to funding and hence mirrors their activities on the liabilities side of the balance sheet. The product or service considered here is the supply of deposit facilities. This retail market is interesting because it is by nature localized, so that the number of competing banks tends to be limited, except for the more recently mushroomed Internet banks.[9] The loan market refers to the main (traditional) activity of banks, lending, which is representative of the assets side of the balance sheet. The credit lending market has mainly a nation-wide or international dimension, as far as we may assume that only smaller amounts are involved in lending to (local) small- and medium-sized enterprises.

1.2 EFFICIENCY AND ITS MEASUREMENT

One of the major effects of banking competition is that it improves banking efficiency. Under perfect competition or market conditions not far removed from that situation, less efficient banks will be driven out of the market.[10] Hence the increase of competition as observed or expected in the EU, as a consequence of deregulation, integration and harmonization, will most probably also affect efficiency. Eventually, the expected increase in competition most probably leads to further consolidation and rationalization in the European banking sectors. Less efficient banks are more likely to run the risk of being taken over. Large-scale rationalization will affect employment. For each of the European nations, the degree of inefficiency of its banks is vitally important for public policy with respect to the viability of its banking industry in the near future.

All these developments have stirred up interest in the measurement of bank efficiency. In more recent years, the emphasis of this research area has shifted from scale and scope economies towards technical and allocative inefficiency. These two measures may be combined to provide a measure of total *economic efficiency*, or, if cost instead of production is considered, *cost efficiency.* The managerial ability to decide on input and output in order to minimize cost or maximize revenues is referred to as X-efficiency.

Like competition, efficiency cannot be observed directly. The cost frontier approach seeks to measure this type of inefficiency as the deviation of costs from the so-called efficient frontier, which is the estimated level of costs under optimal behaviour. Chapter 6 applies the stochastic cost frontier approach to the European banking industry in an attempt to measure its efficiency and compare efficiencies across countries.[11]

Such model-based approaches are rather complicated and time-consuming. Therefore, in practice, efficiency is often estimated using related concepts, such as the cost–income ratio or the interest rate margin. Such simple proxies, however, fall short in properly measuring efficiency. This is what the next section will prove, thereby underlining the need for a more sophisticated approach, as applied in Chapter 6.

As competition and efficiency are often seen as near synonyms, in the sense that competition leads to efficiency, many of the cost–related ratios we will consider here as proxies of efficiency, are in practice also frequently used as proxies of competition. For instance, interest rate margins are often taken as proxies of competition as well.

Table 1.1 presents a number of more or less well-known proxies of – primarily – efficiency for nine European countries, consisting of the largest seven EU countries: Belgium, France, Germany, Italy, the Netherlands, Spain and the UK, plus two smaller countries with important banking sectors: Luxembourg and Switzerland. The figures relate to a year (1996) in the middle of the last decade investigated in this book. The first proxy is the ratio of operating (noninterest-rate) expenses to gross income. The interpretation of this ratio is not unambiguous. As a proxy for efficiency, a high ratio is usually assumed to indicate high efficiency, (forced by) strong competition and (as a result) low average profit rates. This interpretation supposes that tariffs of bank services, such as lending rates,[12] commissions and fees, are dictated by competition or external factors, and hence that, given the output level, revenues are more or less a residual item. An alternative view is that inefficiency causes relatively high costs, whereas profits or profit margins may be seen, to some extent, as accidental or determined by external factors. This would be the case if tariffs of bank services were determined by a mark-up on costs.[13] Here, a high ratio would reflect high costs and would indicate *in*efficiency. As the interpretation of this ratio is not unambiguous, for the moment we do not draw any conclusion from this variable.

The second proxy is the ratio of net interest rate income to the balance sheet total. Low values of this ratio reflect high efficiency, strong competition and low profit rates. In Table 1.1, in order to allow easy identification, the lowest three interest rate margins, indicating the countries with the most efficient banks among the group of nine, are shaded lightly, and the highest three ratios, referring to the countries with the least efficient banks, are shaded darkly.[14] The interest rate margin ratio may be distorted by the composition of assets and liabilities, differences in the yield curve between the countries considered, the relative size of equity capital and book-keeping operations, which enlarges or shortens the balance sheet. Other

Table 1.1 Country-specific ratios and indices related to efficiency and competition (all banks; 1996)

	Cost-income ratio	Interest rate margin	Labour cost share	Labour intensity (balance sheet)	Labour intensity (inhabitants)[a]	Intensity of branches	Index of concentration[b]	Index of competition	Diffusion index
Belgium	0.66	1.21	0.60	59	76	17.7	55	0.92	—
France	0.70	1.08	0.54	73	69	4.5	41	0.91	efficient
Germany	0.64	1.79	0.59	101	87	5.3	16	0.86	inefficient
Italy	0.67	2.53	0.65	120	57	3.7	25	0.93	—
Luxembourg	0.47	0.67	0.50	22	491	8.1	22	0.92	—
Netherlands	0.67	1.73	0.54	75	75	4.4	75	0.66	efficient
Spain	0.62	2.55	0.61	162	62	9.4	44	0.56	inefficient
Switzerland	0.66	1.18	0.52	68	163	5.1	90	—	efficient
UK	0.62	2.07	0.55	156	71	2.1	28	0.72	inefficient
	Correlations								
Cost inc. ratio	1	0.33	0.41	0.30	-0.90	-0.12	0.40	-0.06	
Int. rate margin		1	0.76	0.90	-0.64	-0.27	-0.21	-0.55	
Lab. cost share			1	0.57	-0.62	0.21	-0.31	-0.01	
Lab. int. (b.sh.)				1	-0.64	-0.32	-0.24	-0.62	
Lab. int. (inh.)					1	0.09	-0.18	0.32	
Int. of branches						1	0.13	0.16	
Concentration							1	-0.42	
Competition								1	

Notes to Table 1.1: Ratios and indices with light shading indicate countries where the banks are relatively efficient, whereas dark shading points to countries where the banks are relatively inefficient. Correlations with diagonal shading are expected to be negative, the others should be positive. Expectations with respect to the sign of the cost–income ratio correlations are undetermined.

Sources: OECD Bank Profitability; Financial Statements of Banks (1998). For Luxembourg and the UK: commercial banks, and for other countries: all banks.

[a] IMF International Financial Statistics; [b] Total assets of the five largest banks as share of total (for Switzerland: 1995).

proxies are related to excessive use of labour or branch offices, indicating less developed types of production: labour costs as share of total operating expenses, the number of employees per 10 000 inhabitants, the ratio of the number of employees and balance sheet total, and the number of branches per 10 000 inhabitants. Actually, these indices are rather poor, as they reflect only a minor part of the determinants of efficiency. Finally, we present indices of concentration and competition, which are often assumed to be (positively) related to efficiency. For concentration, the relative balance sheet total of the largest five banks is used and for competition the so-called *H*-value of Panzar and Rosse as calculated by Bikker and Groeneveld (2000).[15]

The results in Table 1.1 are not very helpful in obtaining a unanimous ranking of the efficiency of the banking sectors in the nine countries considered. Virtually every country is indicated as efficient at least once, and each country but one is also labelled as inefficient at least once. There are at least two reasons for this unsatisfactory result. Firstly, all the employed ratios and indices are, at best, remotely related to efficiency or reflect only one of its many aspects; the majority of them does not measure efficiency *directly*. Secondly, many proxies are disturbed by measurement errors or special circumstances. In Luxembourg and Switzerland, for instance, banks can attract foreign funds at lower cost, due to banking secrecy, the lack of tax on income from wealth for non-inhabitants and the stable currency, and they employ a larger part of their countries' population. Another example is the index of concentration, which tends to be higher in smaller countries. The lower part of Table 1.1 presents correlations between the ratios and indices, which are expected to be negative in the diagonal shaded area and positive elsewhere.[16] The low values confirm that the proxies do not coincide but (partly) diverge, whereas the 'wrong' signs even point to opposite patterns. Apparently, most if not all of the proxies are unreliable as indicators of efficiency.[17]

Disregarding these shortcomings, the final column of Table 1.1 presents a plain diffusion index, which just adds plusses (light shading) and minuses (dark shading) to obtain a total score. This indicator suggests that France, the Netherlands and Switzerland are rather efficient, whereas Germany, Spain and the UK are relatively inefficient. Based on direct (partial) observation or on in-depth knowledge of the countries' banking sectors, accepted wisdom has it that banks in France, Germany and, in particular, Southern European countries, such as Italy and Spain, are expected to be less efficient, on average, than banks in the other Western European countries. Stricter regulation, public policy and financial conservatism (Germany), strong direct interference by the government (France and Italy) and lagging economic development (Greece, Spain, Portugal) are cited to explain the – alleged – diverging levels of efficiency. We will refer to this accepted wisdom as the *expert view*, allowing for the possibility that experts may be completely wrong. In general, this view is not supported by any of the indirect proxies of efficiency of Table 1.1. From the preceding, it is obvious that there is a need for a much more convincing empirical assessment of the efficiency of the banking sectors in European countries. As said, the X-efficiency estimates based on the stochastic cost frontier approach of Chapter 6 seek to fill this gap.

Table 1.2 Comparison of two estimates of inefficiency

	Effects of country dummies in cost model		Index of X-inefficiency	
	Cost differences	*Rank*	*X-inefficiency*	*Rank*
Belgium	0.82	8	0.82	7
France	1.17	3	1.35	2
Germany	1.02	5	0.83	6
Italy	1.27	2	1.29	3
Luxembourg	0.66	9	0.63	9
Netherlands	1.11	4	0.93	5
Spain	1.33	1	1.46	1
Switzerland	0.85	7	0.82	7
UK	1.00	6	1.19	4

To round off the assessment of proxies and present a brief preview of more sophisticated efficiency measures, we provide a comparison between the considered simple ratios and model-based efficiency indices. Therefore, two types of the latter more advanced category are used, both stemming from Bikker (2001), see Table 1.2. The first model-based efficiency measure is the *weighted average* effect of the country dummy coefficients in models for bank cost levels (see Section 6.2.1). Note that in this empirical analysis we compare countries, not banks. Here, the average has been taken over the country dummy coefficients of eight distinct models for 'all banks' and seven considered bank categories, that is commercial banks, cooperative banks, savings banks, investment banks, medium- and long-term credit institutions,

Table 1.3 Correlations between simple ratios and more sophisticated efficiency and competition estimates

Ratios: *Sophisticated estimates*	Cost income ratio	Interest rate margin	Labour cost share	Labour intensity (balance sheet)	Labour intensity (inhabitants.)	Intensity branches	Index of concentration	Index of competition
Effects country dummies of bank cost model	0.57	0.30	0.63	0.72	-0.72	-0.34	-0.09	-0.47
Index of X-inefficiency	0.46	0.68	0.50	0.75	-0.62	-0.28	-0.16	-0.39
Index of competition	-0.06	-0.55	-0.01	-0.62	0.32	0.16	-0.42	1

Note: Correlations with light shading are expected to be negative, the others should be positive. Expectations with respect to the sign of the cost-income ratio correlations are undetermined.

real estate and mortgage banks and specialized government credit banks.[18] The index of X-inefficiency is based on the stochastic cost frontier model (see Section 6.2.2). The two measures are highly correlated, the correlation coefficient being 0.91, whereas the ranking of countries in terms of cost efficiency is almost identical. The similarity between the results of the two quite different approaches is striking and raises confidence in the robustness of the results.

The first two lines of Table 1.3 present correlations between the simple ratios and the two more sophisticated efficiency estimates. Not one of these simple ratios provides a ranking that comes close to the ranking we have found in Table 1.2. The correlations in the lightly shaded areas are expected to be negative, whereas the other correlations should be positive. An exception is the cost-income ratio, where we have no a priori expectation. This often-used cost-income ratio appears to be positively correlated, indicating that the second, less common, interpretation of this ratio with respect to its relationship with efficiency, mentioned above, is correct. The interest rate margin is the best proxy of differences in cost levels, based on its correlation of 0.80 with effects of the bank-specific model. With a correlation coefficient of 0.72, the labour intensity index related to the balance sheet total comes second best. In reversed order, these ratios are also the best proxies of our index of X-inefficiencies (correlations are 0.76 and 0.69 for, respectively, labour intensity and interest rate margin). On the whole, the interest rate margin seems to be the best proxy, despite its serious shortcomings, as it heavily overestimates efficiency in France and underestimates efficiency in the UK. In theory, efficiency and competition are closely related. In particular, competition is seen as a condition that forces banks to become efficient. Actually, for 1996, efficiency and competition appeared to be fairly loosely connected phenomena, given the low correlations of around 0.40 between our measures of efficiency and the index of competition.

The last line of Table 1.3 provides correlations with a P–R model-based estimate of competition. These results point out that the cost-income ratio seems to be valueless as indicator of competition. The interest rate margin and the labour intensity index related to the balance sheet total, the best – but not perfect – indicators of efficiency, are also the best – though not perfect – indicators of competition. Other ratios have low correlations or even correlations with the wrong sign. These outcomes underline that none of the popular simple proxies considered is appropriate, and that there is a need for a more direct measurement of competitions and efficiency, as will be performed in Chapters 4–6.

1.3 PERFORMANCE

After market structure and competition, performance is the third panel of the SCP triptych. The SCP paradigm relates structure and conduct to performance. Performance in an industry is explained from the conduct of firms, including degree of collusion, innovation, advertising, and so on. In turn, conduct depends on structural characteristics of the market, such as the number of firms, entry requirements and cost and demand functions. The past twenty years have seen a critical discussion on and general abandonment of the SCP paradigm in the industrial economics literature (see also Bos, 2003). This is due primarily to its low flexibility, as a crucial role is played by the structural variables that are considered exogenous, so that firms cannot modify their behaviour. Also, the paradigm suffers from empirical shortcomings, in particular its insufficient explanatory capability. A major underlying problem of the SCP relationship is the fact that the explanatory variables are not really exogenous and that they, together with the dependent variable, may be affected by third-factor determinants such as institutional, economic and technical changes. An example is the Internet, which may at the same time change the structure (causing new entries), the conduct (causing increase of competition) and performance (benefits from new challenges, costs arising from new IT investment expenses and opportunities or disadvantages resulting from tougher competition).

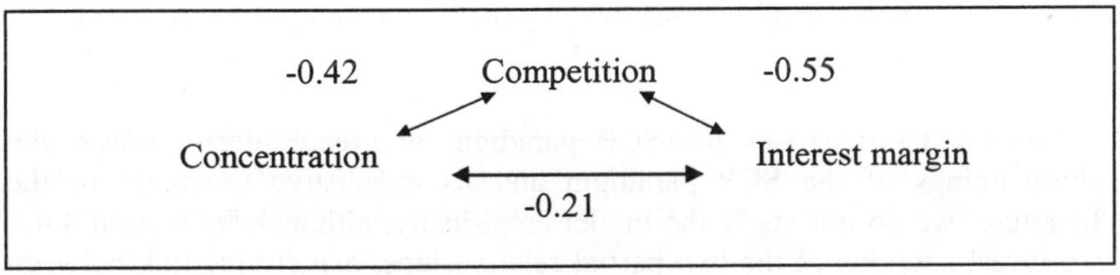

Figure 1.1 Correlations between structure, conduct and performance

A final shortcoming of the SCP paradigm is that its two stepwise relationships, from structure to conduct and from conduct to performance, do not necessarily constitute a meaningful link between structure and performance. This is illustrated in a highly simplified way by Figure 1.1, which presents correlations from Table 1.1 between structure (proxied by concentration), conduct (as reflected by the competition measure *H*) and performance (indicated by interest margin). Although the partial relationships between concentration and competition and between competition and performance show a substantial degree of correlation, a significant final link from concentration to performance (interest margin) is missing.[19] More generally, performance is hardly explained by structure alone. Actually, that is exactly what has generally been done in testing the SCP hypothesis empirically: conduct and hence both partial relationships have been ignored, leaving only the direct effect of structure on performance to be investigated. But correlation is, of course, of fairly limited use as a tool for establishing the existence of a relationship.

In reality, the interrelationships between the considered concepts are more complicated. A more elaborated – though not complete – scheme of relationships is shown in Figure 1.2. The asterisks indicate the links such as identified by the SCP paradigm. The efficiency theory suggests that the more efficient banks may reduce prices at the cost of their (higher) profits in order to improve their competitive positions and to gain larger market shares, thereby affecting the market structure. These relationships are marked by plus signs.[20]

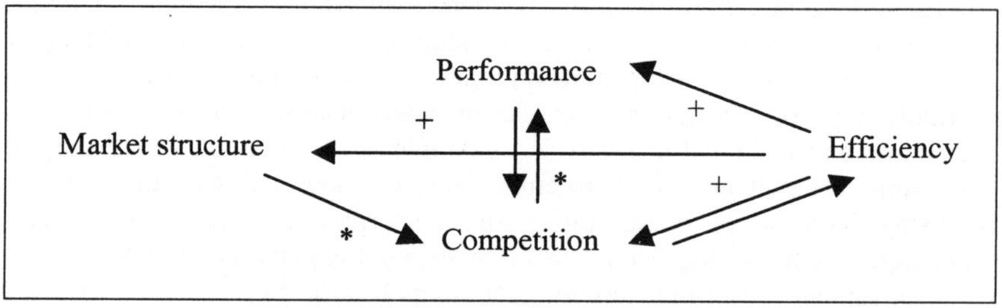

Figure 1.2 Relationships between structure, conduct, performance and efficiency

Section 3.3 discusses the SCP paradigm in greater detail. Given the shortcomings of the SCP paradigm and its exhaustive treatment in the literature, we do not apply the model empirically, although in Section 4.4.2 we investigate one of the two partial relationships, namely the link between market structure and competition.[21] Instead of the complete SCP paradigm, Chapter 7 investigates one aspect of bank performance, namely its cyclicality – and related bank behaviour such as that regarding provisioning and lending – which has attracted new interest in the runup to the new Basel Capital Accord. The new Accord's proposed risk-sensitive minimum requirements have raised concerns about a possible (acceleration of) the procyclical behaviour of banks, which might threaten macroeconomic stability. Chapter 7 analyses the interaction between business cycles and bank behaviour over the past two decades and for 26 industrial countries. As expected, profits appear to move up and down with the business cycle, allowing for accumulation of capital in boom periods. Provisioning for credit losses goes up when the cycle falls, but less so when the net income of banks is relatively high, resulting in reduced procyclicality. Lending also fluctuates with the business cycle, but appears to be driven by demand rather than by supply factors such as (shortage of) capital, which contradicts the assumptions underlying capital crunch theory. All in all, over the past few decades, distortion caused by procyclical behaviour of banks has been limited, banking crises excepted.

NOTES

1. This directive boosted the deregulation and liberalization of international capital flows. Other policy initiatives were lifting of restrictions on interest payments on deposits and the development of a harmonized framework for supervision of the European banks. In the beginning of 1993, all formal restrictions regarding the provision of financial services across the European Union were removed. Banks which are licensed anywhere in the Union are given a 'single banking licence', which allows them to service the entire European market, either by setting up branches in other countries or by offering products across national borders.
2. European Commission (1997) gives a detailed evaluation of the impact of the single market programme on the performance and strategic reaction of the banking sector in European countries. See also Molyneux and Gardner (1997), Vander Vennet (1997), Danthine et al. (1999) and Bos (2002). For a detailed description of the economic integration in the EU, see Vanthoor (2002).
3. European Commission (1997) discusses the increase of competition. Chapter 4 observes only a slight increase of competition. Improved efficiency has been observed by Groeneveld (1999), Altunbas et al. (2001), Maudos et al. (1999, 2001, 2002). This is also confirmed in the Chapter 6.
4. Other nonregulated firms, such as pension funds, do not need to hold capital.
5 An alternative approach is that of Neven and Röller (1995).
6. A survey of the literature is given in Sections 3.4.3 and 5.3.3.
7. For countries with relatively closed banking systems, the *H*-statistic is thus more indicative of the competitive situation in the domestic banking market.
8. Panzar and Rosse (1987) treat banks as single-product firms, using deposits and other funding costs as inputs to produce merely loans and other interest earning assets. This is the so-called intermediation approach to bank modelling, which emphasises the financial intermediation role of banks. Hence, the observed *H* is an index of the overall competitive conditions in the whole banking market. Therefore, this approach cannot be applied to separate segments of the banking market.
9. It should be noted that the Internet is an alternative for some of the customers only.
10. Chapter 4 proves that banks in Europe are indeed operating under monopolistic competition, which is not very far removed from perfect competition.
11. See for other studies the prominent survey on efficiency of financial institutions of Berger and Humphrey (1997) and the studies of Molyneux et al. (1996) and Altunbas et al. (2001).
12. And hence interest margins when funding costs are given.
13. Note that a ratio would be meaningless if the profit margin were proportional to costs (as in the case of a mark-up in terms of a percentage of costs) because the ratio would be constant. The first view assumes that profits are – strongly – negatively correlated with costs, whereas the second assumes that profits are uncorrelated or less than proportionally related to costs.
14. This kind of shading in order to indicate countries with relatively efficient and inefficient banks is also applied to the other proxies of efficiency.
15. These results are similar to the estimates in Chapter 4.
16. Under the assumption that the first interpretation of the cost income ratio would be correct.

17. It is remarkable that the correlation between the cost-income ratio and the interest rate margin has the wrong sign. This issue will be addressed later.
18. The averages are weighted by the corresponding number of observations to take the importance of the categories into account.
19. Although, we will find some evidence on the impact of the number of banks (structure) on Return on Equity (performance) in Chapter 2, see Figure 2.4.
20. Other relationships shown are (i) tougher competition forces banks to become more efficient, and (ii) poor performance may induce banks to soften competition. A link not shown is: poor performance may increase the likelihood of failures, take-overs and mergers, affecting the structure of the market, or: supernormal performance may attract new entries.
21. We also slightly touch upon the structure–performance hypothesis in Section 2.6.

2. Intermediation, integration and internationalization

2.1 INTRODUCTION

The banking world is in a state of turbulence. Advances in information and financial technologies are transforming banking practices and products, institutional and regulatory conditions are changing and shocks from the economic and financial environment are hammering down on banks. Information technology has contributed to the internationalization of the money and capital markets, to the development of new risk management techniques and to the arrival of a spate of new complex financial products. Furthermore, the Internet has created a world of new challenges and threats in banking services and sales potential. The second banking directive in the EU, the establishment of EMU and its new single currency have radically transformed institutional conditions in Europe. Likewise, the Riegle-Neal Act of 1994 and the gradual repeal of the 1933 Glass-Steagull Act have drastically converted the banking landscape in the USA. Shortly, Basel II, a new world-wide regulatory capital requirement regime, will come into force, changing regulatory conditions. Regional crises in Asia (1998), Russia (1999) and Argentina (2002), the near collapse of the Long-Term Capital Management (LTCM) Fund (1998), the burst of the Internet bubble and the nearly unprecedented fall in share prices (2000–03), and the recent world-wide decline in economic growth have created an unfavourable and volatile economic environment with many threats to the banks. Together with continuing disintermediation and increase of international competition, this implies a multitude of challenges to the banks.

This chapter presents a brief survey of the current position and characteristics of the European banking industry, the environment it operates in and its current and recent development, and discusses banking policy and related issues set to become important in the near future. Given the differences between the banking industry in Europe and the USA, it is often elucidating to compare the banking markets in these regions. Therefore, the survey occasionally and indirectly covers the USA and other non-European countries as well. Where possible, data have been collected for 2001 and five or ten preceding years.

Section 2.2 discusses disintermediation and the role of banks in the economy. The internationalization of the banking industry is reviewed in Section 2.3, while Section 2.4 describes the mergers and acquisitions and their causes. Section 2.5 deals with technological developments. Section 2.6 explains revenue and cost measures of banks, which bear relationships with competitive conditions and efficiency. Finally, the question is addressed whether the observed consolidation and increased competition might have impaired financial stability.

2.2 DISINTERMEDIATION: THE ROLE OF BANKS IN THE ECONOMY

The euro area's financial system has often been described as a bank-based system, owing to the prominent role traditionally played by banks in the major economies in the euro area. The US financial system, by contrast, has long been recognized as the foremost example of a market-based system. However, non-financial sectors in the euro area increasingly direct their savings and surplus funds away from banks towards new forms of financial intermediation, such as investment funds, insurance corporations and pension funds, as well as towards the capital markets, to invest in shares or debt instruments. Non-financial enterprises increasingly access the capital markets for their financing and, although still limited, increasingly use debt securities.

On the asset side, financial assets owned by non-financial sectors in the euro area are split almost equally between intermediated and non-intermediated assets (see Figure 2.1). For households, banks are still the most common place to hold financial assets: about 30 per cent in 2000 compared to 37 per cent in 1997. However, in recent years households allocated significant amounts of financial assets into pension funds and insurance corporations as well as into investment funds. Figures indicate that the domestic sectors gradually shift their preferences away from keeping financial assets with banks in favour of other intermediaries and the capital markets.

Many factors have contributed to these developments. Liberalization and the development of information technologies in the 1980s and 1990s have underpinned the development of capital markets and increased the possibilities for asset diversification. The introduction of the euro has led to a

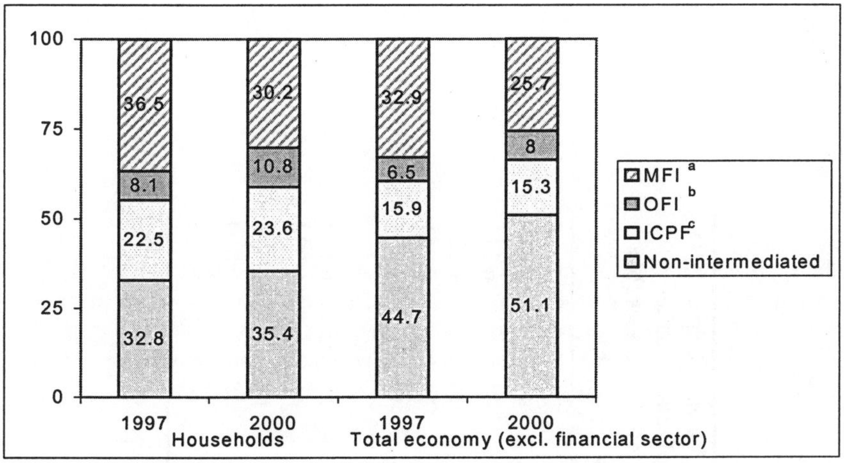

[a] MFI: Banks, investment firms and other monetary financial institutions; [b] OFI: Other ('non-bank') financial intermediaries; [c] ICPF: Insurance corporations and pension funds.

Source: European Central Bank (2002).

Figure 2.1 Distribution of financial assets between intermediated and non-intermediated instruments in the euro area (as per cent of total assets)

further increase in the diversification of investors' portfolios within and between assets classes, while changes in tax regulations have played a role too. Given the recent decrease in interest rates and inflation in recent years, the decline in intermediated instruments also reflects an increased demand among investors for high-yield, though riskier, instruments compared to safer but lower-yield bank deposits. Households also have invested more on the capital markets in an attempt to benefit from the high valuation of equity in recent years: the share of (non-intermediated) invested funds on the capital markets increased from almost 33 per cent in 1997 to 36 per cent in 2000 (see Figure 2.1). The recent fall in share prices has reversed this process somewhat. Finally, demographic trends have heightened incentives to create complementary (private) pension schemes and hence the channelling of funds into investment funds, pension funds and insurance companies.

On the liability side, in the EU, non-intermediated liabilities, such as stock market capitalization and debt securities, are equally important in size as intermediated ones, such as bank loans, especially for non-financial enterprises, whereas non-intermediated liabilities are far more important in Japan and the USA (see Table 2.1). For the non-financial enterprises, there has been a gradual shift also in the EU from bank financing to capital market

Table 2.1 *Capital and bank markets indicators*

	Stock market capitalization, as % of gdp	Debt securities,[a] as % of gdp	Bank loans, as % of gdp	Capital raised on stock markets, as % of gdp	Bank loans, as % of total assets of banks	Gdp at 1995 market prices (bln €)
2001						
EU	87	51	135	1.2[b]	42	7 616
EMU	72	49	130	1.1[b]	44	6 111
of which: UK	152	69	204	2.0	36	1 020
USA	140	38	17	1.1	16	6 911
Japan	94	7	29	0.4	19	4 345
1996						
EU	51	17	117	4.5[c]	50	6 693
EMU	35	14	104	4.9[c]	46	5 384
of which: UK	143	29	208	2.6	68	891
USA	108	6	11	2.7	18	5 860
Japan	118	4	21	0.4	15	4 185

[a] Outstanding amounts; [b] 2000 instead of 2001; [c] 1997 instead of 1996.

Sources: Eurostat, ECB Working Group on Bank Development and OECD Bank profitability.

financing. Particularly in 2001, the value of debt securities has been high due to Universal Mobile Telecommunication System (UMTS) auctions. Of the two forms of capital market financing, bond financing and equity financing, the former has been gradually gaining importance in the major EU countries, from 75 per cent on average in 1996 to 86 per cent on average in 2001 (see Table 2.2). Nevertheless, on the bank balance sheets in the euro area, loans to resident non-banks still constitute the most important asset class and this classical bank intermediation activity remains highly significant (see Table 2.1). This is different in Japan and the USA, where loans take minor positions on the bank balances. Yet bank loans as a percentage of gross domestic product (gdp) are still increasing substantially in most countries and regions, in the EU from 117 per cent in 1996 to 135 per cent in 2001 (see Table 2.1).

Table 2.2 Funds raised in the capital market by non-financial enterprises (US$ bln)[a]

	International bonds and notes by nationality of issuer, net issues				Announced international equity issues by nationality of issuer			
	1996		*2001*		*1996*		*2001*	
France	15.7	(67.7)	96.0	(83.0)	7.5	(32.3)	19.6	(17.0)
Germany	87.0	(90.9)	246.5	(97.7)	8.7	(9.1)	5.9	(2.3)
Italy	6.6	(59.5)	75.1	(92.9)	4.5	(40.5)	5.7	(7.1)
Netherlands	27.3	(80.3)	46.1	(83.4)	6.7	(19.7)	9.2	(16.6)
Spain	8.0	(80.8)	35.0	(93.3)	1.9	(19.2)	2.5	(6.7)
Sweden	5.5	(67.1)	8.8	(80.7)	2.7	(32.9)	2.1	(19.3)
UK	36.4	(80.2)	86.1	(73.7)	9.0	(19.8)	30.8	(26.3)
Total (avgs)	*186.5*	*(75.2)*	*593.6*	*(86.4)*	*41.0*	*(24.8)*	*75.8*	*(13.6)*
USA	138.5	(94.3)	622.1	(96.3)	8.4	(5.7)	23.9	(3.7)

[a] In parentheses: per cent of total capital market financing.

Source: BIS.

An exception is the UK where the high bank loan-to-gdp ratio fell somewhat over time. However, for the EU, the share of loans in total liabilities of non-financial enterprises diminished between 1995 and 2000, from, on average, 39 per cent in 1995 to 28 per cent in 2000 (see Table 2.3). In 2001, less capital was raised on stock markets than in 1996, probably due to the mood on the stock markets which was much more buoyant in 1996 than in 2001 (see Table 2.1).

Apart from a heavier reliance on capital market financing, figures also indicate a heavier reliance on *international* capital markets. This can be seen in Table 2.4, which also shows wide differences from one country to another, with percentages ranging from 12 per cent in Italy and Denmark via 62 per cent in the Netherlands to 75 per cent in Ireland, leaving aside the special case of Luxembourg.

Table 2.3 Liabilities of non-financial enterprises (in %) [a]

	Securities as share of loans and securities		Share of loans in total liabilities	
	1995	*2000*	*1995*	*2000*
Austria	6.1	9.5	74.9	69.3
Belgium	13.8	17.3	35.9	30.0
Denmark	10.5	4.8	47.1	41.8
Finland	8.6	12.5	30.8	14.7
France	20.3	25.7	27.5	14.1
Germany	6.4	4.0	42.5	37.3
Italy	4.0	2.5	54.4	43.3
Netherlands	5.4	11.4	37.8	31.2
Portugal	14.2	12.8	27.7	32.7
Spain	9.7	5.3	37.5	32.3
Sweden	5.1	12.0	40.2	29.9
EU-average [b]	*9.9*	*10.6*	*38.6*	*28.2*

[a] Figures for Greece, Ireland, Luxembourg and the UK were not available; [b] for these eleven countries.

Source: Eurostat (Newcronos).

A driving force behind the growth of debt securities issuance has been the merger and acquisition activity that characterized the telecom sector in particular. On the stock market, the privatization policies in several euro area countries played a role (telecom sector and other utilities). However, the issue of corporate bonds was generally restricted to very large companies that have been closely involved in the wave of mergers and acquisitions. Bank loans remain an important instrument for non-financial firms' funding. Difficulties for the bulk of euro area corporations in accessing debt securities and equity markets for funding are a reason behind the continued importance of loans. Because the euro area economy is dominated by small- and medium-size enterprises (SMEs; see ECB, 2002), traditional bank loans, trade credits and non-listed shares as well as other equity, tend to be primary sources of financing rather than market-based financing, such as publicly listed shares and corporate debt issuance. Moreover, despite a gradual shift towards more transaction or deal-based banking, the relationship between banks and their corporate customers continues to be very important in all EU countries. The continued importance of bank loans might also be explained by the increasing use of syndicated loans, where a number of intermediaries provide funds under pre-specified conditions, giving firms faster and generally easier access to funds than traditional bank loans.

Table 2.4 International debt securities: outstanding amounts as per cent of total debt securities

	1996	2001
Austria	31	41
Belgium	6	15
Denmark	10	12
Finland	39	38
France	14	28
Germany	7	30
Greece	17	23
Ireland	48	76
Italy	4	12
Luxembourg	96	100
Netherlands	49	62
Portugal	15	28
Spain	8	17
Sweden	27	36
UK	31	45
EU average	*27*	*37*

Source: BIS.

All in all it seems that while the importance of traditional banking activities (collecting deposits and granting loans on a retail basis) has diminished in relative terms, banks still remain the predominant players in the euro area financial system. Banks administrate many of the investment funds, are part of the holding companies along with insurance groups and are major participants on the securities markets. This has been accompanied by a restructuring process and a reorientation of activities from traditional bank lending towards investment banking style activities such as enhancing financial market intermediation by creating and selling new capital market products or advising clients on the pricing and structuring of a merger or acquisition. This is in turn reflected in a shift in bank revenue flows from interest income to non-interest income such as fees, commission and profit on trading activities (see also Section 2.6). Hence most euro area companies remain by and large dependent on banks to finance their activities. In this respect it has to be taken into account that banks in the euro area have expanded their role to encompass more market-oriented types of intermediation. Through advising on and managing of initial public offerings and the issue of debt securities by corporations, it would seem that an important part of the financing of euro area companies remains in the hands of financial intermediaries.

2.3 INTERNATIONALIZATION

The steady development towards integrated European financial markets has made the banking sector more international. Banks increasingly are involved in offering financial services to foreign businesses and individuals. Although internationalization has been a long-term trend, it has been fostered by the introduction of the euro, for example the merging of the infrastructures for large-value payments and interbank markets as well as the increasing integration of capital markets. The introduction of the euro has further intensified competition in an already highly competitive environment for financial institutions. The most visible response of financial intermediaries to these pressures has been consolidation either through mergers and acquisitions or through cross-shareholdings. Other ways to internationalize are the development of foreign banking through the direct provision of financial services and through foreign branches. Foreign branches and subsidiaries can result from international take-overs or from 'greenfield' investments, for instance in new activities or in new regions. However, the volume of international mergers and acquisitions (M&As) has been rather modest compared to domestic M&As. As we will see in Section 2.4, domestic M&A transactions accounted for 78 per cent of the total transaction value in 1990–2001. There are significant differences in national legal and regulatory environments, which hinder cross-border mergers. Cultural factors and differences in the framework for corporate governance also tend to discourage cross-border consolidation.

2.3.1 Foreign Ownership of Banks

Table 2.5 provides summary information on the extent of foreign ownership of banks in the EU. The weighted average of the combined market share of foreign branches and subsidiaries amounts to 16 per cent in terms of banking assets for the euro area countries at end 2001 (13 per cent in 1997). This average hides enormous differences across countries. The asset share of foreign banks is almost 95 per cent in Luxembourg compared to around 50 per cent in Ireland and the UK and 25 per cent in Belgium, while it is

Table 2.5 Share of foreign banks (as a per cent of total assets of domestic banks)

	From EEA countries				From third countries				Total	
	Branches		Subsidiaries		Branches		Subsidiaries			
	'97	'01	'97	'01	'97	'01	'97	'01	'97	'01
Austria	0.7	0.8	1.7	18.2	0.0	0.9	0.0	0.5	2.4	19.5
Belgium	8.5	3.8	14.1	18.8	6.1	0.6	1.6	1.6	30.4	24.8
Denmark	4.5	4.2	0.1	12.5	0.0	0.0	0.0	0.0	4.6	16.8
Finland	7.8	5.7	0.0	0.0	0.0	0.0	0.0	0.0	7.8	5.7
France	2.8	3.2	4.7	7.8	1.9	0.6	4.7	7.8	14.1	19.3
Germany	0.9	1.5	1.4	1.8	0.7	0.6	1.2	0.9	4.3	4.7
Greece	9.0	6.0	2.1	8.2	6.8	5.0	0.8	0.6	18.8	19.8
Ireland	*n.a.*[b]	11.0	27.8	27.9	1.0	0.2	7.1	9.3	*n.a.*	48.5
Italy	3.5	5.6	1.9	1.1	1.4	1.0	0.1	0.1	7.0	7.8
Luxembour	19.2	18.2	64.3	69.3	1.4	1.0	7.6	5.4	92.5	93.8
Netherlands	2.1	2.2	2.8	7.6	0.5	0.2	1.8	1.3	7.2	11.3
Portugal	3.9	4.2	5.8	12.1	0.2	0.2	0.9	0.9	10.7	17.5
Spain	4.9	4.1	4.1	4.0	1.6	0.2	1.9	1.2	12.5	9.5
Sweden	1.4	*n.a.*	0.0	*n.a.*	0.1	*n.a.*	0.2	0.0	1.7	*n.a.*
UK	*n.a.*	23.7	*n.a.*	1.2	*n.a.*	20.9	*n.a.*	5.2	*n.a.*	51.1
EU[a]	*2.5*	*8.4*	*4.5*	*6.8*	*1.1*	*5.4*	*1.7*	*3.2*	*9.8*	*23.8*
EMU[a]	*3.2*	*3.7*	*6.0*	*8.6*	*1.4*	*0.6*	*2.3*	*2.8*	*13.0*	*15.7*

[a] Weighted average. [b] n.a. stands for non available.

Source: ECB or authorities represented in the ECB's Banking Supervision Committee.

negligible in some other European countries. The data also indicate that the foreign banks in the EU countries are predominantly subsidiaries of banks in European Economic Area (EEA) countries, followed by branches from the EEA and subsidiaries from third countries. The UK is an exception to this: the number of branches of foreign banking groups is significantly larger than the number of subsidiaries, irrespective of the regions of origin. Viewing from the perspective of the expansion of European banks outside Europe, there seems to be a strong tendency in the recent past to expand into Central and Eastern Europe to anticipate the economic development in these regions and into Latin America, mainly by Spanish banks. Moreover, some important acquisitions have also been made in the USA to benefit from that large market.

For banks planning to enter a new market, there are several considerations to take into account in selecting the appropriate mode. Foreign bank branches often concentrate on corporate finance services, trading activities and private banking rather than retail activities. Branches are commonly used by parent banks to support the activities of home-country clients that operate abroad. Retail businesses are much more difficult to enter. Domestic banks enjoy substantial competitive advantages, because of their widespread branch distribution networks. Moreover, the branch mode is often used to operate in a leading financial centre. The regulatory environment, however, is also a major factor in determining the organizational form of the development of cross-border banking activities. The preference for a branch or a subsidiary may also be linked to differences in national regulation, for example deposit guarantee schemes, tax reasons, restrictions on the foreign ownership of banks, restrictions on the activities of foreign branches, capital use optimization. Thus, the most effective way of gaining access to the retail sector has been to merge with or acquire an existing local bank. A significant number of such operations has indeed taken place over the past three years, as is described in Section 2.4 on M&As. This might be the strongest available indicator that integration is progressing.

2.3.2 External Positions of Banks

Further evidence on the internationalization of banking can be derived from balance sheet data, which reflect the volume of direct cross-border provision of financial services. Data on the external positions of banks in individual countries vis-à-vis the non-banking sectors is represented in Table 2.6.

Table 2.6 presents separate data on the external assets (loans and the ownership of foreign marketable securities, such as government and corporate bonds) and on external liabilities (deposits, bonds and other marketable short-term securities) of national banking systems. These data indicate that the international deposits and liabilities held by non-banks at European banks are rather significant in the EU (respectively, 17 per cent and 16 per cent of gdp in 2001), a substantial increase since 1996, while these figures are much lower for the USA and Japan. Internationalization on the asset side of bank balance sheets can be explained by the integration of the European money market and the increased issuance activity in the corporate debt market, especially by the telecom sector. On the liability side the increased external positions of banks reflects changes in motives for maintaining bank balances abroad, for example, the evasion of domestic income and wealth taxation.

2.3.3 Origin of Bank Income

The existence of significant cross-border activity by financial institutions can be confirmed by the geographical breakdown of the revenues of financial institutions. Van der Zwet (2003) investigated the largest 50 banks and insurance company groups and pointed to significant international diversification. The largest financial groups appear to focus equally on home and foreign markets. Insurance companies seem to have a more explicit foreign bias (earnings in foreign countries being, on average, 65 per cent of their revenues) than banks do (earnings from their home country being 61 per cent of their revenues). From this study, it also appeared that European

Table 2.6 External positions of banks in individual countries (as a per cent of gdp)

	Loans to foreign non-banks		Deposits of foreign non-banks	
	1996	*2001*	*1996*	*2001*
Austria	6.8	15.8	5.0	5.3
Belgium	12.2	20.5	24.2	43.1
Denmark	7.3	8.8	4.3	5.9
Finland	1.4	9.8	0.5	1.9
France	4.7	7.1	3.7	5.1
Germany	5.5	17.5	7.5	17.6
Ireland	35.4	58.7	25.3	35.3
Italy	3.1	2.5	1.3	1.5
Luxembourg	608.1	580.3	939.2	687.1
Netherlands	8.4	12.9	14.1	23.9
Portugal [a]	2.1	6.9	7.2	9.5
Spain	2.9	4.1	7.5	19.3
Sweden	3.7	6.0	3.0	4.8
UK	24.0	34.2	31.2	34.0
EU-15	*8.5*	*15.7*	*10.9*	*16.9*
EU-15 (bln euros)	*775.6*	*1 244.4*	*989.9*	*1 345.1*
Switzerland	18.6	29.7	83.0	125.1
Norway	2.9	3.2	1.5	2.1
USA	1.4	1.7	1.0	1.6
Canada	1.4	1.6	6.0	4.4
Japan	3.1	5.5	0.4	0.8

[a] 1997 figures instead of 1996.

Source: BIS.

financial groups are more strongly internationally diversified than financial groups from the USA, which may be due to the internal market in Europe for financial services. This method points to significant international diversification among the largest financial institutions.

2.4 MERGERS AND ACQUISITIONS

As was mentioned above, the intensified competition on the financial markets, on which banks operate, has given further inducement towards consolidation, for example through mergers and acquisitions. Data on bank mergers in the euro area, including mergers between banks and non-banks (insurance companies and securities firms), are presented in Figure 2.2. The data show that M&A activity has significantly increased in 1998–2001 compared to the beginning of the 1990s. Also, average transaction size sharply increased, suggesting that large banks increasingly became involved in the merger activity, compared to a dominance of mergers between smaller institutions in the beginning of the 1990s. A clear majority of M&A transactions has occurred with other banks.

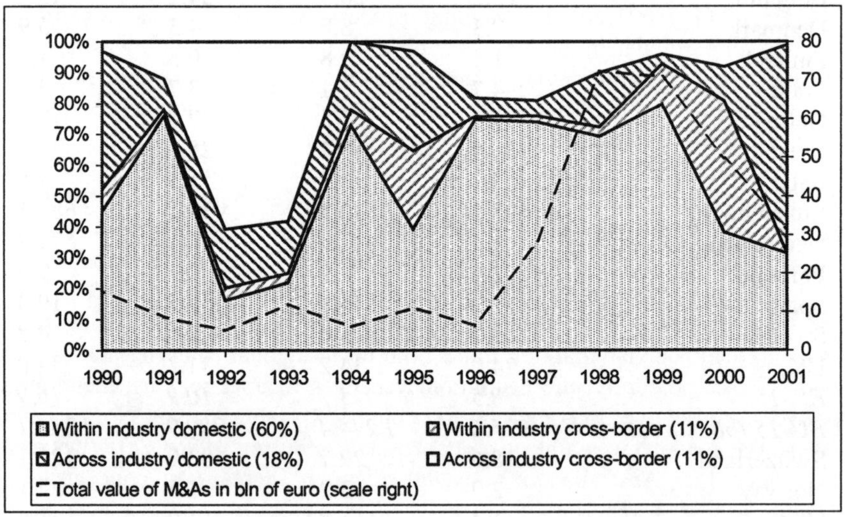

Source: Cabral et al. (2002).

Figure 2.2 Value of mergers and acquisitions involving banks in the euro area

However, financial conglomerates involving banks, insurance companies and securities firms have also been created. During 1990–2001, 30 per cent of the total M&A value was due to cross-sector transactions, in the euro area most prominent in Belgium, Germany, Finland, Ireland and the Netherlands. Domestic mergers continue to dominate international mergers. In the period 1990–2001, domestic transactions accounted for 78 per cent of the total transaction value and 60 per cent within the banking sector.

The relatively modest volume of international mergers could indicate that domestic banking mergers are apparently more advantageous than international mergers. Individual European economies are rather heterogeneous, implying that purely domestic banking mergers offer ample opportunity for asset risk diversification. Domestic mergers will thus be preferred to international mergers, as they avoid the problems related to the mixing of different cultures and languages, while the prospect of increased market power is still offered. Moreover, as we have seen, differences in national regulation, such as regarding deposit insurance systems, tax systems and specific restrictions on banking activities, discourage cross-border consolidation.

Table 2.7 provides concentration indices (CR_5, the share of the five largest banks per country; see Chapter 3) of total assets, lending and deposits for 1996 and 2001. An increase in concentration is shown in almost all EU countries. This reflects the ongoing process of further consolidation in Europe, in particular in the larger countries where consolidation was lagging behind. Figures do not deviate much across the object of measurement: total assets, lending and deposits. The conclusion that concentration is progressing also holds for the entire EU. For such a large region, concentration is still low, reflecting the limited cross-border consolidation in Europe, but it is rising. Concentration in the euro area is substantially lower than in the USA, in part due to the fact that the euro area has a larger population. As said above, consolidation in the EU may also have been lagged by the existence of national and cultural borders. This goes all the more for the entire EU where the CR_5s are lower. The process of concentration in the USA is moving at an even higher pace than that in Europe, both for individual countries and for the entire EU. Apparently, the institutional changes in both regions, mentioned above, are effective. In some non-EU countries, such as Japan, Norway and Switzerland, there was almost no consolidation during 1996–2001, whereas in others, like Australia and Canada, a strong increase in concentration appeared in those years.

For long, consolidation has been a continuing process, moving in waves: years of fewer mergers were followed by years of increased activity. Institutional and other changes may have triggered such waves, which were then often reinforced by herd behaviour. Figure 2.3 provides figures on consolidation during the last decade. The wave behaviour is evident: a strong

Table 2.7 *Concentration indices* (CR_5) *based on total assets, lending and deposits*

	Total assets		Loans		Deposits	
	1996	*2001*	*1996*	*2001*	*1996*	*2001*
Austria	55	66	51	60	56	68
Belgium	67	90	70	91	67	89
Denmark	77	84	78	83	79	84
Finland	96	93	95	94	98	93
France	45	45	46	42	49	44
Germany	25	37	24	33	21	33
Greece	87	84	85	83	88	85
Ireland	59	65	64	69	61	65
Italy	36	46	37	45	39	47
Luxembourg	29	39	35	46	28	38
Netherlands	81	88	80	86	81	93
Portugal	53	76	52	75	54	79
Spain	57	60	54	56	57	57
Sweden	63	76	62	73	84	87
UK	33	41	38	47	36	44
EU region	*10*	*12*	*9*	*11*	*11*	*11*
EMU region	*12*	*16*	*12*	*15*	*13*	*14*
EU average	*58*	*66*	*58*	*66*	*60*	*67*
RoW average [a]	57	61	55	59	61	64
Norway	63	64	60	62	69	68
Switzerland	74	76	66	59	76	77
Australia	68	77	67	77	74	83
Canada	79	86	75	85	78	85
Japan	40	40	43	39	48	41
USA	18	24	18	31	21	30

[a] Rest of World.

Source: Fitch-IBCA.

rise in 1995, a fall in 1996 and an overwhelming rise in 1997, to an unprecedented level which persisted into the next years.

Herd behaviour in connection with mergers and acquisitions is often observed. Apparently, bank managers are often quick to follow competing banks in their merge step, probably for fear of choosing the wrong strategy, due to general uncertainty about future bank market developments. The fact that merge waves in Europe and the USA have been rather similar, reflects this herd behaviour, see Figure 2.3. These regions have the high merge levels of 1995 and 1997–99 in common, and the rise or fall in levels of mergers in both regions is similar in most years considered. Except for 1999, the value involved in the USA has nearly always been much higher than in Europe, roughly twice as high. As also appeared from the concentration indices, USA consolidation leads that of Europe. The role of the Rest of the World – not shown in the graph – is minor and is even decreasing over time.

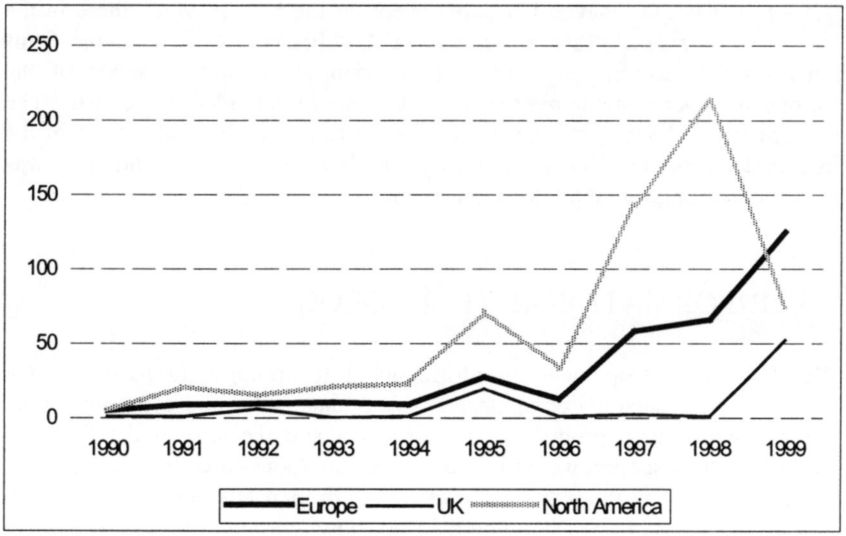

Source: Thomson Financial SDC Platinum and Group of Ten (2001).

Figure 2.3 Total value of bank mergers and acquisitions classified by acquiring or largest firm's region (US$ bln)

Consolidation creates very large financial institutions. Tables 2.A.1–3 in Appendix 2 presents the 20 largest firms in, respectively, 2001, 1996 and 1991, ranged by shareholder value and expressed in US$. In 2001, the shareholder value of the largest banks was twice as high as in 1996 and 3.2 times higher than in 1991. For the balance sheet figures, growth rates were 77 per cent and 155 per cent. These growth rates far exceed the nominal growth of the real economy, as US gdp was 31 per cent higher in 2001 than it was in 1996, and 71 per cent higher than in 1991. Moreover, gdp growth expressed in US$ over the decade was less than 20 per cent in Japan and only just above zero in Europe (for example 3 per cent in Germany). Hence it appears that the process of consolidation and the higher growth rates of financial values compared to real-economic values have been the major forces behind the expanded size of the large banks.

Another issue that attracts attention is the shift in countries dominating the ranking list. Where Japanese banks occupied all four top positions in 1991, they gradually fell back over time, in line with the depressing real-economic developments. This is nevertheless remarkable in the light of the large-scale mergers which have taken place in Japan in order to rescue institutions in distress. US banks show an impressive advance over time: in 1991 only one US bank just made the top 20, but in 1996 the country had five banks in the sub top and in 2001 seven US banks were on the list, of which three in the top five. In recent years a number of US banks and investment firms amalgamated, contributing further to concentration. The presence of the European banks is stable over time, with around ten banks on the chart. The large number of European banks, with fewer representatives at the top of the list, underlines the fact that, during the last decade, consolidation was somewhat stronger in the USA than in Europe.

2.5 INFORMATIONAL TECHNOLOGY

Well-known developments in informational technology, in particular the advance of the personal computer, software, data bases and communication, has changed banks' production and products and the size of the financial markets. In this section we will focus on the Internet, which has the potential to radically change the way banks interact with their customers and to make established markets more vulnerable to new entrants. Many banks are cautious about these developments and are opting for a multi-channel distribution strategy, combining the traditional 'bricks-and-mortar' branch network with remote distribution channels, such as telephone banking and internet banking.

Internet banking is growing but is, with the exception of the Nordic countries, still relatively unimportant. It has its greatest success in securities trading and other standardized transaction-based services, such as savings deposits and mortgage loans. Very few pure Internet banks actually exist in Europe. The lack of an established brand name and security concerns seem to be important hindrances. Moreover, major parts of the public are hardly approachable through the Internet. In practice, internet banking facilities have been integrated into the existing distribution network. Some banks have chosen to pursue a stand-alone venture, for example to break into foreign markets by offering products at very competitive prices.[1] Transaction costs using new distribution channels like the Internet are substantially lower than using branches, which means that banks will have an incentive to develop these channels further.

The branch network remains an important asset for European banks, in line with the multi-channel strategy and despite the ongoing consolidation process and the expansion of alternative distribution channels. This preference may also explain why branch networks are not decreasing as significantly as one would perhaps expect on the basis of banks' investments in information technology. Another reason is that some banking transactions require face-to-face interaction between client and banker, while, in general, banks also aim for a certain geographic coverage of their branch network. Table 2.8 shows that in the EU the numbers of inhabitants per bank branch and per bank employee slowly increased over 1997–2001, although, with substantial differences across countries. Apart from the advent of new distribution networks, important factors behind the development of delivery channels have been the wave of mergers and acquisitions, and an increased focus on profitability and cost management. In that respect, the multi-channel strategy with the branch network as an important cornerstone clearly implies certain risks for the future.

Table 2.8 Numbers of inhabitants per bank branch and per bank employee

	Numbers of inhabitants per bank branch		Numbers of inhabitants per bank employee	
	1997	*2001*	*1997*	*2001*
Austria	1 721	1 781	107	109
Belgium	1 385	1 664	133	135
Denmark	2 319	2 251	110	110
Finland	3 978	4 282[a]	196	206[a]
France	2 289	2 266	141	142[b]
Germany	1 299	1 524	102	102
Greece	4 188	3 560	185	177
Ireland	3 131	3 800[a]	100[b]	110[a]
Italy	2 278	1 976	166	168[a]
Luxembourg	1 349	1 471[a]	22	18
Netherlands	2 302	3 057	140	126
Portugal	2 098	1 450	154	183
Spain	1 035	1 028	153	154
Sweden	3 134	4 141[b]	205	205[b]
UK	3 615	4 206[a]	130	134[a]
EMU[c]	*1 664*	*1 719*	*134*	*135*
EU[c]	*1 850*	*1 933*	*134*	*136*

[a] 2000; [b] 1999; [c] weighted average, possibly over different years.

Source: ECB or authorities represented in the ECB's Banking Supervision Committee.

2.6 REVENUES, COSTS AND COMPETITION

The net interest rate margin is an interesting measure of bank profitability, which allows comparison over time and across countries. It also reflects competitive conditions or efficiency on the banking markets, assuming that competition enforces efficiency and presses the margin down (see also Section 1.2). Table 2.9 presents for all EU countries the net interest rate margin for two recent years, 1997 and 2001, and averages over two recent periods, 1994–1997 and 1998–2001. Two general trends stand out. First, margins in many countries fell over time. The same is apparent from the EU averages, which also reflect the downward trend in the margins. This indicates growing competition, as is commonly assumed to be the case in the EU.[2] Secondly, the level of the margin differs considerably across EU countries. Especially the Southern European countries, Italy, Greece, Spain and Portugal, all face high margins, say around 2.5 per cent, although in Italy and Portugal the margins have declined over time. Finland, recovering from a banking crisis, and Ireland, dealing with high inflation and growth, also had high margins in the earlier years. Margins fell to relatively low levels in Belgium, France and Germany, whereas Luxembourg takes a special position

Table 2.9 Net interest rate margins (in %)

	1997	2001	avg. 94–97	avg. 98–01
Austria	1.5	1.5	1.6	1.7
Belgium	1.5	1.0	1.6	1.3
Denmark	2.0	1.4	2.2	1.6
Finland	2.6	1.8	2.2	2.0
France	1.3	0.9	1.6	1.1
Germany	1.5	0.8	1.7	1.1
Greece	2.6	2.5	2.1	2.6
Ireland	2.1	1.6	2.8	1.7
Italy	2.7	2.2	3.1	2.3
Luxembourg	0.7	0.6	0.8	0.7
Netherlands	1.7	1.5	1.9	1.6
Portugal	2.6	1.9	3.0	2.3
Spain	2.8	3.0	2.9	2.9
Sweden	1.5	1.4	1.9	1.4
UK	1.7	1.3	2.1	1.6
EU average	*1.9*	*1.6*	*2.1*	*1.7*
USA	2.7	2.3	2.7	2.3
Japan	1.1	0.9	1.1	1.3

Source: Fitch-IBCA.

as intermediary of savings escaping fiscal authorities.[3] The USA, sometimes seen as the champion of liberty and competition, has margins well above those of the EU, although they, too, tend to decline over time.[4]

For a long time, interest income has been the major source of banks' income, see Table 2.10. However, this source has become less abundant over time, reflecting, among other things, the process of disintermediation described above. Other sources of income, such as fees, commissions and profit on trading, grew over time for banks of all sizes, especially in the earlier years of the 1990s. On average, in Europe, interest income was of roughly equal importance for all bank sizes in 1990 and 1996, but in 2001 other income was more important for larger banks than for smaller and medium-sized banks, pointing, for the former size class, to greater specialization in non-lending services and trading. Such specialization of large banks was especially manifest in France and the UK. In the USA, interest income already was less dominant before the review period, typifying a market-based banking system, and specialization emerged earlier than it did in Europe.

Table 2.10 Share of net interest revenue for various bank-size classes [a]

	1990			**1996**			**2001**		
	small	*medium*	*large*	*small*	*medium*	*large*	*small*	*medium*	*large*
France	0.79	0.59	0.79	*n.a.*	0.58	0.42	0.58	0.67	0.19
Germany	0.86	1.64	0.97	0.81	0.85	0.85	0.77	0.84	0.79
Italy	0.76	0.78	0.71	0.78	0.70	0.69	0.76	0.65	0.60
Spain	0.86	0.87	0.88	0.81	0.79	0.74	0.75	0.75	0.70
Sweden	0.76	0.91	0.94	0.80	0.81	0.83	0.79	0.90	1.05
UK	0.71	0.79	0.75	0.63	0.52	0.51	0.63	0.59	0.53
'EU'	*0.80*	*1.05*	*0.86*	*0.63*	*0.73*	*0.60*	*0.72*	*0.73*	*0.60*
USA	0.65	0.65	0.46	0.76	0.66	0.49	0.76	0.66	0.61

[a] In the sum of net interest revenue and other operating income.

Notes: 'Small' means below the 75th percentile; 'medium' between the 75th and 95th percentile; 'large' above the 95th percentile. Percentiles are computed on total assets held in 2001. *'EU'* is defined as the average of the six countries considered. Percentages higher than 100 per cent are possible where trading losses or high expenses on commissions occur.

Source: Danthine et al. (1999), Table 1.7, and author's own computations on data from the BankScope data set by Bureau Van Dijk and Fitch-IBCA.

Another determinant of bank profitability is operating expenses. Expressed as a percentage of gross income, it is also often used as a proxy of competitive conditions, although its interpretation is ambiguous (as explained in Section 1.2). This cost-to-income ratio is high – and hence the profit-to-income ratio low – in France, Germany, Italy and Spain, which are indeed often seen as less efficient countries (although that would imply higher profit margins), but also in the Netherlands, a country with fairly efficient banks (see Table 2.11). Staff expenses, the larger part of operational costs, are high in France and Italy, and highest in the Netherlands. The cost-income ratio is low – and profits high – in the Scandinavian and Anglo-Saxon countries. Again, Luxembourg is an outlier.

The cost–income ratio tends to fall over time, as is clear also from the EU average, indicating lower costs compared to income. This is remarkable, particularly in the light of the falling interest rate margins, and indicates cost reduction. Indeed, the staff–costs ratio (not shown here) declines over time too, both in Europe and in the USA, indicating rationalization of the bank production. Evidently, here we observe efficiency effects of increased competitive pressure. In general, interest rate margins have been earned over larger amounts of assets, with bank profit levels sustained until quite recently. The cost–income ratio is also low in the USA. For Japan the ratio is above 100 per cent, reflecting that income does not cover expenses, and hence that losses are being recorded.

Table 2.11 Operating expenses as per cent of gross income

	1997	2001	avg. 94–97	avg. 98–01
Austria	81	60	85	70
Belgium	72	77	76	72
Denmark	65	69	70	67
Finland	69	54	93	57
France	87	77	91	79
Germany	77	94	77	85
Greece	85	73	85	65
Ireland	63	63	64	64
Italy	90	82	95	82
Luxembourg	50	59	50	55
Netherlands	78	84	78	80
Portugal	80	71	84	77
Spain	84	77	82	77
Sweden	61	55	64	59
UK	67	67	67	66
EU average	*74*	*71*	*77*	*70*
USA	67	68	70	67
Japan	151	116	126	115

Source: Fitch-IBCA.

Increased competitive pressure in the EU countries, the burst of the Internet bubble, causing, among other things, a nearly unprecedented fall in share prices with adverse effects on banking activities, and the world-wide downswing in economic conditions, have subjected the banks to a severe test. Going by the banks' profit figure, banks in most countries have firmly stood the test (see Table 2.12). This does not hold for Germany, where the falling profits of recent years indicate the fairly poor condition of many of its banks. The very low German returns on assets (ROA) and on equity (ROE) also reflect the unsteady circumstances of its banking system, due to, among other things, government intervention and lack of consolidation. The disastrous state of the Japanese banks speaks for itself.

Table 2.12 Profit before tax and returns on assets and equity

	Profit before tax (bln US$)		ROA (in %)		ROE (in %)	
	1996	*2001*	*1996*	*2001*	*1996*	*2001*
Austria	1.2	2.1	0.3	0.3	8.3	8.2
Belgium	4.5	3.6	0.3	0.4	11.2	10.1
Denmark	2.5	2.5	0.8	0.4	12.5	8.6
Finland	0.7	3.9	0.4	1.0	6.9	18.3
France	13.1	34.4	0.2	0.4	4.5	10.1
Germany	23.5	14.8	0.2	0.1	5.5	2.7
Greece	0.8	1.7	0.4	0.8	9.6	8.8
Ireland	2.1	2.9	1.1	0.6	14.4	10.2
Italy	12.1	20.7	0.3	0.5	4.0	7.7
Luxembourg	3.3	3.3	0.5	0.4	13.6	11.1
Netherlands	7.0	9.6	0.5	0.5	10.7	11.1
Portugal	1.9	2.6	0.6	0.6	11.1	12.2
Spain	11.4	14.8	0.7	0.9	11.6	12.8
Sweden	5.3	5.4	0.8	0.8	19.5	17.8
UK	35.2	38.1	0.8	0.5	16.9	10.0
EU total	*124.7*	*160.4*	*0.4*	*0.4*	*8.8*	*9.3*
USA	84.5	157.2	1.0	0.9	17.0	14.4
Japan	-0.9	-44.6	-0.6	-0.4	-1.6	-6.9

Source: Fitch-IBCA.

On average, returns on assets in Europe remained nearly constant over the years under consideration: they rose from 0.40 to 0.42. The outcome is even more favourable if Germany is disregarded. This is remarkable, given the observed decline in net interest rate margins, and reflects the increasing non-interest income from non-traditional banking activities, such as asset management, the management of stock and bond issues and trading. The differences across countries are striking too; they depend to some extent on national circumstances, such as market structure (see below), and fluctuate over time. European returns compare unfavourably with those of the USA, which are at least twice as high. In part this is explained by the fact that banks in the USA are riskier than those in Europe (among other things, due to their more expanded investment activities), which is also reflected in the lower rating of the US banks. Besides, the returns on equity in the USA are higher for all sectors.

The ROE figures are shown in the last two columns of Table 2.12. They underline the observed diverging levels of profitability across countries and its volatility over time. Figure 2.4 depicts the relationship between the number of banks (proxying market structure) and ROE, providing some – anecdotal – evidence in support of the well-known Structure–Performance hypothesis (see also Section 1.3). The number of banks (in logarithms) explains more than 50 per cent of the variation in ROE, at a level of significance of no less than 99.85 per cent and has a similar impact on ROA. Various alternative measures of the market structure, such as concentration indices, perform substantially less well in explaining ROE or ROA levels.[5]

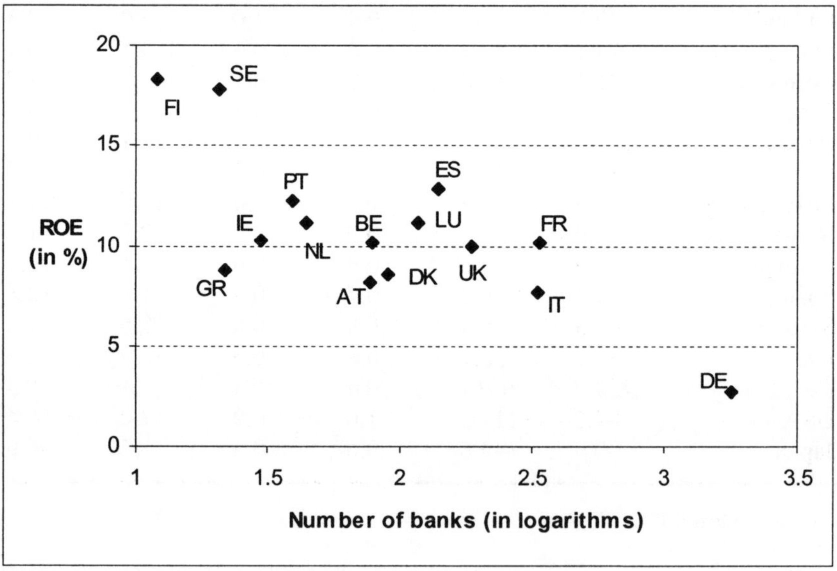

Figure 2.4 Relationship between number of banks and returns on equity

2.7 CONSOLIDATION, COMPETITION AND BANKING STABILITY

This chapter surveys a number of sources of increased competition and consolidation. Although traditional banking business has fallen off in relative terms, due to increased competition from non-bank institutions and capital markets, banks still remain the predominant players in the euro area financial system. Economic and monetary integration in the EU has strongly encouraged both internationalization and concentration. The share of foreign assets and liabilities on the EU banks' balance sheets is still modest, but is sharply rising. Europe has seen large-scale bank mergers and acquisitions, albeit mainly on the domestic level. Information technology has changed banks' products, markets and the way banks interact with customers, and has amplified competition. Increased competition has resulted in smaller margins and profits. Unbridled competition in banking may give rise to the threat of financial instability. At the same time policies to prevent instability may have adverse consequences for competition among banks. Hence, there might exists a trade-off between competition and stability (Canoy et al., 2001).

Consolidation and increased competition raise the question whether banking stability in Europe has been affected seriously by the recent developments discussed in this chapter. The literature on bank instability largely ignores the consequences which different bank-market structures may have for the sector's safety (Carletti and Hartmann, 2002). In the course of their relationship with borrowers, banks invest in the acquisition of private information that generates informational revenue. As long as banks appropriate at least part of this revenue (the so-called charter value), they are encouraged to limit their exposure so as to enjoy the (future) value of the relationship. As soon as the banking market becomes more competitive, relationship banking will decrease in value and banks will take more risks (Besanko and Thakor, 1993, Boot and Thakor, 1993, Allen and Gale, 2000). This is illustrated by events in the USA during the 1980s, when various deregulation measures and market factors reduced monopoly rents. Banks' response to the erosion of profits was excessive risk-taking, thereby increasing the value of the put options on deposit insurance funds (Edwards and Mishkin, 1995). Canoy et al. (2001) and Carletti and Hartmann (2002) present surveys of literature elaborating on the charter value, the impact of deposit insurance and policy reactions. Smith (1984) and Matutes and Vives (2000) found that under various (institutional) conditions, competition for deposits also makes banks fragile.

However, a more recent strand of literature suggests that stronger competition does not necessarily wear out stability. Regarding liability-side risk, some papers argue that problems among depositors causing bank fragility can emerge independently of the degree of competition (Matutes and

Vives, 1996). Others show that bank mergers may lead to a higher probability of possible liquidity shortages in the interbank market (Carletti et al., 2002). Concerning asset-side risk, some writers argue that there are possible circumstances in which concentrated banking markets would be riskier than a competitive sector, indicating that consolidation might be worse than severe competition (Nagarajan and Sealey, 1995, Caminal and Matutes, 2002). On the other hand, Beck et al. (2003) find that systematic banking crises are less likely in economies with more concentrated banking systems. They further find that banking crises are less likely as fewer regulatory restrictions on bank competition and activities exist, and as national institutions encourage competition. All in all, the theoretical literature does not seem to be conclusive as regards the relationship between competition and stability, although only a limited number of studies supports a positive relationship. Theory suggests that adequate policies, such as risk-adjusted deposit insurance premiums,[6] could mitigate a certain trade-off between competition and stability (Carletti and Hartmann, 2002).

The prominent charter-value hypothesis is supported by a number of empirical papers, whereas other writers failed to find evidence for this paradigm (Carletti and Hartmann, 2002). Concentration can go hand in hand with lower risk for individual banks, as shown by several articles on the diversification effects of mergers. Where concentration implies less competition, this would support the trade-off between competition and stability. Other studies indicate, however, that larger (merged) banks do not benefit from lower default probabilities. De Nicolo and Kwast (2001) find evidence that consolidation in the USA might have increased interbank related systematic risk (irrespective of changes in competitiveness). Cross-country comparisons indicate the presence of a trade-off between competition and stability in some country pairs, whereas in many others there seems to be no trade-off.

Increased competition may be welcomed as it contributes to allocative efficiency and social wealth. The literature also makes clear, however, that changes in market structure and competition could be liable to impair financial stability, although, in general, competition does not (necessarily) cause instability. It depends on specific cases and circumstances whether a change in competition and concentration is associated with more or less (in)stability (Group of Ten, 2001). This outcome stresses the importance of well-designed rules for the antitrust and supervisory authorities regarding bank mergers and for the permanent wariness of supervisory authorities where competition is rising or already fierce.

APPENDIX 2 TWENTY LARGEST BANKS IN TERMS OF SHAREHOLDER EQUITY IN 2001, 1996 AND 1991

Table 2.A.1 Twenty largest banks in terms of shareholder equity in 2001

Bank	Country	Shareholder equity [b] ($bln)		Total assets ($bln)		Market capitalization ($bln)	
Citigroup	USA (1)	81.2	1	1 051	2	259.7	1
Mizuho Bank/Mizuho Corp Bank [a]	JP (1)	56.6	2	1 287	1	53.0	9
HSBC Holdings	UK (1)	52.5	3	696	9	109.6	2
Bank of America	USA (2)	48.5	4	622	12	99.0	3
JPMorgan Chase	USA (3)	41.1	5	694	10	71.7	5
Deutsche Bank	DE (1)	41.1	6	813	4	43.9	11
Royal Bank of Scotland Group	UK (2)	40.9	7	535	14	69.4	6
Sumitomo Mitsui Banking Corp [a]	JP (2)	40.2	8	958	3	48.9	10
HypoVereinsbank	DE (2)	31.8	9	645	11	27.9	16
UFJ Bank Ltd [a]	JP (3)	30.3	10	721	8	10.7	19
Groupe Crédit Agricole	FR (1)	29.4	11	499	16	15.1	18
UBS	SW (1)	28.5	12	749	5	64.6	7
Wachovia Corporation	USA (4)	28.5	13	330	18	42.7	12
Wells Fargo & Company	USA (5)	27.2	14	308	20	73.7	4
Santander Central Hispano	SP (1)	27.0	15	317	19	39.1	15
Bank of China	China (1)	26.4	16	406	17	7.6	20
BNP Paribas	FR (2)	25.4	17	731	6	39.6	14
Bank of Tokyo-Mitsubishi	JP (4)	24.7	18	722	7	40.0	13
Barclays Bank	UK (3)	24.0	19	518	15	55.3	8
Crédit Suisse	SW (2)	23.3	20	611	13	19.3	17

[a] Pro-forma; [b] including reserves.

Sources: Euromoney (shareholder equity and total assets) and Datastream (market capitalization).

Table 2.A.2 Twenty largest banks in terms of shareholder equity in 1996

Bank	Country	Shareholder equity ($bln)		Total assets ($bln)		Market capitalization ($bln)	
HSBC Holdings	UK (1)	29.4	1	402	9	19.4	16
Bank of Tokyo-Mitsubishi	JP (1)	28.4	2	720	1	86.3	1
Groupe Crédit Agricole	FR (1)	22.8	3	477	8	—	—
Chase Manhattan	USA (1)	21.0	4	336	12	39.2	7
Citicorp	USA (2)	20.7	5	281	16	29.1	8
BankAmerica	USA (3)	20.7	6	251	17	28.1	9
Dai-Ichi Kangyo Bank	JP (2)	19.5	7	498	5	44.9	3
Sumitomo Bank	JP (3)	18.6	8	500	4	45.2	2
Sanwa Bank	JP (4)	17.7	9	501	3	39.5	6
UBS	SW (1)	16.3	10	325	13	3.9	18
Sakura Bank	JP (5)	16.0	11	478	7	24.4	12
Deutsche Bank	DE (1)	15.6	12	536	2	22.9	13
Fuji Bank	JP (6)	15.6	13	487	6	42.2	5
ABN AMRO Holding	NL (1)	14.4	14	341	11	21.6	14
Wells Fargo	USA (4)	14.1	15	109	20	16.1	17
NationsBank	USA (5)	13.7	16	186	19	28.1	9
National Westminister Bank	UK (2)	13.1	17	310	14	20.8	15
Barclays Bank	UK (3)	12.9	18	306	15	26.4	11
Groupe Caisse d'Epargne	FR (2)	12.7	19	230	18	—	—
Industrial Bank of Japan	JP (7)	12.5	20	361	10	44.0	4

Table 2.A.3 Twenty largest banks in terms of shareholder equity in 1991

Bank	Country	Shareholder equity ($bln)		Total assets ($bln)		Market capitalization ($bln)	
Sumitomo Bank	JP (1)	15.2	1	406	2	53.3	4
Dai-Ichi Kangyo Bank	JP (2)	13.6	2	426	1	60.2	2
Fuji Bank	JP (3)	13.3	3	396	5	57.9	3
Sanwa Bank	JP (4)	13.0	4	401	4	52.0	5
UBS Group	SW (1)	12.9	5	184	15	2.2	15
Mitsubishi Bank	JP (5)	12.0	6	380	6	18.2	8
Barclays Bank	UK (1)	11.7	7	264	10	11.3	9
Sakura Bank	JP (6)	11.6	8	406	3	47.7	6
Deutsche Bank	DE (1)	11.2	9	298	8	18.8	7
Compagnie Financière de Paribas	FR (1)	11.1	10	200	14	—	—
Industrial & Commercial Bank of China	China (1)	10.6	11	180	16	3.7	14
National Westminister Bank	UK (2)	10.4	12	232	12	8.4	10
Crédit Lyonnais	FR (2)	9.7	13	306	7	0.6	16
Citicorp	USA (1)	9.5	14	217	13	4.3	13
Industrial Bank of Japan	JP (7)	9.4	15	288	9	60.6	1
Swiss Bank Corp	SW (2)	9.2	16	153	18	—	—
Caisses d' Epargne Ecureuil (CENCEP)	FR (3)	9.1	17	174	17	—	—
ABN AMRO	NL (1)	9.0	18	243	11	6.5	11
Bank of China	China (2)	8.2	19	140	19	5.4	12
Caisse des Dépots et Consignations	FR (4)	8.1	20	75	20	—	—

NOTES

1. An example is ING Direct, the online banking unit used by ING to enter foreign deposit-taking markets.
2. The interest rate margin tends to move with the level of interest rates. As the interest rates have fallen somewhat between 1997 and 2001, that might have contributed too to the lower margins.
3. High margins in Southern Europe may reflect weaker competition. It is however harder to believe that the low margins in Germany and France point to high competition, as this is contrary to 'accepted wisdom'.
4. The high US margins also violate the simple high competition, low margin theory.
5. See also Section 4.4, where numbers of banks and concentration indices are used to explain competition (conduct) on EU banking markets.
6. See also Garcia (2000) and Bikker and Prast (2001).

3. Measures of competition and concentration in the banking industry

3.1 INTRODUCTION

The deregulation of financial services in the European Union, the establishment of the Economic and Monetary Union (EMU) and the development of information technology are expected to contribute to dramatic changes in European banking markets over the coming years, with vast implications for competition and concentration in the banking and financial sector. The recent wave of mergers in the European banking industry can be seen as a result of these developments. This process of consolidation may affect competition, particularly on local retail markets, and enhances concentration, whereas the size of new global players may cause concerns about financial stability.

To assess the implications of these developments, it is necessary to investigate the impact of consolidation on the market structure and the performance of banks. Measures of concentration and competition are essential for welfare-related public policy towards the banking market. In recent years, however, only a limited number of empirical studies have investigated competition and concentration in European banking markets. The scarcity of analysis in this field is primarily due to a dire shortage of detailed European sub-market banking data. This chapter provides an overview of the tools at hand to investigate competitive conditions and to calculate the degree of concentration in (banking) markets, as presented in the literature. It summarizes the theoretical foundations of the various measures of competition and concentration as well as their empirical application to the European banking industry.

Concentration and competition are linked to product markets and geographical areas, both in theory and in empirical analyses. Banks provide a multitude of products that do not serve a unique market, and defining a relevant market involves making a preliminary decision about potentially relevant structural characteristics, such as concentration and competition (Kottmann, 1974). The relevant market includes all suppliers of a good who are actual or potential competitors, and it has a product dimension and a geographical dimension. The product definition of a market requires the determination of the range of products which can be assigned to a particular market on the basis of their substitutability in terms of consumer demand. Likewise, the geographical boundaries of a market are drawn according to existing and potential contacts between actual and potential market participants. They are determined from the customer's point of view and take into consideration individual consumer as well as product characteristics. The mobility of banking customers, and therefore the geographic boundaries of the market, depend quite crucially on the type of customer and their economic size; the local dimension of a market is relevant for retail banking products and the regional or international dimension is relevant for corporate banking. Product characteristics influence the mobility of customers in that commercial borrowers tend to display greater mobility in their search for financing possibilities than depositors (Kottmann, 1974; Deppe, 1978; and Büschgen, 1993).

The chapter is organized as follows. Section 3.2 presents an overview of market concentration measures, discusses their theoretical characteristics and gives numerical examples to illustrate differences and similarities between concentration indices in operation. The literature on the measurement of competition can be divided into two major streams: structural and non-structural approaches. In the structural approaches, concentration ratios take a central position in order to describe the market structure. Structural approaches are investigated first (in Section 3.3), as they constitute a natural link between concentration and competition. The impact of market concentration on market performance has its roots in both the oligopoly theory and the structure–conduct–performance (SCP) paradigm. Whereas the former approach is founded in economic theory, the latter is an *ad hoc* approach, often criticized in methodological as well as identificational terms, but nevertheless applied empirically ad infinitum. Where an SCP model can be based on any concentration ratio, two formal derivations of the competition–concentration relationship based on oligopoly theory each exactly define the relevant concentration ratio. This section also surveys empirical results of the SCP test for the European banking industry. Section 3.4 provides a theoretical presentation of non-structural approaches to the measurement of competition, some of which share the same theoretical roots as the formal structural methods of the preceding section. Furthermore, this section summarizes the results of the various studies applying those approaches to the European banking industry. Appendix 3 reviews the most important distributional concepts employed in this chapter.

3.2 MEASURES OF CONCENTRATION

The importance of concentration ratios arises from their ability to capture structural features of a market. Concentration ratios are therefore often used in structural models explaining competitive performance in the banking industry as the result of market structure.[1] This feature will be discussed in Section 3.3, where the impact of concentration on competitive performance is investigated. Concentration ratios are also able to reflect changes in concentration as a result of the entry of a bank into the market or its exit from it, or caused by a merge. This feature is used in the USA, for instance, in the enforcement process of anti-trust laws in banking.

The concept of industrial concentration has been extensively treated and lively debated in the economic literature. Despite the many different approaches to its measurement, general agreement prevails about the constituting elements of concentration measures, that is the number of banks and the distribution of bank sizes (or inequality) in a given market. However, the classification of concentration measures in the literature is not systematic. This chapter presents concentration indices (*CI*) exhibiting the general form:

$$CI = \sum_{i=1}^{n} w_i \, s_i \tag{3.1}$$

where s_i is the market share of bank *i*, w_i is the weight attached to the market share and *n* is the number of banks in the market in question. This section considers ten concentration ratios – the *k* bank concentration ratio (CR_k); the Herfindahl–Hirschman index (*HHI*); the Hall–Tideman index (*HTI*); the Rosenbluth index (*RI*); the comprehensive industrial concentration index (*CCI*); the Hannah and Kay index (*HKI*); the U index (*U*); the multiplicative Hause index (H_m); the additive Hause index (H_a); and the Entropy measure (*E*) – and discusses the weighting scheme and structure of each. The theoretical discussion of the properties of the various indices is illustrated by their empirical application to the Dutch mortgage market. In addition, the most frequently used indices, CR_k and *HHI*, are applied to 20 countries in order to assess their ability to measure and, more particularly, to rank bank concentration in these countries.

3.2.1 Classification by Weighting Scheme and Structure

Concentration measures can be classified according to their weighting schemes and structure. Marfels (1971a) and Dickson (1981) discuss the weighting schemes of a number of concentration ratios. The weighting scheme of an index determines its sensitivity towards changes at the tail-end of the bank size distribution. Marfels differentiates between four groups of weights:[2]

1. Weights of unity are attached to the shares of an arbitrarily determined number of banks ranked in descending order ($w_i = 1$, $\forall i \leq k$), and zero weights are attached to the remaining banks in the industry ($w_i = 0$, $\forall i > k$). An example is the *k* bank concentration ratio, probably the most frequently used concentration ratio.
2. Banks' market shares are used as their own weights ($w_i = s_i, \forall i$), so that greater weights are attached to larger banks. These indices take account of all banks in the industry. An example is the Herfindahl–Hirschman index, well-known from both theory and practice.
3. The rankings of the individual banks are used as weights ($w_i = i$, $\forall i$), where banks can be ranked in ascending or descending order. All banks are included in computing this index. Examples are the Rosenbluth index and the Hall–Tideman index.
4. Each market share is weighted by the negative of its logarithm ($w_i = -log\, s_i, \forall i$). A smaller absolute weight is thus attached to larger market shares. An example is the Entropy index.

Dickson's (1981) approach to weighting schemes is somewhat more theoretical. By defining conjectural variation elasticity,[3] he presents the derivation of various weighting schemes embedded in microeconomic theory. Dickson found only six of the 15 indices under investigation consistent with theoretical market models: the CR_k, the *HHI*, the *CCI*, the H_m, the *HKI* and the *U*. Some of the indices presented in this section are more complex and hence consistent with more than one of the weighting schemes; an example is the *CCI*.

The structure of concentration indices can be discrete or cumulative. Discrete measures of concentration correspond to the height of the concentration curve at an arbitrary point.[4] The *k* bank concentration ratio, for instance, belongs to this class of discrete measures. Practical advantages of discrete measures are simplicity and limitation of required data. In the literature, both supporters and critics of discrete concentration measures are numerous. Both parties, however, stress the impact of concentration on the market behaviour of banks. Supporters of discrete measures maintain the view that the behaviour of a market dominated by a small number of banks is very unlikely to be influenced by the total number of enterprises in the market: the calculation of concentration indices on the basis of the entire bank size distribution would be unnecessarily large-scale, while only marginally changing the final results. Critics adhere to the view that every bank in the market influences market behaviour and stress a severe disadvantage of discrete indexes: they ignore the structural changes in those parts of the industry which are not encompassed by the index of concentration. The competitive behaviour of the smaller market players might force the larger players to act competitively as well.

Cumulative or summary measures of concentration, on the other hand, explain the entire size distribution of banks, implying that structural changes in all parts of the distribution influence the value of the concentration index. Of the measures presented in this section, the *HHI*, the *CCI*, the *RI* and the *HTI* as well as the *E* display this feature. Marfels (1971b) showed that it is possible to find corresponding measures of inequality for every summary measure of concentration, but that discrete measures of concentration do not exhibit this duality. Hence, he argues that the behaviour of discrete measures resulting from changes in the number of banks in the industry or in bank size disparity cannot be clearly identified.

3.2.2 Concentration Ratios

3.2.2.1 The *k* bank concentration ratio

Simplicity and limited data requirements make the *k* bank concentration ratio one of the most frequently used measures of concentration in the empirical literature. Summing only over the market shares of the *k* largest banks in the market, it takes the form:

$$CR_k = \sum_{i=1}^{k} s_i \tag{3.2}$$

giving equal emphasis to the *k* leading banks, but neglecting the many small banks in the market. There is no rule for the determination of the value of *k*, so that the number of banks included in the concentration index is a rather arbitrary decision. The concentration ratio may be considered as one point on the concentration curve, and it is a one-dimensional measure ranging between zero and unity. The index approaches zero for an infinite number of equally sized banks (given that the *k* chosen for the calculation of the concentration ratio is comparatively small as compared to the total number of banks) and it equals unity if the banks included in the calculation of the concentration ratio make up the entire industry. If the industry consists of *n* equally sized banks, then $CR_k = \sum_{i=1}^{k} s_i = \sum_{i=1}^{k} 1/n = k/n$, which is a decreasing function of the number of banks in the market, and which yields the *numbers equivalent* as $n_e = k/CR_k$ (White, 1982).[5]

3.2.2.2 The Herfindahl–Hirschman index

The Herfindahl–Hirschman index (*HHI*) is the most widely treated summary measure of concentration in the theoretical literature and often serves as a benchmark for the evaluation of other concentration indices. In the USA, the *HHI* plays a significant role in the enforcement process of antitrust laws in banking. An application for the merger of two banks will be approved without further investigation if the basic guidelines for the evaluation of the concentration in deposit markets are satisfied. Those guidelines imply that the post-merger market *HHI* does not exceed 0.18, and that the increase of the index from the pre-merger situation is less than 0.02 (Cetorelli, 1999). Often called the full-information index because it captures features of the entire distribution of bank sizes, it takes the form:

$$HHI = \sum_{i=1}^{n} s_i^2 \tag{3.3}$$

which is the sum of the squares of bank sizes measured as market shares. As mentioned above, the Herfindahl–Hirschman index stresses the importance of larger banks by assigning them a greater weight than smaller banks, and it incorporates each bank individually, so that arbitrary cut-offs and insensitivity to the share distribution are avoided. The *HHI* index ranges between $1/n$ and 1, reaching its lowest value, the reciprocal of the number of banks, when all banks in a market are of equal size, and reaching unity in the case of monopoly. Davies (1979) analyses the sensitivity of the *HHI* to its two constituent parts, that is the number of banks in the market and the inequality in market shares among the different banks and finds that the index becomes less sensitive to changes in the number of banks the larger the number of banks in the industry.

Several authors propose linking the Herfindahl–Hirschman index to distributional theory by presenting it in terms of the moments of the underlying bank size distribution. A first attempt to present the *HHI* in terms of the distribution's mean and variance has been undertaken by Adelman (1969). Kwoka (1985) rewrites the Herfindahl–Hirschman index as $HHI = \bar{s} + \sum_{i=1}^{n}(s_i - \bar{s})^2$ by defining the mean market share as $\bar{s} = 1/n$. Rearranging yields the *HHI* as an inverse function of the number of banks in the industry and a direct function of the market shares's variance about the mean:

$$HHI = (1/n) + n\sigma^2 \tag{3.4}$$

This presentation points up two features of the Herfindahl–Hirschman index. First, the relation between the number of banks and the value of *HHI* is not a simple one. Given the number of banks in the market, the *HHI* increases with the variance, which is itself a function of the number of banks in the market (Adelman, 1969). Second, this presentation of the *HHI* is ambiguous in that a variety of combinations of the number and sizes of banks can produce the same *HHI* (Kwoka, 1985). However, this need not be a shortcoming and, for instance, holds also for the Lerner index.[6]

In the context of hypothetical market analysis, Rhoades (1995) argues that the inequality of banks' market shares might differ substantially between markets yielding the same *HHI* value. It is possible to calculate the numbers equivalent of the HHI as $n_e = 1/HHI$ for every value of the Herfindahl–Hirschman index (since $HHI = \Sigma_{i=1}^{n} (1/n)^2 = n(1/n)^2 = 1/n$), providing evidence that at least two different bank size distributions can generate the same *HHI*.

Hart (1975) takes a slightly different approach to embedding the Herfindahl–Hirschman index into distributional theory. Arguing that there are cases where the exact number of banks in an industry is unknown but information is available about both the banking market's size and banks' size classification, he proposes to divide the total distribution of bank sizes into classes and to calculate the parameters of the original distribution from the parameters of the first moment distribution if the relationship between the distributions is known. He obtains a definition of *HHI* given by:

$$HHI = (\eta_0^2 + 1) / n \tag{3.5}$$

where η_0^2 is the coefficient of variation (the possible change of the size structure) of the original distribution. As long as the coefficient of variation does not change, an increase in *n* will result in a decrease in the *HHI*. Hart considers the sensitivity to the entrance of very small banks into an oligopolistic market as the greatest disadvantage of the index.

3.2.2.3 The Hall-Tideman index and the Rosenbluth index

The concentration indices developed by Hall and Tideman (1967) and Rosenbluth (Niehans, 1961) resemble one another both in form and in character. Hall and Tideman bring forward a number of properties which concentration measures should satisfy and they accept the *HHI* on the basis of those properties. They emphasize the need to include the number of banks in the calculation of a concentration index, because it reflects to some extent the conditions of entry into a particular industry.[7] Their index takes the form:

$$HTI = 1 / (2\sum_{i=1}^{n} i\, s_i - 1) \tag{3.6}$$

where the market share of each bank is weighted by its ranking in order to ensure that the emphasis is on the absolute number of banks, and that the largest bank receives weight $i = 1$. The *HTI* ranges between zero and unity, being close to zero for an infinite number of equal-sized banks, and reaching unity in the case of monopoly. Like the Herfindahl–Hirschman index, the *HTI* equals 1/n for an industry with *n* equally sized banks and the numbers equivalent of the index is defined as $n_e = 1/HTI$.

Rosenbluth's index is related in an obvious way to the concentration curve,[8] but different from the CR_k, it takes explicit account of each item in the size distribution. The use of the rankings of banks as weights for the calculation of the index, starting with the smallest, makes the index – unlike the CR_k – sensitive to changes in the bank size distribution of smaller banks. The Rosenbluth index is calculated from the area above the concentration curve and below a horizontal line drawn at a level of 100 per cent (entire market) on the vertical scale, defined as C in Figures 3.A.1 and 3.A.2 in Appendix 3. Rosenbluth's index takes the form $RI = 1/(2C)$, which is identical to the *HTI* for $C = \sum_{i=1}^{n} i\, s_i - 1/2$. The only difference between the indices results from the ranking of banks. For a given degree of inequality, the *RI* decreases with the increase in the number of banks. Hause (1977) claims that the value of the Rosenbluth index is heavily influenced by the small banks in the size distribution, so that its usefulness for analysing departures from competition in highly concentrated industries seems quite dubious.

3.2.2.4 The comprehensive industrial concentration index

The comprehensive industrial concentration index (*CCI*) has emerged from the debate on concentration and dispersion of banks (or firms) within various industries. The debate rests on two arguments. Despite the widely recognized convention that the dominance of the largest few banks determines market behaviour, discrete concentration measures have been criticized on the grounds that they ignore changes in market structure occurring elsewhere than among the largest banks. Conversely, dispersion measures, such as the Lorenz curve and the Gini coefficient, are said to undervalue the importance of large banks in the industry. To circumvent the deficiencies of earlier indices, Horvarth (1970) presents the *CCI*, which is capable of reflecting both relative dispersion and absolute magnitude. The *CCI* owes its intellectual heritage to the *HHI* and takes the form:

$$CCI = s_1 + \sum_{i=2}^{n} s_i^{\,2}(1+(1-s_i)) \tag{3.7}$$

It is the sum of the proportional share of the leading bank and the summation of the squares of the proportional sizes of each bank, weighted by a multiplier reflecting the proportional size of the rest of the industry. The index is unity in the case of monopoly and it is higher than the dominant bank's absolute percentage share for a market with a greater number of banks (Horvarth, 1970). The well-established theoretical literature on equilibrium subset cartels serve as a formal underpinning for the appropriateness of the dissimilar treatment of two classes of banks, that is the accentuation of the dominant bank at the expense of the rest.

3.2.2.5 The Hannah and Kay index

Hannah and Kay (1977) propose a summary index of concentration of the form:

$$HKI = (\sum_{i=1}^{n} s_i^{\alpha})^{1/(1-\alpha)} \quad \alpha > 0 \text{ and } \alpha \neq 1 \tag{3.8}$$

where α is an elasticity parameter to be specified and intended to reflect their ideas about changes in concentration as a result of the entry or exit of banks, and the sales transfer among the different banks in the market. The freedom to choose α allows for alternative views on what is the appropriate weighting scheme and for the option to emphasize either the upper or the lower segment of the bank size distribution. Therefore, in addition to the distribution of the banks in the market, the value of the index is sensitive to the parameter α. For $\alpha \to 0$, the index approaches the number of banks in the industry, and for $\alpha \to \infty$, it converges towards the reciprocal of the market share of the largest bank. The numbers equivalent of the *HKI* can be solved for $HKI = (n_e(1/n_e)^{\alpha})^{1/(1-\alpha)}$ as $n_e = HKI$.

Hannah and Kay (1977) show that the entry of a bank, whose size is equal to the effective average size of the existing banks,[9] will result in the greatest reduction in concentration and cause the numbers equivalent of the concentration index to increase by one. If a bank of greater than effective average size enters the industry, the effect of reduction in concentration would be smaller, or could even be reversed (higher concentration because the size effect outweighs the numbers effect). The expansion of a bank whose size exceeds the effective average bank size, would increase the value of the *HKI*, and the expansion of a bank smaller than the effective average bank size would reduce it. The distribution of the *HKI* for a given market and for various values of α is presented in Table 3.1 at the end of this section.

3.2.2.6 The *U* index

Davies (1979) defines his *U* index in terms of inequality and the number of banks in the industry reflecting his perception that most of the concentration indices developed earlier attach too much weight to either inequality or the number of banks in the market. It takes the form $U = I^{a} n^{-1}$, where $a \geq 0$ and *I* is a generally accepted measure of inequality. The index allows flexibility in the weight given to size inequality (*I*) and the number of banks (*n*) by varying *a*, which is an innovation compared to the concentration measures presented earlier. The choice of *a* is not arbitrary. To obtain the value of *a,* Davis proposes to estimate a simple model of inter-industry variance in price cost margins of the form $\pi_i = \alpha C_i^{\beta}$, where π_i and C_i are, respectively, the price-cost margin and concentration in industry *i*.[10] Replacing C_i by the *U* index and taking logarithms, the regression equation can be written as:

$$\log \pi_i = \log \alpha + \beta_1 \log I_i + \beta_2 \log n_i + \upsilon_i \qquad (3.9)$$

Since $\beta_1 = a\beta$ and $\beta_2 = -\beta$, the estimated value of *a* can be obtained as $a = -\beta_1 / \beta_2$. Theoretically, Davies derives the *U* index as:

$$U = (n\Sigma_{i=1}^{n} s_i^2)^a n^{-1} = (n^{(a-1)/a} \Sigma_{i=1}^{n} s_i^2)^a = (\Sigma_{i=1}^{n} s_i (s_i n^{(a-1)/a}))^a \qquad (3.10)$$

by defining inequality as $I = 1 + c^2 = \Sigma_{i=1}^{n} x_i^2 / n\bar{x}^2 = (\Sigma_{i=1}^{n} x_i^2 / n) X^2 / n^2 = n\Sigma_{i=1}^{n} s_i^2$. Hence, *I* is a simple transformation of the coefficient of variation c^2. Davies investigates the reaction of the *U* index to new entries and mergers in order to shed light on the role and the possible values of the *a* parameter. Since mergers and entry can best be measured by introducing a yardstick measure of typical bank size, the Herfindahl average effective size of banks has been applied.[11] Davies proposes that *a* should be constrained to $a \leq 1$ in empirical applications for the index to deliver economically unambiguous and plausible results. For $a \leq 1$, a merger always leads to an increase in the recorded concentration and the proportionate increase will be in line with the size of the merging banks. The magnitude of the parameter *a* furthermore determines the sensitivity of the index to different types of mergers. *U* will thus become more sensitive to mergers as value of *a* increases and the merging banks are larger. The entry of a new bank into the industry will lead to a fall in recorded concentration, provided the entrant is no more than twice the Herfindahl average effective size. The de-concentrating effect is maximized, where the entrant is of exactly the average effective size. The entry of very small banks will generally have only a minimal effect on concentration, and the magnitude of *a* determines the sensitivity of *U* to entry. The restriction $a \leq 1$, however, implies that $0 < s_i n^{(a-1)/a} < s_i$. From a theoretical point of view, this result is implausible. Oligopolistic behaviour becomes possible only if *a* is constrained to $a \geq 1$. It therefore appears as if the *U* index delivers theoretically as well as empirically satisfactory results only if $a = 1$, for which $U = HHI$. The distribution of the *U* index for a given market and various values of *a* are presented in Table 3.1 at the end of this section.

3.2.2.7 The Hause indices

Based on a discussion of the various interpretations of the Cournot model, Hause (1977) introduces six criteria that a theoretically reasonable measure of industrial concentration should satisfy. He claims that none of the earlier measures meets all of his criteria, and he attempts to derive two measures of concentration that do. Both depend on a parameter α that captures the effects of collusion in an oligopoly model. Hause furthermore provides numerical evidence that the tendency towards more competition as n increases is much slower for low values of α, that is a high degree of collusion, than implied by the *HHI* index. The multiplicatively modified Cournot measure takes the form:

$$H_m(\alpha,\{s_i\}) = \sum_{i=1}^{n} s_i^{2-(s_i(HHI-s_i^2))^{\alpha}} \tag{3.11}$$

where *HHI* is the Herfindahl–Hirschman index and α is the parameter capturing the degree of collusion. To ensure that the index is a decreasing, convex function of the equivalent number of equally sized banks implied by the index, it appears necessary to restrict $\alpha \geq 0.15$. The α parameter decreases inversely to the degree of collusion, and for $\alpha \to \infty$ the index approaches the Herfindahl–Hirschman index. Assuming a two-bank industry, Hause derives the range for the expression raised to the power of α as $[0, 2(1/3)^{0.15} = 0.39]$, so that the exponent on s_i always exceeds unity (provided $\alpha > 0$).[12] The validity of the index in theoretical terms depends quite crucially on the specification of α: only if $\alpha \to \infty$ will the weights attached to the banks' market shares grow to equal those of the Herfindahl–Hirschman index. The index equals one in the monopoly case, it converges to zero for an infinite number of equally sized banks in the market and it takes the value $(1/n)^{1-((n-1)/n^3)^{\alpha}}$ if the banks in the industry are of equal size, converging to the Herfindahl result, that is $1/n$, for large n. Hause furthermore proposes the additively adjusted Cournot measure of concentration, which is defined as:

$$H_a(\beta,\{s_i\}) = \sum_{i=1}^{n} (s_i^2 + (s_i(HHI - s_i^2))^{\beta}) \tag{3.12}$$

with $\beta > 1$. This restriction assures the convergence of the index to the Herfindahl–Hirschman index for larger numbers of banks, and the measure becomes $(n^{-1} + n^{1-2\beta}(1-n^{-1})^{\beta})$, if all banks in the market are of equal size.

3.2.2.8 Entropy measure

The Entropy measure has its theoretical foundations in information theory and measures the *ex-ante* expected information content of a distribution.[13] The Entropy measure takes the form:[14]

$$E = -\Sigma_{i=1}^{n} s_i \, log_2 \, s_i \tag{3.13}$$

The index ranges between 0 and $\log_2 n$, and is therefore not restricted to [0, 1], as most of the other measures of concentration presented above. The value of the Entropy varies inversely to the degree of concentration. It approaches zero if the underlying market is monopoly and reaches its highest value, $E = \log n$, when market shares of all banks are equal and market concentration is lowest. For a given number of banks, the index falls with an increase in inequality among those banks (White, 1982), and the weights the index attaches to market share decreases in absolute terms as the market share of a bank becomes larger (Kwoka, 1985). The numbers equivalent of this index takes the form $n_e = 2^E$.

3.2.3 Empirical Illustrations of Concentration Measures

Before concluding the discussion of the various concentration measures, we present a few brief numerical exercises taken from practical experience. The first application demonstrates the diverging results yielded by the various concentration measures when applied to the same underlying market. Table 3.1 presents the values of these indices based on market shares of 16 banks active in the Dutch mortgage market. Even a brief glance reveals the wide spread in these values. The results show clearly that not only does the range of possible values differ strongly across the indices, but so do the values of the indices within this range. For instance, the value is high for the CR_k and low for the *HHI* and in particular for the Rosenbluth index, where the ranges of these indices are identical (see Table 3.1).

Three of the indices, namely the *HKI*, the multiplicatively modified Hause index and the *U* index were calculated for a number of parameter values for α or a. The sensitivity of these indices to changes in those parameter values is displayed in Figures 3.1–3.3. They clearly show that, for a given market structure, the *U* index is an increasing function of the underlying parameters, while the *HKI* and the Hause index are decreasing. The *HHI* is a special case of the *U* index for $a = 1$, whereas the Hause index converges to the *HHI* if $\alpha \to \infty$.

Table 3.1 Application of concentration measures to the Dutch mortgage market

Index type	Range	Parameters	Typical features	Value
CR_3	$0 < CR_k \leq 1$		Takes only large banks into account; arbitrary cut off	0.82
CR_4			—	0.90
CR_5			—	0.96
HHI	$1/n \leq HHI \leq 1$		Considers all banks; sensitive to entrance of new banks	0.24
HTI	$0 < HTI \leq 1$		Emphasis on absolute number of banks	0.25
Rosenbluth	$0 < RI \leq 1$		Sensitive to changes in the size distribution of small banks	0.04
CCI	$0 < CCI \leq 1$		Addresses relative dispersion and absolute magnitude; suitable for cartel markets	0.56
HKI	$1/s_1 \leq HKI \leq n$	$\alpha = 0.005$	Sensitive to size distribution; stresses influence small banks	15.79
		$\alpha = 0.25$	—	9.41
		$\alpha = 5$	—	3.64
		$\alpha = 10$	Sensitive to size distribution; stresses influence large banks	3.40
U index	$1/n \leq U \leq \infty$	$a = 0.25$	Stresses number of banks	0.09
		$a = 1$	For $a = 1$, the U index corresponds to the HHI	0.24
		$a = 2$	—	0.92
		$a = 3$	Stresses inequality distribution of banks	3.51
Hause index	$0 < H_m \leq 1$	$\alpha = 0.25$	Suitable for highly collusive markets	0.44
		$\alpha = 1$	—	0.25
		$\alpha = 2$	Suitable for not collusive markets	0.24
Entropy	$0 \leq E \leq \log n$		Based on expected information content of a distribution	2.35

Concentration ratios are often used as input for public policy rules and measures regarding the banking market structure. Policy makers can select suitable concentration indices depending on (i) the features of their banking market (for example the type or level of concentration), (ii) their perceptions regarding the relative impact larger and smaller banks have on competition in a certain market, and (iii) their perceptions regarding the relative impact of size distribution and number of banks (for instance, reflecting the impact of a new entry). These features and perceptions mainly determine which index is most appropriate. Concentration ratios are also used to measure the impact of concentration on competition. Section 3.2.1 elaborates on the relation between the concentration ratios' weighting schemes and underlying bank conduct.

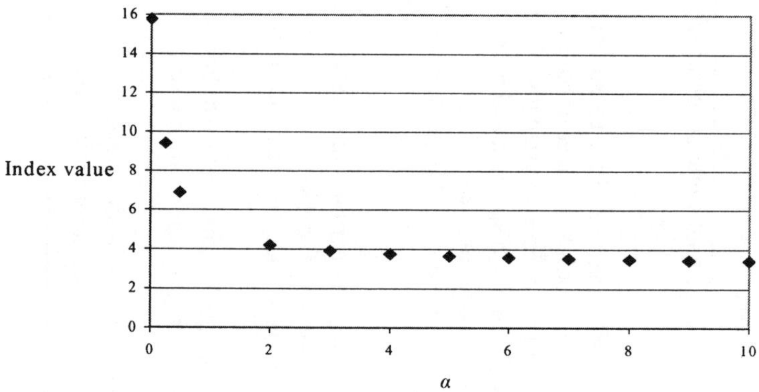

Figure 3.1 The Hannah and Kay index (for different values of α)

The second practical exercise demonstrates the results for two concentration measures when applied to different markets. Table 3.2 shows the values of the most frequently used indices, the Herfindahl–Hirschman index and the k bank concentration ratios, for k = 3, 5 and 10, based on market shares in terms of total assets of banks in 20 countries (for details and background, see Chapter 4). We have already observed the spread caused by differences in weighting schemes which can occur in the (average) levels of the various indices. Differences across countries in the *HHI* relate most heavily to the number of banks (see last column), whereas differences in the CR_k are mainly due to the skewness of the bank-size distribution, in particular of its large-bank end. On the whole, apart from a few exceptions,[15] the rankings of countries are rather similar for the various indices considered, which raises confidence in the appropriateness of these indices. The result is typical for what is observed in the empirical literature. Surprisingly, the

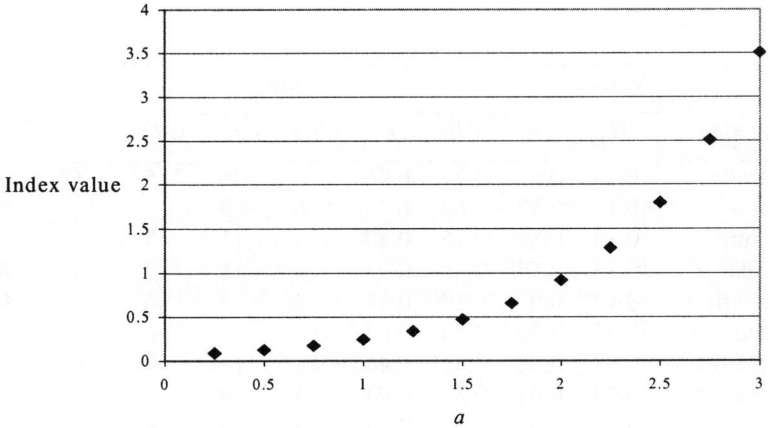

Figure 3.2 *The* U *index (for different values of* a*)*

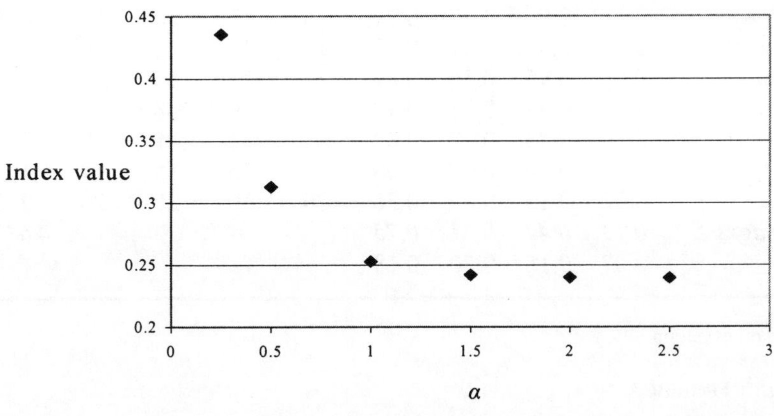

Figure 3.3 *The multiplicatively-modified Hause index (for different values of* α*)*

ranking of the *HHI* and the 3-bank *CR* bear the closest resemblance (with a correlation of 0.98), whereas the ranking of the 5 and 10-bank *CR*s differ more from the *HHI* (with, respectively, correlations of 0.94 and 0.86). The CR_3 and the CR_{10} are least similar. This observation puts into perspective the many ponderous considerations in the literature regarding the neglect of the smaller banks in the *k* bank *CR* indices – compared to the *HHI*, which takes all banks into account.

Table 3.2 *Concentration indices for 20 countries, based on total assets (1997)*

	Values				Rankings				No. of banks
Countries	*HHI*	CR_3	CR_5	CR_{10}	*HHI*	CR_3	CR_5	CR_{10}	
Australia	0.14	0.57	0.77	0.90	6	6	5	6	31
Austria	0.14	0.53	0.64	0.77	6	9	11	12	78
Belgium	0.12	0.52	0.75	0.87	9	11	7	7	79
Canada	0.14	0.54	0.82	0.94	6	8	2	1	44
Denmark	0.17	0.67	0.80	0.91	4	3	4	5	91
France	0.05	0.30	0.45	0.64	16	16	16	15	336
Germany	0.03	0.22	0.31	0.46	18	18	18	19	1 803
Greece	0.20	0.66	0.82	0.94	3	4	2	1	22
Ireland	0.17	0.65	0.73	0.84	4	5	8	8	30
Italy	0.04	0.27	0.40	0.54	17	17	17	17	331
Japan	0.06	0.39	0.49	0.56	14	14	14	16	140
Luxembourg	0.03	0.20	0.30	0.49	18	19	19	18	118
Netherlands	0.23	0.78	0.87	0.93	2	1	1	3	45
Norway	0.12	0.56	0.67	0.81	9	7	10	11	35
Portugal	0.09	0.40	0.57	0.82	12	13	12	9	40
Spain	0.08	0.45	0.56	0.69	13	12	13	13	140
Sweden	0.12	0.53	0.73	0.92	9	9	8	4	21
Switzerland	0.26	0.72	0.77	0.82	1	2	5	9	325
UK	0.06	0.34	0.47	0.68	14	15	15	14	186
USA	0.02	0.15	0.23	0.38	20	20	20	20	717
Averages/Σ	*0.11*	*0.47*	*0.61*	*0.75*	—	—	—	—	*4 612*
σ [a]	0.07	0.18	0.20	0.18					

[a] Standard deviation.

Source: Fitch-IBCA.

3.2.4 Concluding Remarks

With the exception of the *k* bank concentration ratio and the Herfindahl–Hirschman index, the measures of concentration presented in the preceding discussion have been applied only sparingly in the empirical banking literature. The former two indices are also often used as proxies for the market structure in structural approaches to measure competition, namely the structure–conduct–performance paradigm and the efficiency hypothesis, which both will be presented in the next section. The Herfindahl–Hirschman index, furthermore, is a statutory measure to evaluate the impact which a proposed merger in the US banking industry is to have on the market structure in the region concerned. Applied in practice, the various concentration measures may show strongly diverging values for the same market, owing to the use of varying weighting schemes, which reflect mainly different assessment regarding the relative impact of larger and smaller banks on competition in a certain market. Policy makers should choose concentration indices depending on the features of their banking market and their perceptions regarding the relative impact larger and smaller banks have on competition and regarding the relative impact of size distribution and number of banks. Where for the *k* bank *CR*s and the *HHI* the levels may vary, their rankings of banking markets in 20 countries appear (as is often the case) to be quite similar. This adds to the suitability of these indices for public policy rules and measures.

3.3 STRUCTURAL MEASURES OF COMPETITION

The literature on the measurement of competition can be divided into two major streams: structural and non-structural approaches. The *structural approach* to the measurement of competition embraces the structure–conduct–performance paradigm and the efficiency hypothesis, as well as a number of formal approaches with roots in industrial organization theory. The two former models investigate, respectively, whether a highly concentrated market causes collusive behaviour among the larger banks resulting in superior market performance, and whether it is the efficiency of larger banks that enhances their performance. These structural models, which link competition to concentration, are presented in this section. Non-structural models for the measurement of competition, namely the Iwata model (Iwata, 1974), the Bresnahan model,[16] and the Panzar–Rosse model (Panzar and Rosse, 1987), were developed in reaction to the theoretical and empirical deficiencies of the structural models. These New Empirical Industrial Organization approaches test competition and the use of market power, and stress the analysis of banks' competitive conduct in the absence of structural measures. These non-structural approaches, which ignore the impact of concentration, will be discussed in Section 3.4.

Structural measures of competition may, in turn, be divided into two major schools of thought: the formal and non-formal approaches. The study of the relationship between market performance and market structure has its roots in the non-formal framework of the SCP paradigm. Since its origins, this framework has evolved largely independently of ongoing refinements in formal models of imperfectly competitive markets (Martin, 1993). The empirical application of the SCP paradigm in its original form and the recognition that the market structure should be treated as an endogenous variable, led to a reformulation of the empirical tests and to attempts to build a formal theoretical framework for the structural equations. Oligopoly theory has replaced structure–conduct–performance as the organizing framework for industrial economics. In some cases, this work recast structure–conduct–performance arguments in a more formal mould (Martin, 1993). Yet, large discrepancies between the formal and non-formal approaches remain.

The first part of this section discusses two non-formal approaches to the market structure–market performance relationship, the SCP framework and the efficiency hypothesis. These approaches are called non-formal as measures for the market structure are not derived theoretically, but chosen at will. The second part presents two formal derivations of the competition–concentration relationship, one based on the Herfindahl–Hirschman index and one on the *k* bank concentration ratio. These measures of the market structure follow formally from theoretical derivations. Both the formal and the non-formal approaches link competition to concentration, as in every approach a concentration ratio takes up a central position.

3.3.1 Non-formal Structural Approaches to Competition

The SCP and the efficiency hypothesis are the two most common non-formal structural approaches to measure the impact of concentration on competition. In its original form, the SCP explains market performance as the result of an exogenously given market structure, which depends upon basic demand and supply side conditions (Reid, 1987, and Scherer and Ross, 1990) and which influences the conduct of banks in the industry. A higher level of concentration in the market is assumed to foster collusion among the active banks and to reduce the degree of competition in that particular market. The application of the SCP to the banking literature has been criticized by various authors, for instance by Gilbert (1984), Reid (1987), Vesala (1995) and Bos (2002). Their criticism is directed at the form of the model rather than at the specification of the variables used. Much of the criticism is related to the one-way causality – from market structure to market performance – inherent in the original model as it is still being applied in many banking studies, and to the failure by recent studies to incorporate new developments in the theory of industrial organizations. The extensive literature applying the structure–performance paradigm to the banking industry has been summarized by, for instance, Gilbert (1984) and Molyneux et al. (1996). In this context, it should be noted that most of the studies applying the SCP framework to the banking industry do not take explicit account of the *conduct* of banks.[17] This being the case, the remainder of the analysis will focus on the structure–performance (S–P) relationship.

The *efficiency hypothesis*, developed by Demsetz (1973) and Peltzman (1977), challenges the line of reasoning of the traditional S–P paradigm and offers a competing explanation of the relation between market structure and performance. The hypothesis claims that if a bank achieves a higher degree of efficiency than other banks in the market (that is, its cost structure is comparatively more effective), its profit maximizing behaviour will allow it to gain market share by reducing prices (Molyneux and Forbes, 1995). Market structure is therefore shaped endogenously by banks' performance, so that concentration is a result of the superior efficiency of the leading banks (Vesala, 1995).

Empirically, one may distinguish the S–P paradigm from the efficiency hypothesis by looking at the endogenous variable measuring the performance of a particular bank, which is usually estimated as a function of exogenous market structure and control variables, as in:

$$\Pi_{i,t} = \alpha_0 + \alpha_1 CR_{j,t} + \alpha_2 MS_{i,t} + \sum_k \alpha_{k+2} X^k_{i,j,t} \tag{3.14}$$

$\Pi_{i,t}$ is a performance measure for bank i, $CR_{j,t}$ is a measure of concentration in region j (the region to which bank i belongs) and $MS_{i,t}$ is the market share of bank i; t refers to period t. CR and MS each proxies an aspect of the market structure. X^k is a vector of control variables included to account for both bank-specific and region-specific characteristics (Molyneux and Forbes, 1995). The traditional structure–performance relationship would apply to the data if $\alpha_1 > 0$ and $\alpha_2 = 0$, and the efficiency hypothesis holds if $\alpha_1 = 0$ and $\alpha_2 > 0$.

Resulting from the definition of bank performance measures in various empirical studies, the S–P literature as applied to the banking industry can be divided into two groups (Gilbert, 1984; Molyneux et al., 1996; and Bos, 2002). A great variety of articles have employed the *price* of a particular product or service as a measure of bank performance, whereas a smaller number of studies relied on *profitability* measures, such as banks' profit rates.

The first group uses a price measure of some kind – commonly either *average* prices of products or services (average interest rates on loans or deposits, average service charges on demand deposits), or the price of *particular* products or services (for example business loans). The use of average prices as a proxy for bank performance has had its share of criticism. More precisely defined product markets are examined when data on individual product prices is employed. Price measures, however, ignore the (possible) cross-subsidization that is not uncommon for a multi-product bank, so that studies applying these performance measures might present a misleading picture as compared to the overall performance of the bank (Molyneux and Forbes, 1995). The definition of relevant product (and geographical) markets, as discussed in the introduction, is also an issue here.

Apart from the ease with which they can be obtained, profitability measures have the advantage of consolidating product profits and losses of a multi-product bank into one single figure; that is to say, they do include cross-subsidization among products. Like the pricing approach to banking performance, the calculation of profit measures from both stock and flow variables is a drawback (Molyneux et al., 1996). In addition, Vesala (1995) claims that banks' operational inefficiencies can lead to lower profitability, so that market power and profits need not necessarily be positively correlated. Furthermore, the calculation of an aggregated profit measure precludes the estimation of market power in individual markets.

Table 3.3 summarizes a variety of measures that can be used to describe *market structure* in the banking industry. In most studies, banking market structure is proxied by a measure of concentration and the market shares of the banks in the market.[18] The studies applying the S–P to the US banking industry usually define market structure in terms of the Herfindahl–Hirschman index, the *k* bank concentration ratio or the number of banks in the market (Molyneux et al., 1996). Only a very limited number of studies apply the Entropy, the Hall–Tideman index or the Gini coefficient as market structure measure. Not all structure–performance studies account for barriers to entry.

The control variables usually included in the empirical analysis proxy market demand conditions (such as per capita income or wage, levels of population density, immigration into specific markets), cost differences across banks, size-induced differences between banks, such as scale economies (for example measure of individual bank size), different risk categories (Molyneux et al., 1996) and ownership differences (Lloyd-Williams et al., 1994).

The results of the rather limited number of studies investigating the structure–performance relationship for European banking markets are no less ambiguous than those obtained from the US banking industry (Gilbert, 1984; Weiss, 1989; Molyneux et al., 1996; Bos, 2002). The scarcity of those studies is mainly the result of the lack of sub-market banking data for the European banking markets, which makes it extremely difficult to define a meaningful (relevant) market area and a reasonable measure of concentration in universal banking and nationwide banking markets.

3.3.2 Formal Structural Approaches to Competition

The growing body of literature subjecting the choice of profitability measures to formal analysis has been summarized by Martin (1993). Most of these formal studies generalize the Lerner index of monopoly power. They do not stress any one measure of profitability as correct or the best, but provide guidance in selecting tests of market power and profitability. The overall organizing framework, which will now be introduced, has its roots in industrial organizations theory. It provides the basis for the discussion of formal structural and non-structural models in competition theory.

Table 3.3 The structure–performance relationship in banking

Market structure (exogenous)	Concentration	- Herfindahl–Hirschman index - *k* bank concentration ratio - number of banks - other concentration ratios or Gini coefficient
	Market share[a]	- defined for the relevant market
	Barriers to entry[b]	- *regulatory barriers*: bank charters or branches and the conditions related to them - *non-regulatory barriers*: minimal efficient size, product differentiation, scale economies, technology and know-how
	Number of branches	- operating in the relevant market
	⇓	
Performance (endogenous)	Price measures	- price of *particular* products or services (for instance business loans) - *average* prices of products or services (for example average interest rates on loans; average interest rates on deposits; average service charges on demand deposits)
	Profitability measures	- single figure consolidating profits and losses realized with all products offered by a bank

[a] Market shares of individual banks are very often used as a measure indicating the efficiency of banks; [b] Vesala (1995) claims that the correlation between regulatory protection and concentration, as well as the correlation between regulatory protection and profitability may explain the detected positive correlation between concentration and profitability.

The derivations are based on the profit maximization problem for oligopolistic markets presented, for instance, by Cowling (1976) and Cowling and Waterson (1976). There are *n* unequally sized banks in the industry producing a homogeneous product.[19] Bank size differences are incorporated by the shape of the individual banks' cost functions. The profit function for an individual bank takes the form:

$$\Pi_i = px_i - c_i(x_i) - F_i \tag{3.15}$$

where Π_i is profit, x_i is the volume of output, p is the output price, c_i are the variable costs and F_i are fixed costs of bank i. Banks are assumed to face downward sloping market demand functions, the inverse of which is defined as:

$$p = f(X) = f(x_1 + x_2 + \ldots + x_n) \tag{3.16}$$

The first order condition for profit maximizing of bank i yields:

$$d\Pi_i / dx_i = p + f'(X)(dX / dx_i)x_i - c_i'(x_i) = 0 \tag{3.17}$$

and can be written as:

$$p + f'(X)(1 + \lambda_i)x_i - c'(x_i) = 0 \tag{3.18}$$

with $\lambda_i = d\sum_{j \neq i}^{n} x_j / dx_i$. This variable λ_i is called the conjectural variation of bank i and is the change in output of all remaining banks anticipated by bank i in response to an initial change in its own output dx_i. The concept of conjectural variation can parameterize any static or dynamic equilibrium structure in which firms' reaction functions are continuous. It allows differentiation between various market forms, and can be viewed as including expectations about the behaviour of potential entrants as well as actual rivals (Cowling, 1976, p.5). Depending on the underlying market form, λ_i can take values between -1 and $\sum_{j \neq i}^{n} x_j / x_i$. In the case of *perfect competition*, an increase in output by one bank has no effect on the market price and quantity: $dX/dx_i = 0 = (1 + \lambda_i)$, and hence $\lambda_i = -1$. A bank operating in a *Cournot oligopoly* does not expect retaliation from its competitors, that is, it expects other banks to remain inactive in response to an increase in its own output. An increase in output by bank i thus leads to an increase in total industry output by the same amount: $dX/dx_i = 1 = (1 + \lambda_i)$, so that $\lambda_i = 0$. In the case of *perfect collusion*, a bank i expects full retaliation from its competitors, who intend to protect their market share in response to an increase in output by bank i: $dX/dx_i = X/x_i = 1 + \lambda_i$ (an increase in output by bank i by one unit leads to an increase in market output by X/x_i units), and $\lambda_i = (X - x_i)/x_i = \sum_{j \neq i}^{n} x_j / x_i$. In what follows, Equation (3.18) will serve as a starting point both for the discussions of a variety of measures of competition and for the formal derivations of the relationship between measures of concentration and measures of competition.

3.3.2.1 The Herfindahl–Hirschman index in formal structure–performance models

Multiplying Equation (3.18) with x_i and summing the result over all banks yields:

$$\sum_{i=1}^{n} px_i + \sum_{i=1}^{n} f'(X)(dX / dx_i)X^2(x_i^2 / X^2) - \sum_{i=1}^{n} c_i'(x_i)x_i = 0 \quad (3.19)$$

and rearranging gives the price-cost margin as measure of performance for the industry as:

$$\sum_{i=1}^{n} (px_i - c_i'(x_i)x_i) / pX = -\sum_{i=1}^{n} (x_i / X)^2 (f'(X)X^2 / pX)(dX / dx_i) \quad (3.20)$$

which can be rewritten as:

$$\sum_{i=1}^{n} (px_i - c_i'(x_i)x_i) / pX = -\sum_{i=1}^{n} s_i^2 (dx_i / dx_i + d\sum_{j \neq i}^{n} x_j / dx_i) / \eta_D \quad (3.21)$$

or, as $\eta_D = dXp / dpX = p / f'(X)X$,[20]

$$\sum_{i=1}^{n} (px_i - c_i'(x_i)x_i) / pX = -(1+\gamma)HHI / \eta_D \quad (3.22)$$

where $\gamma = \sum_{i=1}^{n} \lambda_i x_i^2 / \sum_{i=1}^{n} x_i^2$. This expression represents the average price-cost margin in terms of η_D, the price elasticity of demand, the Herfindahl–Hirschman index *HHI* and γ, a term capturing the conjectural variation. This derivation conforms with the assumptions of the SCP framework in that a higher degree of concentration in an industry results in higher price-cost margins. In addition, this theoretical derivation justifies the use of the Herfindahl–Hirschman index as a measure of concentration in structure-performance relationships, when γ is known and equal for all banks.

In line with the general derivations presented above, Dickson (1981) introduced the conjectural variation elasticity $t_i = (dX/X)/(dx_i/x_i)$, that is the proportional change in market output anticipated by bank i $(\forall i)$. On the basis of this definition, two statements are possible. First, the degree of expected retaliation allows to draw conclusions about the underlying market structure. Second, there is theoretical justification for concentration measures to determine price-cost margins. Dickson redefined the price-cost margin of Equation (3.22), ignoring the constant η_D, as:

$$A = \sum_{i=1}^{n} s_i t_i \qquad (3.23)$$

with $t_i = s_i\ (1+\lambda_i)$. Note that: $\Sigma_{i=1}^{n} s_i\, t_i = \Sigma_{i=1}^{n}\ s_i^2\ (1+\lambda_i) = HHI + \Sigma_{i=1}^{n} x_i^2 \lambda_i / X^2 = HHI + \gamma \Sigma_{i=1}^{n} x_i^2\ / X^2 = HHI(1+\gamma)$. Just like the definition of the conjectural variation λ_i, the conjectural variation elasticity t_i takes different values depending on the underlying market structure. First, in a Cournot oligopoly, $dX/X = dx_i/X$, such that $t_i = (dX/X)/(dx_i/X)\ (x_i\ /X)$ = s_i. Second, $t_i = 1$ in the case of perfect collusion, since $dX/X = dx_i/x_i$. Third, for perfectly competitive markets $dX/dx_i = 0$ and $t_i = 0$. Measures of concentration can therefore be treated as weighted averages of conjectural variation elasticities.

The results obtained by Dickson for theoretically justifiable measures of concentration presented in Section 3.2 are summarized in Table 3.4. It turns out that the conjectural variation of a bank can take a fixed value, or vary within a certain range. The value of the conjectural variation elasticity thus tells us how the market structure has interacted with firms' decisions to give us a measure that is more directly related to the objectives of policy makers (such as welfare).

Table 3.4 Concentration measures and their conjectural variations

Measure of concentration	Weight w_i	Range of conjectural variation elasticity t_i [a]
HHI	$w_i = s_i$	$w_i = t_i = s_i$
CR_k	$w_i = 1$ for $i \leq k$	$w_i = t_i = 1$
	$w_i = 0$ for $i > k$	$w_i = t_i = 0$
CCI	$w_i = 1$ for s_1 and	$w_i = t_i = 1$
	$w_i = (s_i + (s_i - s_i^2))$ for $i > 1$	$s_i < w_i\ (= t_i\ ) \leq 0.75$
HKI [b]	$w_i = s_i^{\ a-1}$	$0 \leq t_i \leq 1$ [c]
U	$w_i = s_i n^{(a-1)/a}$	$0 < s_i n^{(a-1)/a}\ (= t_i) < s_i$ for $a \leq 1$ and $t_i > 1$ is possible for $a > 1$
H_m	$w_i = s_i^{\,1-(s_i(H-s_i^2))^a}$	$s_i < t_i < 1$

[a] See the text for the market structure corresponding to each of the values of t_i; [b] for the derivation of this weight, Dickson (1981) departs from the expression $HKI = \Sigma\ s_i^{\alpha}$ from which Hannah and Kay derived their index as presented in Equation (3.8); [c] the index can be made compatible by restricting $0 \leq s_i^{\alpha-1} \leq 1$, and $a \geq 1$. The parameter a is equal to 1 in the monopoly case, and the Cournot equilibrium is obtained when $\alpha \to 2$.

3.3.2.2 The k bank concentration ratio in formal structure–performance models

Another approach to the theoretical derivation of the SCP relationship has been proposed by, among others, Saving and Geroski (Reid, 1987) and assumes a *k* bank cartel with fringe competitors. Of the *n* banks in a market, *k* banks are acting as a cartel, and the remaining *n-k* banks are the competitive fringe in the industry. These *n-k* banks are price takers and equilibrate price and marginal cost, $p = c_i$, $\forall i = (k+1),...,n$, for profit maximizing purposes. The supply of these banks can then be written as $c_i^{-1}(p)$, so that the aggregate supply of the competitive fringe is $S_{n-k}(p) = \sum_{i=k+1}^{n} c_i^{-1}(p)$. Industry demand is defined by $D_T(p)$, with $D_T'(p) < 0$. Under the conditions defined above, the k bank cartel faces demand $D_k(p) = D_T(p) - S_{n-k}(p)$, where $S_{n-k}'(p) > 0$ and $D_T'(p) < 0$. Differentiating the above equation and dividing by $D_k(p)/p$ yields $D_k'(p)p / D_k(p) = D_T'(p)p / D_r(p) - S_{n-k}'(p)p / D_r(p)$ which can be written as $\eta_{D_k} = \eta_{D_T} D_T(p) / D_r(p) - \eta_{S_{n-k}} S_{n-k}(p) / D_r(p)$, where η_{D_k}, η_{D_T} and $\eta_{S_{n-k}}$ are, respectively, the elasticities with respect to price of residual demand, industry demand and fringe supply. For profit maximizing reasons, the *k* bank cartel should, in line with the concept of the Lerner index, set its price-marginal cost margin equal to the reciprocal of the elasticity of its demand curve:

$$\frac{p - c'_j}{p} = \frac{1}{\eta_{D_k}} = \frac{1}{\eta_{D_T}(D_T / D_k) - \eta_{S_{n-k}}(S_{n-k} / D_k)} = \frac{C_k}{\eta_{D_T} - \eta_{S_{n-k}}(1 - C_k)} \tag{3.24}$$

since $D_T / D_k = 1 / C_k$ and $S_{n-k} / D_k = (D_T - D_k) / D_k = 1 / C_k - 1 = (1 - C_k) / C_k$. This result shows that the application of the *k* bank concentration ratio for empirical estimations of the structure–performance relationship is theoretically justified for a market with a *k* bank cartel and *n-k* small banks. Hence, if we assume that the market is dominated by a cartel, in a S–P relationship, we should use CR_k.

3.3.3 Concluding Remarks

This section discussed formal and non-formal approaches to the relationships between market structure and market performance. The non-formal structure-performance paradigm and efficiency hypothesis, although lacking formal back-up in micro-economic theory, have frequently been applied to the banking industry and provide policy makers by measures of market structure and performance as well as their interrelationship. The formal approaches presented give evidence of the appropriateness of the CR_k and the *HHI* in the empirical application of structure-performance models. These formal relationships also state that bank conduct plays a role: CR_k is based on the assumption of a *k* bank cartel, *HHI* presupposes that conduct can be described by conjectural variation and similar deductions hold for other concentration ratios. These interpretations help policy makers to select a measure of concentration appropriate to their needs.

3.4 NON-STRUCTURAL MEASURES OF COMPETITION

This section discusses three non-structural measures of competition, namely the Iwata model, the Bresnahan model and the Panzar and Rosse approach. The derivations of the first two measures are based on the results obtained for the oligopoly profit-maximization problem presented in Section 3.3. The Panzar and Rosse method is based on the comparative static properties of the reduced-form revenue approach.

3.4.1 The Iwata Model

The Iwata model allows the estimation of conjectural variation values for individual banks supplying a homogeneous product in an oligopolistic market (Iwata, 1974). Although, to the best of our knowledge, this measure has been applied to the banking industry only once,[21] it is included in the present overview for completeness' sake. Defining the price elasticity of demand as $\eta_D = -(dp/dX)(x/p)$, Equation (3.18) can be written as $p-(1/\eta_D)(p/x)(1+\lambda_i)x_i - c'(x_i) = 0$, which, by re-arranging yields:

$$\lambda_i = \eta_D((c'(x_i) - p)/p)(X/x_i) - 1 \tag{3.25}$$

The numerical value of this conjectural variation will be obtained indirectly. Under the assumptions that p and x_i/X are strict functions of exogenous variables, and that η_D, the elasticity of demand, is constant, the method involves the estimation of a market demand function and cost functions of individual banks to obtain a numerical value of the conjectural variation for each bank. The application of this model to the European banking industry is difficult, especially given the lack of micro-data for the structure of cost and production for homogeneous products of a large number of players in the European banking markets.

3.4.2 The Bresnahan Model

Bresnahan (1982) and Lau (1982) present a short-run model for the empirical determination of the market power of an *average* bank. Based on time-series of industry data, the conjectural variation parameter $\lambda = (1 + d\sum_{i \neq j} x_j / dx_i)/n$, with $0 \leq \lambda \leq 1$, is determined by simultaneous estimations of the market demand and supply curves. Banks maximize their profits by equating marginal cost and perceived marginal revenue. The perceived marginal revenue coincides with the demand price in competitive equilibrium and with the industry's marginal revenue in the collusive extreme (Shaffer, 1993). Under the bank equality assumption of the Bresnahan model, Equation (3.18) can be rearranged to yield $p + f'(X)X\lambda = c'(x_i)$. Consistent with the statements about market forms and the corresponding conjectural variations in the introduction to this section, $\lambda = 0$ for the average bank in a *perfectly competitive* market. Under *Cournot equilibrium*, $d\sum_{i \neq j} x_j / dx_i = 0$, so that $\lambda = 1/n$ and $p + h(\cdot)/n = c'(x_i)$, with $h(\cdot) = f'(X)X$, the semi-elasticity of market demand. $p + h(\cdot) = c'(x_i)$ for *perfect collusion* since $\lambda = (1 + d\sum_{i \neq j} x_j / dx_i)/n = (1 + (X - x_i)/x_i)/n = x/(nx_i) = 1$, $\forall i$.

Empirical applications of the Bresnahan model are rather scarce. It has been estimated by Shaffer (1989 and 1993) for, respectively, the US loan markets and for the Canadian banking industry. Suominen (1994) applied the model in its original one-product version to the Finnish loan market for the period 1960–84 during which the interest rates applied by banks were tightly regulated. Interest rates on loans were deregulated in August 1986, but interest rates on deposits remained effectively restricted until 1990. An adapted two-product version is applied to the Finnish loan market for the period after deregulation (September 1986–December 1989).

Suominen finds coefficient estimates for λ which are close to zero and not significantly different from zero at the 5 per cent level for the period with regulated interest rates in both markets, and values of λ indicating use of market power after the deregulation of the loan market. Swank (1995) estimated Bresnahan's model to obtain the degree of competition in the Dutch loan and deposit markets over the period 1957–90, and found that both markets were significantly more oligopolistic than in Cournot equilibrium.

Chapter 5 presents applications of the Bresnahan model to loans markets as well as deposits markets in nine European countries over the latest two or three decades. Where values of λ appear to be significant different from zero, so that perfect competition should be rejected, they are nevertheless close to zero. In many cases, the hypothesis $\lambda = 0$ (that is, perfect competition) can not be rejected.

3.4.3 The Panzar and Rosse Approach

The method developed by Panzar and Rosse (1987) determines the competitive behaviour of banks on the basis of the comparative static properties of reduced-form revenue equations based on cross-section data. Panzar and Rosse (P–R) show that if their method is to yield plausible results, banks need to have operated in a long-term equilibrium (that is to say, the number of banks needs to be endogenous to the model) while the performance of banks needs to be influenced by the actions of other market participants. Furthermore, the model assumes a price elasticity of demand, *e*, greater than unity, and a homogeneous cost structure. To obtain the equilibrium output and the equilibrium number of banks, profits are maximized at the bank as well as the industry level. That means, first, that bank *i* maximizes it profits where marginal revenue equals marginal cost:

$$R_i'(x_i, n, z_i) - C_i'(x_i, w_i, t_i) = 0 \tag{3.26}$$

x_i being the output of bank *i*, *n* the number of banks, w_i a vector of *m* factor input prices of bank *i*, z_i a vector of exogenous variables that shift the bank's revenue function, and t_i a vector of exogenous variables that shift the bank's cost function. Second, it means that, in equilibrium, the zero profit constraint holds at the market level:

$$R_i^*(x^*, n^*, z) - C_i^*(x^*, w, t) = 0 \tag{3.27}$$

Variables marked with * represent equilibrium values. Market power is measured by the extent to which a change in factor input prices (∂w_{k_i}) is reflected in the equilibrium revenues (∂R_i^*) earned by bank *i*. Panzar and Rosse define a measure of competition, the '*H*-statistic' as the sum of the elasticities of the reduced-form revenues with respect to factor prices:[22]

$$H = \sum_{k=1}^{m} (\partial R_i^* / \partial w_{k_i})(w_{k_i} / R_i^*) \tag{3.28}$$

The estimated value of the *H*-statistic ranges between -∞ and 1. *H* is smaller than zero if the underlying market is monopoly, it ranges between zero and unity for monopolistic competition, and an *H* of unity indicates perfect competition. Shaffer (1983) demonstrated formal linkages between the Panzar–Rosse *H*-statistic, the conjectural variation elasticity and the Lerner index. Only a limited number of studies tests the P–R method for the banking industry. Table 3.5 summarizes the results of those investigations.

Shaffer (1982), in his pioneering study on New York banks, observed monopolistic competition. For Canadian banks, Nathan and Neave (1989) found perfect competition for 1982 and monopolistic competition for 1983-84. Lloyd-Williams et al. (1996) and Molyneux et al. (1996) revealed perfect collusion for Japan. Molyneux et al. (1994) tested the P–R statistic on a sample of French, German, Italian, Spanish and British banks for the period 1986-89 in order to assess the competitive conditions in major EC banking markets. They obtain values for *H* which are not significantly different from zero and from unity for France, Germany (except for 1987), Spain and the UK, thus pointing to monopolistic competition. The *H*-statistic for Italy during 1987–89 is negative and significantly different from zero, hence it was not possible to reject the hypotheses of monopoly. Coccorese (1998), however, who also intends to evaluate the degree of competition in the Italian banking sector, obtains significantly non-negative values for *H*. *H* was also significantly different from unity, except in 1992 and 1994.

Vesala (1995) applies the model to the Finnish banking industry (1985–92) to test for competition and market power in the Finnish banking sector. His estimates of *H* were always positive, but significantly different from zero and from unity only in 1989 and 1990. For Switzerland, Rime (1999) observed monopolistic competition. Hondroyiannis et al. (1999) tested the Greek banking industry for 1993–95 and found also evidence of monopolistic competition. Bikker and Groeneveld (2000) determine the competitive structure of the whole EU banking industry. The estimated values for the *H*-statistic lie between two thirds and one in most countries. The hypothesis $H = 0$ is rejected for all countries, whereas $H = 1$ cannot be rejected for Belgium and Greece at the 95 per cent confidence level. DeBandt and Davis (2000) investigate banking markets in France, Germany and Italy within groups of large and small banks. Aiming to assess the effects of EMU on market conditions, they obtain estimates of *H,* which are significantly different from zero and from unity for large banks in all three countries. The *H*-statistics estimated for the sample with small banks indicate monopolistic competition in Italy, and monopoly power in France and Germany. Chapter 4 considers banks in 23 OECD countries and investigates small, medium-sized and large banks separately. This P–R analysis finds monopolistic competition virtually everywhere, although perfect competition cannot be rejected for some market segments.

Shaffer (2002) analysed the pricing conduct of a small monopoly bank in Jayton, Texas. The estimated values of *H* (for various models) were low but significantly different from zero, thus strongly rejecting static monopolistic behaviour. As monopolistic behaviour is an impossibility per se, a different kind of behaviour must prevail, for instance one related to entry deterrence or one based on an objective function other than that of static profit

Table 3.5 P–R model results in other studies

Authors	Period	Countries considered	Results
Shaffer (1982)	1979	New York	monopolistic competition
Nathan and Neave (1989)	1982–84	Canada	1982: perfect comp.; 1983–84: monopolistic comp.
Lloyd-Williams et al. (1996)	1986–88	Japan	monopoly
Molyneux et al. (1994)	1986–89	France, Germany, Italy, Spain and UK	mon.: Italy; mon. comp.: France, Germany, Spain, UK
Vesala (1995)	1985–92	Finland	monopolistic competition for all but two years
Molyneux et al. (1996)	1986–88	Japan	monopoly
Coccorese (1998)	1988–96	Italy	monopolistic competition
Rime (1999)	1987–94	Switzerland	monopolistic competition
Hondroyiannis et al. (1999)	1993–95	Greece	monopolistic competition
Bikker and Groeneveld (2000)	1989–96	15 EU countries	monopolistic competition
DeBandt and Davis (2000)	1992–96	France, Germany and Italy	large banks: mon. comp. in all countries; small banks: mon. comp. in Italy, monopoly in France, Germany
Shaffer (2002)	1984–99	Jayton, Texas	monopolistic competition
Chapter 4	1988–98	23 OECD countries	monopolistic competition

maximization. Apparently, the P–R approach is intrinsically unable to distinguish among such alternative explanations.

3.5 CONCLUSIONS

This chapter surveys the various approaches to the measurement of concentration and competition, which are fundamental for welfare-related public policy towards structure and conduct in banking markets. The presentation and analysis of ten measures of concentration was supplemented by numerical examples illustrating their properties when applied empirically. The choice of the concentration index is mainly dependent on the policy makers' perception of the relative influence on competition attached to large and small banks. The Herfindahl–Hirschman index and the k bank concentration ratio appear most frequently, both in theory and practice. The simple structure of these indices and the limited data requirement of the CR_k contribute to this success. Applied to various markets, these indices appear to bring forth virtually similar rankings, which adds to their suitability in practise. The theoretical justification of the CR_k and the *HHI* as measures of concentration was derived in connection with the relationship between market structure and market performance. These analyses also elucidate the assumed bank conduct underlying these concentration ratios.

The structure-performance relationship, a simplified version of the traditional SCP paradigm, and the efficiency hypothesis integrate measures of concentration and competition. Formal derivations of this class of relationships provide evidence of the theoretical appropriateness of both the *HHI* and the CR_k as measures of concentration in structural models. Various types of empirical applications of the structure-performance relationship, seeking to find support for either the SCP model or the efficiency hypothesis, were discussed. As was the case for the USA, applications of these tests to the European banking industry have not yielded clear-cut results.

Three non-structural measures of competition were presented. Their derivations are based on oligopoly theory of the industrial organizations approach (Bresnahan and Iwata model), or on the comparative static properties of reduced-form revenue equations (Panzar and Rosse approach). Whereas both the Bresnahan and the Panzar and Rosse methods were applied to the European banking industry, the application of the Iwata model posed difficulties, given the lack of required micro-data on the structure of cost and production of a large number of players in the European banking markets. Since studies applying the Bresnahan method to European markets are scarce, no trends may be observed in their results. Monopolistic competition is the prevailing outcome in the studies applying the Panzar and Rosse method to European countries.

APPENDIX 3 DISTRIBUTIONAL CONCEPTS

This appendix provides a brief glossary of general distributional concepts used in the derivation and description of the various measures of competition and concentration.

1 The Concentration Curve

The concentration curve plots the cumulative market share, $\sum_{i=1}^{n} s_i$, against rank i of the banks in the market. The height of the curve above any point i on the horizontal axis measures the percentage of the industry's total size accounted for by the largest i banks. The curve is continuously rising from left to right, but rises at a continuously diminishing rate. It reaches its maximum height of 100 per cent at a point on the horizontal axis corresponding to the total number of banks in the industry. Figures 3.A.1 and 3.A.2 show examples of the concentration curve for the Dutch mortgage and banking markets measured in terms of total assets. Figure 3.A.1 illustrates the fact that the largest five banks (in terms of market share) hold 95 per cent of the Dutch mortgage market, and Figure 3.A.2 shows that the largest five banks in the Netherlands hold roughly 90 per cent of total assets.

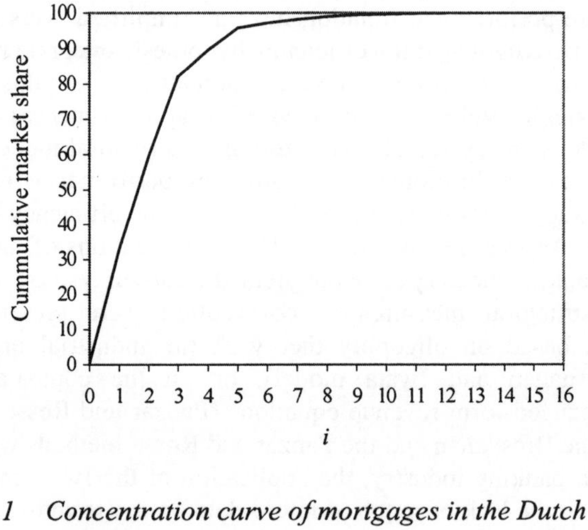

Figure 3.A.1 Concentration curve of mortgages in the Dutch banking industry

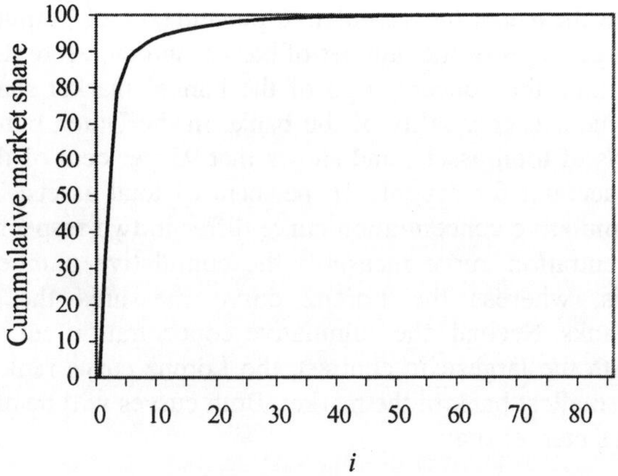

Figure 3.A.2 Concentration curve of total assets in the Dutch banking industry

2 The Numbers-equivalent

The numbers-equivalent has been proposed by Adelman (1969) and translates the measure of concentration, which has been calculated for a particular market, into the number of equally sized banks constituting the same level of concentration. The numbers-equivalent can be derived for each concentration measure by rearranging the index in such a way that the number of banks becomes a function of the value of the concentration index.

3 The Lerner Index

The Lerner index μ, or degree of monopoly power, expresses market power as the difference between the output price and marginal cost in the profit maximum divided by the output price. Profits are maximized where marginal revenues equal marginal costs $c'(X) = r'(X)$, with $r'(X) = p + (dp/dX)X$, such that $p - c'(X) = -(dp/dX)X$, and the Lerner index is then defined as:

$$\mu = (p - c'(X)) / p = -(dp/dX)\, X/p = -1/\eta_D \qquad (3.A.1)$$

$\mu = 0$ indicates perfect competition, since in equilibrium $p = c'(X) = r'(X)$.

4 The Lorenz Curve

The Lorenz curve measures the cumulative percentages of output accounted for by various percentages of the number of banks, and therefore describes the inequality rather than the concentration of the banks' market shares. Figure 3.A.3 illustrates the size inequality of the banks in the Dutch banking sector measured in terms of total assets, and shows that 95 per cent of the banks in the Netherlands account for roughly 16 per cent of total assets. The Lorenz curve and the cumulative concentration curve differ in two respects. First, the cumulative concentration curve measures the cumulative number of banks along the x-axis, whereas the Lorenz curve measures the cumulative percentages of banks. Second, the cumulative concentration curve ranks the banks starting with the largest; in contrast, the Lorenz curve ranks the banks starting with the smallest bank in the market. Both curves will be affected by a change in a bank's market share.

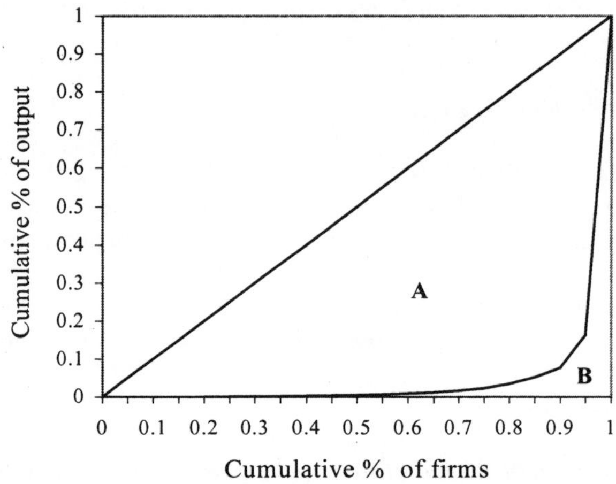

Figure 3.A.3 Lorenz curve for the Dutch banking sector

5 The Gini Coefficient

The Gini coefficient (*G*), a measure of inequality,[23] is defined as the ratio of the area enclosed by the Lorenz curve and the diagonal representing equality in distribution (A) and the entire area under this diagonal (A+B) in Figure 3.A.3, hence $G = A/(A+B)$. The maximum value on both axes is 1, so that the area embraced by the diagram yields unity. Hence, $A+B = 1/2$, and $G = 2A$.

6 Entropy

Consider a set of events E_i, where $i=1,...,n$. Exactly one of these events will occur with probability x_i, where $i=1,...,n$, and $\sum_{i=1}^{n} x_i = 1$. The information content of a realized event is a decreasing function of the ex-ante probability of its occurrence, and is generally defined as $h(x_i) = log(1/x_i) = -\log x_i$. The expected information content for all events can then be calculated before the realization of an event. Since E_i has probability x_i, the message that E_i occurs will be received with the same probability, so that the information content will be $h(x_i)$ with probability x_i. The expected information content of a realized event is therefore $H(x) = \sum_{i=1}^{n} x_i h(x_i) = -\sum_{i=1}^{n} x_i \log x_i$, where x on the left stands for the array of the n probabilities x_i (Theil, 1967). Entropy as a measure of concentration has been presented in this chapter on the basis of a base 2 logarithm as proposed by White (1982). This logarithm can be transformed into the natural logarithm as $\log_2 s_i = \ln s_i / \ln 2$, so that:

$$E_i = -\sum_{i=1}^{n} s_i \log_2 s_i = -(1/\ln 2)\sum_{i=1}^{n} s_i \ln s_i \tag{3.A.2}$$

and similarly into other logarithm bases.

7 Coefficient of Variation

The coefficient of variation is defined as $c = \sqrt{V}/\bar{x}$, where $\bar{x}$ is the mean bank size and V, the variance, is defined as $V = \sum_{i=1}^{n} (x_i - \bar{x})^2 / n$. Unlike the variance, the coefficient of variation remains unchanged if the sizes of all banks are increased proportionately.

NOTES

1. It should be noted, however, that a measure of concentration does not warrant conclusions about the competitive performance in a particular market. Even in a highly concentrated market, competitive behaviour between the leading banks is still possible.
2. Instead of Marfels' fourth group of weighting schemes, in which the shares of individual banks are used as weights in a weighted geometric mean, the present chapter presents the logarithm of the market share of the respective bank (relevant for the calculation of, for

example the Entropy measure). The exponential of the Entropy measure, which uses the former weighting concept, will not be discussed in this chapter.

3. The concept of conjectural variation is explained in Section 3.3.2 below Equation (3.18).
4. Appendix 3 explains the concentration curve.
5. See Appendix 3 for an explanation of the numbers equivalent.
6. Appendix 3 discusses the Lerner index.
7. Entry into an industry is seen as relatively easy, if there are many banks in the industry, and relatively difficult if the market is shielded by a few banks. This argument will gain emphasis in Section 4.4, which discusses the impact of concentration on competition. In empirical investigations of structural models, measures of concentration are often used as the only measure approximating market structure. Many studies reveal the importance of entry barriers for market performance.
8. The Rosenbluth index and the Gini coefficient are related according to $RI = 1/(n(1\text{-}G))$, due to the similarity of the Lorenz curve and the concentration curve. See Appendix 3 for explanation of the Gini coefficient and the Lorenz curve. Rosenbluth (1955), Kellerer (1960), Niehans (1961) and Marfels (1971b) give details and derivations of a theoretical relationship between the concepts of concentration inequality.
9. The effective average size is defined as the market size divided by the numbers equivalent calculated from the concentration index for a specific industry.
10. Note that when data on price-cost margins would be available, the obvious question arises why Davies does not use these data directly as a measure of competition, rather than to try to fit a model that relates it to some other measure.
11. The Herfindahl effective average size is defined as the industry size divided by the numbers equivalent calculated from the Herfindahl–Hirschman index.
12. Actually, we are not able to reproduce Hause's upper bound value for the expression raised to the power of α. In our view, in a two-bank industry, the expression takes its maximum value, $4(1/3)^3$, if $S_1 = 1/3$, which is the square of Hause's maximum.
13. See Appendix 3 for details.
14. The old-fashioned base 2 can be replaced by, for instance, the more common base e (for natural logarithms), which would change the value of the Entropy by a constant (viz. 1/ln 2). An example for this transformation is presented in Appendix 3.
15. Exceptions are related mainly to a deviating bank size distribution of the largest 10 banks. This is especially true where the total number of banks is limited.
16. See Bresnahan (1982) and Lau (1982). This technique is elaborated further in Bresnahan (1989).
17. To the best of our knowledge, only the study by Calem and Carlino (1991) takes explicit account of bank conduct in the empirical application of the SCP framework. They found that strategic conduct of commercial and federal savings banks in the USA was not limited to concentrated markets. Chapter 4, Section 4.4, investigates the structure–conduct relationship.
18. With nerve or imaginary power, market share is often also considered as a proxy for bank efficiency.
19. For a discussion on homogeneity, see Stigler (1964).
20. We assume η_D to have a negative value.
21. Shaffer and DiSalvo (1994) apply this model to a two-banks market.
22. See Panzar and Rosse (1987) of Vesala (1995) for details of the formal derivation of the *H*-statistic.
23. An extensive overview of measures of inequality has been given by Cowell (1995). Only the concepts of importance within the context of this chapter will be briefly discussed here.

4. Competition and concentration in the banking industry and their relationship

4.1 INTRODUCTION

European banking markets are undergoing unprecedented changes, caused by the deregulation of financial services, the establishment of the Economic and Monetary Union (EMU) and developments in information technology, which may well turn out to be dramatic. Many of these changes will have vast implications for competition and concentration in the banking and financial sectors. One of the consequences is already apparent in the recent wave of mergers in the European banking industry. This process of concentration may affect competition, in particular on local markets for retail banking services. Questions may arise such as: should concentration be slowed down? or: are additional measures needed to ensure sufficient competition in local retail markets? Besides, increased concentration and the size of the new global players may cause concerns about financial stability. In order to judge the implications of these developments, one has to examine the banking industry's current market structure, to determine the degree of competition, and to investigate the impact the consolidation is likely to have on the market structure and the behaviour of banks. In recent years, however, relatively few empirical studies have examined competition and concentration in European banking markets. This chapter seeks to measure the degree of competition in the European banking markets, and to investigate the impact of concentration on competition. Moreover, it attempts to compare the situation in Europe with that in the USA and other countries.

The literature on the measurement of competition may be divided into two mainstreams, called the structural and the non-structural approach.[1] The structural approach to model competition includes the structure–conduct–

performance (SCP) paradigm and the efficiency hypothesis, as well as a number of formal approaches with roots in Industrial Organization theory. The SCP paradigm investigates whether a highly concentrated market causes collusive behaviour among larger banks resulting in superior market performance; whereas the efficiency hypothesis tests whether it is the efficiency of larger banks that makes for enhanced performance. In reaction to the theoretical and empirical deficiencies of the structural models, non-structural models of competitive behaviour have been developed, namely the Iwata model, the Bresnahan model, and the Panzar and Rosse (P–R) model.[2] These New Empirical Industrial Organization approaches measure competition and emphasize the analysis of the competitive conduct of banks without using explicit information about the structure of the market. In this chapter we will use one of these non-structural models, the P–R model, to assess the degree of competition in a large number of countries. One of the structural approaches, the SCP paradigm, provides a theoretical relationship between market structure (concentration) and conduct (competition) which has been ignored by the empirical banking literature. We fill in the gap by testing this relationship empirically, using the P–R model's measure of competition.

Ideally, an evaluation of competitive conditions and the degree of concentration in the banking industry should begin by rigorously defining the market under consideration. The relevant market consists of all suppliers of a particular banking service including actual or potential competitors, and it has a product dimension and a geographical dimension. The product definition of a market is based on the equality of the products as regards their ability to fulfil specific consumer wants. The geographical boundaries of a market are determined by actual and potential contacts between actual and potential market participants. These boundaries depend on the products involved: for retail banking, the local dimension of a market is relevant while the regional or international dimension is relevant for corporate banking. The desire to define product and (smaller-scale) geographical markets makes it harder to apply competition and concentration models to the banking industry, especially given the shortage in (European) data with respect to specific banking products or local regions.

This chapter attempts to solve this problem to some extent by applying the P–R model to samples of banks of various sizes, under the assumption that small banks operate mostly at a local scale and that large banks compete more than other banks at the international level, while medium-sized banks occupy an intermediate position. Furthermore, retail banking is assumed to be concentrated mostly in small banks while corporate banking occurs more at large banks. Banking behaviour in geographical markets of various sizes is observed indirectly, through the data of individual banks used in the P–R model. Of course, this is only a first step in the right direction, but we do acquire information about the effect of (the size of) geographical markets on competition.

The ground plan of this chapter is as follows. Section 4.2 introduces and explains the P–R approach. Section 4.3 applies this model to banks in 23 industrialized countries. For each country, four samples are taken: small, medium-sized and large banks and, finally, all banks. This section also displays various concentration indices and applies them to the (same) 23 industrialized countries. Finally, the relationship between competition and concentration is tested empirically.

4.2 THE PANZAR AND ROSSE APPROACH

Rosse and Panzar (1977) and Panzar and Rosse (1987) formulated simple models for oligopolistic, competitive and monopolistic markets and developed a test to discriminate between these models. This test is based on properties of a reduced-form revenue equation at the firm or bank level and uses a test statistic *H*, which, under certain assumptions, can serve as a measure of the competitive behaviour of banks. The test is derived from a general banking market model which determines equilibrium output and the equilibrium number of banks by maximizing profits at both the bank level and the industry level. This implies, first, that bank *i* maximizes its profits, where marginal revenue equals marginal cost:

$$R_i'(x_i, n, z_i) - C_i'(x_i, w_i, t_i) = 0 \tag{4.1}$$

R_i refers to revenues and C_i to costs of bank *i* (the prime denoting *marginal*), x_i is the output of bank *i*, *n* is the number of banks, w_i is a vector of *m* factor input prices of bank *i*, z_i is a vector of exogenous variables that shift the bank's revenue function, t_i is a vector of exogenous variables that shift the bank's cost function. Second, at the market level, it means that, in equilibrium, the zero profit constraint holds:

$$R_i^*\left(x^*, n^*, z\right) - C_i^*\left(x^*, w, t\right) = 0 \tag{4.2}$$

Variables marked with an asterisk (*) represent equilibrium values. Market power is measured by the extent to which a change in factor input prices (dw_{k_i}) is reflected in the equilibrium revenues (dR_i^*) earned by bank *i*. Panzar and Rosse define a measure of competition *H* as the sum of the elasticities of the reduced-form revenues with respect to factor prices:[3]

$$H = \sum_{k=1}^{m} \frac{\partial R_i^*}{\partial w_{k_i}} \frac{w_{k_i}}{R_i^*} \tag{4.3}$$

The first market model Panzar and Rosse investigated describes monopoly. The monopoly analysis includes the case of price-taking competitive firms, as long as the prices they face are truly exogenous, that is, as long as their equilibrium values are unaffected by changes in the other exogenous variables in the model. An empirical refutation of 'monopoly' constitutes a rejection of the assumption that the revenues of the banks in question are independent of the decisions made by their actual or potential rivals. Panzar and Rosse prove that under monopoly, an increase in input prices will increase marginal costs, reduce equilibrium output and subsequently reduce revenues; hence H will be zero or negative. This is a highly generalized result, requiring little beyond the profit maximization hypothesis itself. Along similar lines, Vesala (1995) proves that the same result holds for monopolistic competition without the threat of entry, that is, with a fixed number of banks. Thus, this case also falls under what we call 'monopoly'. In the case where the monopolist faces a demand curve of constant price elasticity $e>1$ and where a constant returns to scale Cobb–Douglas technology is employed, Panzar and Rosse proved that H is equal to e-1. Hence apart from the sign, the *magnitude* of H may also be of importance, as H yields an estimate of the Lerner index of monopoly power $L = (e-1)/e = H/(H-1)$, see Appendix 4.A.

Three other commonly employed models for an industrial market investigated by Panzar and Rosse are monopolistic competition, perfect competition and conjectural variation oligopoly, all of which happen to be consistent with positive values for H. In these models, the revenue function of an individual bank depends upon the decisions made by its actual or potential rivals. For monopolistic and perfect competition, the analysis is based on the comparative static properties of the Chamberlinian equilibrium model. This model introduces interdependence into banks' structural revenue equations via the hypothesis that, in equilibrium, free entry and exit results in zero profits. Under a set of general assumptions,[4] it can be proved that under monopolistic competition, $H \leq 1$. Positive values of H indicate that the data are consistent with monopolistic competition but not with individual profit maximization as under monopoly conditions. In other words, banks produce more and at lower prices than would be optimal in each individual case. A priori, monopolistic competition is most plausible for characterizing the interaction between banks, as it recognizes the existence of product differentiation and is consistent with the observation that banks tend to differ with respect to product quality variables and advertising, although their core business is fairly homogeneous.

In the limit case of the monopolistic competition model, where banks' products are regarded as perfect substitutes of one another, the Chamberlinian model produces the perfectly competitive solution, as demand elasticity approaches infinity. In this perfect competition case, $H = 1$. An increase in input prices raises both marginal and average costs without – under certain conditions – altering the optimal output of any individual firm. Exit of some firms increases the demand faced by each of the remaining firms, leading to an increase in prices and revenues equivalent to the rise in costs.

Finally, analysing the conjectural variation oligopoly case, Panzar and Rosse show that strategic interactions among a fixed number of banks may also be consistent with positive values of *H*. In general, the value of *H* is not restricted. In the special case of *perfect* collusion oligopoly or a perfect cartel, the value of *H* is non-positive, similar to the monopoly model. Table 4.1 summarizes the discriminatory power of *H*.

Table 4.1 Discriminatory power of H

Values of *H*	Competitive environment
$H \leq 0$	Monopoly equilibrium: each bank operates independently as under monopoly profit maximization conditions (*H* is a decreasing function of the perceived demand elasticity) or perfect cartel
$0 < H < 1$	Monopolistic competition free entry equilibrium (*H* is an increasing function of the perceived demand elasticity)
$H = 1$	Perfect competition. Free entry equilibrium with full efficient capacity utilization

The Chamberlinian equilibrium model described above provides a simple link between *H* and the number of banks, so between market behaviour and market structure. The model is based on free entry of banks and determines not only the output level but also the equilibrium number of banks. Vesala (1995) proves that *H* is an increasing function of the demand elasticity *e*, that is, the less market power is exercised on the part of banks, the higher *H* becomes. This implies that *H* is not used solely to reject certain types of market behaviour, but that its magnitude serves as a measure of competition. One of the general assumptions underlying the Chamberlinian equilibrium model mentioned above is that the elasticity of perceived demand facing the individual firm, $e(x, n, w)$, is a non-decreasing function of the number of rival banks. Panzar and Rosse call this a standard assumption, eminently plausible and almost a truism. Vesala's result and this assumption together provide a positive (theoretical) relationship between *H* and the number of banks, or – in a more loose interpretation – an inverse relationship between *H* and banking concentration.

4.2.1 The empirical P–R model

The empirical application of the P–R approach assumes a log-linear marginal cost function (dropping subscripts referring to bank *i*):

$$ln\,MC = \alpha_0 + \alpha_1\, ln\,OUT + \Sigma_{i=1}^{m} \beta_i\, ln\,FIP_i + \Sigma_{j=1}^{p} \gamma_j\, ln\,EX_{COST_j} \qquad (4.4)$$

where *OUT* is output of the bank, *FIP* are the factor input prices (for example regarding funding, personnel expenses and other non-interest expenses) and EX_{COST} are other variables, exogenous to the cost function C_i (*t* in Equation (4.1)). Equally, the underlying marginal revenue function has been assumed to be log-linear of the form:

$$ln\,MR = \delta_0 + \delta_1\, ln\,OUT + \Sigma_{k=1}^{q} \zeta_k\, ln\,EX_{REV_k} \qquad (4.5)$$

where EX_{REV} are variables related to the bank-specific demand function (*z* in Equation (4.1)). For a profit-maximizing bank, marginal costs equal marginal revenues in equilibrium, yielding the equilibrium value for output (denoted by an asterisk):

$$ln\,OUT^* = (\alpha_o - \delta_0 + \Sigma_{i=1}^{m} \beta_i\, ln\,FIP_i + \Sigma_{j=1}^{p} \gamma_j\, ln\,EX_{COST_j} - \Sigma_{k=1}^{q} \zeta_k\, ln\,EX_{REV_k})/(\delta_1 - \alpha_1) \qquad (4.6)$$

The reduced-form equation for revenues of bank *i* is the product of the equilibrium values of output of bank *i* and the common price level, determined by the inverse-demand equation, which reads, in logarithms, as: $ln\,p = \xi + \eta\, ln\,(\Sigma_i\, OUT^*_i)$.

In the empirical analysis, the following operationalization of the reduced-form revenue equation is used:

$$ln\,INTR = \alpha + \beta\, ln\,AFR + \gamma\, ln\,PPE + \delta\, ln\,PCE + \Sigma_j \zeta_j\, ln\,BSF_j + \eta\, ln\,OI + e \qquad (4.7)$$

where *INTR* is the ratio of total interest revenue to the total balance sheet,[5] *AFR* is the ratio of annual interest expenses to total funds, or the Average Funding Rate, *PPE* is the ratio of personnel expenses to the total balance sheet, or the (approximated) Price of Personnel Expenses, *PCE* is the ratio of physical capital expenditure and other expenses to fixed assets, or the (approximated) Price of Capital Expenditure, *BSF* are Bank-Specific exogenous Factors (without explicit reference to their origin from the cost or revenue function), *OI* is the ratio of Other Income to the total balance sheet, and *e* is a stochastic error term. *AFR*, *PPE* and *PCE* are the unit prices of the inputs of the banks: funds, labour and capital, or proxies of these prices. In the notation of Equation (4.7), the *H*-statistic is given by $\beta + \gamma + \delta$. In order to verify whether the competitive structure has changed over time as a result of liberalization and deregulation, model (4.7) is applied to a pooled cross-section (across banks) and time-series analysis over the time span 1988–98. We are assuming that the long-term equilibrium market structure underlying the Panzar–Rosse analysis shifts *gradually* over time due to institutional changes (as mentioned in the introduction) not incorporated into the model equation. Ignoring market dynamics may lead to imprecise parameter estimates and biased *H*-statistics, which could in turn result in wrong inferences about the competitive nature of the banking industry. Therefore, we multiply the elasticities of *H* by a continuous time-curve model $exp(\varepsilon\, TIME)$:

$$ln INTR = \alpha + (\beta\, ln AFR + \gamma\, ln PPE + \delta\, ln PCE)e^{\varepsilon\, TIME} + \Sigma\zeta_j\, ln BSF_j + \eta\, ln OI + e \quad (4.8)$$

H is equal to $(\beta + \gamma + \delta)e^{\varepsilon\, TIME}$. Note that $\varepsilon = 0$ indicates that *H* is constant over time. An alternative specification uses the logistic time-curve:

$$\ln INTR = \alpha + f(\beta, c, TIME)(\ln AFR + \gamma' \ln PPE + \delta' \ln PCE) + \Sigma\zeta_j \ln BSF_j + \eta \ln OI + e \quad (4.9)$$

with $f(\beta,\ \varepsilon,\ TIME) = 1/(1+(1/\beta-1)\exp(\varepsilon\, TIME))$, $\beta \neq 0$,[6] $\gamma' = \gamma / f(\beta,\ \varepsilon,\ TIME)$ and $\delta' = \delta / f(\beta,\ \varepsilon,\ TIME)$. In this model *H* is equal to $f(\beta,\ \tau,\ TIME)\ (1 + \gamma' + \delta')$. Note that $\varepsilon = 0$ indicates that *H* is constant over time and that *H* increases over time, if ε is negative. Without such an assumption of *gradual* change, the results may be implausibly erratic, as found by Molyneux et al. (1994), who applied the P–R model to a series of subsequent years.

The dependent variable is the 'ratio of total *interest* revenue to the total balance sheet', as in Molyneux et al. (1994). The decision to consider only the interest part of the total revenue of banks is consistent with the underlying notion inherent in the P–R model, that financial intermediation is the core business of most banks. However, Shaffer (1982) and Nathan and Neaves (1989) took total revenue as their dependent variable. In our sample, the share of non-interest revenues to total revenues is, on average, only 14 per cent. However, it has increased in recent years, doubling between 1990 and 1998. In order to account for the influence exerted by the generation of other income on the model's underlying marginal revenue and cost functions, we also include the ratio of other income to the total balance sheet (*OI*) as an explanatory variable. Actually, the P–R models we will apply, Equations (4.8) and (4.9), encompass the model of Molyneux et al. for $\eta = 0$ (and $\varepsilon = 0$).

The 'ratio of personnel expenses to the number of employees' (*PENE*) could be a plausible alternative to the 'ratio of personnel expenses to the total balance sheet' (*PPE*) included in our estimations. However, the former ratio is available for only a small subset of our sample. Furthermore, empirical exercises reveal that results based on *PENE* closely approximate those based on *PPE*. This is probably due to the size of the sample used, which makes the results less sensitive to measurement errors. The 'ratio of physical capital and other expenses to fixed assets' is a *proxy* of the price of capital.[7] In particular, the balance sheet item 'fixed assets' appears to be unrealistically low for some banks. However, the exclusion of outliers or a correction for fixed assets, such as applied by Resti (1997), did not lead to remarkable changes in the estimation results.

Bank-specific factors (*BSF*) are additional explanatory variables which reflect differences in risks, costs, size and structures of banks and should, at least theoretically, stem from the marginal revenue and cost functions underlying the empirical P–R equation (4.8) or (4.9). The risk component can be proxied by the ratio of risk capital or equity to total assets (*EQ*), the ratio of loans to total assets (*LO*) and the ratio of non-performing loans to total loans (*NPL*). More than one variable for risk is considered, as there are cases where one of these variables may be unavailable for a particular bank. The ratio of interbank deposits to total customers and short-term funding (*BDEP*) and the ratio of demand deposits from customers to total customer and short-term funding (*DDC*) are used to capture differences in the deposit mix. Correspondent bank activities are taken into consideration when the ratio of cash and due from depository institutions (or banks) to total deposits (*CDFB*) is included. Total assets (*TA*) are used as a scaling factor.

A positive parameter for *LO* is expected, because more loans reflect more potential interest rate income. The coefficient for *OI* is probably negative as the generation of other income may be at the expense of interest income. Regarding the signs of the coefficients of the other explanatory variables, several writers hold conflicting theories[8] while others do not have a priori expectations.

4.3 EMPIRICAL RESULTS

4.3.1 Data

The P–R model has been applied to banks from 23 European and non-European countries, as listed in Table 4.2. The data have been obtained from the database of the International Bank Credit Analysis Ltd (Fitch-IBCA), a London-based bank credit rating agency. In principle, data from individual banks are used for the years 1988–98, but the actual starting dates of the samples vary across countries.[9] For each country, Table 4.2 reports the number of banks and available number of observations.[10] The total number of banks is 5 444 and the total number of observations is almost 29 000. Hence, on average, the sample includes more than five observations (in fact years) for each bank, since some of the observations are lacking due to non-reporting of (*all* relevant) data by banks in their annual reports, mergers or new entries in the sample period.

Table 4.2 Sample period and number of observations per country

Country	Sample period	No. of years	No. of banks	No. of observation per bank type			
				All	Small	Medium	Large
Australia	1991–98	8	39	185	13	115	57
Austria	1989–98	10	95	434	226	176	32
Belgium	1989–98	10	85	479	217	194	68
Canada	1988–98	11	60	363	158	140	65
Denmark	1990–98	9	96	578	466	79	33
Finland	1990–98	9	14	77	10	32	35
France	1988–98	11	393	2 489	812	1 334	343
Germany	1988–98	11	2 219	10 987	6 765	3 764	458
Greece	1990–98	9	22	102	46	37	19
Ireland	1992–98	7	35	143	15	112	16
Italy	1988–98	11	365	1 943	813	897	233
Japan	1989–98	10	148	1 081	17	432	632
Korea (South)	1992–98	7	21	63	1	34	28
Luxembourg	1990–98	9	128	825	333	395	97
Netherlands	1991–98	8	57	307	99	145	63
New Zealand	1990–98	9	10	52	9	23	20
Norway	1989–98	10	39	220	74	120	26
Portugal	1991–98	8	41	268	70	144	54
Spain	1990–98	9	154	831	204	458	169
Sweden	1989–98	10	26	145	18	52	75
Switzerland	1988–98	11	385	1 976	1 414	485	77
UK	1989–98	10	213	1 220	518	491	211
USA	1991–98	8	799	4 190	1 383	2 326	481
Total			*5 444*	*28 958*	*13 681*	*11 985*	*3 292*
In %				*100.0*	*47.2*	*41.4*	*11.4*

For each country, the model has been applied to a sample of all banks, as well as to subsamples of small banks, medium-sized banks and large banks, respectively. The partitioning into small, medium-sized and large is based on total assets of the banks: for each year, the smallest 50 per cent of all banks of the world-wide sample constitute the small-banks sample, the largest 10 per cent of all banks constitute the large-bank sample, whereas the remainder make up the medium-sized sample. The large-bank sample was kept relatively small to ensure that only the really large banks are included. The final numbers of *observations* are affected by the availability of data, which actually appears to be correlated with the size of the bank. Of course, the size distribution differs from one country to another, see Table 4.2. An alternative would be to make the size subdivision per country. However, the border between small and medium-sized banks in, say, 1997 would then range from US$ 166 million in Denmark to US$ 12 660 million in South Korea and between medium-sized and large banks would range from US$ 2 797 million in Germany to US$ 111 280 million in Canada. This alternative is less desirable, because it makes it very hard to compare subsamples across countries[11] and, therefore, has not been considered.

Due to the small number of assumptions (mainly the cost minimization and duality hypotheses) underlying the P–R approach, the validity of the test is fairly general. Nevertheless, a few caveats are in order. As we employ consolidated banking data, the banking market of country *X* is defined as the hypothetical market where banks from country *X* are active and not, say, the banking market within the national borders of that country. Moreover, banks operate in various segments of the market, both geographically and in terms of banking products and, for that matter, also in various input markets as well. This remark is particularly true of large universal banks with sizeable foreign activities. These internationally active banks are obviously confronted by other competitive forces than small regional banks. The P–R result *H* reflects only a kind of average over all these market segments. Finally, in certain segments of the markets, banks face competition from non-bank financial institutions. However, the P–R approach does not require observations of non-banks, as the *H*-statistic is a direct measure of the degree of competition taking competitive effects from other institutions in its stride.

4.3.2 Competition in the EU Banking Industry

In an exploring analysis we apply the P–R model to observations over the sample period 1989-96 of 892 banks from the fifteen EU countries, which, actually, form a subset of the entire data collection.[12] Table 4.3 shows the pooled regression results based on Equation (4.9). To test for the robustness of the estimation results, this table records the outcomes of various model specifications.

Table 4.3 Empirical results of the reduced-form revenue model for the EU

	Standard model		Extra variables		Weighted regression		No time trend	
	Coeff.	*t-value*	Coeff.	*t-value*	Coeff.	*t-value*	Coeff.	*t-value*
INTE	0.68	*92.1*	0.65	*94.0*	0.83	*180.0*	0.67	*93.0*
PE	0.15	*32.2*	0.13	*27.1*	0.09	*42.1*	0.10	*32.5*
CE	0.02	*2.5*	0.03	*5.0*	-0.02	*4.2*	0.01	*2.4*
TIME [a]	1.38	*4.6*	1.09	*4.1*	2.00	*9.1*	—	—
LO	—	—	0.09	*26.9*	—	—	—	—
TA	—	—	-0.02	*10.0*	—	—	—	—
Austria	1.23	*45.2*	0.86	*28.2*	0.91	*48.0*	1.21	*44.9*
Belgium	0.59	*20.0*	0.27	*9.1*	0.34	*20.8*	0.57	*19.7*
Denmark	1.44	*52.4*	1.04	*34.2*	0.94	*52.2*	1.43	*52.2*
Finland	1.23	*32.5*	0.81	*20.9*	0.87	*40.0*	1.21	*32.1*
France	0.49	*18.0*	0.17	*5.9*	0.34	*21.0*	0.47	*17.7*
Germany	0.58	*22.9*	0.31	*10.9*	0.41	*25.1*	0.57	*22.7*
Greece	0.58	*17.5*	0.31	*9.3*	0.33	*16.3*	0.56	*17.0*
Ireland	0.66	*18.6*	0.35	*9.6*	0.61	*26.2*	0.64	*18.2*
Italy	1.28	*48.4*	0.90	*30.4*	0.86	*50.0*	1.26	*48.2*
Luxembourg	0.54	*19.4*	0.33	*11.7*	0.40	*23.7*	0.52	*19.0*
Netherlands	0.73	*25.6*	0.40	*13.2*	0.59	*37.2*	0.71	*26.2*
Portugal	0.63	*21.5*	0.33	*11.3*	0.48	*27.2*	0.61	*21.1*
Spain	0.72	*28.0*	0.43	*16.0*	0.46	*28.1*	0.70	*27.9*
Sweden	1.42	*41.5*	1.01	*27.3*	0.92	*43.3*	1.39	*41.1*
UK	0.52	*18.1*	0.27	*9.1*	0.43	*25.6*	0.50	*17.7*
Adjusted R^2		0.711		0.750		0.998		0.710
H (1989–96)		0.79–0.76		0.75–0.73		0.88–0.86		0.78
# of observ.		5 224		5 207		5 224		5 259

[a] The time-trend coefficients ε are divided by 100 for the sake of presentation.

Note: *t*-values are presented in italics after the coefficients.

The crucial variable *H* depends on *TIME* and the three unit prices of the banks' inputs, see below Equation (4.9). All these unit prices contribute significantly to the explanation of the interest revenue of banks. Given the fact that funding is the main factor in the production function of banks, it is hardly surprising that its elasticity, β, is the largest one, followed by the coefficient of labour. The three factor price elasticities decrease only slightly over time,[13] although statistically significant. For the 'standard model' in Column 1, in the first year (1989), the values of β, γ and δ are 0.675, 0.101 and 0.011, respectively (due to the logistic time-curve model), whereas these parameters amount to 0.653, 0.098 and 0.011, respectively, in the last year (1996). Note that H is hardly effected by deletion of the time trend (last column) or by addition of bank specific variables such as loans (LO) and total assets (TA). Given the deregulation and liberalization in the EU over those years (and before), it is surprising that H declines (from 0.787 to 0.762), rather than increases. Apparently, opposite influences shaping the competitive environment have been at work. The effect of deregulation and liberalization, on the one hand, and the effect of an increase in the degree of concentration, on the other, have probably partly offset each other.[14] Formal tests reveal that H differs significantly from both 0 and 1,[15] providing evidence that a certain degree of monopolistic competition in the European banking market is present. Hence, the hypothesis of either monopoly or perfect competition must be rejected. This finding agrees with our expectation mentioned earlier that competitive interactions between banks can best be characterized by monopolistic competition.

Apart from common factors, the structure of the banking markets in individual EU countries also – still – depends on numerous country-specific features, for example national institutions, the degree of government intervention, the sophistication of the financial system, etc. Moreover, national balance sheet figures are not always perfectly comparable due to existing differences in national accounting practices and definitions. To take these country-specific characteristics into account, we have added dummy variables for the various countries.

The country-specific dummies also contribute significantly to the explanation of the dependent variable. More importantly, the value of the dummies varies considerably across countries and ranges between 0.49 for France and 1.44 for Denmark. A formal test indeed strongly rejects the hypothesis that the dummy parameters are all equal to each other.[16] This points to structural differences between national banking sectors and corroborates the findings of Vives (1991). Interestingly, the dummies are relatively high for countries that have experienced serious problems in their banking systems. Around 1990, the Nordic countries witnessed severe banking crises, due to the collapse of the property markets, where they had accumulated large exposures after the deregulation of traditional banking markets. For Italy, the cause is less clear, but may relate to problems with *Banca di Napoli*.

We also ran regressions where banks are *weighted* according to their size in terms of total assets.[17] This approach is justified by the obvious fact that small banks are less important in the intermediation process than the large ones.[18] Consequently, the competitive behaviour of large banks should have a greater impact on the estimation outcomes in order to obtain a more representative and realistic picture of the actual competitive conditions prevailing in the banking market. The elasticity of funding costs (β) is much higher in the weight-based model (0.83) than in the standard model (0.68). Its effect on H is slightly offset by lower values of the other cost components. On balance, H rises in the weight-based model to 0.88 in 1989 and 0.86 in 1996 (from, respectively, 0.79 and 0.76 in the standard model). From this shift in H it may be concluded that the market environment of the larger banks is more competitive. Presumably, larger banks are relatively more active in international wholesale markets, where competition is generally assumed to be more fierce (Gilibert and Steinherr, 1989). In banking, relatively smaller competitive pressures exist in the retail market and for small-to-medium sized firms in the corporate banking market. The coefficients of the country-specific dummy variables in the weighted model are comparable to those of the standard model.[19]

Two issues remain to be investigated. First, as elaborated in the literature, a critical feature of the H-statistic is that the P–R approach must be undertaken on the basis of observations that are in long-run equilibrium. An equilibrium test uses the fact that in competitive capital markets, risk-adjusted rates of return will be equalized across banks. In such a case, the rates of return will not be correlated with input prices. An equilibrium test is provided by model (4.7), after replacement of the dependent variable by rate of return on total assets (ROA) or return on equity (ROE). $H=0$ would then indicate equilibrium, whereas $H<0$ would point to disequilibrium. Using ROE, we find that the hypothesis of equilibrium ($H=0$) cannot be rejected at the 95 per cent significance level.[20] This justifies the applied methodology.

Second, the P–R methodology refers to the elasticities of the reduced-form or equilibrium revenues with respect to changes in input prices. Like Molyneux et al. (1994), we use revenues scaled by the total balance sheet value as the dependent variable in the estimation to generate estimates of the H-statistic. Vesala (1995) points out that scaling transforms the revenue equation into a pricing equation. The comparative static properties of the reduced-form revenue equation that guide our judgement of competitive conditions do not necessarily hold as such for pricing equations. Vesala (1995) suggests re-estimation using revenues as the dependent variable to see whether the conclusions remain the same. Following this suggestion and in line with Shaffer (1982) and Nathan and Neave (1989), we have (re-) estimated our model with the (unscaled) total revenue as the dependent variable. For the total-revenue model, the value for H is decreasing from 0.68 (in 1989) to 0.66 (in 1996), instead of decreasing from 0.79 to 0.76 as in the scaled-interest-income model. Hence, this change in the dependent variable does not affect the conclusions: in any case H differs significantly from both 0 and 1. Actually, Nathan and Neave (1989) take total revenue *corrected for loan losses* as dependent variable. Also, the impact of this correction appears to be virtually negligible.

4.3.3 Banking Competition in 23 Individual Countries

Judging by the divergent values of the country-specific dummies emerging from the EU-wide analysis, national banking systems clearly exhibit structural differences. This calls for an empirical assessment of the competitive environment encountered by national banking sectors. A closer look at the competitive behaviour of the banking industry in each individual country also enables us to explore a possible relationship between national concentration and national competition. For these reasons, we here apply the P–R analysis to the individual banking sectors of each of the 23 countries considered.

Appendix 4.B presents tables with the estimation results of all individual countries, for 'all banks' as well as for the three considered bank-size categories. Table 4.4 offers an overview of the estimates of *H*. For New Zealand and South Korea, the number of small banks is too small to make adequate estimations. Our basic approach was to create a model for each country and bank size combination, which included all selected bank-specific factors. Actually, for some countries, data are unavailable for part of these variables, or available only for a limited number of banks. In the latter case, we accepted only a slight reduction in sample size and otherwise disregarded that particular variable.[21] Finally, *BSF* were deleted if their coefficients were not significant. This was done mainly to prevent the number of observations from being reduced by the extra explanatory variables, and also for economy's sake. For the latter reason, insignificant coefficients of the time-trend variable were also deleted. Sensitivity analyses confirm that the *H* estimates are only slightly affected, if at all, by the deletion of the non-significant variables.

The central variable *H* is equal to $(\beta+\gamma+\delta)exp(\varepsilon\,TIME)$ and hence depends on *TIME*, provided $\varepsilon \neq 0$. In the latter cases, *H* has been calculated both 1991 and 1997 (see also Table 4.4). The coefficient of the average funding rate, β, appears to be most significant and almost invariably positive and therefore the main contributor to *H*. The coefficient representing labour cost, γ, is also significant and positive in most cases, but usually smaller than β. The coefficient of the price of capital expenses, δ, varies in size, sign and level of significance, and is the least important component of *H*. The elasticity δ may also be small due to the poorer quality of Capital expenses and Fixed assets data, which together constitute the price level of capital expenses.

Finally, the coefficient of *TIME*, ε, also varies in size, sign and level of significance. In fact, ε is zero (because not significant) in 53 per cent of all cases, indicating no significant change in the competitive conditions. Where ε is non-zero, ε is positive in 34 out of the 43 cases, which indicates that

Table 4.4 Empirical results for H *for various bank-size samples and various years*

	All banks		Small banks		Medium sized banks		Large banks	
	1991	*1997*	*1991*	*1997*	*1991*	*1997*	*1991*	*1997*
Australia	0.50[1]	0.57[1]	*-0.14*[2]	—	0.67[1]	0.70[1]	0.63[1]	0.68[1]
Austria	0.87[1]	—	**0.93**[2]	—	0.91[1]	0.89[1]	0.91[3]	—
Belgium	0.89[1]	—	**0.95**[2]	—	0.88[3]	—	0.86[1]	0.88[1]
Canada	0.60[1]	0.62[1]	0.74[1]	—	0.63[1]	—	0.56[1]	0.60[1]
Denmark	0.32[1]	0.36[1]	0.31[1]	0.34[1]	0.75[1]	—	**1.16**[2]	—
Finland	0.78[1]	—	**0.67**[2]	—	0.76[3]	—	0.70[1]	—
France	0.70[1]	—	0.54[1]	0.59[1]	0.74[1]	0.79[1]	**0.89**[2]	—
Germany	0.60[1]	0.63[1]	0.56[1]	0.59[1]	0.68[1]	0.70[1]	**1.05**[2]	**1.03**[2]
Greece	0.76[1]	—	0.41[2]	—	0.66[1]	—	**1.01**[3]	**0.94**[3]
Ireland	0.65[1]	—	**0.99**[2]	—	0.63[1]	—	**0.93**[3]	—
Italy	0.82[1]	—	0.75[1]	—	0.89[1]	0.86[1]	0.83[1]	0.81[1]
Japan	0.58[1]	0.54[1]	**0.43**[2]	—	0.07[3]	0.11[3]	0.64[1]	0.61[1]
Korea (South)	0.68[1]	—	—	—	**0.72**[2]	—	**0.77**[3]	—
Luxembourg	0.93[1]	—	0.94[2]	—	0.94[2]	0.95[2]	0.90[1]	0.91[1]
Netherlands	0.75[1]	—	**0.74**[2]	—	0.87[1]	—	**0.91**[3]	**0.95**[3]
New Zealand	0.86[1]	—	—	—	**1.11**[2]	**1.13**[3]	0.86[4]	—
Norway	0.74[1]	0.77[1]	0.80[1]	—	0.71[1]	0.75[1]	0.66[1]	0.71[1]
Portugal	0.83[1]	—	0.84[2]	—	0.88[1]	0.84[1]	0.91[3]	—
Spain	0.55[1]	0.62[1]	0.56[1]	0.64[1]	0.52[1]	0.59[1]	0.61[1]	0.66[1]
Sweden	0.80[1]	—	0.84[2]	—	0.69[1]	0.76[1]	**0.95**[3]	—
Switzerland	0.55[1]	0.58[1]	0.51[1]	0.54[1]	**0.95**[2]	0.92[3]	**1.01**[4]	—
UK	0.61[1]	0.64[1]	0.41[1]	—	0.81[1]	0.85[1]	1.20[1]	—
USA	0.54[1]	0.56[1]	0.61[1]	0.62[1]	0.53[1]	0.54[1]	0.68[1]	0.72[1]

[1] For each country, the superscripts refer to the acceptance or rejection of the null hypothesis H=0 and H=1, as is explained in the footnotes of the respective tables in Appendix 4.B. These footnotes also explain the use of bold, italic and underscored figures.

competition increases over time in 80 per cent of these cases (see Table 4.4, where H is shown for both 1991 and 1997, as long as $\varepsilon \neq 0$). In the all-bank sample, competition in 1997 was higher than in 1991 in all the 'non-zero ε' cases, except for Japan. However, these changes over time are fairly limited, to 2.3 basis points (bps) on average, which is much less than expected. Increased competition is more often observed for medium-sized and large banks than for small banks or the all-bank sample, but with lower increases (1.9 bps and 1.3 bps, respectively, for medium-sized and large banks versus 3.0 bps and 3.8 bps, respectively, for small banks or all-banks; see Table

4.C.2 in Appendix 4.C). Growth in competition in EU countries has been higher than in non-EU countries for the all-bank sample and small banks, but lower for large banks. The latter result is remarkable as stronger increases in competition for the EU were expected for all bank size samples. Presumably, the rise in European competition, which had been expected for the years around 1997, had not materialized. Absence of clear rise in competition was also found in the pooled EU model of the previous section, which even reveals a (slight but significant) fall in competitiveness.

Loans appear to be the most important *BSF*, both in terms of incidence and level of significance. Apparently, the ratio between loans and total assets, as a proxy of risk, is an important factor in the total interest-to-income ratio. The signs of *Loans* and *Other Income* are in line with expectation (respectively, positive and negative) for all country and sample-size combinations, apart from Greece where implausible signs are found for small and medium-sized banks. In general, the regression results are highly satisfactory, due in part to the large size of the samples: the estimation of H appears to be very robust. Its value is hardly affected by specification choices, such as those regarding *BSFs*. Furthermore, the goodness of fit of the regression equations is satisfactory.

The tables in Appendix 4.B also present the estimated values for H and test results for the hypotheses H=0 and H=1. Table 4.4 reports these values of H for various bank-size samples and – where applicable ($\varepsilon \neq 0$) – for various years. The superscripts refer to the test results in the footnotes of the tables in Appendix 4.B. Values of H for which the hypothesis H=0 is not rejected at a confidence level of 95 per cent are in italics. Values of H for which the hypothesis H=1 is not rejected at the 95 per cent (or 99 per cent) level of confidence are in boldface (or boldface and underlined, respectively).[22]

For the all-banks samples of all 23 countries, both H=0 (perfect cartel[23]) and H=1 (perfect competition) are rejected convincingly, that is, at the 99 per cent level of confidence, and for nearly all countries even at the 99.9 per cent level. This would imply monopolistic competition in all countries, without exception. However, this uniform picture becomes more diversified when the banking market is split into segments: the market for (i) small banks operating mostly on a local scale, (ii) middle-sized banks operating both locally and nationally, and (iii) large banks which also operate internationally. For the small banks of only one country, Australia, the hypothesis H=0 cannot be rejected, which suggests that this market is characterized by perfect collusion. Note, however, that this result is based on an unusually small sample size of 13 observations. In any case, this result suggests a lower level of competition. For a number of bank-size and country combinations, the hypothesis H=1 cannot be rejected, implying that these markets may be characterized by perfect competition. This holds in particular for a number of the large-bank markets. For Danish large banks, H is significantly larger than 1, which may indicate a deviating market structure, such as conjectural variation oligopoly (see Section 4.2).

A shortcoming of the P–R test may be the fact that it is single-tailed, in the sense that a positive value rejects any form of imperfect competition (under the assumption of profit-maximizing behaviour and at least short-term competition), whereas a negative value is consistent with various types of market power.[24] However, this shortcoming is of little consequence for this chapter, as $H \leq 0$ is rejected in all cases but one.

Based on the result of Vesala (1995, page 56), we interpret H between 0 and 1 as a continuous measure of the level of competition, in the sense that higher values of H indicate stronger competition. The values of H are comparable across national or bank-size markets if the revenue equation, the perceived demand elasticity and its sensitivity to the number of banks ($\partial e/\partial n$) are identical for the various markets.[25] In particular, the latter cannot be observed, so the following conclusions are under reservations that the necessary assumptions hold. The averages across all countries (bottom rows of Table 4.4) make clear that H is substantially below average for small-bank markets (0.64), somewhat greater for medium-sized bank markets (0.75) and greatest for large-bank markets (0.86). Apparently, and in line with expectations, smaller banks operate in a less competitive environment than larger banks or, put differently, local markets are less competitive than national and international markets. The 0.64–0.86 spread should be seen as the *lower limit* of the actual difference in competition between local and international markets, as small banks do not solely operate on local markets but may also be active on the national markets; by the same token, large banks do not exclusively operate on international markets. The difference in the degree of competition between local and international markets is not only reflected in the overall averages, but also in many of the national figures. The values of H for small-bank markets range from -0.14 to 0.99, whereas for large banks they range from 0.58 to above 1 (see Table 4.C.2 in Appendix 4.C).

In Europe, all large banks appear to operate in a highly competitive environment. Exceptions are two Scandinavian countries (Finland and Norway) and Spain with H values around 0.7. Competition among smaller banks is weak in Greece, Denmark and the UK, and limited in France, Germany, Spain and Switzerland. In general, competition seems to be weaker in non-European countries. In the USA, Canada and Australia, for instance, H ranges from 0.5 to 0.7, and in Europe from 0.7 to 0.9 (see also Table 4.C.2). Of course, this conclusion does not necessarily hold for all market segments. In Japan competition is, in fact, slightly weaker, while in New Zealand and South Korea it is somewhat stronger. It should be kept in mind, however, that these comparisons of H across countries are based on more far-reaching assumptions than are made in the standard P–R test (see above). The structure of the European banking industry has altered during the 1980s mostly in response to domestic deregulation and in anticipation of EU-wide regulatory changes. One of the major consequences has been increased competition, see Gual and Neven (1993) and Molyneux et al. (1996). Gardener and Molyneux (1990) explained how mergers in Europe often contributed to the forming of groups of local and regional based banks that could compete effectively with the large, dominant banks. In a number of countries outside Europe, liberalization and deregulation took place somewhat later, for example in the USA, where the 1994 Riegle-Neal Act ending a ban on lending and branch operations across state borders, and where in 1999, the Glass-Steagall Act was repealed, which had prevented firms from combining banking and insurance activities. These trends may well have contributed to the observed differences in degrees of competition inside and outside Europe.

In order to show what effect our choice for interest revenue as dependent variable in the P–R model had on the outcome, Table 4.5 contrasts our results with those based on total revenue as dependent variable for the Netherlands, where the share of non-interest revenue in total revenue averages 16 per cent. As the financial intermediation model underlying the P–R theory does not apply to the activities generating non-interest revenues, it comes as no surprise that the fit of the P–R model (measured by the adjusted R^2) is much lower for total revenue (0.60) than for interest revenue (0.90). In the total-

Table 4.5 Empirical results for the Netherlands for interest revenue and total revenue (all banks; 1991–98)

	Interest revenue				Total revenue			
	Including other income		Excluding other income		Including other income		Excluding other income	
	Coeff.	*t-value*	*Coeff.*	*t-value*	*Coeff.*	*t-value*	*Coeff.*	*t-value*
Funding rate	0.75	*48.5*	0.76	*47.8*	0.48	*17.6*	0.47	*17.0*
Wage rate	0.08	*5.0*	0.01	*2.0*	0.07	*2.5*	0.16	*13.3*
Capital price	-0.07	*2.9*	-0.01	*1.6*	0.01	*0.7*	0.02	*1.3*
Loans ratio	0.04	*3.4*	0.04	*3.4*	0.04	*1.6*	0.02	*1.0*
Other income	-0.05	*5.1*	—	—	0.06	*3.5*	—	—
Total assets	0.01	*2.3*	0.01	*1.4*	-0.01	*1.1*	-0.00	*0.4*
Equity	0.12	*8.7*	0.11	*7.6*	0.07	*2.9*	0.08	*3.3*
Intercept	-0.73	*8.8*	-0.67	*8.0*	-0.51	*3.5*	-0.50	*3.4*
Adjusted R^2	0.90		0.90		0.59		0.57	
No. of observ.	296		296		296		296	
H	0.75[1]		0.77[1]		0.56[1]		0.65[1]	

[1] H=0 and H=1 rejected (level of confidence 99.9 per cent).

revenue variant, the estimated value of H is substantially lower, which is plausible because the input price 'funding costs' is generally not relevant for the non-interest revenue activities. Nevertheless, this value of H still points to the same conclusion, which is that the market is characterized by monopolistic competition. Inclusion of 'other income' as an independent variable hardly affects the outcome. Similar results are obtained for other countries. All in all, this sensitivity analysis confirms that total revenue is less appropriate as input for the P–R model than interest revenue.

Table 3.5 in Chapter 3 did present a comprehensive overview of the P–R results in the literature. In some respects, the empirical P–R studies offer far from uniform outcomes. Yet, except in the case of Japan and, according to some authors, Italy, they all point to the existence of monopolistic competition in the countries considered, although for some years and some countries, perfect competition could not be excluded.[26] *Grosso modo*, therefore, our results are in line with those of the literature, namely monopolistic competition for most countries and submarkets, whereby perfect competition can not always be excluded.

4.4 MARKET STRUCTURE AND COMPETITION

Given the current wave of mergers in the EU banking market and the expectation of continued or even accelerating consolidation, concerns have been voiced as to competitive conditions in the EU banking markets, especially in some market segments, such as local and retail markets. More precisely, the question emerges whether market concentration might affect the conduct of banks or the degree of competition. Theoretically, the existence of a relationship between market structure and banks' behaviour is indicated by, among others, the P–R model. Where, in the literature, the impact of the banking market structure on bank performance has been examined exhaustively – employing the structure–conduct–performance paradigm – the relevance of market structure for conduct or competitive conditions has been almost entirely ignored.[27] The present section aims at examining this disregarded relationship and seeks to assess a possible impact of the number of banks and the banking market concentration on competition, by that expanding the existing literature in this field.

4.4.1 Banking Market Concentration

As was observed above, the P–R approach provides a link between the number of banks and competition. However, as a description of the market structure, the number of banks is a limited concept. For instance, it fully ignores the size distribution of banks (or inequality) in a given market. As concentration indices, weighted averages of banks' market shares, take both the size distribution and the number of banks into account, they are often used as a simple proxy of the market structure. Apart from the number of banks itself, we also use two – frequently applied – types of such indices as a proxy.[28] The first is the so-called *k* bank concentration ratio (CR_k) which takes the market shares of the *k* largest banks in the market and ignores the remaining banks in that market. This index is based on the idea that the behaviour of a market is dominated by a small number of large banks. The second index we use is the Herfindahl–Hirschman index (*HHI*), which takes market shares as weights, and stresses the importance of larger banks by assigning them a greater weight than smaller banks. It includes each bank separately and differently, and thereby avoids an arbitrary cut-off and insensitivity to the share distribution.

Table 4.6 presents the 1997 *HHI* and CR_k, for $k = 3$, 5 and 10, for all 23 countries analysed earlier. Total assets have been taken as the measure of bank size. The value of the *k* bank concentration ratios (for various values of *k*) always exceeds the value of the *HHI,* since the latter gives less prominence to the markets shares (the weights again being market shares) than the former (unit weights). The results for the various index values are rather similar, displaying a high degree of correlation. The strongest correlations are found between CR_3 and CR_5, CR_5 and CR_{10}, and, surprisingly, *HHI* and CR_3. In terms of ranking, the correlation between *HHI* and CR_3 is, at 98 per cent, by far the strongest. This demonstrates that the *HHI* is determined mainly by (the squares of the market shares of) the large banks, which puts into perspective the alleged drawback of the CR_k indices vis-à-vis the *HHI,* that is, that they ignore the influence of smaller banks.

For countries where the number of banks in the available sample is low, as in Finland, South Korea and New Zealand, results are less reliable. High concentration rates are found in Denmark, Greece, the Netherlands and Switzerland, where the largest three banks take more than two-thirds of the total market in terms of total assets. In Canada, concentration is high only when at least five banks are taken into consideration. Switzerland is the most highly concentrated country according to *HHI*, which may seem remarkable given the large number of banks in that country. Increasing the sample of Swiss banks to more than three hardly increases the concentration rate. Concentration appears to be low in France, Germany, Italy, Luxembourg and the USA, where the largest three have a combined share of less than one-third. By all measures, concentration is lowest in the USA. Germany, where the number of banks in our sample is largest, takes the last place but one in concentration.

All types of indices appear to be inversely correlated to the number of banks. This is owing to a well-known weakness of concentration indices, namely their dependency on the size of a country or banking market. The

Table 4.6 Concentration indices for 23 countries, based on total assets (1997)

	HHI	CR_3	CR_5	CR_{10}	No. of banks
Australia	0.14	0.57	0.77	0.90	31
Austria	0.14	0.53	0.64	0.77	78
Belgium	0.12	0.52	0.75	0.87	79
Canada	0.14	0.54	0.82	0.94	44
Denmark	0.17	0.67	0.80	0.91	91
Finland	0.24	0.73	0.91	1.00	12
France	0.05	0.30	0.45	0.64	336
Germany	0.03	0.22	0.31	0.46	1 803
Greece	0.20	0.66	0.82	0.94	22
Ireland	0.17	0.65	0.73	0.84	30
Italy	0.04	0.27	0.40	0.54	331
Japan	0.06	0.39	0.49	0.56	140
Korea (South)	0.11	0.45	0.68	0.96	13
Luxembourg	0.03	0.20	0.30	0.49	118
Netherlands	0.23	0.78	0.87	0.93	45
New Zealand	0.18	0.63	0.90	n.a.	8
Norway	0.12	0.56	0.67	0.81	35
Portugal	0.09	0.40	0.57	0.82	40
Spain	0.08	0.45	0.56	0.69	140
Sweden	0.12	0.53	0.73	0.92	21
Switzerland	0.26	0.72	0.77	0.82	325
UK	0.06	0.34	0.47	0.68	186
USA	0.02	0.15	0.23	0.38	717
Averages/total	*0.12*	*0.49*	*0.64*	*0.73*	*4 645*
Standard deviation	*0.07*	*0.18*	*0.20*	*0.18*	

smaller the country or the number of its banks, the larger its measure of concentration. In the empirical analysis below, we attempt to solve this problem by taking the number of banks into account explicitly. Table 4.6 is based on the Fitch-IBCA data set, used for the P–R analysis in Section 4.3.3. This sample does not include all banks, which for some countries might distort the concentration index value. However, this effect is limited as the ignored market segment consists mainly of the smallest banks. This problem, too, is considered in the empirical analysis below. Another shortcoming of concentration indices is that non-bank financial institutions are ignored. As competition from non-banks is mainly related to some segments of the banking market, such as mortgage lending, it is difficult to correct for that in the present broad 'total assets' measure of concentration. Finally, the Fitch-IBCA data set consists of consolidated figures and does not distinguish between domestic and foreign operations. For that reason, the concentration index values for small countries with large international banks are overestimated.[29] This is illustrated in Table 4.7, where market shares for total assets, loans and non-bank deposits are presented for the ten banks with the largest balance-sheet total in the sample.

Table 4.7 Market shares of the ten largest banks in the sample (1997)

	Country	Market shares			National	
		Total assets	*Loans*	*Deposits*	*H*	CR_3
1. UBS AG	Swi	0.36	0.46	0.45	1.01	0.72
2. Deutsche Bank AG	Ger	0.09	0.09	0.12	1.03	0.22
3. HSBC Holdings Plc	UK	0.14	0.14	0.15	1.20	0.34
4. Bayerische Hypo- und Vereinsbank[a]	Ger	0.09	0.07	0.04	1.03	0.22
5. Crédit Agricole CA	Fra	0.14	0.11	0.13	0.89	0.30
6. Dai-Ichi Kangyo Bank Ltd DKB	Jap	0.17	0.14	0.12	0.61	0.39
7. ABN–Amro Holding NV	Neth	0.34	0.39	0.41	0.95	0.78
8. Société Générale	Fra	0.10	0.10	0.11	0.89	0.30
9. Norinchukin Bank	Jap	0.08	0.13	0.11	0.61	0.61
10. Sakura Bank Limited	Jap	0.16	0.13	0.12	0.61	0.61

[a] Pro forma.

The market shares of even the largest banks in France, Germany, Japan and the UK are modest, suggesting that, on a national or market-wide scale, these banks have limited market power. Of course, the situation may be different in particular market segments or local areas. Large banks in small countries, such as UBS of Switzerland and ABN–Amro of the Netherlands, do command substantial market shares, although in the case of ABN-Amro, for instance, domestic business is less than half of total business, while for UBS the ratio is even less than one-quarter. After correction for foreign operations (which, by the way, affects both the denominator and the numerator of the shares), the market shares for ABN–Amro are almost 30 per cent smaller,[30] though still sizeable. To some extent, the indices (such as CR_3) do indeed reflect the higher concentration in the Netherlands and Switzerland. At the same time, ABN–Amro and UBS may be facing stiff competition on other (foreign) markets.

4.4.2 Relationship Between Competition and Market Structure

In order to investigate the relationship between competition and market structure in the banking industry, we related the *H*-statistic for all banks,[31] as a measure of competition, to the concentration index *(CI)* and the logarithm of the number of banks in the markets (log *n*) as representatives of the market structure. Despite the various shortcomings, already noted, which concentration index may have as a proxy of the market structure, we nevertheless, for want of anything better, examined how it acts in the empirical relationship in question. The estimated values of *H* were taken from the 'all-bank' sample. Concentration indices are one-dimensional measures taking account of two dimensions, that is, the number of banks, indicating the 'density' of the banking market, and their size distribution, indicating skewness. Some concentration indices can be rewritten as measures of the distribution and the number of banks. For instance, the Herfindahl–Hirschman index can be rewritten as:[32]

$$HI = (\eta_0^2 + 1)/n \tag{4.10}$$

where η_0^2 is the coefficient of variation (the possible change of the size structure) of the original bank-size distribution. In our empirical analysis, we restore this two-dimensionality, describing the market structure by both the *CI* and the number of banks. Here we have used logarithms to scale the variable *n*. There is another reason why inclusion of the number of banks makes sense. Below Table 4.6, we recorded the dependency of concentration indices on the size of a country or banking market. By including the number of its banks (as proxy of the banking market size) in the regression equation, we correct for this distortion. At the same time, the effect on the *CI* of a limited sample size (as is the case for some countries) is compensated for. Hence, the estimated regression is given by:

$$H = \alpha_0 + \alpha_1\, CI + \alpha_2 \log n + \alpha_3\, Europe \tag{4.11}$$

A dummy variable 'Europe' is included because *H* is substantially higher for Europe than for non-European banking markets, which may be due to economic and institutional conditions. The upper part of Table 4.8 presents regression results for Equation (4.11) for four different *CIs*. Alternatively, the observations for the 23 countries could also be weighted by log *n* as a measure (or proxy) of the respective banking-market size. In this way, we could take account of the magnitude of the banking market in each country, weighting Germany, France and Italy heavier than, say, Greece, Ireland and Sweden. At the same time, lower weights would be allocated to countries where the sample size is limited and the variables might therefore be somewhat less reliable, as is the case for Finland, South Korea and New Zealand. Weighted regression results are shown in the lower part of Table 4.8.

For all eight regressions, the coefficient of the concentration index shows the expected negative sign, indicating that competition is decreasing with increasing market concentration. In the one-sided test, all negative signs are significant. For all concentration indices, the level of significance (expressed in the *t*-value) is much higher in the weighted regression. (This holds, incidentally, also for the other variables.) This outcome is at least a strong indication that concentration does impair competitiveness. The significance of the coefficients of the CR_k's is higher than that of *HHI*, for all *k* and for both the weighted and unweighted regression. This result supports the view that the share of the *k* largest banks (*k* being 3, 5 or 10) rather than the entire size distribution of banks in a market, is the strongest determinant for the competitive conditions in a market.

Table 4.8 Relationship between competition and concentration for the all-bank sample with a Europe dummy

	HHI		CR_3		CR_5		CR_{10}	
Unweighted regression								
Constant	1.01	(7.0)	1.23	(7.1)	1.31	(5.5)	1.54	(4.6)
Concentration index	-0.93	(1.9)	-0.53	(2.9)	-0.47	(2.3)	-0.65	(2.5)
Log *n*	-0.07	(2.8)	-0.09	(3.6)	-0.10	(3.2)	-0.11	(3.0)
'Europe'	0.15	(2.3)	0.16	(2.8)	0.14	(2.3)	0.17	(2.9)
Adjusted R^2	0.25		0.37		0.30		0.35	
Weighted regression								
Constant	1.01	(10.2)	1.17	(10.4)	1.33	(9.3)	1.69	(9.0)
Concentration index	-0.79	(3.4)	-0.44	(4.2)	-0.52	(4.2)	-0.80	(5.0)
Log *n*	-0.07	(4.7)	-0.08	(5.6)	-0.10	(5.6)	-0.13	(6.3)
'Europe'	0.14	(5.3)	0.17	(6.3)	0.20	(6.3)	0.24	(7.0)
Adjusted R^2	0.996		0.997		0.997		0.997	

Note: T-values in parenthesis. At a confidence level of 95 %, the critical value of the one sided *t*-value test is 1.73 and that of the two-sided *t*-value test is 2.09. At a confidence level of 99 %, these figures are 2.54 and 2.85, respectively.

In principle, a larger number of banks indicates more potential for competition. For that reason for log *n* one would expect to see a coefficient with a positive sign. Yet wherever the size distribution is heavily skewed and just a few banks dominate the market, a large number of banks merely indicates that there is a broad fringe of powerless dwarfs. The larger the number of banks, the less opportunity each has to assert its influence and increase competition. The latter effect appears to be dominant, as the net effect of the number of banks on competition is negative.[33] Obviously, in situations typically measured by the CR_k indices, where a few large banks occupy a large share of the market, market power is exercised more heavily. The dummy variable for Europe proves to be significant for all eight regression equations, indicating the different institutional and economic conditions faced by European banks, which are disregarded by the other explanatory variables.

It is no easy task to find out which differences cause the diverging levels of competition between European and non-European banks. We found that in Equation (4.11) the 'share of bank demand deposits in total assets' is an alternative for 'Europe', see Table 4.9. After inclusion of that variable, the Europe dummy becomes insignificant and may be dropped. This share reflects an aspect of banks' average funding habits: European banks make more extensive use of the interbank market for funding. We may have hit on an important variable here,[34] but a convincing theoretical explanation is lacking. One possible explanation is that where banking and financial markets are more developed, (i) the interbank market is more developed and (ii) competition is more intense. If this is true, then the share of bank deposits acts as an indicator of financial sophistication.

Table 4.9 Relationship between competition and concentration for the all-bank sample with 'share of bank deposits'

	HHI		CR_3		CR_5		CR_{10}	
Unweighted regression								
Constant	0.90	(7.0)	1.05	(6.6)	1.14	(5.3)	1.33	(4.5)
Concentration index	-0.71	(1.8)	-0.38	(2.4)	-0.37	(2.1)	-0.51	(2.4)
Log *n*	-0.07	(3.1)	-0.08	(3.6)	-0.09	(3.3)	-0.10	(3.1)
Share of bank deposits	0.85	(3.6)	0.83	(3.7)	0.80	(3.5)	0.89	(4.0)
Adjusted R^2	0.42		0.48		0.45		0.50	
Weighted regression								
Constant	1.07	(11.4)	1.24	(11.9)	1.40	(10.4)	1.67	(9.2)
Concentration index	-0.86	(4.0)	-0.47	(5.0)	-0.54	(4.8)	-0.73	(4.9)
Log *n*	-0.08	(5.6)	-0.09	(6.7)	-0.11	(6.5)	-0.13	(6.5)
Share of bank deposits	0.57	(6.2)	0.70	(7.4)	0.79	(7.2)	0.91	(7.2)
Adjusted R^2	0.997		0.997		0.997		0.997	

The above provides evidence that conduct such as competitive behaviour may indeed be related to characteristics of the market structure such as concentration and number of banks. A Wald test, which assesses the significance of the coefficients of the *CI* and the number of banks simultaneously, confirms this conclusion.[35] The evidence is only modest, however, as Equation (4.11) is not very robust. For instance, if the Europe dummy is deleted, the significance of the other parameters drops dramatically. Nevertheless, the continuing process of consolidation in the banking industry may raise the policy makers' concern about competitive conditions in the banking markets. This concern, however, is very often related not so much to entire markets as to market segments, such as, for instance, deposits or certain geographical areas. Unfortunately, the limited availability of data makes it impossible to make more refined analyses.

4.5 CONCLUSIONS

The ongoing dramatic structural changes in the banking industry, particularly in Europe, may affect competition, especially on local markets and for banks' retail services. This chapter sought to assess competitive conditions and concentration in the banking markets of as many as 23 industrialized countries both inside and outside Europe over a time span of more than 10 years. In addition, it investigated the interaction between competition and concentration. The Panzar–Rosse approach was applied to obtain a measure of competitive conditions for the entire EU, as well as for each of the countries considered. The resulting *H*-statistic provides strong evidence that the banking markets in the EU and in each of the examined industrialized countries are characterized by monopolistic competition or certain forms of partial collusion,[36] at least as long as the entire markets for all banks are considered. The absence of variation in the *H*-estimates across countries is remarkable. Bresnahan and Reiss (1991) have found that almost all variation in competitive conduct occurs with the entry of the second and third firm into a market.

We have attempted to take account of the geographical and even the product dimension of banking operations by defining three sub-markets in terms of bank sizes for each country and have estimated their degree of competition. Competition is stronger among large banks – operating predominantly in international markets – and weaker among small banks – operating mainly in local markets – while medium-sized banks take an intermediate position. In some countries, perfect competition has been found among large banks.

The competitive measure *H* has been assumed to be time-dependent. For a number of countries, estimates of the *H*-statistic over time indicate a significant increase in competition. However, these improvements in competition appear to be only slight, that is to say smaller than expected. Competition seems to be somewhat stronger in Europe than in countries such as the USA, Canada and Japan. Thanks to the large sample and the pooled regression approach, our results are fairly robust. Generally speaking, our findings are in keeping with comparable studies in the literature, which also point to monopolistic competition in most countries.

Concentration in the banking markets of 23 industrialized countries was measured using various *k* bank concentration ratios and the Herfindahl–Hirschman index. Empirical studies concerning the impact of market structure on banks' conduct are rare. In order to investigate this relationship, the estimated *H*-values indicating competition are used as proxies of conduct and are related both to the concentration indices considered and to the absolute number of banks operating in these markets, acting together as a proxy of the market structure. The impact of both market structure measures on competition appears to be significant, most markedly so when the *k* bank concentration indices are used. The latter finding confirms the observation that a few large (cartel) banks can restrict competition and that a multitude of fringe competitors is unable to engender competition.

APPENDIX 4.A THE PANZAR–ROSSE APPROACH IN A SIMPLE MONOPOLY MODEL

An illustration of the practical application of the Panzar–Rosse approach can be obtained from the analysis of a simple single product monopoly model (Panzar and Rosse, 1987, page 446). Suppose that the monopolist faces a demand curve of constant price elasticity $e > 1$, that reads as:

$$y = (\gamma^{-1} z^{-\alpha} p)^{-e} \qquad (4.A.1)$$

where y is the demand for the single product, p is its price and z is a vector of exogenous variables, that shift the firm's demand function, with parameters α. In that case the firm's revenue function (R) is equal to:

$$R(y,z) = y\,p = y(\gamma\, z^{\alpha} y^{-1/e}) = \gamma\, z^{\alpha} y^{(e-1)/e} \qquad (4.A.2)$$

For simplicity, we assume also that the monopolist employs a constant return to scale Cobb–Douglas technology, so that its cost function (C) can be written as:

$$C(y,w,x) = y\, x^{\beta} \prod_i w_i^{ai} \quad \text{with } a_i > 0 \text{ and } \Sigma\, a_i = 1 \qquad (4.A.3)$$

where w is a vector of factor prices, exogenous to the firm, with parameters a_i, and x is a vector of exogenous variables that shift the firm's cost function, with parameters β. Profit maximization follows from the first derivative of profit, R-C:

$$\partial(R - C)/\partial y) = \gamma\, z^{\alpha} (e-1)/e\, y^{-1/e} - x^{\beta} \prod_i w_i^{ai} = 0 \qquad (4.A.4)$$

The equilibrium output is (asterisks refer to equilibrium values):

$$y^{*} = (x^{\beta} \prod_i w_i^{ai} /(\gamma\, z^{\alpha} (e-1)/e))^{-e} \qquad (4.A.5)$$

This leads to the nonstochastic version of the firm's reduced-form revenue equation:

$$\ln R(y^*,z,x) = \gamma_0 + e\,\alpha\, \ln z - (e\text{-}1)\,\beta \ln x - (e\text{-}1) \sum a_i \ln w_i\,, \qquad (4.A.6)$$

where the intercept γ_0 is equal to $(e \ln \gamma - (1 - e) \ln((e - 1)/e))$. So, $H = -(e - 1) \sum a_i = 1 - e \leq 0$. H must be negative if the marginal cost curve is to cut the marginal revenue curve below, as required by the second order condition for monopoly profit maximization. Note that in this case, because of the simple structure of the example, estimation of the reduced-form equation not only allows one to test the hypothesis of monopoly profit maximization, it also provides the analyst with estimates of all structural parameters of interest, if the hypothesis is maintained. In particular, this example indicates that the magnitude, as well as the sign of H may be of interest. Here, because it provides an estimate of the price elasticity of demand, H also yields an estimate of the Lerner index of monopoly power $L = (e - 1)/e = H/(H - 1)$.

APPENDIX 4.B ESTIMATION RESULTS OF P–R MODELS FOR 23 COUNTRIES AND VARIOUS SIZE CLASSES

Table 4.B.1 Empirical results for Australia (1991–98)

	All banks		Small banks		Medium-sized banks		Large banks	
	Coeff.	*t-value*	*Coeff.*	*t-value*	*Coeff.*	*t-value*	*Coeff.*	*t-value*
Funding rate	0.44	*9.7*	0.01	*0.1*	0.66	*13.5*	0.52	*10.9*
Wage rate	0.03	*3.6*	-0.16	*1.0*	0.03	*3.0*	0.05	*3.0*
Capital price	-0.00	*0.9*	0.01	*0.0*	-0.05	*4.0*	0.02	*1.5*
Time	17.64	*3.8*	—	—	7.58	*2.3*	13.15	*4.3*
Loans	0.35	*10.6*	—	—	0.25	*7.0*	—	—
Other income	—	—	-0.80	*5.8*	—	—	-0.05	*2.9*
Total assets	—	—	—	—	—	—	0.02	*2.4*
Equity	—	—	1.63	*3.7*	-0.06	*3.4*	—	—
Cash & DFB	—	—	—	—	—	—	-0.02	*2.5*
Intercept	-0.80	*6.4*	11.4	*4.3*	0.06	*0.3*	1.19	*6.8*
Adjusted R^2	0.67		0.85		0.82		0.91	
No. of observ.	168		13		104		56	
H (1991/1997)	0.50[1]	0.57[1]	-0.14[2]		0.67[1]	0.70[1]	0.63[1]	0.68[1]

[1] *H*=0 and *H*=1 rejected (level of confidence 99.9%); [2] *H*=0 accepted (level of confidence 95%).

Table 4.B.2 Empirical results for Austria (1989–98)

	All banks		Small banks		Medium-sized banks		Large banks	
	Coeff.	*t-value*	*Coeff.*	*t-value*	*Coeff.*	*t-value*	*Coeff.*	*t-value*
Funding rate	0.62	*34.3*	0.55	*14.6*	0.76	*32.3*	0.82	*34.1*
Wage rate	0.20	*12.0*	0.32	*10.1*	0.14	*7.6*	0.08	*10.2*
Capital price	0.05	*5.8*	0.07	*4.7*	0.03	*2.6*	0.01	*1.1*
Time	—	—	—	—	-3.89	*3.0*	—	—
Loans	0.09	*8.8*	0.12	*7.0*	—	—	—	—
Other income	-0.12	*9.6*	-0.21	*9.5*	-0.05	*3.5*	—	—
Total assets	—	—	—	—	-0.03	*3.3*	—	—
Bank deposits	-0.02	*3.2*	—	—	-0.05	*5.4*	-0.05	*3.7*
Equity	—	—	—	—	0.06	*2.4*	—	—
Dem. Dep. C.	—	—	0.4	*2.7*	0.01	*2.2*	—	—
Cash & DFB	—	—	—	—	—	—	0.01	*2.7*
Intercept	-0.44	*5.2*	-0.43	*2.3*	0.01	*0.1*	0.08	*1.2*
Adjusted R^2	0.82		0.77		0.96		0.99	
No. of observ.	426		189		170		32	
H (1991/1997)	0.87[1]		0.93[2]		0.91[1]	0.89[1]	0.91[3]	

[1] *H*=0 and *H*=1 rejected (level of confidence 99.9%); [2] *H*=1 not rejected (level of confidence 95%); the F-statistic is 2.53 and the probability level (of the null hypothesis) is 11.4%; [3] *H*=0 and *H*=1 rejected (level of confidence 99%).

Table 4.B.3 Empirical results for Belgium (1989–98)

	All banks		Small banks		Medium-sized banks		Large banks	
	Coeff.	*t-value*	*Coeff.*	*t-value*	*Coeff.*	*t-value*	*Coeff.*	*t-value*
Funding rate	0.76	*32.5*	0.88	*21.7*	0.77	*24.9*	0.77	*32.1*
Wage rate	0.07	*6.2*	0.03	*1.1*	0.10	*7.1*	0.07	*7.6*
Capital price	0.06	*5.3*	0.04	*2.4*	0.01	*1.4*	0.00	*0.1*
Time	—	—	—	—	—	—	4.37	*3.7*
Loans ratio	0.14	*10.1*	0.10	*6.6*	0.11	*6.7*	—	—
Other income	—	—	—	—	—	—	-0.01	*2.1*
Total assets	—	—	0.05	*2.8*	—	—	—	—
Bank deposits	—	—	-0.03	*4.7*	-0.02	*4.2*	—	—
Equity	—	—	—	—	—	—	0.07	*4.3*
Cash & DFB	0.02	*2.4*	—	—	0.02	*2.5*	0.02	*2.7*
Intercept	0.17	*1.7*	-0.20	*-1.0*	0.28	*2.2*	-0.12	*1.4*
Adjusted R^2	0.78		0.79		0.83		0.99	
No. of observ.	407		191		156		64	
H (1991/1997)	0.89[1]		0.95[2]		0.88[3]		0.86[1]	0.88[1]

[1] *H*=0 and *H*=1 rejected (level of confidence 99.9%); [2] *H*=1 not rejected (level of confidence 95%); the F-statistic is 0.65 and the probability level (of the null hypothesis) is 42.3%; [3] *H*=1 rejected (level of confidence 99%).

Table 4.B.4 Empirical results for Canada (1988–98)

	All banks		Small banks		Medium-sized banks		Large banks	
	Coeff.	*t-value*	*Coeff.*	*t-value*	*Coeff.*	*t-value*	*Coeff.*	*t-value*
Funding rate	0.55	*20.6*	0.69	*29.2*	0.60	*16.0*	0.52	*19.7*
Wage rate	0.08	*5.4*	0.08	*4.4*	0.09	*4.5*	0.03	*0.8*
Capital price	-0.04	*4.0*	-0.02	*1.6*	-0.06	*3.3*	-0.02	*0.9*
Time	5.90	*3.2*	—	—	—	—	10.99	*4.7*
Loans ratio	0.18	*8.1*	—	—	0.40	*9.4*	0.17	*3.4*
Total assets	—	—	-0.05	*3.8*	—	—	—	—
Bank deposits	—	—	-0.02	*2.8*	—	—	—	—
Equity	0.04	*2.2*	—	—	—	—	—	—
Cash & DFB	0.03	*5.2*	—	—	—	—	—	—
Intercept	-0.45	*4.6*	-0.05	*0.4*	-0.30	*2.0*	-0.76	*4.6*
Adjusted R^2	0.77		0.86		0.70		0.96	
No. of observ.	304		140		140		59	
H (1991/1997)	0.60[1]	0.62[1]	0.74[1]		0.63[1]		0.56[1]	0.60[1]

[1] *H*=0 and *H*=1 rejected (level of confidence 99.9%).

Table 4.B.5 Empirical results for Denmark (1990–98)

	All banks		Small banks		Medium-sized banks		Large banks	
	Coeff.	*t-value*	*Coeff.*	*t-value*	*Coeff.*	*t-value*	*Coeff.*	*t-value*
Funding rate	0.32	*11.0*	0.33	*10.7*	0.60	*17.5*	0.64	*20.4*
Wage rate	-0.01	*1.0*	-0.03	*2.7*	0.16	*12.2*	0.48	*11.3*
Capital price	-0.02	*3.6*	-0.02	*2.2*	-0.01	*0.9*	0.04	*1.6*
Time	21.37	*4.2*	17.31	*3.2*	—	—	—	—
Loans ratio	0.28	*20.1*	0.27	*19.7*	0.27	*10.8*	—	—
Total assets	0.04	*7.1*	—	—	—	—	—	—
Bank deposits	-0.01	*3.0*	-0.02	*4.7*	—	—	—	—
Equity	0.06	*3.2*	—	—	0.15	*4.6*	—	—
Dem. Dep. C.	0.04	*2.8*	0.04	*2.6*	—	—	—	—
Intercept	-1.05	*9.5*	-1.19	*14.3*	-0.21	*1.4*	1.37	*7.0*
Adjusted R^2	0.79		0.77		0.92		0.97	
No. of observ.	514		415		79		26	
H (1991/1997)	0.32[1]	0.36[1]	0.31[1]	0.34[1]	0.75[1]		1.16[2]	

[1] *H*=0 and *H*=1 rejected (level of confidence 99.9%); [2] *H*=1 not rejected (level of confidence 95%); the F-statistic is 6.55 and the probability level (of the null hypothesis) is 1.8%.

Table 4.B.6 Empirical results for Finland (1990–98)

	All banks		Small banks		Medium-sized banks		Large banks	
	Coeff.	*t-value*	*Coeff.*	*t-value*	*Coeff.*	*t-value*	*Coeff.*	*t-value*
Funding rate	0.67	*18.0*	1.08	*5.1*	0.51	*9.3*	0.75	*29.7*
Wage rate	0.12	*3.7*	-0.13	*0.7*	0.22	*3.8*	-0.04	*2.4*
Capital price	-0.01	*1.0*	-0.28	*2.6*	0.03	*1.0*	-0.01	*-0.6*
Loans ratio	0.22	*6.1*	—	—	—	—	0.09	*2.0*
Other income	-0.07	*2.3*	—	—	-0.15	*2.6*	—	—
Bank deposits	-0.03	*2.1*	—	—	—	—	-0.15	*6.6*
Equity	-0.11	*2.8*	—	—	—	—	-0.16	*3.1*
Intercept	-0.21	*1.3*	-0.17	*0.1*	-0.85	*3.8*	-0.65	*5.6*
Adjusted R^2	0.88		0.79		0.80		0.97	
No. of observ.	67		10		32		34	
H	0.78[1]		0.67[2]		0.76[3]		0.70[1]	

[1] *H*=0 and *H*=1 rejected (level of confidence 99.9%); [2] *H*=1 not rejected (level of confidence 95%); the F-statistic is 3.03 and the probability level (of the null hypothesis) is 13.2%; [3] *H*=0 and *H*=1 rejected (level of confidence 99%).

Table 4.B.7 Empirical results for France (1988–98)

	All banks		Small banks		Medium-sized banks		Large banks	
	Coeff.	*t-value*	*Coeff.*	*t-value*	*Coeff.*	*t-value*	*Coeff.*	*t-value*
Funding rate	0.59	*54.0*	0.41	*16.3*	0.56	*30.4*	0.82	*20.1*
Wage rate	0.09	*12.2*	0.08	*5.8*	0.11	*11.6*	0.00	*0.0*
Capital price	0.02	*3.7*	0.01	*1.5*	0.04	*5.3*	0.07	*3.9*
Time	—	—	14.42	*3.9*	10.05	*6.6*	—	—
Loans ratio	0.13	*21.9*	0.16	*13.0*	0.09	*12.6*	0.14	*8.0*
Total assets	-0.03	*7.5*	—	—	—	—	—	—
Bank deposits	—	—	—	—	-0.02	*3.0*	-0.09	*4.9*
Equity	-0.05	*5.5*	-0.06	*4.7*	—	—	0.13	*4.0*
Intercept	-0.09	*1.5*	-0.58	*5.6*	-0.28	*4.3*	-0.52	*3.4*
Adjusted R^2	0.60		0.57		0.67		0.70	
No. of observ.	2 416		759		1 313		340	
H (1991/1997)	0.70[1]		0.54[1]	0.59[1]	0.74[1]	0.79[1]	0.89[2]	

[1] *H*=0 and *H*=1 rejected (level of confidence 99.9%); [2] *H*=1 rejected (level of confidence 99%); the F-statistic is 5.36 and the probability level (of the null hypothesis) is 2.1%.

Table 4.B.8 Empirical results for Germany (1988–98)

	All banks		Small banks		Medium-sized banks		Large banks	
	Coeff.	*t-value*	*Coeff.*	*t-value*	*Coeff.*	*t-value*	*Coeff.*	*t-value*
Funding rate	0.45	*74.1*	0.39	*53.7*	0.50	*50.9*	0.92	*28.1*
Wage rate	0.13	*35.9*	0.13	*27.5*	0.16	*25.4*	0.14	*17.2*
Capital price	0.00	*0.3*	0.01	*4.8*	-0.01	*2.3*	0.00	*0.1*
Time	7.07	*19.0*	9.68	*18.8*	4.72	*9.3*	-2.32	*2.6*
Loans ratio	0.07	*32.0*	0.09	*33.0*	0.04	*10.0*	—	—
Other income	-0.05	*23.6*	-0.06	*21.0*	-0.05	*13.7*	—	—
Total assets	-0.01	*8.9*	—	—	—	—	-0.03	*4.7*
Bank deposits	-0.01	*6.8*	-0.00	*2.1*	-0.01	*6.0*	-0.12	*12.5*
Equity	-0.04	*12.5*	-0.02	*5.3*	-0.03	*5.4*	-0.22	*18.5*
Dem. Dep. C.	0.01	*4.5*	0.02	*8.2*	—	—	—	—
Cash & DFB	0.01	*7.3*	0.01	*7.0*	0.01	*5.4*	—	—
Intercept	-0.64	*26.3*	-0.83	*27.6*	-0.45	*11.2*	1.05	*8.8*
Adjusted R^2	0.69		0.69		0.71		0.84	
No. of observ.	10 513		6 523		3 672		458	
H (1991/1997)	0.60[1]	0.63[1]	0.56[1]	0.59[1]	0.68[1]	0.70[1]	1.05[2]	1.03[2]

[1] *H*=0 and *H*=1 rejected (level of confidence 99.9%); [2] *H*=1 not rejected (level of confidence 95%).

Table 4.B.9 Empirical results for Greece (1990–98)

	All banks		Small banks		Medium-sized banks		Large banks	
	Coeff.	*t-value*	*Coeff.*	*t-value*	*Coeff.*	*t-value*	*Coeff.*	*t-value*
Funding rate	0.62	*17.2*	0.49	*6.8*	0.61	*11.4*	0.91	*15.1*
Wage rate	0.11	*4.8*	0.05	*0.7*	0.02	*0.4*	0.08	*3.1*
Capital price	0.03	*1.7*	-0.13	*1.8*	0.04	*1.1*	0.09	*4.8*
Time	—	—	—	—	—	—	11.70	*4.6*
Loans ratio	—	—	-0.20	*3.4*	—	—	—	—
Other income	—	—	—	—	0.08	*3.2*	—	—
Total assets	—	—	—	—	—	—	-0.08	*5.7*
Bank deposits	—	—	0.08	*3.7*	—	—	—	—
Equity	—	—	0.15	*2.7*	—	—	—	—
Dem. Dep. C.	—	—	0.04	*2.4*	—	—	—	—
Cash & DFB	—	—	0.12	*4.1*	—	—	—	—
Intercept	-0.31	*2.6*	-0.69	*2.1*	-0.39	*1.7*	0.80	*4.9*
Adjusted R^2	0.80		0.92		0.85		0.99	
No. of observ.	102		29		35		19	
H (1991/1997)	0.76[1]		0.41[2]		0.66[1]		1.01[3]	0.94[3]

[1] *H*=0 and *H*=1 rejected (level of confidence 99.9%); [2] *H*=0 and *H*=1 rejected (level of confidence 95%); [3] *H*=1 not rejected (level of confidence 95%).

Table 4.B.10 Empirical results for Ireland (1992–98)

	All banks		Small banks		Medium-sized banks		Large banks	
	Coeff.	*t-value*	*Coeff.*	*t-value*	*Coeff.*	*t-value*	*Coeff.*	*t-value*
Funding rate	0.71	*17.9*	0.49	*6.0*	0.76	*20.0*	0.54	*19.4*
Wage rate	0.02	*0.8*	0.08	*1.4*	-0.01	*0.4*	0.37	*11.9*
Capital price	-0.08	*2.6*	0.43	*4.5*	-0.12	*3.8*	0.01	*0.3*
Loans ratio	—	—	—	—	0.05	*1.9*	—	—
Total assets	—	—	—	—	-0.14	*3.7*	—	—
Bank deposits	-0.07	*2.4*	—	—	-0.07	*2.1*	0.05	*2.7*
Equity	0.12	*3.5*	—	—	—	—	—	—
Non-perf. loans	—	—	—	—	—	—	0.04	
Intercept	-0.78	*4.6*	-1.43	*3.9*	0.62	*1.8*	0.84	*6.7*
Adjusted R^2	0.71		0.74		0.84		1.00	
No. of observ.	127		15		96		14	
H	0.65[1]		0.99[2]		0.63[1]		0.93[3]	

[1] *H*=0 and *H*=1 rejected (level of confidence 99.9%); [2] *H*=1 not rejected (level of confidence 95%); the F-statistic is 0.00 and the probability level (of the null hypothesis) is 97.0%; [3] *H*=1 not rejected (level of confidence 95%); the F-statistic is 4.25 and the probability level (of the null hypothesis) is 7.3%.

Table 4.B.11 Empirical results for Italy (1988–98)

	All banks		Small banks		Medium-sized banks		Large banks	
	Coeff.	*t-value*	*Coeff.*	*t-value*	*Coeff.*	*t-value*	*Coeff.*	*t-value*
Funding rate	0.64	*58.6*	0.64	*39.0*	0.76	*44.2*	0.68	*14.2*
Wage rate	0.19	*19.6*	0.12	*8.9*	0.17	*22.2*	0.26	*8.1*
Capital price	-0.00	*0.4*	-0.01	*1.5*	-0.02	*2.2*	-0.09	*5.3*
Time	—	—	—	—	-4.68	*6.2*	-4.02	*2.1*
Loans ratio	0.58	*8.5*	0.11	*12.9*	0.02	*3.4*	—	—
Total assets	-0.03	*15.4*	-0.03	*4.8*	-0.06	*8.2*	-0.07	*5.0*
Equity	—	—	—	—	-0.06	*5.6*	-0.08	*3.1*
Dem. Dep. C.	-0.01	*2.8*	—	—	—	—	—	—
Cash & DFB	-0.01	*3.5*	—	—	—	—	-0.08	*6.8*
Intercept	0.27	*6.1*	0.14	*1.7*	0.79	*9.7*	0.71	*3.4*
Adjusted R^2	0.72		0.66		0.80		0.72	
No. of observ.	1 780		812		897		225	
H (1991/1997)	0.82[1]		0.75[1]		0.89[1]	0.86[1]	0.83[1]	0.81[1]

[1] *H*=0 and *H*=1 rejected (level of confidence 99.9%).

Table 4.B.12 Empirical results for Japan (1989–98)

	All banks		Small banks		Medium-sized banks		Large banks	
	Coeff.	*t-value*	*Coeff.*	*t-value*	*Coeff.*	*t-value*	*Coeff.*	*t-value*
Funding rate	0.56	*21.9*	0.73	*5.6*	0.19	*4.5*	0.56	*24.4*
Wage rate	0.05	*3.0*	-0.54	*2.6*	-0.11	*5.8*	0.08	*6.2*
Capital price	0.01	*0.8*	0.24	*2.8*	-0.03	*6.0*	0.04	*3.4*
Time	-11.9	*6.2*	—	—	72.43	*4.5*	-9.59	*5.6*
Loans ratio	0.08	*2.6*	—	—	0.36	*9.2*	0.10	*4.0*
Total assets	-0.05	*8.7*	—	—	—	—	—	—
Bank deposits	—	—	—	—	—	—	-0.01	*3.2*
Equity	0.04	*3.1*	—	—	—	—	0.05	*4.2*
Dem. Dep. C.	0.04	*4.1*	—	—	—	—	—	—
Cash & DFB	0.02	*3.0*	-0.13	*2.9*	0.07	*3.6*	0.03	*6.9*
Intercept	-0.37	*3.7*	-2.50	*5.1*	-2.40	*23.5*	-0.76	*7.9*
Adjusted R^2	0.91		0.67		0.77		0.95	
No. of observ.	915		17		429		583	
H (1991/1997)	0.58[1]	0.54[1]	0.43[2]		0.07[3]	0.11[3]	0.64[1]	0.61[1]

[1] *H*=0 and *H*=1 rejected (level of confidence 99.9%); [2] *H*=0 not rejected (level of confidence 95%); the F-statistic is 4.29 and the probability level (of the null hypothesis) is 6.0%; [3] *H*=0 and *H*=1 rejected (level of confidence 99%).

Table 4.B.13 Empirical results for South Korea (1992–98)

	All banks		Small banks[0]		Medium-sized banks		Large banks	
	Coeff.	*t-value*	*Coeff.*	*t value*	*Coeff.*	*t value*	*Coeff.*	*t value*
Funding rate	0.61	*7.0*	—	—	0.58	*4.2*	0.76	*6.7*
Wage rate	0.04	*2.0*	—	—	0.09	*3.8*	0.01	*0.5*
Capital price	0.03	*2.2*	—	—	0.05	*4.1*	-0.01	*0.3*
Other income	—	—	—	—	-0.14	*5.7*	—	—
Total assets	—	—	—	—	0.17	*6.0*	-0.08	*2.1*
Equity	—	—	—	—	0.29	*5.1*	—	—
Cash & DFB	—	—	—	—	-0.05	*3.6*	—	—
Intercept	-0.70	*2.6*	—	—	-3.29	*7.3*	0.31	*0.6*
Adjusted R^2	0.43				0.79		0.63	
No. of observ.	63				27		28	
H	0.68[1]				0.72[2]		0.77[3]	

[0] Number of observations is too low; [1] *H*=0 and *H*=1 rejected (level of confidence 99%); [2] *H*=1 not rejected (level of confidence 95%); the F-statistic is 3.31 and the probability level (of the null

hypothesis) is 8.5%; [3] *H*=1 not rejected (level of confidence 95%); the F-statistic is 2.78 and the probability level (of the null hypothesis) is 10.9%.

Table 4.B.14 Empirical results for Luxembourg (1990–98)

	All banks		Small banks		Medium-sized banks		Large banks	
	Coeff.	*t-value*	*Coeff.*	*t-value*	*Coeff.*	*t-value*	*Coeff.*	*t-value*
Funding rate	0.84	*107.9*	0.85	*70.5*	0.80	*52.4*	0.84	*46.9*
Wage rate	0.08	*12.3*	0.07	*6.0*	0.11	*12.0*	0.06	*7.0*
Capital price	0.01	*4.6*	0.02	*3.4*	0.02	*4.3*	-0.01	*0.8*
Time	—	—	—	—	1.84	*2.0*	2.66	*2.8*
Loans ratio	0.01	*3.8*	0.01	*3.0*	0.01	*2.5*	—	—
Other income	-0.05	*11.7*	-0.06	*6.7*	-0.05	*8.2*	-0.03	*3.4*
Total assets	0.02	*5.9*	—	—	0.06	*8.3*	—	—
Equity	0.02	*2.9*	—	—	—	—	—	—
Dem. Dep. C.	—	—	—	—	—	—	-0.02	*2.9*
Cash & DFB	—	—	—	—	-0.02	*3.5*	—	—
Intercept	-0.39	*8.1*	-0.21	*3.8*	-0.60	*8.3*	-0.20	*3.7*
Adjusted R^2	0.94		0.94		0.94		0.98	
No. of observ.	774		308		358		93	
H (1991/1997)	0.93[1]		0.94[2]		0.94[2]	0.95[2]	0.90[1]	0.91[1]

[1] *H*=0 and *H*=1 rejected (level of confidence 99.9%); [2] *H*=0 and *H*=1 rejected (level of confidence 99%).

Table 4.B.15 Empirical results for the Netherlands (1991–98)

	All banks		Small banks		Medium-sized banks		Large banks	
	Coeff.	*t-value*	*Coeff.*	*t-value*	*Coeff.*	*t-value*	*Coeff.*	*t-value*
Funding rate	0.75	*48.5*	0.70	*23.1*	0.85	*48.9*	0.67	*19.1*
Wage rate	0.08	*5.0*	-0.01	*0.2*	0.06	*4.7*	0.09	*9.2*
Capital price	-0.07	*2.9*	0.05	*0.3*	-0.05	*2.2*	0.12	*4.3*
Time	—	—	—	—	—	—	6.80	*4.4*
Loans ratio	0.04	*3.4*	—	—	0.04	*4.76*	0.27	*4.8*
Other income	-0.05	*5.1*	-0.06	*3.1*	-0.03	*2.9*	—	—
Total assets	0.01	*2.3*	—	—	0.03	*3.2*	0.02	*3.1*
Equity	0.12	*8.7*	0.14	*5.6*	0.07	*4.5*	—	—
Intercept	-0.73	*8.8*	-1.31	*7.9*	-0.44	*4.5*	-0.20	*1.6*
Adjusted R^2	0.75		0.90		0.95		0.95	
No. of observ.	296		96		139		61	
H (1991/1997)	0.75[1]		0.74[2]		0.87[1]		0.91[3]	0.95[3]

[1] *H*=0 and *H*=1 rejected (level of confidence 99.9%); [2] *H*=1 not rejected (level of confidence 95%); the F-statistic is 2.33 and the probability level (of the null hypothesis) is 13.0%; [3] *H*=1 not rejected (level of confidence 95%); the F-statistic is, respectively, 2.72 and 0.92, and the probability level (of the null hypothesis) is, respectively, 10.5% and 34.1%.

Table 4.B.16 Empirical results for New Zealand (1990–98)

	All banks		Small banks[0]		Medium-sized banks		Large banks	
	Coeff.	*t-value*	*Coeff.*	*t-value*	*Coeff.*	*t-value*	*Coeff.*	*t-value*
Funding rate	0.67	*25.3*	—	—	0.80	*32.4*	0.65	*25.6*
Wage rate	0.15	*5.9*	—	—	0.30	*10.6*	0.16	*5.2*
Capital price	0.04	*3.1*	—	—	-0.01	*0.5*	0.05	*2.0*
Time	—	—	—	—	3.66	*4.0*	—	—
Loans ratio	0.12	*7.6*	—	—	—	—	—	—
Other income	—	—	—	—	-0.13	*4.9*	—	—
Total assets	-0.04	*8.5*	—	—	0.05	*4.9*	—	—
Equity	—	—	—	—	-0.23	*10.0*	—	—
Dem. Dep. C.	0.20	*7.1*	—	—	—	—	0.17	*5.1*
Intercept	0.47	*3.8*	—	—	0.15	*1.0*	0.06	*0.4*
Adjusted R^2	0.95				0.99		0.98	
No. of observ.	52				22		20	
H (1991/1997)	0.86[1]				1.11[2]	1.13[3]	0.86[4]	

[0] Number of observations is too low; [1] *H*=0 and *H*=1 rejected (level of confidence 99.9%); [2] *H*=1 not rejected (level of confidence 95%); the F-statistic is 3.84 and the probability level (of the null hypothesis) is 7.0%; [3] *H*=1 not rejected (level of confidence 99%); the F-statistic is 6.24 and the probability level (of the null hypothesis) is 2.6%; [4] *H*=0 and *H*=1 rejected (level of confidence 99%).

Table 4.B.17 Empirical results for Norway (1989–98)

	All banks		Small banks		Medium-sized banks		Large banks	
	Coeff.	*t-value*	*Coeff.*	*t-value*	*Coeff.*	*t-value*	*Coeff.*	*t-value*
Funding rate	0.58	*19.2*	0.69	*38.8*	0.57	*15.1*	0.63	*14.0*
Wage rate	0.13	*7.5*	0.14	*7.6*	0.13	*9.7*	-0.05	*1.0*
Capital price	0.0	*1.4*	-0.03	*2.1*	-0.02	*2.1*	0.03	*3.0*
Time	7.41	*3.6*	—	—	9.78	*3.9*	14.20	*3.1*
Other income	-0.02	*2.2*	—	—	—	—	—	—
Total assets	—	—	-0.07	*3.8*	0.05	*4.1*	-0.09	*4.2*
Bank deposits	-0.03	*5.7*	-0.02	*2.9*	-0.02	*2.3*	—	—
Equity	—	—	—	—	0.07	*3.0*	—	—
Dem. Dep. C.	0.04	*3.9*	—	—	—	—	0.16	*4.0*
Intercept	-0.27	*2.7*	0.47	*3.3*	-0.67	*4.4*	0.23	*0.7*
Adjusted R^2	0.93		0.96		0.92		0.99	
No. of observ.	179		72		113		26	
H (1991/1997)	0.74[1]	0.77[1]	0.80[1]		0.71[1]	0.75[1]	0.66[1]	0.71[1]

[1] *H*=0 and *H*=1 rejected (level of confidence 99.9%).

Table 4.B.18 Empirical results for Portugal (1991–98)

	All banks		Small banks		Medium-sized banks		Large banks	
	Coeff.	*t-value*	*Coeff.*	*t-value*	*Coeff.*	*t-value*	*Coeff.*	*t-value*
Funding rate	0.76	*48.5*	0.83	*17.4*	0.85	*22.6*	0.66	*23.0*
Wage rate	0.10	*7.3*	-0.01	*0.1*	0.08	*4.3*	0.25	*8.8*
Capital price	-0.02	*2.6*	0.01	*0.4*	-0.02	*2.3*	0.00	*0.0*
Time	—	—	—	—	-7.98	*3.7*	—	—
Loans ratio	0.07	*8.9*	—	—	0.08	*9.2*	—	—
Other income	-0.03	*3.6*	—	—	-0.05	*5.2*	-0.06	*2.4*
Total assets	—	—	-0.08	*2.1*	0.03	*2.8*	—	—
Bank deposits	-0.05	*4.8*	-0.08	*2.1*	-0.03	*3.2*	—	—
Equity	—	—	—	—	0.03	*2.3*	—	—
Dem. Dep. C.	—	—	0.09	*3.1*	-0.02	*2.0*	—	—
Non-perf. loans	—	—	—	—	—	—	0.06	*3.8*
Cash & DFB	—	—	—	—	0.02	*3.1*	0.03	*3.1*
Intercept	-0.15	*2.3*	0.29	*1.0*	-0.45	*2.9*	0.51	*3.7*
Adjusted R^2	0.92		0.87		0.96		0.97	
No. of observ.	257		53		137		49	
H (1991/1997)	0.83[1]		0.84[2]		0.88[1]	0.84[1]	0.91[3]	

[1] *H*=0 and *H*=1 rejected (level of confidence 99.9%); [2] *H*=1 rejected (level of confidence 95%); the F-statistic is 4.31 and the probability level (of the null hypothesis) is 4.3%); [3] *H*=1 rejected (level of confidence 95%); the F-statistic is 6.26 and the probability level (of the null hypothesis) is 1.6%.

Table 4.B.19 Empirical results for Spain (1990–98)

	All banks		Small banks		Medium-sized banks		Large banks	
	Coeff.	*t-value*	*Coeff.*	*t-value*	*Coeff.*	*t-value*	*Coeff.*	*t-value*
Funding rate	0.42	*18.0*	0.42	*9.3*	0.39	*11.4*	0.44	*11.3*
Wage rate	0.06	*7.3*	0.04	*2.0*	0.09	*7.5*	0.11	*6.8*
Capital price	0.02	*3.1*	0.04	*3.4*	-0.01	*1.2*	0.02	*1.0*
Time	20.00	*7.8*	21.17	*3.6*	20.85	*5.5*	14.41	*4.4*
Loans ratio	0.11	*16.0*	0.16	*10.8*	0.06	*5.7*	0.12	*8.3*
Total assets	-0.01	*2.5*	—	—	-0.03	*3.2*	-0.04	*6.8*
Bank seposits	-0.03	*8.1*	-0.03	*3.2*	-0.03	*5.9*	—	—
Equity	—	—	—	—	—	—	0.08	*3.3*
Dem. Dep. C.	—	—	—	—	—	—	-0.06	*4.3*
Cash & DFB	—	—	—	—	—	—	0.02	*2.8*
Intercept	-0.66	*9.4*	-0.71	*4.8*	-0.52	*4.4*	-0.21	*1.2*
Adjusted R^2	0.81		0.79		0.83		0.93	
No. of observ.	801		179		453		152	
H (1991/1997)	0.55[1]	0.62[1]	0.56[1]	0.64[1]	0.52[1]	0.59[1]	0.61[1]	0.66[1]

[1] *H*=0 and *H*=1 rejected (level of confidence 99.9%);

Table 4.B.20 Empirical results for Sweden (1989–98)

	All banks		Small banks		Medium-sized banks		Large banks	
	Coeff.	*t-value*	*Coeff.*	*t-value*	*Coeff.*	*t-value*	*Coeff.*	*t-value*
Funding rate	0.71	*29.2*	0.72	*18.2*	0.49	*9.5*	0.90	*27.7*
Wage rate	0.06	*6.9*	0.17	*5.4*	0.14	*4.7*	0.05	*4.6*
Capital price	0.02	*3.6*	-0.05	*2.1*	0.01	*0.8*	-0.00	*0.0*
Time	—	—	—	—	16.38	*3.8*	—	—
Loans ratio	—	—	—	—	—	—	0.07	*2.7*
Other income	—	—	—	—	-0.04	*2.4*	—	—
Total assets	—	—	—	—	0.13	*3.9*	—	—
Bank deposits	-0.04	*3.6*	—	—	-0.05	*3.0*	-0.09	*3.5*
Equity	—	—	—	—	—	—	0.09	*3.3*
Intercept	-0.30	*3.3*	0.32	*2.8*	-1.44	*4.8*	1.01	*3.2*
Adjusted R^2	0.86		0.97		0.87		0.93	
No. of observ.	145		18		44		75	
H (1991/1997)	0.80[1]		0.84[2]		0.69[1]	0.76[1]	0.95[3]	

[1] *H*=0 and *H*=1 rejected (level of confidence 99.9%); [2] *H*=0 and *H*=1 rejected (level of confidence 99%);[3] *H*=1 not rejected (level of confidence 95%); the F-statistic is 1.60 and the probability level (of the null hypothesis) is 21.0%.

Table 4.B.21 Empirical results for Switzerland (1988–98)

	All banks		Small banks		Medium-sized banks		Large banks	
	Coeff.	*t-value*	*Coeff.*	*t-value*	*Coeff.*	*t-value*	*Coeff.*	*t-value*
Funding rate	0.43	*32.8*	0.38	*24.3*	0.82	*32.5*	0.74	*28.1*
Wage rate	0.06	*6.1*	0.07	*5.1*	0.09	*4.7*	0.20	*4.8*
Capital price	0.03	*7.3*	0.02	*4.6*	0.06	*10.1*	0.07	*4.6*
Time	8.87	*6.2*	12.18	*6.0*	-5.87	*5.3*	—	—
Loans ratio	0.09	*16.0*	0.08	*11.0*	0.08	*9.2*	0.08	*3.4*
Other income	-0.04	*5.1*	-0.04	*3.9*	-0.08	*5.8*	-0.10	*4.0*
Total assets	—	—	0.03	*4.2*	—	—	—	—
Bank deposits	-0.01	*3.8*	-0.01	*2.8*	-0.01	*2.9*	-0.04	*4.2*
Equity	—	—	-0.03	*3.3*	0.04	*3.0*	0.08	*2.9*
Cash & DFB	—	—	—	—	0.03	*4.2*	—	—
Intercept	-1.35	*27.0*	-1.52	*17.4*	-0.34	*3.4*	-0.29	*2.1*
Adjusted R^2	0.73		0.71		0.88		0.94	
No. of observ.	1 805		1 257		470		71	
H (1991/1997)	0.55[1]	0.58[1]	0.51[1]	0.54[1]	0.95[2]	0.92[3]	1.01[4]	

[1] *H*=0 and *H*=1 rejected (level of confidence 99.9%); [2] *H*=1 not rejected (level of confidence 95%); [3] *H*=1 rejected (level of confidence 99%); the F-statistic is 8.03 and the probability level (of the null hypothesis) is 0.5%; [4] *H*=1 not rejected (95%).

Table 4.B.22 Empirical results for the United Kingdom (1989–98)

	All banks		Small banks		Medium-sized banks		Large banks	
	Coeff.	*t-value*	*Coeff.*	*t-value*	*Coeff.*	*t-value*	*Coeff.*	*t-value*
Funding rate	0.50	*21.8*	0.34	*10.6*	0.66	*15.8*	0.91	*31.6*
Wage rate	0.08	*4.3*	0.05	*1.5*	0.09	*4.6*	0.22	*6.6*
Capital price	0.02	*2.4*	0.02	*1.4*	0.03	*2.2*	0.07	*3.4*
Time	6.68	*2.7*	—	—	8.21	*2.9*	—	—
Loans ratio	0.20	*21.9*	0.18	*13.2*	0.18	*11.2*	0.23	*9.2*
Other income	-0.03	*2.7*	-0.05	*2.3*	—	—	-0.19	*6.0*
Total assets	—	—	-0.06	*3.2*	-0.05	*2.4*	—	—
Equity	0.13	*8.5*	0.18	*6.3*	—	—	—	—
Cash & DFB	—	—	—	—	0.03	*3.4*	0.04	*7.6*
Intercept	-1.03	*-11.2*	-1.65	*8.5*	0.51	*2.5*	0.49	*4.5*
Adjusted R^2	0.62		0.45		0.69		0.90	
No. of observ.	1 114		458		383		193	
H (1991/1997)	0.61[1]	0.64[1]	0.41[1]		0.81[1]	0.85[1]	1.20[1]	

[1] *H*=0 and *H*=1 rejected (level of confidence 99.9%).

Table 4.B.23 Empirical results for the United States (1991–98)

	All banks		Small banks		Medium-sized banks		Large banks	
	Coeff.	*t-value*	*Coeff.*	*t-value*	*Coeff.*	*t-value*	*Coeff.*	*t-value*
Funding rate	0.40	*46.7*	0.40	*29.0*	0.40	*35.8*	0.43	*19.6*
Wage rate	0.07	*13.7*	0.18	*16.1*	0.06	*8.4*	0.13	*8.7*
Capital price	0.06	*19.7*	0.02	*3.2*	0.06	*14.1*	0.10	*15.4*
Time	3.62	*4.4*	3.08	*2.9*	3.52	*3.0*	8.01	*4.8*
Loans ratio	0.12	*20.0*	0.09	*11.2*	0.12	*14.1*	0.21	*18.3*
Other income	—	—	-0.04	*6.4*	—	—	—	—
Total assets	-0.02	*10.1*	—	—	-0.02	*4.5*	—	—
Equity	0.06	*7.4*	0.03	*2.5*	0.05	*4.7*	—	—
Non-perf. loans	0.01	*4.3*	—	—	0.01	*3.7*	—	—
Cash & DFB	0.03	*11.9*	0.02	*5.2*	0.04	*9.6*	—	—
Intercept	-0.76	*16.3*	-0.63	*8.3*	-0.76	*11.2*	-0.02	*2.6*
Adjusted R^2	0.51		0.48		0.52		0.70	
No. of observ.	3 835		1 350		2 216		463	
H (1991/1997)	0.54[1]	0.56[1]	0.61[1]	0.62[1]	0.53[1]	0.54[1]	0.68[1]	0.72[1]

[1] *H*=0 and *H*=1 rejected (level of confidence 99.9%).

APPENDIX 4.C VARIOUS EXPLANATORY TABLES

Table 4.C.1 Number of banks and observations per country in EU analysis

	Number of banks	Number of observations
Austria	58	399
Belgium	55	316
Denmark	37	240
Finland	10	61
France	89	584
Germany	88	624
Greece	22	131
Ireland	50	64
Italy	92	633
Luxembourg	104	570
Netherlands	45	209
Portugal	38	238
Spain	80	603
Sweden	27	140
United Kingdom	97	447
Total	*892*	*5 259*

Table 4.C.2 Empirical results for H *for various bank-sizes: averages over 1991 and 1997*

Banks:	All		Small		Medium		Large	
	Avg *H*	*Change*	Avg *H*	*Change*	Avg *H*	*Change*	Avg *H*	*Change*
Australia	0.54	*0.07*	-0.14	—	0.69	*0.03*	0.66	*0.05*
Austria	0.87	—	0.93	—	0.90	*-0.02*	0.91	—
Belgium	0.89	—	0.95	—	0.88	—	0.87	*0.02*
Canada	0.61	*0.02*	0.74	—	0.63	—	0.58	*0.04*
Denmark	0.34	*0.04*	0.32	*0.03*	0.75	—	1.16	—
Finland	0.78	—	0.67	—	0.76	—	0.70	—
France	0.70	—	0.56	*0.05*	0.76	*0.05*	0.89	—
Germany	0.61	*0.03*	0.58	*0.03*	0.69	*0.02*	1.04	*-0.02*
Greece	0.76	—	0.01	—	0.75	—	0.98	*-0.07*
Ireland	0.65	—	0.99	—	0.63	—	0.93	—
Italy	0.82	—	0.75	—	0.88	*-0.03*	0.82	*-0.02*
Japan	0.56	*-0.04*	0.43	—	0.09	*0.04*	0.63	*-0.03*
Korea (South)	0.68	—	—	—	0.72	—	0.77	—
Luxembourg	0.93	—	0.94	—	0.95	*0.01*	0.90	*0.01*
Netherlands	0.75	—	0.74	—	0.87	—	0.93	*0.04*

(Continued)

Table 4.C.2 (Concluded)

Banks:	All		Small		Medium		Large	
	Avg *H*	*Change*	Avg *H*	*Change*	Avg *H*	*Change*	Avg *H*	*Change*
New Zealand	0.86	—	—	—	1.12	*0.02*	0.86	—
Norway	0.76	*0.03*	0.80	—	0.73	*0.04*	0.68	*0.05*
Portugal	0.83	—	0.84	—	0.86	*-0.04*	0.91	—
Spain	0.59	*0.07*	0.60	*0.08*	0.55	*0.07*	0.64	*0.05*
Sweden	0.80	—	0.84	—	0.72	*0.07*	0.95	—
Switzerland	0.57	*0.03*	0.53	*0.03*	0.94	*-0.03*	1.01	—
UK	0.61	*0.03*	0.41	—	0.83	*0.04*	1.20	—
USA	0.55	*0.02*	0.61	*0.01*	0.53	*0.01*	0.70	*0.04*
Averages	*0.70*	*0.03*	*0.63*	*0.04*	*0.75*	*0.02*	*0.86*	*0.01*
Standard deviation	0.14	—	0.30	—	0.20	—	0.17	—
Maximum	0.93	—	0.99	—	1.12	—	1.20	—
Minimum	0.34	—	-0.14	—	0.09	—	0.58	—
Averages Europe	0.72	*0.04*	0.68	*0.04*	0.79	*0.02*	0.91	*0.01*
Averages RoW [a]	0.63	*0.02*	0.41	*0.01*	0.63	*0.03*	0.70	*0.03*

[a] RoW is Rest of the World.

APPENDIX 4.D DESCRIPTIVE STATISTICS OF THE DATA

Table 4.D.1 Descriptive statistics of the data of Australia (1991–98)

Banks:	All		Small		Medium-sized		Large	
	Mean	St.dev	Mean	St.dev	Mean	St.dev	Mean	St.dev
Int. rate rec.[a]	0.079	0.023	0.042	0.032	0.081	0.022	0.082	0.015
Funding rate	0.065	0.031	0.063	0.081	0.066	0.025	0.064	0.017
Wage rate	0.010	0.008	0.004	0.007	0.009	0.009	0.013	0.006
Capital price	10.32	47.21	6.46	5.10	5.99	9.89	19.93	83.04
Loans ratio	0.73	0.18	—	—	0.75	0.19	—	—
Other inc.r.[b]	—	—	0.168	0.184	—	—	0.016	0.010
Total assets	—	—	—	—	—	—	50 381	34 123
Equity ratio	—	—	20.98	23.50	6.62	3.64	—	—
C & DFB[f]	—	—	—	—	—	—	0.022	0.044
No. of obs.[g]	*185*		*13*		*115*		*57*	

[a] Interest rate received; [b] other income to real assets ratio; [f] cash & due from depository banks to total assets ratio; [g] *no. of obs.* is the number of observations per variable or the range of this number across the variables. Generally, this number may be somewhat higher – never lower – than the number of observations of the estimated equations, as for estimation none of the variables can be missed.

Table 4.D.2 Descriptive statistics of the data of Austria (1989–98)

Banks:	All		Small		Medium-sized		Large	
	Mean	St.dev	Mean	St.dev	Mean	St.dev	Mean	St.dev
Int. rate rec.[a]	0.064	0.023	0.066	0.025	0.063	0.021	0.054	0.010
Funding rate	0.047	0.024	0.048	0.027	0.047	0.023	0.044	0.010
Wage rate	0.015	0.016	0.020	0.020	0.012	0.005	0.007	0.003
Capital price	1.09	1.66	1.52	2.15	0.61	0.58	0.62	0.36
Loans ratio	0.52	0.22	0.47	0.24	—	—	—	—
Other inc.r.[b]	0.015	0.028	0.022	0.037	0.008	0.005	—	—
Total assets	—	—	—	—	2 763	1 970	—	—
Bank dep. r.[c]	0.39	0.30	—	—	0.43	0.28	0.57	0.23
Equity ratio	—	—	—	—	4.64	1.35	—	—
Dem. dep. r.[d]	—	—	0.18	0.14	0.14	0.09	—	—
C & DFB[f]	—	—	—	—	—	—	0.034	0.039
No. of obs.[g]	*434*		*224/226*		*176*		*32*	

[c] Bank deposits to total customer ratio; [d] Demand deposits to total customer ratio. See also notes to Table 4.D.1.

Table 4.D.3 Descriptive statistics of the data of Belgium (1989–98)

Banks:	All		Small		Medium-sized		Large	
	Mean	St.dev	Mean	St.dev	Mean	St.dev	Mean	St.dev
Int. rate rec.[a]	0.071	0.024	0.069	0.024	0.073	0.024	0.071	0.024
Funding rate	0.058	0.036	0.056	0.046	0.059	0.026	0.063	0.026
Wage rate	0.010	0.008	0.012	0.009	0.008	0.007	0.007	0.003
Capital price	2.98	12.74	2.22	2.69	4.56	19.69	0.91	0.67
Loans ratio	0.37	0.22	0.38	0.23	0.36	0.22	—	—
Other inc.r.[b]	—	—	—	—	—	—	0.006	0.004
Total assets	—	—	256	174	—	—	—	—
Bank dep. r.[c]	—	—	0.28	0.31	0.33	0.33	—	—
Equity ratio	—	—	—	—	—	—	2.84	0.98
C & DFB [f]	0.005	0.018	—	—	0.005	0.022	0.003	0.004
No. of obs.[g]	*473/ 479*		*212/ 217*		*193/ 194*		*68*	

Note: See also notes to Tables 4.D.1 and 4.D.2.

Table 4.D.4 Descriptive statistics of the data of Canada (1988–98)

Banks:	All		Small		Medium-sized		Large	
	Mean	St.dev	Mean	St.dev	Mean	St.dev	Mean	St.dev
Int. rate rec.[a]	0.070	0.022	0.069	0.024	0.071	0.023	0.070	0.014
Funding rate	0.060	0.031	0.057	0.028	0.068	0.037	0.051	0.013
Wage rate	0.011	0.008	0.011	0.010	0.009	0.006	0.013	0.002
Capital price	3.75	4.19	4.56	4.85	3.95	3.91	1.33	0.59
Loans ratio	0.66	0.20	—	—	0.65	0.20	0.67	0.10
Total assets	—	—	317	211	—	—	—	—
Bank dep. r.[c]	—	—	0.47	0.34	—	—	—	—
Equity ratio	7.70	4.00	—	—	—	—	—	—
C & DFB [f]	0.014	0.033	—	—	—	—	—	—
No. of obs.[g]	*324/ 363*		*155/ 158*		*140*		*65*	

Note: See also notes to Tables 4.D.1 and 4.D.2.

Table 4.D.5 Descriptive statistics of the data of Denmark (1990–98)

Banks:	All		Small		Medium-sized		Large	
	Mean	St.dev	Mean	St.dev	Mean	St.dev	Mean	St.dev
Int. rate rec.[a]	0.086	0.024	0.089	0.023	0.074	0.026	0.071	0.017
Funding rate	0.044	0.035	0.043	0.037	0.048	0.023	0.055	0.017
Wage rate	0.024	0.024	0.026	0.026	0.015	0.007	0.011	0.005
Capital price	1.18	2.30	0.93	1.26	2.83	5.13	0.64	0.22
Loans ratio	0.53	0.16	0.53	0.16	0.54	0.18	—	—
Total assets	3 020	11 261	—	—	—	—	—	—
Bank dep. r.[c]	0.14	0.21	0.08	0.14	—	—	—	—
Equity ratio	11.94	4.49	—	—	8.16	3.00	—	—
Dem. dep. r.[d]	0.46	0.18	0.49	0.17	—	—	—	—
No. of obs.[g]	*549/ 578*		*450/ 466*		*79*		*33*	

Note: See also notes to Tables 4.D.1 and 4.D.2.

Table 4.D.6 Descriptive statistics of the data of Finland (1990–98)

Banks:	All		Small		Medium-sized		Large	
	Mean	St.dev	Mean	St.dev	Mean	St.dev	Mean	St.dev
Int. rate rec.[a]	0.069	0.025	0.070	0.035	0.071	0.025	0.068	0.022
Funding rate	0.067	0.045	0.100	0.089	0.065	0.034	0.059	0.030
Wage rate	0.009	0.007	0.014	0.012	0.009	0.006	0.007	0.003
Capital price	4.58	17.55	19.18	44.23	3.99	6.89	0.94	0.99
Loans ratio	0.50	0.18	—	—	—	—	0.51	0.10
Other inc.r.[b]	0.012	0.011	—	—	0.011	0.008	—	—
Bank dep. r.[c]	0.27	0.26	—	—	—	—	0.31	0.23
Equity ratio	7.75	10.38	—	—	—	—	4.75	1.10
No. of obs.[g]	*77*		*10*		*32*		*35*	

Note: See also notes to Tables 4.D.1 and 4.D.2.

Table 4.D.7 Descriptive statistics of the data of France (1988–98)

Banks:	All		Small		Medium-sized		Large	
	Mean	St.dev	Mean	St.dev	Mean	St.dev	Mean	St.dev
Int. rate rec.[a]	0.081	0.038	0.084	0.043	0.081	0.035	0.079	0.034
Funding rate	0.064	0.083	0.066	0.134	0.061	0.038	0.072	0.034
Wage rate	0.018	0.021	0.027	0.033	0.015	0.008	0.010	0.006
Capital price	2.79	9.22	3.37	4.93	2.82	11.93	1.31	1.84
Loans ratio	0.52	0.26	0.52	0.28	0.54	0.25	0.46	0.25
Total assets	11 436	45 038	—	—	—	—	—	—
Bank dep. r.[c]	—	—	—	—	0.37	0.30	0.40	0.25
Equity ratio	7.21	10.11	10.73	15.70	—	—	4.70	2.83
No. of obs.[g]	*2 485/ 2 489*		*809/ 812*		*1 333/ 1 334*		*343*	

Note: See also notes to Tables 4.D.1 and 4.D.2.

Table 4.D.8 Descriptive statistics of the data of Germany (1988–98)

Banks:	All		Small		Medium-sized		Large	
	Mean	St.dev	Mean	St.dev	Mean	St.dev	Mean	St.dev
Int. rate rec.[a]	0.069	0.014	0.069	0.015	0.068	0.014	0.064	0.015
Funding rate	0.044	0.035	0.043	0.043	0.045	0.015	0.054	0.014
Wage rate	0.015	0.014	0.017	0.017	0.013	0.004	0.006	0.005
Capital price	1.27	6.38	1.00	1.91	1.74	10.51	1.48	3.47
Loans ratio	0.59	0.16	0.59	0.16	0.59	0.17	—	—
Other inc.r.[b]	0.010	0.027	0.011	0.033	0.008	0.013	—	—
Total assets	3 469	21 840	—	—	—	—	62 021	88 460
Bank dep. r.[c]	0.22	0.20	0.18	0.17	0.25	0.21	0.49	0.26
Equity ratio	5.42	5.88	5.87	6.34	4.75	4.13	4.19	9.38
Dem. dep. r.[d]	0.15	0.09	0.16	0.09	—	—	—	—
C & DFB[f]	0.023	0.017	0.024	0.016	0.023	0.018	—	—
No. of obs.[g]	*10816/ 10987*		*6 663/ 6 765*		*3 762/ 3 764*		*458*	

Note: See also notes to Tables 4.D.1 and 4.D.2.

Table 4.D.9 Descriptive statistics of the data of Greece (1990–98)

Banks:	All		Small		Medium-sized		Large	
	Mean	St.dev	Mean	St.dev	Mean	St.dev	Mean	St.dev
Int. rate rec.[a]	0.112	0.026	0.113	0.028	0.114	0.024	0.104	0.018
Funding rate	0.100	0.038	0.098	0.038	0.108	0.044	0.092	0.023
Wage rate	0.020	0.010	0.022	0.012	0.017	0.007	0.017	0.005
Capital price	0.74	0.46	1.00	0.48	0.57	0.36	0.45	0.13
Loans ratio	—	—	0.45	0.15	—	—	—	—
Other inc.r.[b]	—	—	—	—	0.026	0.013	—	—
Total assets	—	—	—	—	—	—	24204	13267
Bank dep. r.[c]	—	—	0.23	0.25	—	—	—	—
Equity ratio	—	—	13.01	8.81	—	—	—	—
Dem. dep. r.[d]	—	—	0.09	0.11	—	—	—	—
C & DFB[f]	—	—	0.071	0.050	—	—	—	—
No. of obs.[g]	*102*		*37/46*		*37*		*19*	

Note: See also notes to Tables 4.D.1 and 4.D.2.

Table 4.D.10 Descriptive statistics of the data of Ireland (1992–98)

Banks:	All		Small		Medium-sized		Large	
	Mean	St.dev	Mean	St.dev	Mean	St.dev	Mean	St.dev
Int. rate rec.[a]	0.068	0.027	0.059	0.021	0.068	0.029	0.073	0.014
Funding rate	0.054	0.025	0.053	0.038	0.054	0.024	0.050	0.011
Wage rate	0.007	0.007	0.004	0.005	0.006	0.006	0.016	0.007
Capital price	10.54	79.47	4.40	2.52	12.72	89.66	1.02	0.97
Loans ratio	—	—	—	—	0.54	0.24	—	—
Total assets	—	—	—	—	2649	1881	—	—
Bank dep. r.[c]	0.45	0.35	—	—	0.46	0.35	0.18	0.16
Equity ratio	11.02	14.21	—	—	—	—	—	—
Non-perf. l.[e]	—	—	—	—	—	—	0.015	0.011
No. of obs.[g]	*143*		*15*		*112*		*16*	

[e] Non-performing loans to total loans ratio.

Note: See also notes to Tables 4.D.1 and 4.D.2.

Table 4.D.11 Descriptive statistics of the data of Italy (1988–98)

Banks:	All		Small		Medium-sized		Large	
	Mean	St.dev	Mean	St.dev	Mean	St.dev	Mean	St.dev
Int. rate rec.[a]	0.090	0.026	0.092	0.024	0.090	0.029	0.083	0.014
Funding rate	0.065	0.030	0.061	0.028	0.068	0.033	0.069	0.018
Wage rate	0.019	0.007	0.021	0.007	0.018	0.008	0.015	0.006
Capital price	1.07	1.74	1.48	2.29	0.83	1.22	0.55	0.48
Loans ratio	0.48	0.17	0.44	0.12	0.51	0.20	—	—
Total assets	5866	19138	271	186	2505	2009	38329	42803
Equity ratio	—	—	—	—	9.56	7.16	6.32	2.23
Bank dep. r.[c]	0.40	0.18	—	—	—	—	—	—
C & DFB[f]	0.010	0.012	—	—	—	—	0.008	0.008
No. of obs.[g]	*1845/ 1943*		*813*		*897*		*232/ 233*	

Note: See also notes to Tables 4.D.1 and 4.D.2.

Table 4.D.12 Descriptive statistics of the data of Japan (1989–98)

Banks:	All		Small		Medium-sized		Large	
	Mean	St.dev	Mean	St.dev	Mean	St.dev	Mean	St.dev
Int. rate rec.[a]	0.038	0.013	0.021	0.005	0.035	0.013	0.040	0.013
Funding rate	0.022	0.014	0.022	0.009	0.018	0.011	0.024	0.015
Wage rate	0.019	0.029	0.110	0.021	0.031	0.038	0.009	0.004
Capital price	1.10	3.97	1.26	0.71	1.87	6.18	0.57	0.25
Loans ratio	0.66	0.17	—	—	0.65	0.19	0.67	0.15
Total assets	22779	62214	—	—	—	—	—	—
Bank dep. r.[c]	—	—	—	—	—	—	0.03	0.08
Equity ratio	7.88	12.09	—	—	—	—	4.37	3.50
Dem. dep. r.[d]	0.18	0.05	—	—	—	—	—	—
C & DFB[f]	0.068	0.150	0.266	0.193	0.110	0.212	0.033	0.053
No. of obs.[g]	*928/ 1081*		*17*		*431/ 432*		*605/ 632*	

Note: See also notes to Tables 4.D.1 and 4.D.2.

Table 4.D.13 Descriptive statistics of the data of South Korea (1992–98)

Banks:	All		Small		Medium-sized		Large	
	Mean	St.dev	Mean	St.dev	Mean	St.dev	Mean	St.dev
Int. rate rec.[a]	0.081	0.015	—	—	0.079	0.014	0.085	0.016
Funding rate	0.076	0.017	—	—	0.071	0.014	0.083	0.017
Wage rate	0.007	0.005	—	—	0.007	0.006	0.006	0.004
Capital price	2.98	13.62	—	—	5.12	18.26	0.47	0.35
Other inc.r.[b]	—	—	—	—	0.008	0.014	—	—
Total assets	—	—	—	—	3821	2344	35882	20233
Equity ratio	—	—	—	—	6.88	2.28	—	—
C & DFB[f]	—	—	—	—	0.065	0.078	—	—
No. of obs.[g]	*63*				*32/34*		*28*	

Note: See also notes to Tables 4.D.1 and 4.D.2.

Table 4.D.14 Descriptive statistics of the data of Luxembourg (1990–98)

Banks:	All		Small		Medium-sized		Large	
	Mean	St.dev	Mean	St.dev	Mean	St.dev	Mean	St.dev
Int. rate rec.[a]	0.072	0.033	0.067	0.037	0.075	0.028	0.078	0.035
Funding rate	0.070	0.037	0.062	0.038	0.075	0.032	0.079	0.045
Wage rate	0.006	0.011	0.010	0.016	0.004	0.003	0.003	0.002
Capital price	2.98	3.93	3.75	4.28	2.86	3.89	0.86	0.62
Loans ratio	0.20	0.17	0.20	0.18	0.20	0.17	—	—
Other inc.r.[b]	0.010	0.048	0.013	0.075	0.008	0.010	0.007	0.006
Total assets	3701	6156	—	—	2971	2319	—	—
Equity ratio	5.37	5.83	—	—	—	—	—	—
Dem. dep. r.[d]	—	—	—	—	—	—	0.13	0.12
C & DFB[f]	—	—	—	—	0.002	0.010	—	—
No. of obs.[g]	*825*		*333*		*393/ 395*		*97*	

Note: See also notes to Tables 4.D.1 and 4.D.2.

Table 4.D.15 Descriptive statistics of the data of the Netherlands (1991–98)

Banks:	All		Small		Medium-sized		Large	
	Mean	St.dev	Mean	St.dev	Mean	St.dev	Mean	St.dev
Int. rate rec.[a]	0.064	0.020	0.058	0.027	0.066	0.017	0.069	0.011
Funding rate	0.055	0.022	0.047	0.031	0.059	0.017	0.060	0.014
Wage rate	0.010	0.010	0.014	0.013	0.008	0.009	0.008	0.005
Capital price	1.80	2.66	2.55	3.25	1.78	2.61	0.68	0.27
Loans ratio	0.54	0.25	—	—	0.52	0.28	0.69	0.14
Other inc.r.[b]	0.015	0.024	0.024	0.034	0.011	0.018	—	—
Total assets	21062	64344	—	—	3298	1977	94571	115581
Equity ratio	7.48	7.23	11.93	11.15	5.62	2.18	—	—
No. of obs.[g]	*306/ 307*		*99*		*145*		*63*	

Note: See also notes to Tables 4.D.1 and 4.D.2.

Table 4.D.16 Descriptive statistics of the data of New Zealand (1990–98)

Banks:	All		Small		Medium-sized		Large	
	Mean	St.dev	Mean	St.dev	Mean	St.dev	Mean	St.dev
Int. rate rec.[a]	0.088	0.017	—	—	0.089	0.019	0.088	0.015
Funding rate	0.069	0.017	—	—	0.070	0.015	0.069	0.015
Wage rate	0.012	0.004	—	—	0.013	0.004	0.013	0.003
Capital price	1.24	1.78	—	—	0.98	0.77	0.90	0.23
Loans ratio	0.72	0.17	—	—	—	—	—	—
Other inc.r.[b]	—	—	—	—	0.018	0.006		
Total assets	6680	5214	—	—	4034	1862	—	—
Equity ratio	—	—	—	—	0.83	0.50	—	—
Dem. dep. r.[d]	0.78	0.22	—	—	—	—	0.80	0.14
No. of obs.[g]	*52*				*23*		*20*	

Note: See also notes to Tables 4.D.1 and 4.D.2.

Table 4.D.17 Descriptive statistics of the data of Norway (1989–98)

Banks:	All		Small		Medium-sized		Large	
	Mean	St.dev	Mean	St.dev	Mean	St.dev	Mean	St.dev
Int. rate rec.[a]	0.080	0.024	0.082	0.027	0.079	0.023	0.079	0.019
Funding rate	0.057	0.026	0.056	0.029	0.057	0.025	0.059	0.019
Wage rate	0.011	0.005	0.012	0.004	0.010	0.006	0.012	0.002
Capital price	1.58	1.85	1.83	1.56	1.55	2.00	1.03	1.78
Other inc.r.[b]	0.009	0.007	—	—	—	—	—	—
Total assets	—	—	338	147	2554	1544	20314	6635
Bank dep. r.[c]	0.15	0.17	0.14	0.19	0.15	0.18	—	—
Equity ratio	—	—	—	—	6.80	2.36	—	—
Dem. dep. r.[d]	0.54	0.25	—	—	—	—	0.47	0.16
No. of obs.[g]	*183/ 220*		*74*		*120*		*26*	

Note: See also notes to Tables 4.D.1 and 4.D.2.

Table 4.D.18 Descriptive statistics of the data of Portugal (1991–98)

Banks:	All		Small		Medium-sized		Large	
	Mean	St.dev	Mean	St.dev	Mean	St.dev	Mean	St.dev
Int. rate rec.[a]	0.093	0.034	0.104	0.046	0.088	0.030	0.091	0.022
Funding rate	0.079	0.037	0.094	0.049	0.075	0.033	0.071	0.020
Wage rate	0.012	0.006	0.013	0.008	0.011	0.006	0.013	0.003
Capital price	0.92	1.55	1.02	0.94	1.04	1.98	0.47	0.16
Loans ratio	0.44	0.17	—	—	0.44	0.19	—	—
Other inc.r.[b]	0.012	0.010	—	—	0.011	0.007	0.011	0.004
Total assets	—	—	346	189	2551	2026	—	—
Bank dep. r.[c]	0.42	0.26	0.56	0.25	0.42	0.27	—	—
Equity ratio	—	—	—	—	7.10	4.36	—	—
Dem. dep. r.[d]	—	—	0.12	0.10	0.16	0.10	—	—
Non-perf. l.[e]	—	—	—	—	—	—	0.021	0.009
C & DFB[f]	—	—	—	—	0.032	0.046	0.048	0.047
No. of obs.[g]	*267/ 268*		*68/ 70*		*144*		*49/54*	

Note: See also notes to Tables 4.D.1, 4.D.2 and 4.D.10.

Table 4.D.19 Descriptive statistics of the data of Spain (1990–98)

Banks:	All		Small		Medium-sized		Large	
	Mean	St.dev	Mean	St.dev	Mean	St.dev	Mean	St.dev
Int. rate rec.[a]	0.087	0.026	0.089	0.032	0.085	0.025	0.091	0.020
Funding rate	0.062	0.056	0.068	0.106	0.057	0.024	0.067	0.020
Wage rate	0.017	0.007	0.018	0.008	0.017	0.006	0.015	0.005
Capital price	0.67	1.32	1.06	1.44	0.61	1.46	0.37	0.15
Loans ratio	0.50	0.20	0.48	0.27	0.50	0.17	0.51	0.14
Total assets	10317	28308	—	—	3118	2294	41913	51637
Bank dep. r.[c]	0.21	0.26	0.25	0.34	0.19	0.24	—	—
Equity ratio	—	—	—	—	—	—	5.95	1.85
Dem. dep. r.[d]	—	—	—	—	—	—	0.14	0.08
C & DFB [f]	—	—	—	—	—	—	0.011	0.012
No. of obs.[g]	*831*		*204*		*458*		*164/ 169*	

Note: See also notes to Tables 4.D.1 and 4.D.2.

Table 4.D.20 Descriptive statistics of the data of Sweden (1989–98)

Banks:	All		Small		Medium-sized		Large	
	Mean	St.dev	Mean	St.dev	Mean	St.dev	Mean	St.dev
Int. rate rec.[a]	0.097	0.057	0.153	0.134	0.082	0.026	0.094	0.025
Funding rate	0.089	0.050	0.132	0.107	0.076	0.034	0.088	0.027
Wage rate	0.007	0.014	0.024	0.032	0.005	0.006	0.004	0.004
Capital price	16.94	66.60	5.90	5.55	4.48	5.28	28.22	91.01
Loans ratio	—	—	—	—	—	—	0.77	0.22
Other inc.r.[b]	—	—	—	—	0.007	0.012	—	—
Total assets	—	—	—	—	3074	1653	—	—
Bank dep. r.[c]	0.49	0.33	—	—	0.56	0.37	0.46	0.27
Equity ratio	—	—	—	—	—	—	3.69	1.23
No. of obs.[g]	*145*		*18*		*52*		*75*	

Note: See also notes to Tables 4.D.1 and 4.D.2.

Table 4.D.21 Descriptive statistics of the data of Switzerland (1988–98)

Banks:	All		Small		Medium-sized		Large	
	Mean	St.dev	Mean	St.dev	Mean	St.dev	Mean	St.dev
Int. rate rec.[a]	0.047	0.018	0.046	0.017	0.051	0.021	0.048	0.010
Funding rate	0.040	0.044	0.038	0.051	0.043	0.020	0.042	0.011
Wage rate	0.020	0.023	0.023	0.026	0.013	0.012	0.008	0.003
Capital price	2.91	13.78	2.97	15.08	3.13	10.43	0.53	0.33
Loans ratio	0.61	0.29	0.61	0.29	0.59	0.28	0.69	0.18
Other inc.r.[b]	0.035	0.049	0.040	0.054	0.023	0.027	0.010	0.007
Total assets	—	—	205	170	—	—	—	—
Bank dep. r.[c]	0.26	0.32	0.26	0.33	0.28	0.30	0.18	0.13
Equity ratio	—	—	16.03	15.61	8.59	4.56	4.97	1.49
C & DFB[f]	—	—	—	—	0.020	0.020	—	—
No. of obs.[g]	*1963/ 1976*		*1402/ 1414*		*484/ 485*		*77*	

Note: See also notes to Tables 4.D.1 and 4.D.2.

Table 4.D.22 Descriptive statistics of the data of the UK (1989–98)

Banks:	All		Small		Medium-sized		Large	
	Mean	St.dev	Mean	St.dev	Mean	St.dev	Mean	St.dev
Int. rate rec.[a]	0.074	0.037	0.077	0.046	0.075	0.031	0.066	0.025
Funding rate	0.067	0.161	0.066	0.099	0.073	0.232	0.056	0.021
Wage rate	0.016	0.060	0.024	0.091	0.010	0.008	0.010	0.007
Capital price	2.22	3.76	2.72	4.95	1.97	2.48	1.56	2.50
Loans ratio	0.53	0.30	0.52	0.31	0.53	0.29	0.55	0.26
Other inc.r.[b]	0.022	0.102	0.034	0.154	—	—	0.013	0.010
Total assets	—	—	276	182	3250	2366	—	—
Equity ratio	11.23	11.21	16.09	13.92	—	—	—	—
C & DFB[f]	—	—	—	—	0.024	0.165	0.030	0.068
No. of obs.[g]	*1199/ 1220*		*511/ 518*		*430/ 491*		*201/ 211*	

Note: See also notes to Tables 4.D.1 and 4.D.2.

Table 4.D.23 Descriptive statistics of the data of the USA (1991–98)

Banks:	All		Small		Medium-sized		Large	
	Mean	St.dev	Mean	St.dev	Mean	St.dev	Mean	St.dev
Int. rate rec.[a]	0.070	0.022	0.071	0.026	0.070	0.019	0.067	0.017
Funding rate	0.039	0.018	0.041	0.025	0.037	0.012	0.039	0.014
Wage rate	0.014	0.011	0.015	0.012	0.013	0.011	0.014	0.007
Capital price	3.12	25.41	1.65	5.54	3.77	33.01	4.18	16.11
Loans ratio	0.62	0.18	0.64	0.18	0.62	0.17	0.59	0.20
Other inc.r.[b]	—	—	0.012	0.032	—	—	—	—
Total assets	6350	23270	—	—	2637	2103	—	—
Equity ratio	9.00	4.50	10.21	6.17	8.61	3.40	—	—
Non-perf. l.[e]	0.006	0.017	—	—	0.006	0.012	—	—
C & DFB[f]	0.148	3.356	0.035	0.078	0.231	4.503	—	—
No. of obs.[g]	*4138/ 4190*		*1383*		*2312/ 2326*		*481*	

Note: See also notes to Tables 4.D.1, 4.D.2 and 4.D.10.

NOTES

1. For an overview, see Chapter 3.
2. Hyde and Perloff (1995) discuss the pros and cons of the P–R approach together with two other methods estimating market power, namely the structural model and the Hall method. They conclude that an advantage of the P–R approach is that it is less sensitive to assumptions and specification choices. A disadvantage might be that it cannot distinguish between certain forms of partial collusion and monopolistic competition.
3. See Panzar and Rosse (1987) or Vesala (1995) for details on the formal derivation of *H*.
4. One of the assumptions is that the market is in long-run equilibrium. This assumption can be tested empirically.
5. Here we follow the specification of the dependent variable of Molyneux et al. (1994). Other authors use unscaled revenues. Re-estimation of the equation with unscaled revenues yields similar results, particularly if one of the bank-specific factors is 'total assets'.
6. If $\beta = 0$ or $\beta \approx 0$, the model can be reparameterized, for example: $1/(1+(1/\gamma -1)\exp(\varepsilon\ \mathrm{TIME}))\ (ln\ PE + \beta'\ ln\ INTE + \delta'\ ln\ CE)$. Also, if $\beta = 1$, the model needs to be reformulated.
7. Capital expenses' includes the cost of premises, equipment and information technology.
8. For example, Molyneux et al. (1994) expect a negative coefficient for *EQ*, because less equity implies more leverage and hence more interest income. However, capital requirements increase proportionally with the risk on loans and investment portfolios, suggesting a positive coefficient.
9. Data relating to earlier years would be less useful due to serious free entry restrictions in European countries.
10. Note that ignoring observations of non-financial institutions, which also provide financial intermediation in some subdivision of the banking market, does not distort the current analysis, as the actual (overall) competitive conditions are observed directly, irrespective of the providers of intermediation services.
11. Then, for instance, 'large' banks in Denmark, Germany or Switzerland could be smaller than 'small' banks in Finland, Japan or Korea.
12. For larger countries, subsamples of (only) the largest banks are taken, see Table 4.C.1 in Appendix 4.C.
13. The time-trend coefficient ε is significant.
14. Changes over time in the interest rate yield curve may also have affected the time trend shift. This could be avoided by including a measure of the interest rate spread as an additional explanatory variable.
15. The χ^2-statistic of the Wald test performed on $1/(1+(1/\beta -1)\exp(\tau\ 4.5))(1+\gamma' + \delta')=1$ is 533.6 (probability value: 0.0000 per cent).
16. A reduction from 15 country dummies to one dummy for Scandinavian countries, one for Italy and Austria and one for the remaining countries would also be rejected.
17. Dependent and explanatory variables (including dummies) are all multiplied by 'total assets'. Total assets for each country are normalized to correct for the currency unit. The coefficients of the country-specific dummy variables are corrected for this currency unit-related normalization.
18. Weighting can also be justified on econometric grounds. Based on the central-limit theory, large banks are expected to behave more 'normally' than smaller ones. We found empirical evidence that disturbance terms of big banks are indeed (somewhat) smaller than those of smaller banks. Weighted estimation is then more efficient.
19. All the dummy coefficients are lower, due to a decline in the implicit overall intercept.
20. The χ^2-statistic of the Wald test performed on $1/(1+(1/\beta -1)\exp(\tau 4.5))(1+\gamma' + \delta')=0$ is 1.75 (probability value: 18.6 per cent).

21. For this reason, the number of observations of small, medium-sized and large banks of a country do not necessarily add up to the number of all banks. This would only be the case if the model specification were the same for all bank-size types.
22. Where the probability of the null hypothesis is 5 per cent or more the null hypothesis is accepted or not rejected; if the probability of the null hypothesis is below 1 per cent, the null hypothesis is rejected, and if the probability of the null hypothesis is between 1 and 5 per cent we posit that the null hypothesis is rejected at the (stringent) 99 per cent confidence level.
23. In all countries, the number of banks is far greater than 1. Hence, H=0 reflects perfect collusion or cartel rather than monopoly.
24. See for example Bresnahan (1989), Shaffer and DiSalvo (1994) and Toolsema (2002).
25. These are sufficient but not necessary requirements.
26. Molyneux et al. (1994), who over the years found strong (and less plausible) shifts in H and the markets structure, observed also monopoly in Germany for 1987, whereas deBandt and Davis (2000) found monopoly power for smaller banks in France and Germany.
27. See Calem and Carlino (1991) for an example of the empirical approximation of conduct.
28. Both indices, CR_k and *HHI*, can be derived as proxies for market structure in theoretical SCP relationships, see Chapter 3, Section 3.2.
29. This is, by the way, similar to what happens under the P–R approach, where each country is defined as 'the market where its banks operate', including domestic and foreign bank activities, and where competition in a country is defined as the average level of competition on these 'markets'.
30. Not 50 per cent lower, due to the denominator effect.
31. It would not be sensible to split the concentration index into indices for small, medium-sized and large banks. Hence the analysis is based on the all-banks sample of H and the concentration indices.
32. See Chapter 3, Equation (3.5).
33. An alternative formulation is that the effect of the number of banks, as taken into account by the *CI*, is overestimated (implying low values for the *CI* value in large countries and vice versa).
34. As suggested, for instance, by the better fit in Table 4.9 when the share of interbank deposits is included.
35. For all (sixteen) regressions in Tables 4.9 and 4.10, and also in the weighted regressions (not shown), a hypothetical value of zero for both coefficients is rejected at the 95 per cent level of confidence.
36. Hyde and Perloff (1995) found as a disadvantage of the P–R approach that it cannot distinguish between certain forms of partial collusion and monopolistic competition.

5. Competition on EU deposit and loan markets

5.1 INTRODUCTION

In recent years, numerous developments have affected the markets where banks operate: deregulation, liberalization, globalization and various technological innovations. Each of these developments has influenced the competitive conditions of banks. Adding to this, monetary and financial integration in Europe, including the introduction of the euro, has contributed to a further increase of foreign competition in the region. As banks' market power affects their profitability, competitive conduct also has an impact on the soundness and stability of the financial sector. Healthy competition and a sound market structure are also important for social welfare, implying as they do low prices, low interest rates and adequate lending to consumers and firms, in particular small and medium-sized enterprises. Market imperfections would cause allocative inefficiency and so detract from the prosperity which society derives from banking services. Of course, it should be kept in mind that competitive conditions differ across product and geographical markets and are also subject to continuous changes over time. Finally, the competitive structure of financial markets has major implications for the effectiveness of certain instruments of monetary power, such as the discount rate and required cash reserves. The effects of monetary policy on financial prices and quantities depend crucially on the extent to which individual banks are in a position to exploit credit demand and deposit supply functions (Swank, 1994). Remarkably enough, given the vital importance of competition for social welfare and policy making, the economic literature provides only limited information about competitive conduct in the European banking markets. Apart from measurement problems – competition cannot be observed directly – a lack of sufficient data also impedes a clear view on bank market structure, especially outside the USA. Therefore, various measurement approaches are needed to squeeze the limited data sources dry.

In reaction to the theoretical and empirical deficiencies of structural approaches to the measurement of competition as explained in Chapter 3, non-structural models for the measurement of competition were developed, namely the Iwata model (Iwata, 1974), the Bresnahan model[1] and the Panzar–Rosse model (Panzar and Rosse, 1987). These New Empirical Industrial Organization approaches test competitive conduct and the use of market power, and stress the analysis of banks' competitive conduct in the absence of structural measures.

The Iwata model has hardly been used empirically, an exception being Shaffer and DiSalvo (1994), who apply it to a two-bank market. In Chapter 4, the Panzar and Rosse (P–R) model has proven to be a useful tool for observing competition. The P–R model uses data for individual banks, which tend to be available in ample quantities, allowing fairly precise estimates of competition. However, a disadvantage of the P–R approach is its assumption that banks provide one banking product only. Hence, it does not allow us to distinguish between different product or geographical markets, which by the way would also be hampered by a lack of required data, for example bank-level interest rates and production figures. This is precisely where Bresnahan's model can play a supplementary role, as it allows the investigation of submarkets, due both to its nature and to its data requirements. On the other hand, Bresnahan's model uses macroeconomic data, which limits its possibilities, because these data are made available on an annual basis only.

The present chapter applies Bresnahan's model to two submarkets, deposits and loans, in nine countries of the European Union (EU). For each submarket, we apply the model to all countries together as well as to each of the nine individual countries. This survey is unique in this body of literature in that it compares market power for so many countries. The deposit market reflects banks' competitive conditions with respect to funding and hence mirrors their activities on the liabilities side of the balance sheet. The product or service considered here is the supply of deposit facilities. This retail market is interesting as it is by nature localized, so that the number of competing banks tends to be limited, except for the more recently mushroomed Internet banks. The introduction of Internet banking may have increased competition in this market. On the other hand, it should be noted that the Internet is an alternative for part of the customers only. The loan market refers to the main (traditional) activity of banks, lending, which is representative of the assets side of the balance sheet. The lending market has mainly a nation-wide or international dimension, assuming that only smaller amounts are involved in lending to (local) small and medium-sized enterprises. These markets may be assumed to be fairly competitive, as banks in this business usually face many foreign competitors. Given the data requirements of Bresnahan's model, the choice for deposits and loans is also determined by the availability of the pivotal prices on these markets: the deposit and lending rates.

This chapter has been organized as follows. Section 5.2 sets out the theoretical structure of the Bresnahan model and its empirical application to the deposit and loan markets. Section 5.3 describes the data and estimation methods used and presents the estimation results for both markets in the whole EU region, as well as in each of the nine EU countries separately. Finally, a comparison is made to other studies employing Bresnahan's model or related approaches.

5.2 THE BRESNAHAN MODEL

In order to seek to determine the degree of market power of the *average* bank in the short run, Bresnahan (1982) and Lau (1982) developed an Industrial Organizations type of model of profit maximizing oligopoly banks. The Bresnahan model we will use is based on the intermediation paradigm of a bank, as in Shaffer (1989, 1993), who furthermore assumes that banks produce only one product and use several input factors.[2] As proposed by Shaffer, our cost functions are based on factor input prices. Taking for granted that factor inputs are not the same for loans and deposits, our Bresnahan model separates the costs of both banking activities, that is to say it ignores the interdependence of cost functions for the two products. We estimate the demand and supply relations separately for the deposit and loan markets, assuming that banks try to maximize profits at the product level rather than taking advantage of possible cross-subsidization between products. This section begins by describing the general theoretical structure of the Bresnahan model, as used by Shaffer, and then differentiates to empirical models for the deposit and loan markets, respectively.

5.2.1 Theoretical Structure of the Bresnahan Model

Assuming n banks in the industry supplying a homogeneous product, the profit function of the average bank i takes the form:

$$\Pi_i = px_i - c_i\left(x_i, EX_{S_i}\right) - F_i \tag{5.1}$$

where Π_i is profit, x_i is the volume of output, p is the output price, c_i are the variable costs, EX_{S_i} are exogenous variables affecting the marginal costs, but not the industry demand function, and F_i are the fixed costs of bank i. In the loan market, the output price p can be defined as the difference between the lending rate and the rate of risk-free investment (such as government bonds). An alternative would be to assume that p is equal to the lending rate and to include the funding rate as a cost factor. In the deposit market, the output price p is the difference between the risk free rate and the deposit rate, hence the discount banks receive when they fund with deposits instead of other types of funding.

Banks face a downward sloping market demand function, the inverse of which is defined as:

$$p = f(X, EX_D) = f(x_1 + x_2 + ... + x_n, EX_D) \tag{5.2}$$

where EX_D is a vector of exogenous variables affecting industry demand but not marginal costs. The first order condition for profit maximizing of bank i yields:

$$\frac{d\Pi_i}{dx_i} = p + f'(X, EX_D)\frac{dX}{dx_i}x_i - c_i'(x_i, EX_{S_i}) = 0 \tag{5.3}$$

Taking averages over all banks produces:

$$p + f'(X, EX_D)\frac{dX}{dx_i}\frac{1}{n}X - \Sigma_i c_i'(x_i, EX_{S_i})/n = 0$$

so that:

$$p = -\lambda f'(X, EX_D)X + \Sigma_i c_i'(x_i, EX_{S_i})/n \tag{5.4}$$

where $\lambda = (dX/dx_i)/n = (1 + d\Sigma_{i \neq j} x_j / dx_i)/n$. Thus, λ is a function of the conjectural variation of the average firm in the market. The conjectural variation of firms is defined as the change in output of all remaining firms anticipated by firm i in response to an initial change in its own output. For the average bank in a *perfectly competitive* market, the restriction $\lambda = 0$ holds, as, in a competitive equilibrium, price equals marginal cost. Since prices are assumed to be exogenous to the firm in a perfectly competitive market, an increase in output by one firm must lead to an analogous decrease in output by the remaining firms, in line with Equation (5.4). The *Cournot equilibrium* describes noncooperative optimization where agents who mutually influence each other act without explicit cooperation. Under that type of equilibrium, the conjectural variation ($d\Sigma_{i \neq j} x_j / dx_i$) for firm i would equal zero. The Cournot model assumes that a firm does not *expect* retaliation from other firms in response to changes in its own output, so that $\lambda = 1/n$.[3] Under *perfect collusion*, an increase in output by one of the colluders leads to a proportional increase in output by all other colluders, yielding $\lambda = \left(1 + d\Sigma_{i \neq j} x_j / dx_i\right)/n = \left(1 + (X - x_i)/x_i\right)/n = X/x_i n = 1$, $\forall i$. Hence, under normal conditions, the λ parameter takes values between zero and unity. The λ-parameter in Bresnahan's model plays a role similar to that of the *H*-parameter in the P–R approach, where *H*<0 points to monopoly, 0<*H*<1 indicates monopolistic competition and *H*=1 reflects perfect competition.

As mentioned above, we apply the Bresnahan model to the two most prominent submarkets of the banking industry: the loan and deposit markets. To assess the degree of market power, we simultaneously estimate market quantity and price curves, obtaining the value of λ which indicates the degree of competition.

5.2.2 Empirical Equations for the Deposit and Loan Markets

For the empirical model of the deposit market, the theoretical demand function (5.2) is redefined as a linear aggregate demand function for deposit *facilities* offered to non-banks and reads:

$$DEP = \alpha_0 + \alpha_1 r_{dep} + \alpha_2 EX_D + \alpha_3 EX_D r_{dep} + \varepsilon \qquad (5.5)$$

where *DEP* is the real value of total deposits, r_{dep} is the market deposit rate,[4] EX_D are exogenous variables affecting industry demand for deposits but not marginal costs, such as disposable income, unemployment, the number of bank branches[5] and interest rates for alternative investment (that is the money market rate and the government bond rate) and ε is the error term. Equation (5.5) should also include one or more cross-terms between the deposit rate and at least one of the exogenous variables determining demand for deposit facilities (on the identifiability of the λ parameter, see below). The time subscripts in Equation (5.5) and later equations are deleted for convenience.

The marginal cost function for bank *i* – $c'(x_i, EX_X)$ in Equation (5.3) – is defined as:

$$MC_i = \beta_0 + \beta_1 DEP_i + \beta_2 EX_{Si} + v_i \qquad (5.6)$$

where EX_S are exogenous variables influencing the supply of deposits (costs of input factors for the production of deposits, for instance, wages) and v is the error term. Re-arranging the aggregate demand function (5.5) yields the price function as:

$$r_{dep} = \frac{1}{\alpha_1 + \alpha_3 EX_D}\left[DEP - \alpha_0 - \alpha_2 EX_D - \varepsilon\right] \tag{5.7}$$

which, multiplied by the deposits of bank *i* yields its total revenue as:

$$TR_i = \frac{1}{\alpha_1 + \alpha_3 EX_D}\left[DEP - \alpha_0 - \alpha_2 EX_D - \varepsilon\right]DEP_i \tag{5.8}$$

and, derived with respect to the deposits at bank *i*, its marginal revenues:

$$\begin{aligned} MR_i = \frac{dTR_i}{dDEP_i} &= \frac{1}{\alpha_1 + \alpha_3 EX_D}\left[DEP - \alpha_0 - \alpha_2 EX_D - \varepsilon\right] \\ &+ \frac{1}{\alpha_1 + \alpha_3 EX_D}\frac{dDEP}{dDEP_i}DEP_i = r_{dep} + \frac{\lambda n}{\alpha_1 + \alpha_3 EX_D}DEP_i \end{aligned} \tag{5.9}$$

where λ is defined as below Equation (5.4). Market equilibrium requires the equality of marginal revenues and marginal costs, so that for each bank:

$$r_{dep} + \frac{\lambda n}{\alpha_1 + \alpha_3 EX_D}DEP_i = \beta_0 + \beta_1 DEP_i + \beta_2 EX_{S_i} + \nu_i \tag{5.10}$$

The equilibrium price equation for deposit *facilities* by the banks, that is the deposit rate, follows from taking averages:

$$r_{dep} = -\lambda\frac{DEP}{\alpha_1 + \alpha_3 EX_D} + \beta_0 + \beta_1^* DEP + \beta_2^* EX_S + \nu \tag{5.11}$$

where $\beta_1^* = \beta_1/n$, $\beta_2^* = \beta_2/n$ and $EX_S = \Sigma_i\ EX_{S_i}$. In order to determine λ, the degree of competition of the average bank in the deposit markets of the countries considered, the quantity[6] and price equations, (5.5) and (5.11), respectively, must be estimated simultaneously, as the parameters α_1 and α_3 occur in both equations. Lau (1982) and Bresnahan (1982) show that, whereas both the demand (α) and supply (β) parameters are identified, the λ parameter is identifiable only if the demand function includes the endogenous interest rate (or 'price') and a cross-term with one of the explanatory (other) variables and this interest rate.[7] In other words, λ is identified only, if the assumptions $\alpha_1 \neq 0$ and $\alpha_3 \neq 0$ both hold. Note that α_1 is expected to be positive, so the first term of the right-hand side of Equation (5.11) is λ times a *markdown*. This implies a *lower* deposit rate in the case of no or limited competition, as seems plausible.

Note that, in principle, Equations (5.5) and (5.11) can generate an estimate of competition, even where the corresponding market is facing competition from financial institutions not included in the national samples, such as non-banks, traditional foreign banks and Internet banks. After all, even where competition from other banks is limited, banks are unable to widen the margin between price (or interest rate) and costs when competition from non-banks is heavy or even is only a serious potential threat.

In a similar manner, the aggregate demand (or quantity) function for *loans* by households and banks can be defined as:

$$LOANS = \alpha_0 + \alpha_1 r_{lend} + \alpha_2 EX_D + \alpha_3 EX_D r_{lend} + \varepsilon \qquad (5.12)$$

where real *LOANS* are explained by r_{lend}, the lending rate, by EX_D, exogenous variables influencing the demand for loans, such as income, unemployment, the number of bank branches, the share of labour in total value added and the utilization rate of capital, and by ε, the error term. Again, the equation should contain at least one cross-term consisting of the lending rate and one of the other variables determining demand for loans facilities in order for the λ parameter to be identified. On the analogy of the price equation for deposits presented above, the price relationship for loans may be derived as:

$$r_{lend} = -\lambda \frac{LOANS}{\alpha_1 + \alpha_3 EX_D} + \beta_0 + \beta_1 LOANS + \beta_2 EX_S + \nu \qquad (5.13)$$

The simultaneous estimation of Equations (5.12) and (5.13) generate the value of λ, provided this parameter is identified. Note that α_1 is expected to be negative, thus the first term of the right-hand side of Equation (5.13) is λ times a *markup*. This means a *higher* lending rate in the case of no or limited competition, as seems plausible.

5.3 ESTIMATION RESULTS

The empirical Bresnahan model, developed above, has been applied to the deposit and loan markets of nine EU countries: Belgium, France, Germany, Italy, the Netherlands, Portugal, Spain, Sweden and the UK, both separately and jointly. Other EU countries are not included due to unavailability of data.[8] For practical reasons, we assume here that national markets correspond with the national borders. We do realise that this need not always be the case, as foreign banks and Internet banks may affect domestic competitive conditions. The models are based on time series of quarterly data from a variety of databases and institutions: the International Financial Statistics (*IFS*), the Bank of International Settlements (*BIS*), the Organization of Economic Cooperation and Development (*OECD*), Data Stream (*DS*), the Dutch Central Planning Bureau (*CPB*), the Statistics Netherlands (*CBS*) and several central banks; see Appendix 5.C.

For a number of countries and variables, the availability of the required data and the length of the series are limited. In many cases, there is a trade-off between quality (series without breaks) and quantity (longer series). Special attention is paid to the German data with respect to the German unification. The time series used for our estimations cover both the pre- and the post-unification period. Data for the Western states have been available until 1990; as from 1991, both data for the Western states and aggregate data for the entire country are available. We used the data covering the entire country after 1990 and adjusted the data for the period preceding unification. For real deposits, gross domestic product (gdp) and unemployment we did not have overlapping data at our disposal, hence we exploited dummies to take account of the (imprecise or unknown) adjustments.

The data constraints, furthermore, hamper complete consistency in the definition of the underlying market across countries: deposit and loan volumes are available for the *banking* market in all countries except Belgium, where a broader definition of the market, that is, one accounting for all credit institutions, is applied. The variables deposits, gdp, loans and wage rate are expressed in real terms in order to avoid interference from inflation. For the all-countries sample, all volumes are expressed in 'Deutsche Marks' whereas, in the individual country estimations, these variables are in the countries' own currencies.[9]

The quantity and price equations form a simultaneous system, as each equation includes the endogenous variable of the other equation as explanatory variable. Therefore, the equations have been estimated by the 2SLS method.[10] Account of the cross-equation restrictions has been taken by estimating the price equation conditional on the estimated values of α_1 and α_3 in the quantity equation. Because of the existence of these cross-equation restrictions, a system estimator such as 3SLM or FIML would be a more efficient – but also a more complicated – alternative (Toolsema, 2002).

All equations for all countries and the EU region contain all explanatory variables occurring in the theoretical model. For the quantity equations, real deposits and real loans, we consider two cross-terms throughout, consisting of the price (deposit or lending rate) and one of the other explanatory variables.[11] We need at least one cross-term, whereas inclusion of all cross-terms would be excessive and could cause multicollinearity. Hence, the choice of two cross-terms takes an intermediate position. In some equations, there is the choice between money market and government rates[12] and also an option to include other explanatory variables. In every case, the choice is based primarily on national economic and institutional circumstances, such as characteristics of the money and capital markets. Where a choice is arbitrary, we seek to find significant values for α_1 and α_3, which is a *conditio sine qua non* for our analysis, or to reduce autocorrelation. Seasonal dummies are included only, when one or more of the equation variables have a seasonal pattern and are maintained, when the dummies appear to be jointly significant.

Initial estimation has revealed that the error terms of some equations exhibit serial correlation, as indicated by the Durbin–Watson (DW) or Durbin's h test, and Breusch–Godfrey's Lagrange Multiplier (LM) test. Autocorrelation may leads to overestimating of the coefficients' t-values and hence to wrong inferences (Kennedy, 1998). This feature has been dealt with either through inclusion in the model of the lagged dependent variable as an explanatory variable, a so-called Koyck lag (Theil, 1971), or through inclusion of an autoregressive term in the error. A Koyck lag model assumes that the actual dependent variable adjusts gradually over time to its assumed model value (Nerlove, 1958, discusses various possible underlying adjustment processes).[13] Going by the DW or Durbin's h test, and the Breusch–Godfrey LM test, the autocorrelation problem has been solved in a number of cases. In all cases, we calculate the Newey and West correction for heteroscedasticity and autocorrelation-consistent covariances, which correct the t-values of the coefficients for any possible remaining heteroscedasticity and autocorrelation. This prevents us from making wrong inferences from these t-values, for example regarding significance (Greene, 2000).

5.3.1 The Market for Deposit Facilities

Quantity equation (5.5) determines the volume of deposits in terms of its price (the deposit rate) and exogenous variables from the demand function, such as the money market rate or the government debt rate, the volume of gdp, unemployment and inflation. Deposits are defined as the sum of time deposits and savings, whereas *real* deposits are deflated by the available price index. The coefficient of the deposit rate should have a positive sign, since a higher return on deposits makes deposits more attractive. The return on government debt and the money market rate are the prices of two substitutes for deposits. They have negative coefficients, because the opportunity cost of holding money in deposit increases with the price of any of the substitutes. Real gdp proxies income or wealth and should reflect the positive relationship between income and the propensity to save, or between wealth and investment. The coefficient of unemployment will be positive if the increased probability of facing unemployment encourages savings, but can also be negative, if dis-saving supplements a decline in incomes in the case of unemployment. Hence, a priori predictions about its sign cannot be made. A similar conclusion can be drawn for nonemployment, which would be an alternative to the unemployment variable (Blanchard, 2000, pp. 106ff.). Nonemployment also takes into account the effect of the prudential motives people living on benefits may have for saving money. The impact of inflation on the demand for deposits, too, can swing either way. The direct effect of inflation on deposits is negative, the argument being that higher inflation increases consumers' propensity to spend money now rather than to engage in long-term investments. However, if the deposit rate (almost) fully compensates for inflation, the effect on deposits can also be positive, due to money illusion. The signs of cross-term coefficients are fairly unpredictable, as they reflect non-linear effects.[14] We have no a priori ideas either about the signs of country dummy coefficients or, in many cases, time trend coefficients, when and where they occur. Table 5.1 recapitulates the expected signs of the coefficients of the deposit model and also presents the coefficient signs for the other models to be discussed below.

Table 5.1 Expected coefficient signs of the determinants of the various models

	Deposits	Deposit rate	Loans	Lending rate
Lagged endogenous	+	+	+	+
Deposit rate	+			+
Gdp, real	+		+	
Government rate	–	+		+
Money market rate	–	+		+
Consumer confidence	+			
Unemployment	i		–	
Nonemployment	i			
Inflation	i	+	i	+
Cross-terms	i		i	
Time trend	i	i	i	i
Country dummies	i	i	i	i
Intercept	i	i	i	i
Markdown/up ($-\lambda$)		–		–
Deposits		–		
Wages, real		–		+
Loan growth		+		
Lending rate			–	
Labour share			i	
Utilization grade			+	
Loans, real		+		+

Note: i stands for a priori indeterminacy.

Price equation (5.11) determines the deposit rate as a function of the volume of deposits, the main input price 'wage rate', other exogenous variables, such as inflation and the markup function, that is, output divided by the first derivative of the demand function with respect to r_{dep}. The coefficient of the markup, $-\lambda$, is the measure of deposit market competition, which we set out to find. For the coefficient of the volume of deposits, we expect a negative sign, because banks will pay a lower rate on deposits the more deposits they have already attracted. The coefficient of wages of bank employees should also be negative, as a higher input price has a negative impact on the deposit rate. Consumers need to be compensated for inflation by the deposit rate. Therefore, its coefficient is expected to be positive.

A few other explanatory variables which do not directly follow from the theoretical framework above have also been considered, such as alternative interest rates, which act as a reference for the bank's deposit rate, and loan growth or real loans, which reflects the need for the bank to acquire funding. These variables do not really conflict with the theoretical model for in fact taking deposits is not the sole funding instrument of the bank.[15] The alternative interest rates, the money market or government rate, are related to alternative investment possibilities for the private sector and cannot be ignored. Therefore, we expect positive signs. Higher than normal loan level or loan growth may encourage the bank to raise its deposit rate, in order to increase funding. Again, positive signs would be plausible.

5.3.1.1 EU-wide results for deposit facility markets

The complete estimation results for deposit markets in the nine EU countries combined, as well as in each of these nine EU countries separately, are presented in Appendix 5.A. We first discuss the EU-wide estimation results of the *real deposit* equation, see Table 5.A.1 in this appendix. This cross-section and time series – or panel data – regression is based on the sample with the highest informational content, namely 774 observations. At the same time, such a model is restrictive, since per variable identical coefficients are assumed for all countries involved. In order to deal with possible autocorrelation, we included the lagged dependent variable and an autoregressive term in the error. The coefficient of the lagged dependent variable has been set at 0.95 to avoid a higher and less plausible value. The estimation results of this equation are conditional on this interference. Such a high Koyck lag value points to a slow adjustment process, reflecting that 'real deposits' is a stock variable. Furthermore, it indicates that deposit saving is, in part, based on certain consistent behavioural patterns (such as conservative saving behaviour, price insensitivity, irresponsiveness to alternative investment opportunities), which is not picked up fully by the included explanatory variables. Besides, 'real deposits' also include long-term time deposits, which are in part fixed by definition. The autocorrelation tests indicate that the resulting errors are free of serial correlation.

All demand variables have significant coefficients with the right signs.[16] The cross-term is also significant. Together with the coefficient of the deposit rate, this coefficient is important, as it constitutes the markdown variable in the deposit rate equation. Adding nonemployment to this equation would yield a insignificant coefficient. Substitution of unemployment by nonemployment would result in a lower level of significance.[17] Five country dummy coefficients show a significant deviation from the Dutch deposits level,[18] indicating a higher (Belgium, France, Spain and the UK) or lower (Sweden) savings level, after taking the other variables into account. This outcome reflects differences across countries and suggests that country-specific estimates might add new insights. The country dummies are jointly significant, as shown by the F-test in the bottom of Table 5.A.1. A second F-test reveals that the whole equation is also jointly significant. We conclude that these estimation results make a good basis to construct the markdown variable, as required in the second equation.

Table 5.A.2 in Appendix 5.A presents the EU-wide estimates of the *deposit rate* equation. As the autocorrelation tests show mixed results which indicates possible serial correlation in the errors, we have to rely on *t*-values, based on Newey and West's autocorrelation consistent covariances. This equation also includes a lagged dependent variable, but its coefficient indicates a relatively quick adjustment process. The major explanatory variable is the government rate with a long-term coefficient of $0.423/(1-0.342) = 0.642$. This is a plausible outcome: the deposit rate is approximately two-thirds of the government rate. Other marginal cost or supply variables have hardly any effect. In the centre of our interest is the coefficient λ of the markdown, representing the banks' (use of) market power in offering deposit facilities. This coefficient is highly significant, indicating, in principle, absence of fully perfect competition and use of at least some market power, but its value is small. Actually, λ is so small that the observed use of market power is virtually negligible. Apparently, the EU deposit markets are characterized by a high degree of competition. However, this conclusion may hold true only for the national or local markets. The fact is that we also observe differences in the level of the deposit rates across the EU countries, as four country dummy coefficients are significant. Probably, during this pre-euro period under investigation, cross-border competition on the EU deposit markets has been limited. Under a Cournot equilibrium, λ is assumed to be equal to the reciprocal of the total EU number of banks ($\lambda = 1/n$), see above.[19] A test on $\lambda = 1/n$ makes clear that a Cournot equilibrium must be rejected. Actually, a test does not make much sense (on the EU level), now we have observed that the EU deposit market is at least segmented into national submarkets.

5.3.1.2 Single-country results for deposit facility markets

Table 5.2 summarizes the estimated values of λ for deposit markets in the nine countries under consideration. The table furthermore indicates the number of observations for each estimation exercise and the respective sample periods. The values for λ in Cournot equilibrium ($\lambda = 1/n$, for n banks) are calculated for 1987 and 1997 on the basis of the number of banks obtained from the OECD (1999). By the way, the figures make clear that, over this period, the number of banks has declined considerably, by around 25 per cent, illustrating the current and recent process of consolidation in most EU countries.

Apart from the deposit rate, at least one cross-term variable proved significant in the *real deposits* equation for each country, see Table 5.A.1 in Appendix 5.A. An exception is Belgium, where neither the deposit rate coefficient nor the cross-term coefficients are significant. For that reason we do not estimate a deposit rate equation for that country, unable as we are to determine a useful 'markdown'. The main demand variable real gdp is significant with the right sign in all countries. Also the government rate coefficient has the right sign wherever it is significant. The sign of the unemployment coefficient differs across countries, as expected. For the UK, nonemployment was a good alternative for unemployment. The tests do not indicate – significant – autocorrelation problems in any of the countries considered. The degree of fit – the adjusted R^2 – is satisfactory. Hence, these estimation results constitute a good basis to construct the markdown variable, as needed in the second equation.

For most countries, the *deposit rate* equation is rather plain in the sense that the number of explanatory variables is low, see Table 5.A.2 in Appendix 5.A. Apart from, in a number of countries, the lagged dependent variable, either the government rate or the money market rate is the main significant variable. In a few countries, the input price 'real wages' is also significant. In these cases all signs are in line with expectations. The tests on autocorrelation do not indicate any problem in any country except Sweden, where we rely on Newey and West's autocorrelation consistent covariances. The degree of fit is very satisfactory with levels above 94 per cent for all countries.

Somewhat disappointingly, the major output of the two deposit market model equations, the degree of competition λ, is significantly only for Germany and Spain, see also Table 5.2. For the other countries this indicates, in principle, absence of the use of market power, in fact perfect competition. Note that we should keep in mind that, since the perfect competition hypothesis ($\lambda = 0$) is the null hypothesis, the approach favours this hypothesis: a 95 per cent level of significance is required to reject perfect competition. For that reason we do not 'accept' perfect competition (where λ does not deviate from zero) but consider both perfect competition and some kind of oligopoly with high competition (including Cournot equilibrium) as

Table 5.2 Market power and summary of the estimates of the deposit rate model

	No. of obser-vations	Estimation period	λ[a]	t-value	Number of banks (n)			
					1987		1997	
					n	$1/n$	n	$1/n$
'EU wide'	774	varying[a]	0.000002	*** 5.2	7346	0.0001	5646	0.0002
Belgium	—	—	—	—	120	0.0083	131	0.0076
France	109	1971:2–98:2	0.000106	1.3	2021	0.0005	1288	0.0008
Germany	84	1978:1–98:4	0.000627	** 2.2	4089	0.0002	3284	0.0003
Italy	64	1983:1–98:4	0.000314	0.7	391	0.0026	255	0.0039
Netherlands	83	1978:2–98:4	0.000023	0.7	170	0.0059	169	0.0059
Portugal	80	1978:1–97:4	-0.000139[b]	1.6	29	0.0345	44	0.0227
Spain	82	1978:3–97:4	0.000504	** 2.6	333	0.0030	307	0.0033
Sweden	110	1971:3–98:4	0.009889	1.3	144	0.0069	124	0.0081
UK	90	1976:3–98:4	0.000001	0.7	49	0.0204	44	0.0227

Note: See Tables 5.A.1 and 5.A.2 in Appendix 5.A for the complete estimation results, the explanation of **, and so on.

[a] By country; [b] a negative value for λ indicates the existence of a supra-negative market condition. This is a nonequilibrium situation in which bank output exceeds a competitive level and prices are too low, so that over time output in these markets will fall and prices will rise.

conceivable. Furthermore, we cannot exclude the possibility that the Bresnahan approach might not be sensitive enough to measure market power accurately, given the limited number of available observations on the country level and the possibility of trend breaks during the lengthy observation periods. For Germany and Spain, we find at least nonperfect competition, but the use of market power is limited.

In the case of a Cournot equilibrium, we assume $\lambda = 1/n$. In that respect, we note that the relevant number of banks, n, is not always known exactly. For instance, there is a substantial difference between the number of banks with a banking licence and the number of actually active banks. For Spain the value of λ is significantly below that of Cournot equilibrium, so we can reject the latter. For the other countries, it is less easy to draw a conclusion, although values of λ and $1/n$ make Cournot less likely in Italy, the Netherlands, Portugal and the UK. For Germany, the value of λ appears to be somewhat higher than $1/n$, but we cannot reject the hypothesis of a Cournot equilibrium. The Swedish value of λ is even equal to $1/n$, as under Cournot, but given the t-value of λ, it is again impossible to reject, for example, perfect competition. Possibly, banks in Germany and Sweden (and in some of the other countries) do not expect retaliation from other banks as response to changes in their own deposit facilities output, as the Cournot model assumes. While allowing for the possible insensitivity of the Bresnahan approach, we conclude that the markets for deposit facilities in the EU countries considered are most probably highly competitive, as we also found for the EU-wide sample.

5.3.2 The Markets for Loans

The second market we investigate employing the Bresnahan model is the loan market. Quantity equation (5.12) determines the volume of real loans. The variable loans is negatively related to its price, the lending rate, and positively related to increasing investment activity as indicated by a higher real gdp income and a higher capital utilization rate. Unemployment may be another indicator of economic activity or sentiment, which in addition reflects structural disequilibrium. Its coefficient is expected to be negative. A high profit income share (or a low labour income share) indicates high profits and favourable expectations of future profits. This indicates attractive investment opportunities and, by implication, increasing demand for new loans. On the other hand, if profits are high, new investment activities may also be financed internally, weakening the demand for loans. All in all, we have no way of knowing the sign of the coefficients of the labour share in advance. The propensity of economic agents to take out loans is encouraged when – expected – inflation is higher, so that the real value of funds decreases. Conversely, however, the lending rate might also rise on account of inflation, cancelling out the effects. So the sign of the inflation coefficient is indeterminate. The expected signs are summarized in Table 5.1.

Price relationship (5.13) determines the lending rate by real loans, input items such as wages and the deposit rate, as well as other exogenous variables such as the money market rate, the government rate, inflation and the markup: output divided by the first derivative of the demand function with respect to r_{lend}. The coefficient of the latter, $-\lambda$, is the crucial variable in our analysis, the measure of competitive conduct on the loans market. As the value of λ is expected to fall in the range of 0 to 1, $-\lambda$ will be negative. Banks are expected to translate the risk associated with a larger loan portfolio into a higher lending rate. Likewise, increasing costs related to the provision of loans, namely higher wages, and higher costs of funding increase the operating costs of banks and will probably be reflected in higher lending rates. The money-market rate and the rate on government debt were included in the price relation as a comparative measure for product pricing, and are expected to exert a positive influence on the lending rate. In fact, they also reflect funding cost, such as costs related to interbank and capital market borrowing. Finally, banks will take account of real losses associated with higher inflation by adjusting their lending rate accordingly. Hence, all coefficients are expected to be positive, be it that we anticipate a negative sign for $-\lambda$.

5.3.2.1 EU-wide results for loan markets

The complete estimation results for loan markets in the region of nine EU countries, as well as in each of these nine EU countries separately, are presented in Appendix 5.B. We first discuss the EU-wide estimation results of the *real loans* equation, see Table 5.B.1 in this Appendix. In order to prevent possible autocorrelation, we included the lagged endogenous variable with a coefficient of 0.95, which was fixed to avoid a higher and less plausible value. Other estimation results of this equation are conditional on this interference. This high Koyck lag value points to a slow adjustment process, which is obvious, as 'real loans' is a stock variable. The loans have diverging terms, in some cases up to ten years and more. The loan volume of a country may also depend on certain consistent behavioural or omitted variables, which are not picked up fully by the included explanatory variables. The autocorrelation tests indicate that the errors are free of serial correlation.

All major demand variables have significant coefficients with the right signs. The two cross-term coefficients are also significant, which is important as, together with the coefficient of the lending rate, they constitute the markup variable in the lending rate equation. Five country dummy coefficients show a significant deviation from the Dutch loans level, indicating a higher (Portugal and Spain) or lower (France, Italy and Sweden) lending level, after taking the other variables into account. These differences across countries suggest that country-specific estimates would be worthwhile.

Both the country dummies and the whole equation are jointly significant, as shown by the F-tests in the bottom of Table 5.B.1.

Table 5.B.2 in Appendix 5.B presents the EU-wide estimates of the *lending rate* equation. The test statistics indicate absence of autocorrelation. This equation does not include a lagged dependent variable. Apparently, the lending rate adjusts within one quarter. The major explanatory variable is the government rate with a coefficient of 0.964. Real loans is the only other marginal cost or supply variable with a significant coefficient. The crucial result is the parameter λ of the markup, measuring the use of market power of EU banks in offering loans. This coefficient is significantly pointing to rejection of perfect competition on the EU lending markets. The value of λ is larger than $1/n$, as in the Cournot equilibrium, but the latter cannot be rejected. Significant country dummy coefficients indicate differences in the level of the lending rates across the EU countries. This underlines the conclusion above of less than perfect competition in the EU. Obviously, during this pre-euro period under investigation, cross-border competition on the EU loan markets has been limited.

5.3.2.2 Single-country results for loan markets

Table 5.3 summarizes the estimated values of λ for loans markets in the nine individual countries. Apart from the lending rate, at least one cross-term variable proved significant in the *real loans* equation for all countries, see Table 5.B.1 in Appendix 5.B. An exception is the UK in the sense that its lending rate coefficient is significant at the 94 per cent level of confidence only, instead of the 95 per cent level. Nevertheless, we assume that for this country also a meaningful 'markup' may be constructed. The major demand variables, real gdp and unemployment, are significant with the right sign in most countries. The respective tests do not reveal significant autocorrelation in any of the countries considered.

Apart from the lagged dependent variable, one or more interest rates – the deposit or funding rate, on the one hand, and the government or money market rate as market rates on the other – are the main significant variables in the *lending rate* equation, see Table 5.B.2 in Appendix 5.B. In a number of countries, the quantity real loans and the input price 'real wages' are also significant, with signs in line with expectations. Mixed evidence regarding autocorrelation occurs for the UK only, where we rely on *t*-values, based on Newey and West's autocorrelation-consistent covariances. The degree of fit is high with R-squares above 95 per cent for all countries, except Sweden (92 per cent).

The essential output of the two loan market equations, the degree of competition λ, is significantly in not less than five countries: Germany, Portugal, Spain, Sweden and the UK, see also Table 5.3. For the other countries, in principle, this suggests the absence of use of market power, that

Table 5.3 Market power and summary of the estimates of the lending rate model

	No. of observations	Period	λ		*t*-value	Inverse of no. of banks ($1/n$) 1987	1997
'EU-wide'	718	varying[a]	0.000429	**	2.5	0.0001	0.0002
Belgium	75	1980:1–98:3	0.000064		1.4	0.0083	0.0076
France	81	1978:2–98:2	0.000002		0.2	0.0005	0.0008
Germany	84	1978:1–98:4	0.000000	**	2.7	0.0002	0.0003
Italy	64	1983:3–98:4	0.000147		0.5	0.0026	0.0039
Netherlands	83	1978:2–98:4	0.000000		0.1	0.0059	0.0059
Portugal	79	1978:2–97:4	0.001128	**	2.2	0.0345	0.0227
Spain	82	1978:3–98:4	0.000000	**	2.5	0.0030	0.0033
Sweden	76	1980:1–98:4	0.000492	**	2.3	0.0069	0.0081
UK	87	1976:3–98:1	0.020572	**	2.4	0.0204	0.0227

[a] By country.

is, perfect competition or in any case a high degree of competition.[20] In Germany, Portugal, Spain, Sweden and the UK we find nonperfect competition, but with limited use of market power only. For Germany, Portugal, Spain and Sweden, the value of λ appears to be significantly smaller than according to the λ value in Cournot equilibrium ($\lambda = 1/n$), so we reject this equilibrium for these countries. For the UK, λ appears to be equal to $1/n$, so that we cannot reject Cournot equilibrium. Apparently, banks in the UK do not expect retaliation from other banks as response to changes in their own lending output. For the other countries, a Cournot equilibrium is less likely. With certain reservations, we draw the conclusion that the loans markets in the EU countries investigated are most probably highly (but not always perfect) competitive, as we found also for the EU-wide sample.

5.3.3 Earlier Applications of Bresnahan in the Literature

The few existing empirical applications of the Bresnahan model to the banking industry are difficult to compare with our results.[21] The model has been estimated by Shaffer (1989, 1993) for, respectively, the US loan markets and for the Canadian banking industry. In both cases, values of λ were found to be not significantly different from zero, implying perfect competition or Cournot oligopoly. Zardkoohi and Fraser (1998) use the model to test whether geographical deregulation in the USA had affected the market structure in the individual states. Perfect competition was found in most states, but imperfect competition in the others. Ribon and Yosha (1999) investigated the highly concentrated Israeli banking market and found significant – but declining – market power in both the deposit and loan markets.

As far as we were able to find out, only three studies have applied the Bresnahan method to European banks, namely Suominen (1994) to the Finish banking deposit and loan markets, Swank (1995) to the Dutch mortgage and savings deposit markets and Toolsema (2002) to the Dutch revolving consumer credit market. Suominen finds estimates for λ, which are not significantly different from zero for the years until 1985, with regulated interest rates, and values of λ indicating the use of market power after the deregulation of the loan market. Swank used a dynamic version of the Bresnahan model for the mortgage and savings deposit markets during the years 1955–90. He detects that both markets under consideration were significantly more oligopolistic than under Cournot equilibrium. However, the degree of market power on the mortgage market falls sharply over time, being close to zero in the years we investigate in this chapter. This is in line with the view that deregulation over time has contributed to less oligopoly. In Swank's study, the market power parameter on the deposit market remains close to zero, although rising slightly over time, owing to the increasing concentration of (deposit taking) banks. However, in more recent years, many new suppliers of deposit services have entered the Dutch market. Toolsema (2002) employs monthly data of the consumer credit market over 1993–99. None of the various specifications she tries provide significant values for λ. So she concludes that Dutch banks do not use market power on the consumer credit market.

Our results from the Bresnahan model can be compared with results from the P–R approach. Chapter 4 found for most European countries that the entire banking market was characterized by monopolistic competition and for a few countries, they even observed perfect competition. The same conclusion applies to submarkets of small, medium-sized and large banks. Chapter 4, Section 4.3, also investigates the EU market as a whole, with monopolistic competition as result. Similar outcomes have been found by other authors (for an overview, see Table 3.5 in Chapter 3). According to the Bresnahan model, for the deposit and loan submarkets competition appears to be at least that heavy. Possibly, due to the limited available data sets and the longer estimation periods, with raising risks of trend breaks, the Bresnahan model has more difficulties in distinguishing between perfect competition and oligopoly or monopolistic competition than the P–R approach.

5.4 SUMMARY AND CONCLUSIONS

Application of Bresnahan's market power model indicates a high degree of competition on both the deposit and loan markets in the nine EU countries under consideration, both apart and jointly. The hypothesis of perfect competition ($\lambda = 0$; no markup on the lending rate or no markdown for the deposit rate) can be rejected for the deposit market of the 'entire' EU, for the deposit markets of Germany and Spain and for the lending markets of Germany, Portugal, Spain, Sweden and the UK. Nevertheless, these markets are characterized by high competition, as the use or abuse of market power is very limited. In the other country-market combinations, where we cannot reject perfect competition, we conclude that competition is high, leaving open the question of whether these markets face perfect competition or a kind of oligopoly with competition fairly close to that. This assessment of highly competitive banking markets in EU countries for deposit facilities and loans is in line with the results of the P–R model, which also indicates (at least) the existence of monopolistic competition for almost all European countries and cannot reject perfect competition in some countries.

For the deposit markets of the entire EU and Spain, and the loans markets of Germany, Portugal Spain and Sweden, we can reject the hypothesis of a Cournot equilibrium ($\lambda = 1/n$). Also in a number of other country-market combinations, such equilibrium is less likely. An exception is the loan market in the UK, where we cannot reject Cournot equilibrium. Apparently, banks in the UK do not expect retaliation from other banks in response to changes in their own lending output. Further, Cournot equilibrium is conceivable in the deposit markets of Germany and Sweden.

It should be kept in mind that the estimation results reflect the average market structure and competitive conditions over the last two decades. The general feeling is that competition has increased over time. That suggests that – keeping other caveats aside – our estimation results form an underbound of the current competitive situation.

With respect to both social welfare and monetary policy, these results are rather comforting. A high level of competition implies that banks contribute substantially to the prosperity of the society and suggests that new policy to boost banking market competition may not be a top priority. A high level of competition also means that banks have limited latitude to respond to monetary policy, which makes the monetary instruments more successful in producing the intended effects on intermediate and ultimate target variables.

Of course, in this chapter, only deposit and loan markets are considered, so that other submarkets may have less favourable competitive conditions. Moreover, the situation found locally may deviate from our national analysis. In particular, this might be the case for lending to small and medium-sized enterprises.

The other side of perfect competition is that in the absence of market power, banks do not benefit from excess margins on prices. This might lead to lower profit rates, which could make banks more vulnerable to shocks (see also Section 2.7). Particularly under perfect competition, banks and their supervisors need to be alert and forward-looking in order to maintain financial stability.

APPENDIX 5.A ESTIMATION RESULTS OF THE BRESNAHAN MODELS FOR DEPOSIT MARKETS

Table 5.A.1 Empirical results for the real deposits equation

	'EU-wide'		Belgium		France		Germany		Italy	
	Coeff.	*t*-value [a]	Coeff.	*t*-value	Coeff.	*t*-value	Coeff.	*t*-value	Coeff.	*t*-value
Intercept	13.248	*** *4.2*	-0.050	*0.1*	-0.116	** *1.5*	0.446	*** *3.1*	12.449	*** *8.5*
Deposits, lagged	0.950	—	—	—	0.900	—	—	—	—	—
Deposit rate	1.994	*** *4.1*	-0.002	*0.0*	0.038	** *2.0*	0.043	** *2.3*	0.177	*** *5.1*
Gdp, real	0.096	*** *3.7*	1.359	*** *3.5*	0.265	*** *3.3*	0.639	*** *5.3*	0.748	*** *2.6*
Money market rate	—	—	—	—	-0.002	*** *3.6*	—	—	—	—
Government rate	-1.172	*** *2.8*	-0.031	*** *4.1*	—	—	-0.017	*** *2.8*	-0.010	*1.1*
Unemployment	-1.117	** *2.4*	-0.010	*** *3.0*	0.002	*1.1*	0.012	*** *6.9*	0.014	**1.8*
Inflation	-0.964	*** *3.1*	0.015	*0.7*	-0.001	*0.3*	-0.009	** *2.0*	-0.006	*1.3*
Dep. rate*Real gdp	-0.005	** *2.5*	0.008	*0.1*	-0.043	** *2.1*	-0.034	** *2.1*	-0.190	*** *5.7*
Dep. rate*Inflation	—	—	-0.001	*0.4*	0.000	*0.2*	—	—	—	—
Dep. rate*Gov. rate	—	—	—	—	—	—	-0.000	*0.4*	0.001	*0.7*
Time trend	—	—	—	—	—	—	—	—	-0.022	*** *8.7*
Belgium	6.400	** *2.0*	—	—	—	—	—	—	—	—
France	13.495	** *2.0*	—	—	—	—	—	—	—	—
Germany	18.117	* *1.7*	—	—	—	—	—	—	—	—

Netherlands	—	—	—	—	—	—	—	—	—	—
Italy	-14.745	* *1.8*	—	—	—	—	—	—	—	—
Portugal	-1.898	*0.8*	—	—	—	—	—	—	—	—
Spain	25.363	*** *3.8*	—	—	—	—	—	—	—	—
Sweden	-43.757	** *2.6*	—	—	—	—	—	—	—	—
UK	19.837	*** *2.7*	—	—	—	—	—	—	—	—
Season 1	—	—	—	—	-0.000	*0.1*	—	—	—	—
Season 2	—	—	—	—	-0.023	*** *6.9*	—	—	—	—
Season 3	—	—	—	—	-0.013	*** *3.6*	—	—	—	—
Dum-dep-de [b]	—	—	—	—	—	—	-0.153	*** *9.3*	—	—
Dum-gdp-de [b]	—	—	—	—	—	—	-0.003	*0.4*	—	—
Dum-unempl-de [b]	—	—	—	—	—	—	-0.028	** *2.0*	—	—
AR (1)	0.256	*** *3.2*	—	—	—	—	—	—	0.905	*** *20.1*
No. of observations	774		75		108		86		63	
Adjusted R^2 [c]	0.72		0.96		0.76		0.98		1.00	
F-test	*** 133.2		*** 230.3		*** 32.8		*** 448.5		*** 1934	
F-test on dummies	*** 20.9									
DW/Durbin's *h* [d]	2.03	— [e]	2.31		2.08	-0.45	1.61		1.82	
Breusch–Godfrey [f]	—	1.6	* 2.9	* 3.1	0.2	* 3.6	2.6	*3.1	—	0.0

[a] *t*-values are based on Newey and West's heteroscedasticity and autocorrelation-consistent covariances; one, two and three asterisks indicate a level of confidence of 90%, 95% and 99%, respectively; the level of confidence is based on two-sided testing for all *t*-values; [b] Dum-dep-de reflects a break in the deposit rate of Germany and is 1 for 1970:2–90:1; dum-gdp-de indicates a break in the gdp of Germany and is 1 during 1970:1–90:4; and dum-unempl-de points to a break in unemployment in Germany and is 1 for 1970:1–91:4; [c] the adjusted R-squared is exclusive of the contribution to the explanation of the dependent variable by the fixed lagged dependent variable; [d] the DW test is 'valid' only for equations without a lagged dependent variable. In those cases,

the Durbin's *h*-test applies; [e] a hyphen means that the Durbin's *h*-test statistic could not be calculated (see Green, 2000); [f] the F-test statistic and the number of observations times the R-squared (which has a χ^2 distribution), respectively. A hyphen reflects that the test statistic could not be calculated.

Table 5.A.1.a Empirical results for the real deposits equation (continuation)

	Netherlands		Portugal		Spain		Sweden		UK	
	Coeff.	*t*-value	Coeff.	*t*-value	Coeff.	*t*-value	Coeff.	*t*-value	Coeff.	*t*-value
Intercept	-0.092	* *1.7*	-0.515	*1.7*	-1.222	*** *3.1*	0.113	** *2.1*	0.305	*1.2*
Deposits, lagged	0.975	*** *29.9*	—	—	0.943	*** *11.3*	0.826	*** *13.9*	0.900	—
Deposit rate	0.024	** *2.3*	0.033	*** *2.8*	0.139	** *2.6*	0.016	*** *3.2*	0.027	** *2.1*
Gdp, real	0.110	** *2.4*	1.304	*** *6.8*	0.858	*** *3.3*	0.097	** *2.3*	0.400	*** *4.4*
Government rate	—	—	0.015	*1.2*	-0.002	*1.5*	-0.003	*1.0*	-0.002	*0.7*
Money market rate	0.000	*0.2*	—	—	—	—	—	—	—	—
Unemployment	-0.002	*1.5*	0.030	*1.6*	0.005	** *2.3*	0.000	*0.1*	—	—
Nonemployment	—	—	—	—	—	—	—	—	-1.048	** *2.2*
Inflation	0.003	*1.1*	-0.006	*0.5*	0.025	* *1.9*	-0.007	*** *4.0*	0.002	*1.0*
Consumer conf.	—	—	—	—	0.001	*1.3*	—	—	—	—
Dep. rate*Real gdp	-0.019	** *2.2*	—	—	-0.103	** *2.2*	—	—	-0.027	** *2.0*
Dep. rate*Inflation	-0.001	** *2.5*	0.000	*0.1*	-0.003	** *2.0*	0.001	*** *2.9*	-0.000	** *2.3*
Dep. rate*Gov. rate	—	—	-0.002	** *2.3*	—	—	—	—	—	—
Dep. rate*mm rate[a]	—	—	—	—	—	—	-0.001	*** *4.6*	—	—
Season 1	—	—	0.019	*1.6*	0.001	*0.2*	-0.037	** *2.2*	—	—

Season 2	—	—	0.012	*1.6*	-0.003	*0.8*	-0.051	*** *5.3*	—	—
Season 3	—	—	0.016	*** *3.7*	0.011	*** *3.1*	-0.027	** *2.0*	—	—
S 1 [b]	0.010	*1.7*	—	—	—	—	—	—	—	—
S 2	0.020	*** *4.3*	—	—	—	—	—	—	—	—
S 3	-0.002	*0.4*	—	—	—	—	—	—	—	—
S 4	-0.028	*** *4.4*	—	—	—	—	—	—	—	—
AR (1)	-0.232	* *1.7*	0.573	*** *3.8*	0.090	*0.7*	-0.450	*** *5.5*	—	—
No. of observations	83		46		49		110		91	
Adjusted R^2	0.99		0.97		1.00		0.81		0.72	
F-test	*** 1 226		*** 127.4		*** 890.3		*** 40.3		*** 33.8	
DW/Durbin's *h*	1.98	0.07	2.06		1.76	0.90	1.95	0.26	1.64	1.72
Breusch–Godfrey	—	0.1	0.2	0.3	1.8	* 3.5	0.1	0.3	*3.8	* 3.1

[a] Money market rate; [b] S 1–S 4 indicate a deviating seasonal pattern for some series in the Netherlands during 1982:1–86:1.

Note: See also notes to Table 5.A.1.

Table 5.A.2 Empirical results for the deposit rate equation

	'EU-wide'		Belgium[a]		France		Germany		Italy	
	Coeff.	*t*-value	Coeff.	*t*-value	Coeff.	*t*-value	Coeff.	*t*-value	Coeff.	*t*-value
Intercept	0.577	*0.9*	—	—	2.195	* *1.7*	10.366	*** *2.7*	6.860	** *2.5*
Markdown (-λ)	-0.000	*** *5.2*	—	—	-0.000	*1.3*	-0.001	** *2.2*	0.000	*0.7*
Dep. rate, lagged	0.342	*** *5.5*	—	—	0.947	*** *18.2*	—	—	0.934	*** *16.7*
Deposits	-0.000	*0.2*	—	—	-0.400	*1.3*	-1.792	* *1.9*	0.371	*1.1*
Wages, real	-0.001	*0.1*	—	—	-3.970	* *1.7*	-9.425	*** *2.7*	-0.075	** *2.5*
Inflation	0.043	*1.5*	—	—	0.050	*** *3.6*	0.061	** *2.0*	-0.025	*0.8*
Money market rate	—	—	—	—	—	—	0.803	*** *33.8*	—	—
Government rate	0.423	*** *6.6*	—	—	0.046	*** *2.8*	—	—	0.186	*** *7.6*
Loan growth	—	—	—	—	—	—	31.033	*** *3.8*	23.738	*** *3.5*
Belgium	-0.970	** *2.3*	—	—	—	—	—	—	—	—
France	-1.395	** *2.0*	—	—	—	—	—	—	—	—
Germany	-0.595	*0.4*	—	—	—	—	—	—	—	—
Netherlands	—	—	—	—	—	—	—	—	—	—
Italy	-0.359	*0.3*	—	—	—	—	—	—	—	—
Portugal	2.502	** *2.3*	—	—	—	—	—	—	—	—
Spain	-1.422	*** *3.3*	—	—	—	—	—	—	—	—
Sweden	-0.168	*0.4*	—	—	—	—	—	—	—	—
UK	0.225	*0.2*	—	—	—	—	—	—	—	—
Season 1	—	—	—	—	0.054	*0.5*	-0.728	*** *2.4*	-1.741	*** *3.4*

Season 2	—	—	—	—	-0.049	0.7	-0.346	* 1.7	-0.795	*** 3.1
Season 3	—	—	—	—	-0.102	** 2.1	0.105	0.5	-0.887	*** 3.1
AR	0.872	*** 25.9	—	—	—	—	0.408	*** 2.8	—	—
No. of observations	774				109		84		64	
Adjusted R^2	0.98				0.96		0.98		0.98	
F-test	*** 2 342				*** 304.6		*** 331.4		*** 378.0	
F-test on dummies	*** 9.0									
DW/Durbin's *h*	2.18	-2.54			2.17	-1.21	2.29		2.13	-0.51
Breusch–Godfrey	*** 16.9	*** 20.3			0.8	0.4	—	2.5	—	0.8

[a] This equation has not been estimated, as we do not have a good measure of the 'markdown'.

Note: See also notes to Tables 5.A.1 and 5.A.1 a.

Table 5.A.2.a Empirical results for the deposits rate equation (continuation)

	Netherlands		Portugal		Spain		Sweden		UK	
	Coeff.	*t*-value	Coeff.	*t*-value	Coeff.	*t*-value	Coeff.	*t*-value	Coeff.	*t*-value
Intercept	2.321	*1.0*	-18.775	*** *4.7*	0.385	*0.3*	127.991	*** *2.7*	-2.047	* *0.3*
Markdown (-λ)	-0.000	*0.7*	0.000	*1.6*	-0.001	** *2.6*	0.010	*1.3*	-0.000	*0.7*
Dep. rate, lagged	0.481	*** *3.5*	—	—	0.886	*** *10.5*	0.543	*** *6.4*	0.226	** *2.1*
Deposits	-1.462	* *1.9*	2.357	*1.1*	-0.421	*0.4*	2.096	*1.5*	-0.790	* *1.7*
Wages, real	-0.115	*0.1*	11.700	* *1.8*	0.137	*0.1*	-0.469	*0.5*	0.558	*0.1*
Inflation	0.063	*1.6*	0.575	*** *6.6*	0.033	*0.9*	0.102	* *1.9*	-0.071	*1.9*
Money market rate	0.319	*** *3.4*	0.700	*** *4.2*	0.037	** *2.3*	0.241	** *2.5*	0.930	*** *8.6*
Real loans	—	—	0.001	** *2.0*	—	—	—	—	—	—
Time trend	—	—	—	—	—	—	-0.065	*** *2.7*	—	—
AR (1)	0.397	*** *3.4*	—	—	0.690	*** *5.4*	0.365	*** *3.1*	0.616	*** *3.8*
No. of observations	83		80		82		110		90	
Adjusted R^2	0.97		0.94		0.99		0.96		0.96	
F-test	*** 412.0		*** 197.3		*** 1 087		*** 330.0		*** 310.5	
DW/Durbin's *h*	2.00	0.03	1.90		1.77	1.05	2.22	-1.14	1.91	0.43
Breusch–Godfrey	—	0.0[a]	—	0.1	2.0	2.3	*** 10.2	*** 11.6	—	0.3

Note: See also notes to Tables 5.A.1 and 5.A.1.a.

APPENDIX 5.B ESTIMATION RESULTS OF THE BRESNAHAN MODELS FOR LOAN MARKETS

Table 5.B.1 Empirical results for the real loans equation

	'EU-wide'		Belgium		France		Germany[a]		Italy	
	Coeff.	*t*-value	Coeff.	*t*-value	Coeff.	*t*-value	Coeff.	*t*-value	Coeff.	*t*-value
Intercept	-11.587	*1.4*	24.094	** *2.2*	23.248	*0.0*	7.542	*** *76.2*	33.223	*** *3.3*
Loans, lagged	0.950	—	—	—	0.950	—	—	—	—	—
Lending rate	-4.208	*** *4.9*	-0.073	*** *3.2*	-41.972	** *2.0*	-0.033	** *2.6*	-2.502	*** *3.6*
Gdp, real	0.279	*** *6.9*	1.554	*** *6.1*	90.744	*0.8*	-0.212	*1.6*	16.849	*** *10.0*
Utilization grade	—	—	—	—	7.688	** *2.3*	—	—	—	—
Unemployment	-0.732	** *2.1*	-0.082	*** *4.1*	-45.720	** *2.3*	-0.003	*0.5*	-3.437	*** *4.3*
Inflation	-1.778	*** *3.4*	0.030	*1.4*	-30.649	* *1.9*	-0.026	** *2.1*	-0.678	*** *3.2*
Lending rate*Rgdp	—	—	—	—	—	—	0.033	** *2.5*	—	—
Lending rate*Ut.gr.	0.053	*** *4.0*	—	—	—	—	—	—	—	—
Lending rate*Infl.	0.060	*** *2.6*	0.002	*1.3*	1.883	*1.6*	0.002	*1.5*	0.034	*** *2.8*
Lending rate*Unem.	—	—	0.005	*** *3.0*	3.819	*** *2.4*	—	—	0.217	*** *3.6*
Time trend	—	—	-0.012	** *2.2*	—	—	—	—	—	—
Belgium	3.331	*1.4*	—	—	—	—	—	—	—	—
France	-32.526	** *2.2*	—	—	—	—	—	—	—	—
Germany	-25.929	*1.4*	—	—	—	—	—	—	—	—

(Continued)

Table 5.B.1 *(Concluded)*

	'EU-wide'		Belgium		France		Germany		Italy	
	Coeff.	*t*-value	Coeff.	*t*-value	Coeff.	*t*-value	Coeff.	*t*-value	Coeff.	*t*-value
Netherlands	—	—	—	—	—	—	—	—	—	—
Italy	-59.926	*** *4.3*	—	—	—	—	—	—	—	—
Portugal	8.112	** *2.4*	—	—	—	—	—	—	—	—
Spain	15.887	*** *2.6*	—	—	—	—	—	—	—	—
Sweden	-11.509	*** *4.4*	—	—	—	—	—	—	—	—
UK	-11.531	*0.8*	—	—	—	—	—	—	—	—
Season 1	23.701	*** *6.1*	—	—	-79.664	*** *6.6*	—	—	—	—
Season 2	10.176	*** *3.5*	—	—	-48.536	*** *6.3*	—	—	—	—
Season 3	9.739	*** *4.5*	—	—	-56.694	*** *7.5*	—	—	—	—
AR (1)	—	—	—	—	—	—	0.840	*** *11.1*	—	—
No. of observations	719		75		81		85		64	
Adjusted R^2	0.83		0.73		0.69		1.00		0.88	
F-test	*** 212.1		*** 30.4		*** 18.7		*** 1 127		*** 75.4	
F-test on dummies	*** 35.6						-			
DW/Durbin's *h*	2.05	—	2.23		2.11	—	1.91		2.14	
Breusch–Godfrey	* 3.6	* 3.2	—	1.5	0.4	0.3	0.2	0.1	0.5	0.6

[a] Dependent variable (loans) and real gdp are expressed in logarithms.

Note: See also notes to Tables 5.A.1 and 5.A.1.a.

Table 5.B.1.a Empirical results for the real loans equation

	Netherlands		Portugal		Spain		Sweden		UK	
	Coeff.	*t*-value	Coeff.	*t*-value	Coeff.	*t*-value	Coeff.	*t*-value	Coeff.	*t*-value
Intercept	0.635	** *2.4*	2.550	*1.6*	31.456	*** *3.3*	0.668	** *2.1*	-3,808	*** *5.9*
Loans, lagged	0.950	—	0.888	*** *14.1*	0.917	*** *13.3*	0.950	—	0.900	—
Lending rate	-0.058	*** *3.1*	-0.243	*** *3.1*	-1.496	*** *5.6*	-0.067	*** *3.0*	-1.893	* *1.9*
Gdp, real	0.504	*** *9.3*	1.158	** *2.4*	2.340	*0.3*	0.021	*0.3*	0.048	*** *3.1*
Labour share	—	—	0.035	*1.5*	-0.329	*** *3.7*	-0.009	** *2.5*	—	—
Utilization grade	—	—	—	—	—	—	0.002	*1.1*	—	—
Unemployment	-0.076	** *2.2*	0.020	*0.8*	-0.169	*** *5.9*	-0.008	*** *3.9*	-3.547	*** *3.7*
Inflation	-0.054	*** *2.8*	-0.038	*1.4*	-0.191	*** *3.4*	0.001	*0.3*	-0.509	* *1.7*
Lending rate*Ut.gr.	—	—	—	—	0.001	*0.5*	—	—	0.015	* *1.9*
Lending rate*Infl.	0.005	*** *2.9*	0.001	*1.1*	—	—	-0.000	*0.9*	—	—
Lending rate*Unem.	0.004	*1.5*	—	—	—	—	—	—	0.206	** *2.2*
Lending rate*Lab.sh	—	—	0.003	*** *2.7*	0.019	*** *4.7*	0.001	*** *2.9*	—	—
Time trend	—	—	—	—	—	—	—	—	1.928	*** *5.8*
Season 1	—	—	—	—	-0.009	*0.1*	0.004	*0.6*	—	—
Season 2	—	—	—	—	-0.227	** *2.2*	-0.015	** *2.0*	—	—
Season 3	—	—	—	—	0.066	*0.9*	0.017	*1.3*	—	—
S 1	-0.029	*1.1*	—	—	—	—	—	—	—	—

(Continued)

Table 5.B.1.a *(Concluded)*

	Netherlands		Portugal		Spain		Sweden		UK	
	Coeff.	*t*-value	Coeff.	*t*-value	Coeff.	*t*-value	Coeff.	*t*-value	Coeff.	*t*-value
S 2	0.104	*** *3.7*	—	—	—	—	—	—	—	—
S 3	0.067	** *2.2*	—	—	—	—	—	—	—	—
S 4	-0.030	*1.0*	—	—	—	—	—	—	—	—
AR (1)	—	—	—	—	0.510	****3.2*	—	—	0.321	*** *3.0*
No. of observations	84		80		83		76		87	
Adjusted R^2	0.75		0.99		1.00		0.47		0.95	
F-test	*** 26.4		*** 707.2		*** 8 364		*** 7.4		*** 209.3	
DW/Durbin's *h*	2.0	—	2.09	—	1.96	—	1.84	—	2.08	—
Breusch–Godfrey	0.1	0.3	—	0.3	—	0.2	—	0.4	1.7	1.6

Note: See also notes to Tables 5.A.1 and 5.A.1.a.

Table 5.B.2 Empirical results for the lending rate equation

	'EU-wide'		Belgium		France		Germany		Italy	
	Coeff.	*t*-value	Coeff.	*t*-value	Coeff.	*t*-value	Coeff.	*t*-value	Coeff.	*t*-value
Intercept	1.624	***2.1*	-0.749	*0.8*	-8.903	*** 2.5*	0.281	*0.1*	2.529	*1.6*
Markup ($-\lambda$)	-0.000	*** 2.5*	0.000	*1.4*	-0.000	*0.2*	-0.000	*** 2.3*	-0.000	*0.7*
Lending rate lagged	—	—	0.821	**** 9.2*	—	—	0.658	**** 15.5*	0.478	**** 5.3*
Loans, real	0.003	**** 3.7*	0.000	**** 3.1*	0.002	*** 2.4*	0.000	*1.1*	0.000	*0.1*
Wages, real	0.103	** 1.7*	-0.226	*0.4*	16.668	**** 2.3*	0.190	*0.1*	-0.010	*0.8*
Deposit rate	—	—	—	—	0.668	*** 2.1*	0.313	**** 9.2*	0.379	**** 3.0*
Money market rate	—	—	0.233	**** 2.7*	0.176	**** 2.7*	—	—	0.201	**** 4.3*
Government rate	0.964	**** 8.9*	—	—	—	—	0.171	*** 2.5*	—	—
Inflation	0.035	*0.4*	-0.038	*1.1*	0.065	*1.0*	-0.002	*0.1*	-0.015	*0.5*
Belgium	0.012	*0.6*	—	—	—	—	—	—	—	—
France	-4.225	**** 3.7*	—	—	—	—	—	—	—	—
Germany	-3.953	*1.6*	—	—	—	—	—	—	—	—
Netherlands	—	—	—	—	—	—	—	—	—	—
Italy	-13.294	*** 2.0*	—	—	—	—	—	—	—	—
Portugal	2.678	**** 4.0*	—	—	—	—	—	—	—	—
Spain	-0.775	*0.7*	—	—	—	—	—	—	—	—

(Continued)

Table 5.B.2 *(Concluded)*

	'EU-wide'		Belgium		France		Germany		Italy	
	Coeff.	*t*-value	Coeff.	*t*-value	Coeff.	*t*-value	Coeff.	*t*-value	Coeff.	*t*-value
Sweden	0.769	*1.3*	—	—	—	—	—	—	—	—
UK	-5.058	*** *5.9*	—	—	—	—	—	—	—	—
Season 1	—	—	—	—	0.024	*0.2*	—	—	—	—
Season 2	—	—	—	—	0.061	*0.5*	—	—	—	—
Season 3	—	—	—	—	0.188	*** *2.9*	—	—	—	—
Dum-unempl-de	—	—	—	—	—	—	-0.464	*** *3.1*	—	—
AR (1)	—	—	—	—	0.787	*** *8.8*	0.139	*1.1*	—	—
No. of observations	718		75		81		84		64	
Adjusted R^2	0.91		0.97		0.96		0.99		0.99	
F-test	*** 26.0		*** 353.5		*** 190.9		*** 657.2		*** 930.6	
F-test on dummies	*** 3.7									
DW/Durbin's *h*	2.07		1.98	0.08	1.83		1.94	0.27	1.97	0.13
Breusch–Godfrey	—	0.4	—	0.0	—	1.0	—	1.5	—	0.0

Note: See also notes to Tables 5.A.1 and 5.A.1.a.

Table 5.B.2.a Empirical results for the lending rate equation

	Netherlands		Portugal		Spain		Sweden		UK	
	Coeff.	*t*-value	Coeff.	*t*-value	Coeff.	*t*-value	Coeff.	*t*-value	Coeff.	*t*-value
Intercept	-9.283	*** *3.1*	-5.163	*1.2*	-4.953	** *2.1*	5.985	* *1.7*	-235.03	*0.5*
Markup (-λ)	-0.000	*0.1*	-0.001	** *2.2*	-0.000	** *2.5*	-0.000	** *2.3*	-0.021	** *2.4*
Lending rate lagged	0.561	*** *5.1*	0.625	*** *5.8*	0.897	*** *12.4*	0.349	*** *3.1*	—	—
Loans, real	0.004	*** *2.8*	0.000	** *2.4*	-0.000	*0.2*	0.001	*0.6*	-0.012	*1.1*
Wages, real	6.751	*** *2.9*	1.034	*0.2*	4.180	* *1.8*	-3.684	*1.2*	13.631	* *1.9*
Deposit rate	—	—	—	—	-0.190	*1.1*	—	—	0.679	*** *7.1*
Government rate	0.637	*** *5.1*	0.525	*** *3.5*	0.244	*** *4.3*	0.337	*** *3.3*	0.029	*0.2*
Inflation	-0.089	*1.3*	0.069	*1.5*	0.101	** *2.1*	0.360	*** *4.9*	0.145	** *2.6*
Time trend	—	—	—	—	—	—	—	—	0.114	*0.5*
AR (1)	0.576	*** *4.0*	0.365	** *2.4*	0.003	*0.0*	0.166	*1.2*	0.576	*** *7.0*
No. of observations	83		79		82		76		87	
Adjusted R^2	0.95		0.97		0.99		0.92		0.95	
F-test	*** 218.2		*** 314.6		*** 780.1		*** 135.3		*** 206.7	
DW/Durbin's *h*	1.77	1.06	2.04	-0.18	1.63	1.69	2.01	-0.06	1.71	
Breusch–Godfrey	2.3	2.5	—	0.6	* 3.4	—	—	0.2	—	** 4.7

Note: See also notes to Tables 5.A.1 and 5.A.1.a.

APPENDIX 5.C DEFINITIONS AND SOURCES OF THE DATA

Table 5.C.1 Data sources for Belgium

Time series	Definition	Source
Deposits	Savings and time deposits in bef (nsa)	Own calculations based on BIS data
Loans	Claims of credit institutions on non-financial residents (nsa)	IFS
Deposit rate	Deposit rate	IFS
Lending rate (1970:1–84:4)	Interest rate on investment loans by national industry credit company (credits of 4 years or more with rate flexibility every 5 years), end month data, disc.	BIS
Idem (1985:1–99:4)	Prime lending rate	IFS
GDP	GDP, 1995 prices (nsa)	BIS
Money market rate	3-months treasury bill rate	OECD
Government bond rate	5 year central government bond	OECD
Unemployment rate	Unemployment rate	BIS
Nonemployment rate	Formula: 1- (employment/population)	—
Employment	Employment, domestic (ECB def.) in 1000s pers., Q-av (sa)	BIS
Population	Population	IFS
Price deflator	CPI all items (nsa)	OECD
Wages	Normalized unit labour costs (sa)/Labour cost survey 1996	OECD/Eurostat
Labour share	Labour share	Dutch central bank
Capital utilization	Capital utilization in industry	BIS
Consumer confidence	Consumer confidence indicator (sa)	DS

Table 5.C.2 Data sources for France

Time series	Definition	Source
Deposits	Other than demand deposits (national residency)	IFS
Loans	Claims of banking institutions on other resident sectors; break 1978:1 corrected on the basis of yearly growth	IFS
Deposit rate	Deposit rate; 1986:1 and 1986:2 non available (n.a.) – calculated by taking the average of period before and after	IFS
Lending rate	Lending rate; 1986:1 and 1986:2 n.a. – calculated by taking the average of period before and after	IFS
GDP	GDP, 1995 prices (sa), 1970:1–77:4 calculated with GDP index	BIS (index: IFS)
Money market rate	Treasury bill rate	IFS
Government bond rate	Yield on long term (> 7 years) government bonds on secondary market	BIS
Unemployment rate	Unemployment rate (sa)	IFS
Nonemployment rate	Formula: 1- (employment/population)	—
Employment	Employment total (excl. conscripts) (ECB proxy) in 1000s pers., (sa-disc)	BIS
Population	Population	IFS
Price deflator	GDP total index, 1980 prices (sa)	BIS
Wages	Unit labour cost index, total economy (sa)	BIS/Eurostat
Consumer confidence	Consumer confidence indicator (sa)	DS

Table 5.C.3 Data sources for Germany

Time series	Definition	Source
Deposits	Non-demand deposits of other resident sectors with banks	IFS
Deposit dummy	1970:2 until 1990:1 (time period where series includes only GDP of the western states)	—
Loans	Claims of banks on other resident sectors	IFS
Deposit rate	3–months deposits (< 1 mio DM)	IFS
Lending rate	Lending rate on CA credit (< 1 mio DM)	IFS
GDP	GDP at 1995 prices, market prices (nsa), until 1990:4 GDP only for the western states	BIS
GDP dummy	1970:1 until 1990:4	—
Money market rate	Interest rates on 3-months loans (money market)	BIS
Government bond rate	Redemption yield, 10 year benchmark bond	DS
Unemployment rate	Unemployment rate, dependent labour (sa)	DS
Unemployment dummy	1970:1 until 1991:4 (time period where the unemployment series has been corrected)	—
Nonemployment rate	Formula: 1- (employment/population)	—
Employment	Employment, domestic W and W+E (ECB def.) in 1000s pers., Q-av (nsa)	BIS
Population	Population	IFS
Price deflator	GNP implicit price deflator (nsa)	DS
Wages	Unit labour cost index, temporarily discontinued (sa)	DS/ Eurostat
Consumer confidence	Consumer confidence indicator (sa)	DS

Table 5.C.4 Data sources for Italy

Time series	Definition	Source
Deposits	Savings and time deposits with banks (end-month) in M2 (nsa)	BIS
Loans	Domestic loans by banks (nsa)	BIS
Deposit rate	Interest rate on total deposits, quarterly average	BIS
Lending rate	Interest rate on bank loans, quarterly average	BIS
GDP	GDP, 1995 prices, market prices, (nsa)	BIS
Money market rate	3-months treasury bill rate	IFS
Government bond rate	Italian government long-term bond yield (9–10 year)	IFS
Unemployment rate	Unemployment rate (nsa)	BIS
Nonemployment rate	Formula: 1- (employment/population)	—
Employment	Employment total (ECB def.) in 1000s pers., Q-beg (sa)	BIS
Population	Population	IFS
Price deflator	(GDP, current prices)/(GDP, 1995 prices)	BIS
Wages	Unit labour costs in whole economy (sa)	BIS/Eurostat
Labour share	Labour share	Dutch central bank
Consumer confidence	Consumer confidence indicator (sa)	DS

Table 5.C.5 Data sources for the Netherlands

Time series	Definition	Source
Deposits	Other than demand deposits with banks from non-bank institutions with banks, discontinued	IFS
Loans	Claims of banks on other resident sectors than government, discontinued	IFS
Deposit rate	Rate on deposits 2 years (fixed)	DNB
Lending rate	Lending rate	IFS
GDP	GDP, 1995 prices, purchaser's value (nsa)	BIS
Money market rate	3-months money market rate, discontinued, mean (nsa)	DS: Eurostat
Government bond rate	Medium term (5-8 yr) central government bond yield, secondary market, month-end data	BIS
Unemployment rate	Unemployment rate	OECD
Nonemployment rate	Formula: 1- (employment/population)	—
Employment	Employment, domestic (ECB def.) in 1000s pers., Q-mid (nsa)	BIS
Population	Population	IFS
Price deflator	GDP price deflator, market prices (nsa)	BIS
Wages	Hourly wage rates in private sector, dicontinued, completed with series hourly wage rates in manufacturing sector	DS: CBS/Eurostat
Utilization grade	Utilization grade of industry	CBS
Labour share	Labour share market sector	CPB
Consumer confidence	Consumer confidence indicator (sa)	DS

Table 5.C.6 Data sources for Portugal

Time series	Definition	Source
Deposits	Time and savings deposits, (bln PE)	IFS database
Loans	Claims on private sector	IFS database
Deposit rate	Average interest rate on time deposits	DS: IFS
Lending rate	Average lending rate, excl. doubtful debt	DS: IFS
GDP	GDP, 1990=100, from 1998:1 completed on the basis of growth of data series 18299B.PYF	DS: IFS
Government bond rate	Government bond yield	DS: IFS
Unemployment rate	Unemployment rate, originally yearly data	OECD
Nonemployment rate	Formula: 1- (employment/population)	—
Employment	Employment total (nsa)	BIS
Population	Population	IFS
Price deflator	GDP price deflator, from 1998:4 completed	DS: IFS
Wages	Unit labour cost index, total economy, originally yearly figures	OECD/Eurostat
Labour share	Labour share	Dutch central bank
Consumer confidence	Consumer confidence indicator (sa)	DS

Table 5.C.7 Data sources for Spain

Time series	Definition	Source
Deposits	Savings and time deposits, average of month-end data	BIS
Loans	Total credit to private sector, month average (nsa)	BIS
Deposit rate	Weighted average of rate on savings deposits and rate on time deposits	own calculations
Lending rate	Interest rate on medium-term credit (1–3 yr), month-end	BIS
GDP	Constant GDP, 1990 prices (sa); quarterly data calculated from quarterly data on yearly basis	DS: IFS
Money market rate	Interest rate money market, 3–month interbank deposits, month average	BIS
Government bond rate	Monthly average bond yield (bonds 2 yr maturity)	DS: IFS
Unemployment rate	Unemployment rate, in % of total labour force (nsa)	BIS
Nonemployment rate	Formula: 1- (employment/population)	—
Employment	Employment, domestic (ESA 95), Q-av	BIS
Population	Population	IFS
Price deflator	GDP implicit price deflator index, calculated from yearly data	DS: OECD
Wages	Hourly wages (nsa)	DS: IFS/ Eurostat
Labour share	Labour share	Dutch central bank
Capital utilization	Capacity utilization in industry, excl. construction (nsa)	BIS
Consumer confidence	Consumer confidence indicator (sa)	DS

Table 5.C.8 Data sources for Sweden

Time series	Definition	Source
Deposits	Demand, time, savings and foreign currency deposits	IFS
Loans	Claims of private banks on private sector	IFS
Deposit rate	Deposit rate	IFS
Lending rate	Lending rate	IFS
GDP	GDP, 1991 prices (nsa)	BIS
Money market rate	Treasury bill rate	IFS
Government bond rate	Central government bonds yield, 10 yr bonds	OECD
Unemployment rate	Unemployment rate (nsa)	BIS
Nonemployment rate	Formula: 1- (employment/population)	—
Employment	Employment total in 1000s pers., Q-av (sa)	BIS
Population	Population	IFS
Price deflator	CPI, all items, 1995=100 (nsa)	DS: OECD
Wages	Hourly labour cost (nsa)	OECD/Eurostat
Capital utilization	Capital utilization in economy (sa)	BIS
Labour share	Labour share	Dutch central bank
Consumer confidence	Consumer confidence indicator (sa)	DS

Table 5.C.9 Data sources for the UK

Time series	Definition	Source
Deposits	Sterling deposits from public and private sectors with banks (nsa)	BIS
Loans	UK bank lending to residents – private sector, discontinued	IFS
Deposit rate	UK instant access savings accounts interest rate	IFS
Lending rate	UK minimum base rate of London clearing banks	IFS
GDP	GDP, 1995 prices, market prices (nsa)	BIS
Money market rate	Interest rate money market, treasury bills, 91-day, average allotment rate, end-month	BIS
Government bond rate	Medium-dated (10-year) government stock yield, secondary market, month-end	BIS
Unemployment rate	Unemployment rate (nsa)	BIS
Nonemployment rate	Formula: 1- (employment/population)	—
Employment	Employment total, Q-end (sa)	BIS
Population	Population	IFS
Price deflator	GDP price deflator, 1995=100, discontinued series, market prices (nsa)	BIS
Wages	Unit wage and salary costs in whole economy (index) (sa)	BIS/Eurostat
Utilization grade	Utilization grade, volume, mean of stock	BIS
Labour share	Labour share firms	Dutch central bank
Consumer confidence	Consumer confidence indicator (sa)	DS

Table 5.C.10 Descriptive statistics of the data of the Bresnahan models over 1983–97 [a]

	EU-wide	Belgium	France	Germany	Italy	Nether-lands	Portugal	Spain	Sweden	UK
Deposits, real, bln	426	151	744	1 186	230	253	69	356	140	701
DM, 1990 prices [b]	*365*	*29*	*85*	*102*	*87*	*36*	*9*	*40*	*9*	*236*
Deposit rate	7.4	5.4	4.9	4.8	8.5	5.6	14.6	7.2	7.8	7.8
	4.2	*1.4*	*1.2*	*1.7*	*2.5*	*1.3*	*6.9*	*1.6*	*2.7*	*3.4*
Gdp, real, bln DM	264	77	465	651	423	112	26	143	86	388
1990 prices [b]	*212*	*7*	*41*	*76*	*45*	*14*	*3*	*17*	*6*	*45*
Money market rate	9.6	7.8	8.4	5.9	11.8	6.1	14.6	12.3	10.1	9.1
	4.1	*2.6*	*2.7*	*2.0*	*3.0*	*1.9*	*4.8*	*3.8*	*2.9*	*2.8*
Government rate	10.0	8.7	8.9	7.0	11.7	7.0	14.7	12.0	10.6	9.5
	3.4	*1.9*	*2.1*	*1.0*	*2.6*	*1.2*	*4.7*	*3.0*	*1.9*	*1.5*
Unemployment	10.2	12.1	10.5	10.9	11.1	7.2	6.5	20.1	4.4	9.1
	4.6	*1.5*	*1.2*	*1.3*	*0.8*	*1.3*	*1.5*	*2.5*	*2.7*	*2.2*
Inflation	5.1	3.0	3.5	2.6	6.9	1.6	12.4	6.5	5.2	4.5
	4.5	*1.9*	*2.4*	*1.3*	*3.3*	*1.1*	*7.1*	*2.7*	*3.2*	*2.1*
Loans, real, bln	804	195	1 548	2 460	895	380	65	568	148	977
DM, 1990 prices	*771*	*35*	*255*	*435*	*185*	*92*	*15*	*103*	*29*	*352*

(Continued)

Table 5.C.10 *(Concluded)*

	EU-wide	Belgium	France	Germany	Italy	Nether-lands	Portugal	Spain	Sweden	UK
Lending rate	12.3	10.7	9.7	10.5	13.5	9.1	19.6	14.6	13.2	9.5
	4.4	*2.2*	*1.7*	*1.6*	*2.7*	*2.1*	*5.9*	*2.9*	*2.8*	*2.9*
Utilization grade	79	78	83	84	91	84	80	77	87	46
	13	*2*	*2*	*4*	*3*	*2*	*2*	*3*	*3*	*11*
Wages, real, index	1.00	1.29	1.15	1.32	1.01	1.05	0.35	0.74	1.23	0.69
	0.19	*0.10*	*0.11*	*0.04*	*0.06*	*0.05*	*0.02*	*0.04*	*0.07*	*0.02*
No. of observations	540	60	60	60	60	60	60	60	60	60

[a] Means (in normal font) and standard deviations (in italics); [b] the estimation of the separate countries is based on index values of deposits and gdp (with 1990=1).

NOTES

1. See Bresnahan (1982) and Lau (1982). This technique is elaborated further in Bresnahan (1989).
2. Alternatively, Suominen (1994) and Swank (1995) employ two-product models (deposits and loans) and assume the interdependence of product demand and marginal cost functions, but neither of them employs cost functions including factor input prices.
3 The assumptions underlying the Cournot oligopoly theory according to Hause (1977) are: homogeneous products, *n* firms with strictly increasing marginal cost functions (which need not be identical), independent (noncooperative) behaviour of firms to maximize their own profits, no entry, and industry demand is strictly decreasing.
4. As suggested above, an alternative would be to define the price as the difference between the risk-free (or money market) rate and the deposit rate. In our empirical application, the alternative model would be equivalent to the current model, because alternative rates (such as the money market rate) are also included as an explanatory variable.
5. Data on branches were unavailable for our empirical analysis.
6. The equilibrium version of the demand equation for Deposits, that is Equation (5.5) after substitution of the equilibrium price r_{dep} from Equation (5.11).
7. This is obvious from equation (5.11): if $\alpha_3 = 0$, λ and β_l are indistinguishable from each other.
8. For the other EU countries, we could not find data for all essential model variables. In particular, appropriate lending rates are unavailable for a number of countries.
9. Volumes are expressed in billions of 'Deutsche Marks'. Inflation and interest rates are in percentages.
10. We use Eviews 4.0, which employs the Marquardt algorithm for non-linear estimation. Everywhere, all potential exogenous explanatory variables have been included as instrumental variables.
11. An exception is the EU-wide real deposit equation.
12 Inclusion of both rates would cause multicollinearity.
13. Besides, this model structure, like autocorrelation, may indicate that at least one explanatory variable with lasting effects has been omitted.
14. Note that the signs of cross-terms are difficult to assess, as they consist of two terms, price or interest rate and demand factor. Furthermore, the respective demand factor occurs twice, separately and multiplied by the price. The sign of both coefficients should be judged coherently.
15. Alternatives are the interbank market (deposits) and the capital market (bills, bonds and shares).
16. By significant (or very significant) we mean, in this chapter, at the 95% (or 99%) level of confidence.
17. We found similar results for the single-country estimates, except for the UK where nonemployment was a better explanatory variable, see Table 5.A.1.a in Appendix 5.A.
18. The intercept estimates the Dutch deposit level, after taking the other variables into account.
19. The Cournot model assumes that a firm does not expect retaliation from other firms in r esponse to changes in its own output.
20. Note, once again, that the employed approach is favourable for the perfect competition hypothesis, as it is the null hypothesis.
21. Bresnahan's model has also been applied to other industries, for example, Alexander (1988), Graddy (1994), Genesove and Mullin (1998) and Steen and Salvanes (1999).

6. Efficiency and cost differences across countries

6.1 INTRODUCTION

The banking industry is exposed to a multitude of new developments and challenges. Deregulation, liberalization, information technology and the entry of new types of competitors have contributed to the internationalization of existing capital markets and to the development of new markets for sophisticated financial instruments. The benefits of operating on a larger scale have prompted a wave of mergers. The banking landscape is changing even more radically in Europe, where the introduction of the 'European passport' (the EU-wide banking permission) in 1992 and the single currency (for EMU countries) in 1999 has removed institutional and practical obstacles for banks to operating in other EU countries.[1] In the near future, the (prospect of a) new Basel Capital Accord might contribute to a further increase in scale, as large banks are in a better position to develop sophisticated risk measurement methods, such as the advanced internal rating-based approach.

This changing banking environment focuses attention on competitive conditions in Europe and on the viability of its – until recently – sheltered banks. After all domestic banks have long enjoyed comparative advantages on the domestic markets for bonds and equity in the field of underwriting and trading activities, based on the existence of national currencies. Nowadays, in particular after the introduction of the euro, the efficiency of European banks will become more and more crucial in the light of the current and expected increase in competition,[2] which is particularly evident in the wholesale market segment. Less efficient banks run the risk of being pushed out of the market. Efficiency is also a decisive element in the game of mergers and take-overs, where inefficient banks are an easy and sought-after prey.[3]

This chapter seeks to discover the level and spread of bank efficiency in Europe. In particular, it focuses on differences across countries, various sizes of banks, and various bank type categories and on changes over time. Furthermore, it considers two related but diverging dimensions of efficiency. *Differences between countries* are contemplated, as national discrepancies in terms of institutions, supervisory rules, government interference, customer preferences and level of development may help to explain differences in efficiency. For each of the European nations, the degree of inefficiency of its banks is vitally important for public policy with respect to the viability of its banking industry in the near future, including the design and application of antitrust policies. In addition, they all have to face the consequences of ongoing consolidation and rationalization in their banking sectors.

Size differences between banks may be important, as banks do not operate in a single, unified banking market. Large, international banks concentrate their activities in international (or wholesale) markets, whereas small, national banks conduct their business mainly in local (or retail) markets. Competitive conditions, and hence the need to reduce cost and to increase efficiency, may vary strongly between these markets, as has already been noted in Chapter 4. Because banking data provide insufficient information to make precise distinctions between the various markets, this chapter uses the size of banks to capture such differences by approximation. *Differences between banking categories* are important as well, since the activities of diverging types of bank can be quite dissimilar and should not be ignored. Neglecting the impact of sizes and categories may lead to biased results if the distribution of sizes and categories is not the same for all countries. Finally, *movement of efficiency over time* is interesting as the banking landscape has been undergoing (and will continue to undergo) many shocks, necessitating ongoing efficiency improvement.

Many definitions of efficiency exist. Nowadays, *X-efficiency*, that is, the managerial ability to decide on input and output in order to minimize cost (or maximize revenues), is seen as the most important type of efficiency, much more than scale and scope effects, for example. Most econometric models on efficiency of banks focus on *cost* X-efficiency (Berger and Humprey, 1997). These models take the input prices and the level of output or its components as given. Alternative concepts are (standard) *profit* X-efficiency, which uses input prices and output prices as given, and alternative profit efficiency, which has the same explanatory variables as the cost function. Each efficiency concept adds some independent informational value (Berger and Mester, 1997). As profit can take a negative value, the models for profit efficiency, being logarithmic in nature, are less satisfactory. For Europe and the USA, Bos (2002) proves that one single cost frontier exists (which allows comparison of efficiency across countries or regions), but that this does not hold true for the profit frontier, due to markedly different market conditions. Hence the profit efficiency approach does not allow comparison across countries or regions. For these reasons, and in line with most of the literature, this chapter concentrates on cost efficiency.

Apart from X-efficiency, this chapter also considers *differences in cost levels* controlled for input prices and types of activities, which reflect the diversity of national conditions banks are facing. Cost differences between countries may be seen as indicators of national inefficiencies, caused by country-specific circumstances for banks, as mentioned above. In principle, managerial (in)ability and country-specific obstacles for banks may reflect mutually independent features of (in)efficiency. In practice, they may overlap in part, when differences in national conditions affect the measurement of X-efficiencies (that is, when unfavourable conditions are mistaken for X-inefficiency) and where differences in average managerial abilities between countries exist (and then are confused with cost differences).[4]

The literature is a treasury of single-country studies on efficiency in the banking industry. However, it is not difficult to prove that single-country studies are totally unsuitable for international comparisons and will yield misleading results. A bank's X-efficiency is commonly measured as its cost level compared to that of the best-practice banks of similar size (the so-called frontier), controlled for its types of banking activities and the input prices it faces. It can be shown that the performance of best-practice banks strongly diverges between countries. Thus, for an international comparison of X-efficiency, one needs to compare efficiency of banks with the European best-practice banks, not with the best-practice banks of the respective countries.[5] The number of studies on proper international comparison of efficiency, on the other hand, is limited.[6] In fact, such an international comparison is a truly heroic attempt, as the differences between countries in banking behaviour and in economic and institutional conditions are huge. As activities of banks diverge strongly and as some of these activities are highly complicated, capturing bank behaviour in a single model is a daunting task, even for a single country. Moreover, international comparisons are easily distorted by national differences in the distribution of banks over sizes and categories, a problem which will be dealt with in this chapter.

The organization of this chapter is as follows. Section 6.2 is of a methodological nature and introduces the translog multiproduct cost model, which will be used to estimate cost level differences, and the stochastic cost frontier approach which will be applied to determine X-inefficiencies. Section 6.3 discusses the model specification, the data employed and some econometric tests regarding specification choices. Section 6.4 presents Europe-wide empirical results for efficiency and cost level differences. The next two sections examine the impact on efficiency of, respectively, bank size classes and bank type categories. Section 6.7 investigates changes in efficiency and cost level differences over time.

6.2 METHODOLOGY

We seek to measure two dimensions of efficiency of banks: (i) X-efficiency, the managerial ability to decide on input and output in order to minimize cost, and (ii) national inefficiencies or differences in cost levels, reflecting national economic and institutional banking conditions. Cost differences are based on the translog cost function and X-inefficiencies are based on the stochastic cost frontier model, which is an extension of the translog cost function model. This section describes these models and explains their economic background.

6.2.1 Differences in Bank Cost Levels

The measurement and analysis of differences in bank cost levels is based on the assumption that the technology of an individual bank can be described by a production function which links the various types of banking output to input factors. Under proper conditions, a dual cost function can be derived, with output levels and factor prices as arguments. In line with most of the literature, this chapter uses the translog multiproduct function to describe costs. Christensen et al. (1973) proposed the translog multiproduct cost function as a second-order Taylor expansion, usually around the mean, of a generic function with all variables appearing as logarithms.[7] This translog cost function (TCF) is a flexible functional form and has proven to be an effective tool for the empirical assessment of efficiency. A Cobb–Douglas function would be too simple, whereas a Fourier transformation would be unnecessary complicated. The TCF reads as:

$$c_{it} = \alpha + \sum_j \beta_j x_{ijt} + \sum_j \sum_k \gamma_{jk} x_{ijt} x_{ikt} + v_{it} \tag{6.1}$$

The dependent variable c_{it} is the logarithm of the cost of production of the ith firm (i=1, ..., N) in year t (t=1, …, T). The explanatory variables x_{ijt} consist of output or output components and input prices. The two sum terms constitute the multiproduct translog cost function: the linear terms on the one hand and the squares and cross-terms on the other, each accompanied by the unknown parameters β_j and γ_{jk}, respectively. The last element of Equation (6.1), v_{it}, is the error term which accounts for random effects caused by the model specification.

The appropriate definition of output in banking has been a frequent topic of discussion, the two mainstreams being the *intermediation* approach and the *production* approach. The former assumes that a bank attracts deposits and other funds and transforms them into loans and investment in securities, using inputs such as labour, capital and materials. Interest payments are seen as part of the costs and the corresponding dual cost function includes not deposits but the interest rate paid on deposits as an input factor. Loans and investment are the output components. Examples of this view are Altunbas et al. (1994, 1995) and Barr et al. (1994). The latter approach assumes that a bank provides services related to loans and deposits. In this view, interest payments are not regarded as banking costs. The output components comprise loans and deposits. Examples of this approach can be found in Swank (1996), Resti (1997) and Berger and DeYoung (1997), among others. Since operating costs appear to make up the bulk of banks' cost inefficiency (Berger and Humphrey, 1991), this analysis, in line with most of the literature, takes the production approach.

Apart from loans, savings accounts and demand deposits are distinguished as production factors, each with its own range of services. The number of branches, regarded as an indicator of additional service of a bank to its clients, could also be seen as a production factor, but limited availability of data forms an impediment. To an increasing extent banks provide non-traditional services, such as trade in securities, asset management and investment funds for clients, proprietary trading, derivatives, guarantees and credit lines, securitization, and equity and bond emissions. This type of production is hardly if at all related to balance-sheet items, whereas other public information about the volume of these services is not available for individual banks. Following the examples of Resti (1997) and Berger and DeYoung (1997), this chapter approximates this type of off-balance sheet output as 'other (non-interest) income'. Two kinds of factor prices are included in the TCF, namely wages and the price of physical capital. The TCF can be used to estimate cost differences across countries or banking categories or over time, by adding dummy variables for countries, banking categories or years.

6.2.2 X-inefficiency

Two components of efficiency may be distinguished: *technical efficiency,* the ability to obtain maximum output from a given set of inputs, and *allocative efficiency*, the skill to use the inputs in optimal proportions, given their respective prices and the available production technology (Farrell, 1957). These two measures may be combined to provide a measure of total *economic efficiency*, or, if cost instead of production is considered, *cost efficiency*. Banks with the lowest costs, controlled for output volumes and input price level levels, form the efficient frontier. Errors, lags between the adoption of the production plan and its implementation, human inertia, distorted communications and uncertainty cause deviations from this efficient frontier of best-practice banks. These deviations reflect *X-inefficiency* (Leibenstein, 1966).[8]

Various approaches are available to estimate X-inefficiency (see for example Lozano-Vivas, 1998). All methods involve determining an efficient frontier on the basis of observed (sets of) minimal values rather than presupposing certain technologically determined minima. Each method, however, maintains different assumptions and may result in diverging estimates of inefficiency. Berger and Humphrey (1997) report a roughly equal split between applications of non-parametric and parametric techniques. *Non-parametric* approaches, such as data envelopment analysis (DEA) and free disposable hull (FDH) analysis, have the practical advantage that no functional form needs to be specified. At the same time, however, they do not allow for specification errors, so that such errors if they do exist, may be measured as inefficiency, raising the inefficiency estimate. The results of the DEA method are also sensitive to the number of constraints specified. An even greater disadvantage of these techniques is that they generally ignore prices and can, therefore, account only for technical rather than economic inefficiency. Technical inefficiency does not correspond to the concept of cost efficiency.

One of the various *parametric* methods is the stochastic frontier approach, which assumes that the error term is composed of the sum of a specification error and an inefficiency term. These two components can be distinguished by making one or more assumptions about the asymmetry of the distribution of the inefficiency term. Although such assumptions are not very restrictive, they are nevertheless criticized for being somewhat arbitrary. A flexible alternative for panel data is the distribution-free approach, which avoids any assumption regarding the distribution of the inefficiency term, but supposes that the error term for each bank over time is zero. Hence, the average predicted error of a bank is its estimated inefficiency. The assumption under this approach of – on average – zero specification errors for each bank is a very strong one, and, hence, a drawback. Moreover, shifts in time remain unidentified. Finally, the thick frontier method does not compare single banks with the best-practice banks on the frontier, but produces an inefficiency measure for the whole sample. The 25th percentile of the bank cost distribution is taken as the 'thick' frontier and the range between the 25th and 75th percentile as inefficiency. This approach avoids the influence of outliers, but at the same time assumes that all errors of the 25th percentile reflect only specification errors, not inefficiency. All approaches have their pros and cons. All in all, the stochastic frontier approach, which has been applied widely, is selected as – in principle – being the least biased. Berger and Mester (1997) have found that the efficiency estimates are fairly robust to differences in methodology, which fortunately makes the choice of efficiency measurement approach less critical.

The first stochastic frontier function for production was independently proposed by Aigner, Lovell and Schmidt (1977) and Meeusen and Van den Broeck (1977). Schmidt and Lovell (1979) presented its dual as a stochastic cost frontier (SCF) function. This SCF model elaborates on the TCF, splitting the error term into two components, one to account for random effects due to the model specification and another to account for cost X-inefficiencies:

$$c_{it} = \alpha + \sum_j \beta_j x_{ijt} + \sum_j \sum_k \gamma_{jk} x_{ijt} x_{ikt} + v_{it} + u_{it} \quad (6.2)$$

The v_{it}s are the specification errors of the TCF, which are assumed to be identically and independently $N(0,\sigma_v^2)$ distributed and the u_{it}s are *non-negative* random variables which describe cost inefficiency and are assumed to be identically and independently half-normally ($|N(0,\sigma_u^2)|$) distributed and to be independent from the v_{it}s. In other words, the density function of the u_{it}s is (twice) the positive half of the normal density function. The truncated-normal, gamma and exponential distributions are more general alternatives to describe u_{it}.[9] The exponential and the half-normal distributions assume that the density of observations of u_{it}s is highest at the frontier and declines gradually when moving away from the frontier, whereas the gamma distribution presupposes that the density of observations at first gradually increases when moving away from the frontier. In what follows, the more general truncated normal distribution $N(\mu,\sigma_v^2)$, with zero as the truncation point, has been applied, which provides a rich family of distributions, based on the ranges of parameters μ and σ_v^2, causing fewer technical problems than some of the alternative distributions. The cost inefficiency term may be constant over time for each bank ($u_{it} = u_i$ for all t), as it is assumed to be in the major part of this chapter; it may depend on time in a structural way ($u_{it} = u_i\,\text{f}(t)$), as in Section 6.7; or it may be wholly unrestricted.

Cost efficiency of a bank relative to the cost frontier estimated by model (6.2) is calculated as follows. As c_{it} is expressed in logarithms, costs are defined as $C_{it} = \exp(c_{it})$, where 'exp' refers to the exponential function. X is the matrix containing the explanatory variables. Cost efficiency is defined as:[10]

$$EFF_{it} = E(C_{it} \mid u_{it} = 0, X) \,/\, E(C_{it} \mid u_{it}, X) = 1/\exp(u_{it}) \quad (6.3)$$

In other words, efficiency is the ratio of expected costs on the frontier (where production would be completely efficient, or $u_{it} = 0$) and expected costs, conditional upon the observed degree of inefficiency.[11] Numerator and denominator are both conditional upon X, the given level of output components and input prices. Values of EFF_{it} range from 0 to 1. The inverse of EFF_{it} is inefficiency, $INEFF_{it} = \exp(u_{it})$, which is bounded between 1 and ∞.

The SCF model encompasses the TCF in cases where the inefficiencies u_{it} can be ignored. A test on the restriction, which reduces the former to the latter, is available after reparameterization of the model of Equation (6.2) by replacing σ_v^2 and σ_u^2 by, respectively, $\sigma^2 = \sigma_v^2 + \sigma_u^2$ and $\lambda = \sigma_u^2/(\sigma_v^2 + \sigma_u^2)$, see Battese and Corra (1977). The λ parameter can be employed to test whether an SCF model is essential at all. Acceptance of the null hypothesis $\lambda = 0$ would imply that $\sigma_u = 0$ and hence that the term u_{it} should be removed from the model, so that Equation (6.2) narrows down to the TCF of Equation (6.1).

6.3 MODEL SPECIFICATION, DATA AND ECONOMETRIC ISSUES

For each bank, the translog cost model aims at linking the level of the multiproduct output and the prices of the input factors as closely as possible to total operating costs, excluding interest rate income. There is, of course, the trade-off between the advantage of having more output factors, allowing a higher degree of accuracy in explaining costs, on the one hand, and the possible disadvantage of increased multicollinearity between these output factors, on the other. After examining the results of preliminary calculations, the output components loans, savings and demand deposits are taken, as well as other income as proxy for other services. For the USA, in any case, Berger and Mester (1997) have found that functional form and choice of variables usually make fairly little difference in terms of either average efficiency or the ranking of individual banks.

The definitions of the variables are as follows: costs are operational expenses,[12] loans consist of commercial, consumer and mortgage loans, demand deposits include current accounts, savings is made up of savings accounts, savings deposits and time deposits, and non-interest income consists mainly of commission and revenues from financial transactions. For each bank, the wage rate is calculated as the ratio of total wages and the number of employees, whereas the price of capital is the ratio of 'other non-interest expenditure' and 'premises and fixed assets'. Both variables are approximations, as interbank differences in labour productivity and average working time are ignored,[13] while price of capital should be interpreted broadly, as 'other non-interest expenditure' includes also outlay on information technology and materials. The balance item premises and fixed assets (PFA) may also be rather unreliable, due to book-keeping tricks, but, further on, a solution is proposed and applied to mitigate this problem.

To estimate inefficiency, the model has been applied to data on banks in the 15 countries currently making up the European Union, plus Switzerland, where many prominent banks are domiciled. Austria is not represented in the sample, as data on demand deposits were lacking. The sample of banks consists of all banking categories, such as enumerated in the lower part of Table 6.A.1 in Appendix 6.A, in both foreign and domestic hands, over the years 1990–97, in as far as they are included in the IBCA-Fitch database. For all countries, the value series are expressed in one currency, namely Deutsche Marks. Any bank-year combination, for which at least one of the dependent or explanatory variables is zero or missing, has been deleted from the sample.[14] In particular, the absence of data on (one of) the two input prices reduced the sample. This selection resulted in a sample of 2 563 banks and 6 358 bank-year observations. Table 6.A.1 presents the distribution of these numbers over the countries as well as other country-specific characteristics of the selected European banks.

Reliable and simple indicators of efficiency are very hard to find. The cost-income ratio, the interest-rate margin, the labour-cost share and many other indices or ratios which are often used, fail as efficiency indicators, as was proven in Section 1.2.[15] Table 6.A.1 provides useful information on the national banking systems, but none of the shown ratios stand up as an all-embracing indicator of inefficiency. In order to have a reference for the discussion on the empirical results in later sections, we here present a piece of accepted wisdom on the ranking of the inefficiency of countries' banking sectors, based on direct observation, in-depth knowledge or, perhaps, prejudice. According to this wisdom, banks in France, Germany and, in particular, Southern European countries, such as Greece, Italy, Portugal and Spain, are less efficient, on average, than banks in the other Western European countries. Arguments for the alleged diverging level of efficiency are more severe regulation by the supervisory authorities, interference by local government in the German *Länder,* which reduces competition, financial conservatism, a low level of consolidation and an extended network of branches (Germany), strong direct interference by the government (France and Italy) and lagging economic development (Greece, Spain, Portugal).[16] Banks in the UK are often seen as more advanced and exposed to stronger competition.[17] It remains to be seen how and to what extent these diverging national institutional and economic conditions affect inefficiency. Of course, in each country there may exist large differences in efficiency between, for instance, the major international banks and the small local banks. Furthermore, the banking industry is developing quickly, so that established popular opinions may now be obsolete. It is obvious that a convincing empirical assessment of the efficiency of the banking sectors in the European countries would be highly welcome and the remainder of this chapter seeks to provide just such a yardstick.

6.3.1 Model Specification and Econometric Issues

The specification of the translog cost function, which also constitutes the core of the SCF model, requires a number of choices. As mentioned above, loans, savings, demand deposits and other income (as a proxy for other services) have been chosen as output components. Some alternative choices are discussed here in order to further justify the model used in the rest of this chapter. Table 6.1 presents the statistics that have helped to select one of the various models considered, viz. the logarithms of the likelihood (ln L) for, respectively, the SCF model and the TCF, ditto per observation (ln L/n)[18] and the corresponding standard deviations. For the SCF model, the latter includes both the specification error and the inefficiency term. Note that the more expanded models encompass the elementary ones.

Table 6.1 Specifications of the SCF and TCF models

	No input prices	Wages	Capital prices		Wages and capital prices			
				corrected		corrected		
							incl. loans/assets	
								restrict.
columns	*1*	*2*	*3*	*4*	*5*	*6*	*7*	*8*
no.	6 358	6 358	6 358	6 358	6 358	6 358	6 350	6 350
Stochastic cost frontier (SCF)								
ln L	-626.1	-504.2	-516.1	-455.4	-425.8	-331.8	97.5	88.9
ln L/n	-0.098	-0.079	-0.081	-0.072	-0.067	-0.052	0.015	0.014
σ^2	0.289	0.300	0.280	0.269	0.288	0.287	0.260	0.261
Translog cost function (TCF)								
ln L	-2 130	-2 039	-1 952	-1 967	-1 896	-1 868	-1 330	-1 373
ln L/n	-0.335	-0.321	-0.307	-0.309	-0.298	-0.294	-0.209	-0.216
σ^2	0.115	0.112	0.109	0.109	0.107	0.106	0.090	0.091

According to economic theory, the models considered should include input prices. Data concerning wage rate and price of capital are available, but the quality of the observed prices may be somewhat poor. Both variables are rough approximations, as interbank differences in labour productivity and average working time are ignored, and the price of capital is proxied as the ratio of 'other non-interest expenditure' and the balance sheet item 'premises and fixed assets' (*PFA*), whereas the latter may be rather unreliable, due to book-keeping operations. Nevertheless, despite these shortcomings in the data, none of the two considered input prices could be deleted, for either the SCF or the TCF: the likelihood falls significantly when wages or capital prices are omitted. By far, the best result is obtained when both input prices are included.

In order to correct for the alleged poor quality of *PFA*, we follow Resti (1997) in replacing the original data of this variable by the model values of the translog regression of *PFA* on costs (C) and total assets (TA):

$$\ln PFA = \alpha_0 + \alpha_1 \ln C + \alpha_2 \ln TA + \alpha_3 (\ln C)^2 + \alpha_4 (\ln TA)^2 + \alpha_5 \ln C \ln TA + \varepsilon$$
$$(\bar{R}^2 = 0.84) \qquad (6.4)$$

This correction brings the book-keeping values of *PFA* more in line with the size of the bank, proxied by costs and total assets. In general, the adjustments are small, but they are influential, as they avoid close-to-zero values of *PFA*, which has a major effect on the respective ratio.[19] The correction leads to a significant increase in the logarithm of the likelihood of both models. In the remainder of this chapter we therefore use corrected instead of original capital price data.

The relation between efficiency and the risk inherent in the bank's asset behaviour is usually ignored in the literature on efficiency in the banking industry. In general, banks which grant loans to more risky borrowers will also incur additional monitoring costs, for instance, by employing more skilled labour or using advanced information technology to manage these risks (Diamond, 1984). Hence, higher risk goes with additional operating costs. Ruthenberg and Elias (1996) discuss three available risk variables and find that the ratio of loans to total assets (*L/A*) is the most appropriate for European banks. Indeed, inclusion of this risk measure tremendously improves the models in terms of increase of the logarithm of their likelihood.[20] Hence, this risk variable is included in the models we will use.

Two standard properties of cost functions are linear homogeneity in the input prices and cost-exhaustion (Jorgenson, 1986). They imply the following restrictions on the parameters, assuming – without loss of generality – that the index j in Equation (6.1) is 1 and 2, respectively, for wages and capital prices:

$$\beta_1 + \beta_2 = 1,\ \gamma_{11} + \gamma_{12} = \gamma_{21} + \gamma_{22} = 0, \text{ and } \gamma_{k,1} + \gamma_{k,2} = 0 \quad \text{for } k = 3, \ldots, 7 \quad (6.5)$$

The index k refers to output components and other explanatory variables, such as the risk variable. The first restriction stems from cost exhaustion, reflecting that the sum of cost shares is equal to unity. In other words, the value of the two inputs is equal to total cost. Linear homogeneity in the input prices requires that cost shares and cost flexibility are homogeneous of degree zero in the input prices. This is reflected in the second and third sets of restrictions in (6.5). These eight restrictions reduce the logarithm of the likelihood of the SCF by 8.6 points. According to the likelihood ratio test, which as a matter of fact holds only asymptotically, these restrictions would be rejected at the 5 per cent significance level but accepted at the 2.5 per cent level.[21] However, it is well-known that restrictions tend to be rejected as the sample size increases. This holds in particular in this case, where the inaccuracy of the data prevents exact fulfilment of the restrictions. Henceforth, based on economic theory as well as on the 'nearby fulfilment' of the restrictions, both price homogeneity and cost exhaustion have been imposed. This is equivalent to rewriting cost and prices using one of the prices as a numerary. By this method, the number of parameters is reduced from 35 to 27. For this reason, the model in the far-left column of Table 6.1 is selected for the next analysis.

6.4 MEASUREMENT OF EFFICIENCY

As a first step to assessing banking efficiency in Europe and to establish efficiency differences across countries, the SCF model was applied to all banks. For each country, the level of efficiency was calculated as an average across its banks, see Table 6.2. For Finland, Ireland and Sweden, these numbers may be less reliable, as they are based on less than 20 observations, and, as a matter of fact, on even fewer banks. Therefore, the outcomes for

Table 6.2 European-wide estimates of X-efficiency using the SCF model

Countries	Number of observations	Standard SCF	Ranking	Extended SCF	Ranking
Belgium	44	0.521	14	0.484	14
Denmark	57	0.597	9	0.543	13
Finland	13	0.690	5	0.677	5
France	964	0.568	12	0.552	12
Germany	2 983	0.740	2	0.755	1
Greece	40	0.500	15	0.395	15
Ireland	20	0.798	1	0.697	4
Italy	1 221	0.578	11	0.601	10
Luxembourg	177	0.738	3	0.717	2
Netherlands	164	0.641	8	0.623	8
Portugal	67	0.685	6	0.649	6
Spain	105	0.548	13	0.577	11
Sweden	17	0.590	10	0.617	9
Switzerland	299	0.731	4	0.705	3
UK	187	0.666	7	0.649	6
Weighted Averages		*0.690*		*0.696*	
λ		*0.909*		*0.916*	
σ^2_{mle}		*0.260*		*0.261*	
σ^2_{ols}		*0.090*		*0.086*	
R^2		*0.965*		*0.966*	

Notes: 'Standard' is the stochastic cost frontier model and 'Extended' also includes dummy variables for banking categories. Shading refers to countries with a limited number of observations.

these three countries will be ignored in the following discussions and to indicate this, their results in Tables 6.2 and 6.3 are shaded.

Towards the end of Section 6.2, a test was described to compare the SCF, as a model of the cost structure of banks, with the TCF. The former appears to be superior because the hypothesis of the test, $\sigma_u^2 = 0$ or no inefficiency, is rejected at a higher level of significance. Hence, efficiency differences are of great importance in explaining cost differences between banks.

The average efficiency in Europe is estimated at 69 per cent. This implies that 31 per cent of costs could be avoided by improving efficiency. This loss is high compared to many other studies, which indicate a loss of around 20 per cent (Berger and Humphrey, 1997, Altunbas et al., 2001). As a matter of fact, the range of estimates in the literature is wide (see also Gehrig and Sheldon, 1999). The use of a single model for banks in such a large number of countries may lead to an overestimation of inefficiency, as the differences across countries may contribute to the heterogeneity of the sample, see Mester (1996).[22]

These first results indicate that banks from Germany, Luxembourg, Switzerland and Portugal are amongst the most efficient ones, whereas, on average, banks in Greece, Belgium, Spain and France are least efficient. Banks from the UK, the Netherlands, Italy and Denmark take up intermediate positions in these respects.[23] Part of the results coincides with the accepted-wisdom expectations described above. Banks in Greece, Spain and France are often mentioned as being less efficient. Higher efficiency estimates of banks in Luxembourg and Switzerland are somewhat misleading, as they do not necessarily reflect higher managerial performance but are due to special circumstances including bank secrecy, zero tax rates for foreigners and a stable currency in their country, which makes it easier to attract (foreign) investment cheaply.[24]

Not all results are in keeping with common belief (not that this necessarily makes them less true). Germany is commonly reputed to be probably less efficient, but the efficiency estimates in Table 6.2 suggest otherwise. For that matter, the favourable efficiency assessment for Germany is also supported by the low cost share in Table 6.A.1 in Appendix 6.A. Probably, the German efficiency estimate is strongly affected by the composition of the German banking sample in terms of categories, where savings and cooperative banks outnumber the commercial banks more commonly found elsewhere. This matter will be investigated in greater detail in Section 6.6.[25]

Actually, due to the low level of consolidation and the size of Germany, the German banks dominate the Europe-wide sample numerically. The question may arise whether this German overrepresentation in any way affects the results of Table 6.2. To find this out, we analysed three alternative samples with a strongly reduced number of German observations (or banks). The effects on both the spread in efficiency estimates and the ranking are very limited,[26] even in the sample where the number of German observations is reduced by more than three quarters, see Table 6.C.1 in Appendix 6.C. German banks continue to rank among the most efficient ones. Hence, the overrepresentation of German banks has not distorted the results.

Other unexpected results may be that British banks, on average, take an intermediate position only and that Belgian banks are among the least efficient ones. Probably, many would not expect to see Portugal among the more efficient countries. However, the liberalization of the Portuguese banking system in 1987 and 1992, which prompted increased competition and strong investment in information technology, may have contributed to a substantial increase in efficiency.

Empirically, the SCF approach appears to be a superior tool in explaining costs. However, this does not imply that this method is best able to explain differences in cost efficiency *across countries*. For this reason, the next section presents an alternative approach.

6.4.1 Differences in Cost Levels across Europe

The preceding section considered *X-efficiency*, that is the managerial ability to decide on input and output quantities in order to minimize cost. This section looks at *differences in cost levels*, controlled for types of activities and input prices, which reflect diverging national institutional and economic conditions banks are facing. Cost differences between countries can be interpreted as *national inefficiencies*, due to country-specific obstacles for banks. In principle, managerial (in)ability and country-specific obstacles for banks can reflect mutually independent features of (in)efficiency. In practice, they may overlap in part, when differences in national conditions affect the measurement of X-efficiencies (that is when unfavourable conditions are mistaken for X-inefficiency) or when differences in average managerial abilities between countries exist (and then are mixed up with cost differences). Differences between countries are measured by adding country dummies to Equation (6.1).

The left-hand side of Table 6.3 presents the estimates of the relative cost levels in the countries considered. The 97 per cent goodness of fit indicates a satisfactory model performance. On the whole, the ranking of countries based on cost levels corresponds to that based on X-inefficiencies, which is rather remarkable given the different underlying concepts. This is also clear from Figure 6.1, where cost levels are plotted against X-inefficiencies, showing a strong linear relationship. Apparently, these concepts show a certain degree of overlap or they are tangled up. For some countries, however, this cost-based ranking is more in line with 'accepted wisdom' than the ranking based on inefficiency. According to the cost-related criterion, the German banks are no longer among the most efficient ones, their place in the 'top 4' now being taken by the British banks. Evidently, cost inefficiency in Germany is not

Table 6.3 Europe-wide estimates of cost effects using a translog cost model

	Standard TCF				Extended TCF			
Countries	*Dummy coeff.*[a]		*Cost effects*[b]	*Ranking*	*Dummy coeff.*[a]		*Cost effects*	*Ranking*
Belgium	0.093	(1.6)	1.15	11	0.156	(2.7)	1.16	13
Denmark	0.088	(2.0)	1.14	10	0.135	(3.1)	1.13	10
Finland	-0.214	(2.6)	0.84	4	-0.146	(1.8)	0.86	4
France	0.114	(4.4)	1.17	12	0.154	(5.9)	1.16	12
Germany	-0.048	(1.9)	1.00	7	-0.019	(0.7)	0.97	8
Greece	0.234	(3.9)	1.32	15	0.386	(6.4)	1.46	15
Ireland	-0.299	(4.4)	0.77	2	-0.173	(2.5)	0.83	3
Italy	0.114	(4.4)	1.17	12	0.149	(5.5)	1.15	11
Luxembourg	-0.240	(6.7)	0.82	3	-0.209	(6.0)	0.80	2
Netherlands	0	—	1.04	9	0	—	0.99	9
Portugal	-0.124	(2.8)	0.92	5	-0.080	(1.9)	0.91	6
Spain	0.172	(4.5)	1.24	14	0.203	(5.3)	1.21	14
Sweden	-0.039	(0.5)	1.00	7	-0.048	(0.6)	0.94	7
Switzerland	-0.337	(10.1)	0.75	1	-0.254	(7.4)	0.77	1
UK	-0.116	(3.6)	0.93	6	-0.117	(3.7)	0.88	5
Bank type categories								
Commercial					0	—	1.03	
Cooperative					0.007	(0.6)	1.04	
Savings					0.066	(5.0)	1.10	
Investment					0.175	(6.9)	1.23	
M & L term					-0.355	(8.1)	0.72	
Real Estate					0.091	(2.4)	1.13	
Spec. Gov.					-0.347	(9.2)	0.73	
σ^2_{ols}	0.080				0.077			
Adjusted R^2	0.969				0.970			

[a] T-values between parenthesis; [b] geometric mean for 'cost effects' is set at 1.

Notes: 'Standard' is the translog cost model and 'Extended' also includes dummy variables for banking categories. Shading refers to countries with a limited number of observations.

attributable to weak managerial behaviour – indeed, X-efficiency is high – but to institutional or economic conditions, in line with what is observed directly (severe regulation, interference by government, financial conservatism, and so on). The 'outlier' position of Germany in this respect is also clear from Figure 6.1. In 8th position, the cost-based ranking of the Belgian banks is less humble than its X-efficiency ranking (11th).

Apparently, managerial performance in Belgium may be relatively weak, whereas the institutional or economic conditions with regard to costs are not far from the average level in Europe.

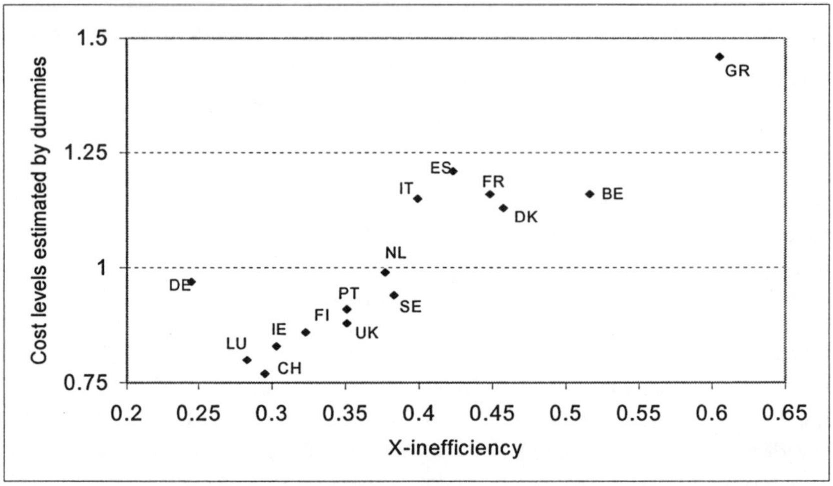

Figure 6.1 Relationships between X-inefficiency and cost levels estimated by dummies

The right-hand side of Table 6.3 takes also the various banking categories into account by using dummies. The results in terms of rankings are rather similar. The dummy estimates indicate that, on average, costs are significantly lower for some specialized (medium- and long-term credit institutions) or privileged (specialized government credit) banks, while they are substantially higher for other (especially investment) banks.

This section presented European-wide estimates of X-efficiency and cost level differences using a extended sample of banks of various size classes and bank type categories and from many countries. Mester (1996) pointed out that the heterogeneity of such samples might affect the estimates – more in particular, that they may cause overestimation of inefficiency. Besides, such an all-bank sample may distort the comparison across countries, when certain size classes or bank type categories show deviant behaviour in terms of efficiency or costs and, in addition, are over- or under-represented in certain countries. Single country studies would reduce heterogeneity, but they would not enable us to make useful comparisons across countries. Therefore, in the next section, heterogeneity is reduced by examination of, respectively, separate size-classes and separate bank type categories.

6.5 EFFICIENCY FOR VARIOUS BANK SIZES

In order to obtain more homogeneous samples, the SCF model has been applied to bank sizes and bank category classes. A simultaneous analysis of sizes and categories is impossible, because we cannot break up the sample into both bank size and bank type classes – the resulting samples would simply be too small, see Table 6.4. Both types of refined analysis are similar in nature but different in direction. This section deals with bank sizes, whereas the next section investigates the various bank categories. We distinguish four bank size classes, where the volume of total assets was used to split the all-bank sample. The small-bank class runs up to 500 million Deutsche Marks (DM) in total assets, the large-bank class contains banks with assets above 5 billion DM and the two intermediate classes are split at 1 250 million DM.

Table 6.4 Distribution of banks over size and categories classes

Total assets [a]	Commercial	Co-operative	Savings	Invest-ment	Others	All banks
0–500	193	606	86	29	1	915
500–1 250	189	289	214	19	14	725
1 250–5 000	191	134	325	18	21	689
5 000+	205	62	99	21	50	437
Total	778	1 091	724	87	86	2 766

[a] Millions of Deutsche Marks.

The average efficiency estimates for countries are presented in Table 6.5. Of course, the break-up into size classes reduces the available number of banks in each cell.[27] Where less than 10 banks are involved, (light) shading indicates that the estimate of the country efficiency is based on a (too) small sample. Note that the estimation results themselves are based on large samples, and hence are steady, and that only the reliability of estimated country effects may suffer from the sometimes small (country-specific) samples. For the latter reason, we do not investigate the detailed country effects in Table 6.5, but only draw general conclusions.

Differences in efficiency between size classes appear to be substantial. Efficiency is high for the smallest banks at 76.8 per cent and low for the largest banks at 41.5 per cent. As larger banks are more complex and therefore more difficult to manage it is no surprise that differences between strong and weak management increase with bank size. An alternative

Table 6.5 *Mean X-efficiency by country and by bank-size class*

	Class 1			Class 2			Class 3			Class 4					
Total assets [a]	*<500*			*500-<1 250*			*1 250-<5 000*			*5 000+*			*Weighted* [b]		
	Effi-ciency	*# of banks*	*Rank-ing*	*Effi-ciency*	*# of banks*	*Rank-ing*	*Effi-ciency*	*# of banks*	*Rank-ing*	*Effi-ciency*	*# of banks*	*Rank-ing*	*effi-ciency*	*Rank-ing* [c]	*Ran-king* [d]
Belgium	0.88	3	1	0.51	2	13	0.26	3	14	0.35	10	9	0.44	11	11
Denmark	0.57	6	10	0.57	8	11	0.51	5	9	0.24	6	14	0.48	10	14
Finland	—	—	—	0.62	2	8	0.73	1	1	0.27	4	13	0.44	13	13
France	0.64	65	7	0.59	63	10	0.44	93	13	0.37	100	7	0.49	8	12
Germany	0.80	599	2	0.78	468	4	0.70	375	2	0.52	104	3	0.75	1	2
Greece	0.57	4	11	0.50	7	14	0.20	4	15	0.17	5	15	0.37	15	15
Ireland	—	—	—	0.79	2	2	0.69	6	3	0.53	3	2	0.67	4	1
Italy	0.71	125	5	0.61	78	9	0.48	92	12	0.33	60	10	0.56	6	9
Luxembourg	0.67	10	6	0.73	23	6	0.63	25	6	0.65	27	1	0.67	3	3
Netherlands	0.63	14	8	0.83	6	1	0.63	12	5	0.45	18	5	0.59	5	5
Portugal	0.57	2	9	0.79	5	3	0.58	10	8	0.31	14	11	0.49	9	10
Spain	—	—	—	0.56	2	12	0.48	8	11	0.40	27	6	0.43	14	6
Sweden	0.50	1	12	—	—	—	0.64	2	4	0.36	6	8	0.44	12	7
Switzerland	0.77	65	3	0.72	42	7	0.61	33	7	0.46	23	4	0.68	2	4
UK	0.76	21	4	0.74	17	5	0.50	20	10	0.28	30	12	0.53	7	8
Total [e]	*0.77*	*915*		*0.73*	*725*		*0.61*	*689*		*0.42*	*437*		*0.66*		

Number of observations	1910	1664	1581	1195
σ^2_{mle}	0.138	0.196	0.474	1.459
λ	0.888	0.912	0.979	0.994
σ^2_v	0.015	0.017	0.010	0.009
σ^2_{ols}	0.052	0.065	0.077	0.113
R^2, adjusted	0.874	0.787	0.825	0.941

[a] Millions of Deutsche Marks; [b] weighted average over the four size classes; [c] ranking of preceding column; [d] ranking of weighted average of rankings over the four size classes; [e] for efficiencies: weighted average over the countries.

Notes: Shading refers to countries with a limited number of banks in the respective class. The total number of banks is 2 766, which is higher than the sample total 2 558. This is due to the fact that over the years some banks move from one size class in another (and hence are counted twice).

explanation could be that small banks are more similar to one another, while large banks constitute a less homogeneous class, where assuming one common underlying frontier may cause overestimation of inefficiency (Mester 1996). Remarkably, however, the results indicate that the translog cost function itself fits better for the larger banks (see, in Table 6.5, the lower values of σ^2_v for the last two classes), in spite of their relatively more complex production structure. This makes the alternative explanation less plausible, as – in a sense – a better fit implies similarity, not heterogeneity. The distribution of banks over size and category classes in Table 6.4 also does not indicate similarity within bank size classes, since each class contains banks in various categories. In any case, the results should be interpreted with caution.

The limited reliability of country effects due to the small country-specific samples does not prohibit a (rough) comparison of inefficiency levels across countries. For each country, the last columns in Table 6.5 present, respectively, the weighted average of efficiencies over the four classes, the country's ranking and the ranking of the weighted average of rankings over the four classes, in short: weighted rankings. In principle, this weighted efficiency and its ranking are more precise than the results in Table 6.2, as they are based on more refined estimates (implying a separate frontier for each class). For a number of countries, the ranking is somewhat different, but the general picture does not change substantially. An important issue is that if the size distribution of banks over the classes within each country is not uniform, a systematic distortion may occur, due to the correlation between inefficiency and bank size. Weighted ranking aims at avoiding this type of distortion. An eloquent case in point is Spain, where 73 per cent of the observed banks fall into the highest size class. Since these large banks, on average, are estimated to be highly inefficient, Spain ranked as a country with rather inefficient banks (13th in Table 6.2, 14th in Table 6.5). However, in terms of efficiency, the Spanish large banks perform well compared to other large banks, resulting in a favourable 6th ranking in Class 4, and also in the 'ranking of the weighted average of rankings over the four classes'. A similar major shift occurs also in the case of Sweden, although based on a much smaller sample.

We conclude that the bank-size class efficiency estimates for the countries considered are more accurate, as they use more homogeneous samples. Even more important is the weighted ranking, although it is a rather forced index, sensitive to the small country-specific samples, which nevertheless is able to correct for systematic distortion if the bank-size distribution for certain countries deviates from the average one.

Table 6.C.2 in Appendix 6.C presents a similar exercise for cost effects based on the application of the translog cost model for the various bank-size classes. The various cost functions fit very well, as indicated by high adjusted R^2 values; the goodness of fit is even the highest for the largest banks (0.95).

Nonetheless, different from the SCF approach, residual errors increase with the bank size, so some heterogeneity exists even in this logarithmic specification. The weighted cost differences and the *weighted ranking* based on the four size classes (last column in Table 6.C.2) are rather similar to the results based on the all-banks sample in Table 6.3. Exceptions are Belgium, ranking 6th instead of 11th ranking, and Portugal (9th instead of 5th). These countries have mainly large banks and the more refined large-bank estimation results differ from those of the all-bank sample. Here we do not find the kind of systematic distortion we observed in the inefficiency estimates above.

6.6 EFFICIENCY FOR VARIOUS BANK CATEGORIES

As the assumption of one frontier for all bank type categories may cause overestimation of inefficiency, this section aims at reducing heterogeneity by applying the SCF model to separate bank categories.[28] Table 6.6 reveals that efficiency estimates appear to vary strongly across categories. Cooperative banks form a category of mainly small and less complex banks,[29] where the estimated inefficiencies are small only: 16 per cent on average. Savings banks, too, have limited inefficiencies: 20 per cent on average. Although these banks are often rather large, their structure is still less complex. Increasing inefficiency is found in investment banks, 'other categories' (taken together because the samples of the three other categories are too small for a separate SCF model to be estimated) and commercial banks, respectively. Probably, commercial banks are more complex than other banks, as is also indicated by the lower model fit (or the higher σ^2_v).[30] Apart from that, this category may also still be too heterogeneous, causing overestimation of inefficiency.

Note that the observed inefficiency differences across the various categories deviate distinctly from the cost level differences as estimated above, see last row in Table 6.6. For instance, savings banks are efficient, but have higher costs than other bank type categories (for instance costs related to branches), whereas commercial banks are inefficient but face an average cost level. Here it is evident that efficiency and costs measure different phenomena.

The estimation results themselves are based on large samples, and hence are steady. However, the reliability of estimated country effects may suffer from the sometimes small country-specific samples. For this reason, we do not investigate the country effects in Table 6.6 in detail, but only draw general conclusions. The last two columns present, respectively, the weighted average of efficiencies and the 'ranking of the weighted average of rankings', both over the five categories. In principle, these weighted efficiencies are

Table 6.6 Mean X-efficiency by country and by bank categories (1990–97)

	Commercial			Cooperative			Savings			Investment			Other categor.[a]			Weighted [b]	
	Effic.	#[c]	*rank*	*Effic.*	#	*rank*	*Effic.*	#	*rank*	*Effic.*	#	*rank*	*Effic.*	#	*rank*	*Effic.*	*rank*[d]
Belgium	0.252	14	13	0.916	1	2	0.372	1	14				0.710	2	3	0.347	13
Denmark	0.278	20	11				0.830	1	2							0.305	12
Finland	0.336	4	8	0.895	1	4	0.688	1	8				0.034	1	13	0.423	9
France	0.330	166	9	0.762	68	7	0.759	21	6	0.559	2	7	0.536	8	7	0.483	10
Germany	0.388	113	6	0.855	799	5	0.825	560	3	0.685	1	5	0.387	30	8	0.799	5
Greece	0.265	13	12										0.189	2	12	0.255	15
Ireland	0.519	6	2				0.666	1	9	0.740	1	3	0.339	2	9	0.520	4
Italy	0.244	66	14	0.794	164	6	0.583	63	11	0.486	3	9	0.580	15	6	0.621	11
Luxembourg	0.548	67	1	0.701	2	9	0.987	1	1	0.749	3	2	0.961	1	2	0.572	1
Netherlands	0.444	32	3	0.656	1	10	0.802	1	5	0.524	6	8	0.965	1	1	0.482	3
Portugal	0.323	18	10	0.903	1	3	0.704	3	7	0.783	4	1	0.279	1	10	0.453	8
Spain	0.223	9	15	0.718	3	8	0.664	19	10	0.359	1	10	0.645	2	4	0.542	14
Sweden	0.361	7	7				0.508	1	12							0.379	7
Switzerland	0.442	86	4	0.982	3	1	0.821	12	4	0.701	33	4	0.584	16	5	0.557	2
UK	0.415	52	5				0.465	1	13	0.651	19	6	0.222	2	11	0.471	6
Total[e]	*0.375*	*673*		*0.839*	*1043*		*0.793*	*686*		*0.666*	*73*		*0.487*	*83*		*0.688*	

λ	0.983	0.819	0.965	0.966	0.995
σ^2_{mle}	1.477	0.061	0.087	0.306	1.067
σ^2_v	0.025	0.011	0.003	0.010	0.005
σ^2_{ols}	0.166	0.027	0.017	0.076	0.137
R^2, adjusted	0.958	0.985	0.985	0.961	0.942
Cost levels [f]	—	+1%	+7%	+19%	-17%

[a] Medium- and long-term credit institutions, real estate and mortgage banks and specialized government banks; [b] weighted average across banks; [c] number of banks; [d] ranking based on weighted average of category related rankings; [e] for efficiency: weighted averages across banks; [f] see Table 6.3.

Note: Shading refers to countries with a limited number of banks for the respective category.

more precise than the results in Table 6.2, as they are based on more refined estimates (where each class has its own implied frontier).

An important issue is that, if the size distribution of banks over the classes within each country is not uniform, a certain systematic distortion may occur, due to the correlation between inefficiency and bank category. The *weighted rankings* aim at avoiding this type of distortion. Actually, across countries, banks are distributed quite differently over the various banking categories. A striking example is Germany, where more than 90 per cent of the banks are of the cooperative and savings bank type: plain banking institutions, where inefficiency is limited (or the estimates of inefficiency are low due to the fact that these categories are less heterogeneous). This strong concentration of relatively efficient cooperative and savings banks in Germany resulted in a high average level of efficiency (see Table 6.2 or Table 6.6, second column from right). However, within these categories – and among the other categories – German banks are not the most efficient ones.[31] After correction for this category effect, the German efficiency turns out to be just slightly above average (see last column in Table 6.6). A similar bias manifested itself for Italy and Spain where, respectively, 73 per cent and 64 per cent of the banks are cooperative and savings banks.[32] A big ranking shift in the opposite direction occurs for the Dutch banks, 78 per cent of which are commercial banks. Commercial banks have, on average, high inefficiencies but *relatively,*

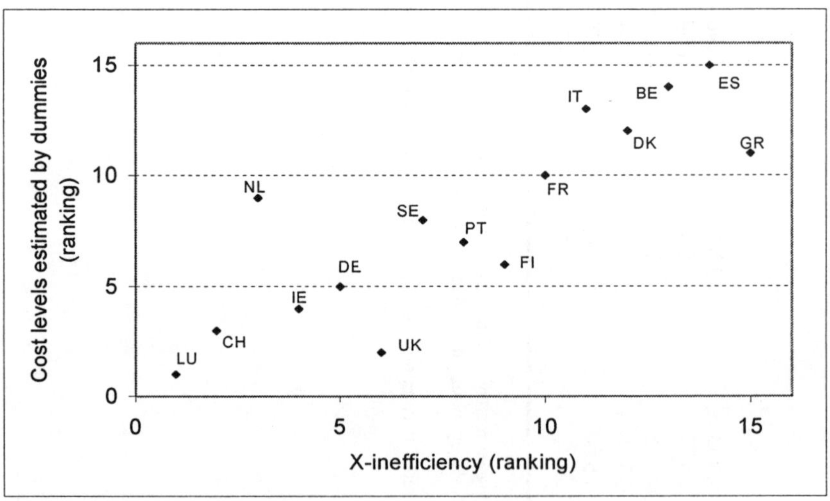

Figure 6.2 Relationships between the rankings of X-inefficiency and cost levels

the Dutch commercial banks are among the most efficient. After correction, the Dutch ranking is 3rd (see Table 6.6) instead of 8th (as in Table 6.2).

Table 6.C.3 in Appendix 6.C presents a similar exercise for cost effects based on the application of the translog cost model for the various bank type categories. The weighted cost differences, their rankings and the *weighted ranking* based on the five bank type categories (lowest left-hand section of the table) are rather similar to the results based on the all-banks sample in Table 6.6. Here we do not find systematic distortions as observed with the inefficiency estimates above. The weighted cost difference rankings are similar to the weighted X-inefficiency rankings from Table 6.6, as is clear from Figure 6.2, where both bank-category weighted rankings are plotted. In the Netherlands, the X-inefficiency is lower than expected given the cost levels, whereas the X-inefficiency is somewhat higher than expected in the UK, Finland and Greece.

We conclude that the separate bank-type category efficiency estimates for the countries considered are more accurate because they use more homogeneous samples. More importantly, the weighted ranking, despite its artificial nature, is able to reveal systematic distortion in countries where there is an unusual concentration of certain bank type categories, as in Germany. We regard this yardstick as the most 'reliable' measure of X-efficiency ranking across countries.

6.7 CHANGES IN EFFICIENCY AND COST LEVEL DIFFERENCES OVER TIME

It is plausible, especially in Europe, that the degree of banks' inefficiency is not constant over the years but falls off gradually over time, either thanks to managers' increased knowledge and experience, or enforced by increased competition and pressure from shareholders. There are various ways to investigate whether and how efficiency and cost differences have changed over time. One way to reveal the dynamics in efficiency is to extend model (6.1) in order to allow the inefficiency terms to become time dependent:

$$c_{it} = \alpha + \sum_j \beta_j x_{ijt} + \sum_j \sum_k \gamma_{jk} x_{ijt} x_{ikt} + v_{it} + u_i \exp(-\eta(t-T)) \qquad (6.6)$$

so that u_i is replaced by $u_{it} = u_i \exp(-\eta\,(t-T))$, where t refers to the time period ($t = 1, ..., T$) and η is an unknown parameter (see Battese and Coelli, 1992). The non-negative random variable u_{it}, which reflects inefficiency, decreases gradually over time if $\eta > 0$, or increases if $\eta < 0$. For the application of this panel data model, one does not need to have observations of the full panel set at one's disposal.

The third column of Table 6.7 presents estimation results of the time-dependent version of the employed stochastic frontier model. The time-trend coefficient appears to be positive, indicating a decrease in inefficiency, as expected, and in fact highly significant. The same pattern emerges if average efficiencies are calculated for the eight years considered. Apart from a small U-turn in the first years, where the number of observations was rather limited and the results are therefore less reliable, a continuous and strong improvement of efficiency over time shows up. Actually, this improvement is truly remarkable: between 1990 and 1997, average inefficiency in Europe has fallen by no less than 43 per cent. This is somewhat more than observed by Altunbas et al. (2001).

Table 6.7 Changes in efficiency and cost level differences over time

	No. of banks	SCF	TCF	
Time trend (η)		0.0229 (7.5)		
Linear time trend			-1.837 (6.0)	
		Efficiency	*Year dummies*	*Cost effect (%)*
1990	31	0.563	—	—
1991	52	0.543	-0.010	-1.0
1992	220	0.563	-0.040	-3.9
1993	364	0.564	-0.117	-11.0
1994	515	0.590	-0.030	-3.0
1995	1 126	0.653	-0.069	-6.7
1996	2 135	0.733	-0.105	-10.0
1997	1 907	0.739	-0.133	-12.5

Similar results can be obtained with respect to the cost level, using the applied translog cost function (fourth column). When a linear time trend is included in the TCF model, the downward slope in the average cost level, controlled for the banking activities considered, is highly significant. When, alternatively, year dummies are introduced, a similar trend of lower costs over time emerges, be it less regular over the years. The average cost level in 1997 appears to be 12.5 per cent below that in 1990 (last column). Average costs have fallen much less than inefficiency, which may point to a reduction in the spread between good and poor management. Note that inefficiency is a relative measure – efficiency of an individual bank compared to the best practice bank – whereas cost level is an absolute yardstick. As has been explained in Section 6.1 and in Appendix 6.B, there may be an overlap in the

Table 6.8 Europe-wide estimates of X-efficiency for two sub-periods

	1990–95			1996–97			1990–97	
	Efficiency	*Rank*	*# banks*[b]	*Efficiency*	*Rank*	*# banks*	*Efficiency*	*Rank*
Belgium	0.515	14	6	0.650	10	23	0.484	14
Denmark	0.564	11	15	0.601	13	21	0.543	13
Finland	0.557	12	1	0.746	3	7	0.677	5
France	0.576	10	256	0.601	14	111	0.552	12
Germany	0.728	1	399	0.773	1	1490	0.755	1
Greece	0.352	15	10	0.578	15	15	0.395	15
Ireland	0.685	2	3	0.723	5	10	0.697	4
Italy	0.638	7	267	0.652	8	306	0.601	10
Luxembourg	0.629	8	41	0.647	11	73	0.717	2
Netherlands	0.643	5	37	0.604	12	36	0.623	8
Portugal	0.640	6	15	0.723	4	27	0.649	6
Spain	0.542	13	22	0.651	9	33	0.577	11
Sweden	0.665	4	5	0.718	6	7	0.617	9
Switzerland	0.666	3	57	0.772	2	145	0.705	3
UK	0.623	9	49	0.691	7	73	0.649	6
Total[a]	*0.650*		*1183*	*0.734*		*2377*	*0.696*	
λ	0.910			0.907			0.916	
σ^2_{mle}	0.359			0.207			0.261	
σ^2_{v}	0.032			0.019			0.022	
σ^2_{ols}	0.118			0.078			0.086	
R^2, adjusted	0.961			0.965			0.966	

Footnotes to Table 6.8: [a] For efficiency: weighted averages; [b] number of banks.

Note: Shading refers to countries with a limited number of banks.

X-efficiency and cost difference results: differences in national cost conditions may affect the measurement of X-efficiencies whereas differences in average managerial abilities between countries can be mistaken for cost differences. Particularly, the observed relatively small cost reduction may in part reflect the substantial fall in X-inefficiency. Anyhow, these results show how the changing institutional and economic environment for banks in terms of deregulation, liberalization and globalization, and the prospect of the single currency in the Economic and Monetary Union in 1999, has, in some way or other, favourably affected efficiency and – most probably – competition in the European banking industry.

The question arises whether the structural changes over time have been similar for all countries. Or, in other words, whether the ranking of countries in terms of efficiency has been affected. In principle, this could be investigated by re-estimation of the models for shorter periods, or even single years. However, as the number of observations for the earlier years is rather low, particularly where the analysis aims at establishing efficiency levels for individual countries, the possibilities for estimating more detailed changes over time are limited. In order to keep the number of observations per country at an acceptable level, the sample has been split into (only) two shorter periods, 1990–95 and 1996–97. The results for efficiency and cost levels are presented in Table 6.8 and Table 6.C.4 in Appendix 6.C. Both the statistical distortion observed in Section 6.6 and the limited number of observations for some countries, might impair the clear view on developments over time for some countries. Therefore, only some of the most remarkable developments are discussed below.

In line with earlier observations, average efficiency appears to improve over time, inefficiency dropping by one quarter in the later period. Greece, the country lagging furthest behind in both periods, has shown the largest improvement, although not in ranking. Spanish banks also improved their position in terms of efficiency, even in terms of ranking. The average efficiency of Dutch banks deteriorated over time, relative to other countries, both in ranking and in absolute figures. However, since the Dutch banking market is dominated by a few large banks, the average over 37 banks considered incorporates many small banks, which may make this overall result less representative. The rank position of French banks took a turn for the worse.

In short, the results reveal that, in most European countries, both inefficiencies and cost levels have been, on average, substantially lower in recent years than in the earlier 1990s. Apparently, deregulation, liberalization and ongoing financial and monetary integration in the EU have increased competitive pressures and forced European banks to operate more economically.

6.8 SUMMARY AND CONCLUSIONS

This chapter assesses the cost efficiency of the European banking industry, examines efficiency and cost level differences across European countries and provides sensitivity analyses with respect to bank size, bank type category and developments over time. As is well-known, the *level* of cost inefficiency estimates depends in part on the methodology applied, whereas the estimates may also be affected by data inaccuracy; therefore the results should be interpreted with some caution. Using the stochastic cost frontier approach, we observe that average X-inefficiency in Europe is rather high at 30 per cent, generally higher than the 20 per cent often found in the literature. However, most of the earlier studies analyse only a single country, ignoring foreign best-practice banks and thereby seriously underestimating inefficiency.

We pay special attention to differences across countries. In terms of X-efficiency, banks in Luxembourg and Switzerland are the most efficient, which however is owing at least in part to their privileged position as tax havens for foreign investors and, by implication, less to managerial ability. Most German banks belong to the very efficient categories of cooperative and savings banks. However, compared to their banking category peers, the efficiency of German banks is only just above the European average. Banks in Denmark, the Netherlands, Portugal and the UK rank among the more efficient ones, whereas banks in Belgium, France, Greece and Italy are typically less efficient. Most Spanish banks are large banks and hence belong to a class of relatively inefficient institutions. However, compared to their peers, the efficiency of Spanish banks is close to the European average.

Apart from X-efficiency, a related but distinct measure of efficiency is employed, namely the cost level. Where the former measures managerial competence, the latter rather reflects institutional and economic conditions. Cost levels in Luxembourg and Switzerland, corrected for input prices and banking activities, are 20 per cent below those in Germany, the Netherlands, Portugal and the UK. Of course, many banks in the former two countries are branches of foreign banks with relatively low costs. Costs in Belgium, Denmark, France and Italy are 15 per cent higher and in Spain and Greece as much as 25 per cent and 35 per cent higher, respectively. This points up the vast differences that exist in institutional and economic conditions among European banks.

Estimated inefficiency appears to be proportional to bank size. Large banks are twice as inefficient as small banks. Apparently, shortcomings in managerial ability are manifested earlier in large financial institutions. If mergers aim to reduce inefficiency, this should be seen as a challenge rather than taken for granted. Estimated inefficiency is also dependent on the type of bank. On average, the inefficiency of cooperative and savings banks is relatively small, at 15 per cent and 20 per cent, respectively, whereas commercial banks typically have two or three times higher inefficiencies. Inefficiencies and cost levels show different patterns with respect to categories, as savings and investment banks face 10 per cent and 20 per cent higher costs, respectively, than cooperative and commercial banks, whereas some specialized bank types operate 30 per cent more economically.

Differences over time also appear to be vast. Inefficiencies were nearly 45 per cent lower in 1997 than in 1990, whereas the cost level also fell by more than 10 per cent. Apparently, deregulation, liberalization and ongoing financial and monetary integration in the EU have increased competitive pressures and forced European banks to operate more economically.

The large spread in inefficiencies and cost levels, which of course is much wider across banks than across countries, indicates that the process of scaling up and rationalization in preparation for increased foreign competition has, for at least part of the banks, only just begun. Poorly managed and inefficient banks abound and are an easy prey for institutions with better-performing management, hunting for take-over game. Especially in countries where banks are less efficient, large-scale consolidation and rationalization of the banking industry will be inevitable and even necessary in order to improve the banking system's soundness and survival prospects.

APPENDIX 6.A COUNTRY-SPECIFIC CHARACTERISTICS OF EUROPEAN BANKS

Table 6.A.1 presents an overview of some country-specific characteristics of the European banks in our sample. For most (especially some smaller) countries, the banks in the sample are a limited subset of the banks in the IBCA-Fitch database. This is the price to be paid for applying a more extensive model to explain costs.[33] On the other hand, for most of these countries, the remaining banks constitute a fairly large sample, which in most cases contains at least the larger banks. Results based on this sample still allow for clear and general conclusions to be drawn, except for Finland, Ireland and Sweden, where the sample is too small.

Table 6.A.1 Country-specific characteristics of selected European banks

	Belgium	Denmark	Finland	France	Germany	Greece	Ireland	Italy	Luxembourg	Netherlands	Portugal	Spain	Sweden	Switzerland	UK	*Total*
IBCA, 1990–97																
Number of banks	94	99	12	392	1 826	22	48	611	128	66	42	189	22	350	317	*4 218*
No. of banks in sample	23	21	7	265	1 503	15	10	311	74	41	27	34	8	150	74	*2 563*
No. of observations	44	57	13	964	2 983	40	20	1 221	177	164	67	105	17	299	187	*6 358*
Balance sheet total [a]	0.77	0.32	0.21	3.14	8.13	0.08	0.13	2.26	0.61	1.60	0.35	0.95	0.60	0.53	3.45	*23.14*
	Shares in balance sheet total (in %)															
Costs	1.2	2.0	2.1	2.1	1.3	2.9	1.8	2.8	0.6	2.0	2.3	2.4	1.6	2.1	2.3	*2.0*
Loans	19.7	47.1	49.3	47.7	43.1	40.2	66.6	50.9	20.1	48.9	41.4	45.0	61.3	56.1	56.1	*47.0*
Savings	51.1	26.6	23.6	35.1	30.5	70.2	39.5	20.7	31.4	24.7	44.9	39.9	5.9	25.5	27.1	*30.0*
Demand deposits	8.3	24.8	25.8	10.5	8.2	6.6	26.3	24.5	9.2	26.5	16.5	9.1	26.2	29.3	30.2	*16.4*
Other income	0.5	0.7	1.4	1.0	0.5	1.9	0.9	1.2	0.1	0.3	1.2	1.1	0.9	2.0	1.4	*0.9*
	Shares in number of observations (in %)															
Commercial	66	95	62	69	7	85	55	24	92	78	69	36	88	57	70	*32*
Cooperative	16	0	15	23	48	0	0	46	2	4	4	8	0	2	0	*35*
Savings	2	5	15	5	43	0	10	26	1	1	13	52	12	7	1	*27*
Investment	0	0	0	1	0	0	10	1	3	15	9	2	0	22	27	*3*
M&l term credit [b]	11	0	0	2	0	15	25	2	2	0	0	1	0	0	0	*1*
Real estate/mortg. [c]	5	0	0	1	1	0	0	0	0	2	4	1	0	2	2	*1*
Spec. gov. credit [d]	0	0	8	0	1	0	0	2	0	0	0	0	0	10	0	*1*

OECD, 1997[e]																
Number of banks	131	92	348	567	3111	51	52	935	215	169	237	307	124	360	468	*7167*
Id. per capita[f]	13	17	68	10	38	5	14	16	512	11	24	8	14	51	8	*19*
#, excl. coop. banks	131	92	54	440	691	44	52	283	215	169	67	210	124	360	468	*3400*
Id. per capita[f]	13	17	11	8	8	4	14	5	512	11	7	5	14	51	8	*9*
Id., sample as %[g]	17	23	11	45	102	34	19	52	33	24	39	15	6	41	16	*45*
No. of inhabitants[h]	10.2	5.3	5.1	58.4	81.9	10.5	3.6	57.4	0.4	15.5	9.9	39.3	8.8	7.1	58.8	*372.2*
Balance-sheet total[i]	1.42	0.34	0.22	4.26	7.91	0.24	0.40	3.08	1.06	1.94	0.43	1.59	0.49	2.15	7.27	*32.79*
Id. per capita[j]	140	64	43	73	97	22	110	54	2529	125	43	40	55	304	124	*88*
Id. sample as %[k]	54	96	93	74	103	35	34	73	57	82	82	60	123	25	48	*71*

[a] Balance sheet total of all banks in the sample of 1997, in trillions of Deutsche Marks; [b] medium- and long-term credit institutions; [c] real estate and mortgage banks; [d] specialized government credit banks; [e] source: OECD, 1999, Bank profitability: financial statements of banks; [f] number of banks divided by the number of inhabitants, per million; [g] number of non-cooperative banks of IBCA sample as a % of the OECD number; [h] in millions; [i] balance-sheet total of all banks, in trillions of Deutsche Marks; [j] in thousands; [k] balance sheet total of IBCA sample as a % of OECD balance sheet total.

Cost as a share in the balance sheet total is an indicator of efficiency, even though, of course, costs are explained in part by output composition and input prices. The average cost level is high in Greece, Italy, Portugal and Spain, which are sometimes regarded as countries with less efficient banks, but also in Switzerland and the UK, which are considered as countries with more advanced banks, and low in Belgium, Germany and, especially, Luxembourg. Most banks in Luxembourg are branches of foreign banks with relatively low costs. Loans as a share of total assets range from 20 per cent in Belgium and Luxembourg to 67 per cent in Ireland. The share of savings and demand deposits varies from 32 per cent in Sweden to 77 per cent in Greece. In most countries, the universal 'commercial' bank is the most widespread type. However, in Germany and Italy, most banks – and in France many banks – are of the cooperative category, hardly found in the other countries.[34] In Germany and Italy a substantial share of banks is of the traditional 'savings bank' type; in Spain, in terms of numbers, this is, in fact, the predominant banking category. Investment banks occur mainly in the Netherlands, the UK and Switzerland. Many of these differences between countries are caused by institutional or regulatory conditions.

The lower part of Table 6.A.1 presents OECD figures for the entire banking sector of each country, offering a closer view on the relative size of our IBCA sample. The fifth row of the lower part of the table shows the *number of banks* in the sample as a percentage of the OECD number, excluding the non-cooperative banks. Except for Finland, Ireland and Sweden, as mentioned earlier, the volume of the sample used is substantial in terms of the number of banks – on average, half of the total is included. The last row gives the *balance sheet total* of IBCA sample as a percentage of the OECD balance sheet total. For all countries, but Switzerland, our sample in terms of the balance sheet total is larger, being, on average, more than 70 per cent of the total. For Switzerland, a few of the largest banks (among which UBS) are missing in our sample, due to lack of data. Hence, our sample contains a larger share of the bigger banks. Apparently, larger banks publish more data and provide the data set employed in this chapter more frequently. We conclude that our sample covers the larger part of the balance sheet total of the banking industry.

The data also provide some additional information on the national banking systems. Therefore, Table 6.A.1 presents numbers of banks and balance sheet totals, both per capita. In this respect, Luxembourg, in particular, and Switzerland appear to be outliers. This is mainly because of the privileged position banks in these countries occupy with respect to attracting funding from foreigners, due to banking secrecy, the absence of tax on income from wealth for non-inhabitants and the stable currency.[35] This phenomenon has prompted many foreign banks to establish branches in these countries.

The number of banks, whether or not per capita, is at times said to reflect certain aspects of the national history of banking evolution in terms of mergers and acquisitions. Germany is an example of a country with relatively many banks of limited average size, reflecting a lagging position in the scaling-up process. For that reason – and several others – efficiency in part of the German banking industry is often seen as lower than in countries where mergers and acquisitions have already reduced the banking population. This may also hold for Finland and Portugal. On the other hand, a low number of banks such as in Greece may also indicate a less developed financial system. Probably, the balance sheet total per inhabitant provides a better indication of banking development. Low values for Greece, Italy, Portugal and Spain and the Scandinavian countries may reflect a late development of banking and low banking efficiency, where high values for Belgium, the Netherlands, Ireland and the UK could point to a more mature financial system.

APPENDIX 6.B DISTURBING EFFECTS OF COUNTRY DUMMIES IN REGIONAL SCF MODELS

In an earlier study, a comparison was made between Europe-wide estimates using an SCF model with and without dummies on the one hand, and single country estimates on the other (see Bikker, 2001). A remarkable shift in the countries' levels of efficiency estimates was observed when country dummies were included in the Europe-wide SCF model (see first columns of Table 6.B.1). After inclusion of the dummies, the ranking of the efficiency of banks in Luxembourg and Belgium fell from very high to dismally low, whereas the status of Italian banks rose from very low to sky-high. The ranking of most other countries also changed. The country ranking in the Europe-wide model with dummies turned out to be rather similar to that of single country estimates (see last column). This is remarkable as in the Europe-wide model a single frontier is estimated for all countries, whereas in the country-specific application nine frontiers are estimated, one for each country.

Table 6.B.1 Europe-wide and single country estimates of efficiency

	Europe wide				Single country	
	Standard		*Country dummies*			
	Eff.	Rank	Eff.	Rank	Eff.	Rank
Belgium	0.431	2	0.196	9	0.524	5
France	0.261	8	0.361	5	0.268	9
Germany	0.424	4	0.523	1	0.691	2
Italy	0.273	7	0.483	2	0.781	1
Luxembourg	0.560	1	0.344	7	0.436	7
Netherlands	0.382	5	0.408	3	0.498	6
Spain	0.242	9	0.341	8	0.533	4
Switzerland	0.430	3	0.393	4	0.659	3
UK	0.297	6	0.359	6	0.364	8
Weighted avgs.	*0.381*		*0.460*		*0.615*	

Note: Lightly shaded ratios and indices indicate countries where banks are relatively efficient, whereas dark shading points to countries with relatively inefficient banks.

This remarkable phenomenon is related to an often ignored[36] technical intricacy of an SCF model with country dummies. Equation (6.2) with added country dummies reads:

$$c_{it} = \alpha + \textstyle\sum_j \beta_j x_{ijt} + \sum_j \sum_k \gamma_{jk} x_{ijt} x_{ikt} + \sum_r \delta_r D_r + v_{it} + u_{it} \qquad (6.7)$$

Dummy coefficient δ_r measures the deviation of the cost level in country *r* from the Europe-wide cost level.[37] An OLS estimate of δ_r would be based on the group averages of the variables (countries seen as groups):

$$\hat{\delta}_r = (1/N_r) \sum\sum_{i,t\in\{R\}} (c_{it} - \hat{\alpha} - \sum_j \hat{\beta}_j x_{ijt} - \sum_j \sum_k \hat{\gamma}_{jk} x_{ijt} x_{ikt})$$
$$= (1/N_r) \sum\sum_{i,t\in\{R\}} [(\alpha - \hat{\alpha}) + \sum_j (\beta_j - \hat{\beta}_j) x_{ijt} + \sum_j \sum_k (\gamma_{jk} - \hat{\gamma}_{jk}) x_{ijt} x_{ikt} + v_{it} + u_{it}] \quad (6.8)$$

Estimates are denoted by hats. The summation is over all bank-year combinations of banks from country *r*, denoted by the set $\{R\}$, which contains N_r observations. In panel data analysis, Equation (6.7) is denoted as *fixed-effects model* and Equation (6.8) is called *between-group estimator*, as this estimator is based on variance between observations of banks of country *r* only. All other coefficients of Equation (6.7) are based on the *within-group (or within-country) variance* of Equation (6.9):

$$\bar{c}_{it} = \sum_j \beta_j \bar{x}_{ijt} + \sum_j \sum_k \gamma_{jk} \bar{x}_{ijt} \bar{x}_{ikt} + \bar{u}_{it} + \bar{v}_{it} \quad (6.9)$$

where $\bar{c}$ denotes '*c* in deviation from the respective country mean'. Country-specific variance is swept away. Note that, via c_{it}, the average level of X-inefficiency of country *r*, which we seek to measure, is one of the determinants of the dummy coefficient of this country (see Equation (6.8)), and that the average level of X-efficiency of country *r* cannot be distinguished separately. In the SCF approach, the coefficients are not estimated by OLS,[38] but by a numerical procedure which takes account of the complicated (truncated normal) distribution of u_{it}. The split up of variance in between- and within-group variance, as explained above, applies to the estimates of the translog cost model parameters and the specification error v_{it}, but not necessarily to the random term u_{it}, which represents X-inefficiency. Its truncated normal-distributed character obstructs a plain and clear view on the effects of the insertion of country dummies on the estimates of X-inefficiency. Nevertheless, it is likely that the measurement of the two concepts, that is, a country's relative cost level and its X-inefficiency, are mixed up in the stochastic frontier model with country dummies. This is illustrated empirically by the results of Table 6.B.1: if dummies are included, the estimates of the countries' average X-inefficiency shift from a plausible ranking to a less convincing one.

As mentioned, the ranking of the countries' X-efficiency levels in Table 6.B.1, based on country-specific estimation, shows a strong similarity to the ranking of the Europe-wide estimation, based on a model with country dummies. This similarity is probably due to the fact that the country-specific model's intercept is estimated in the same way as a dummy coefficient in a Europe-wide application. Expressed in other words, the effect of country dummies is identical to shifts in the countries' frontiers from the European one. However, this lack of uniqueness of the estimated country-specific frontier, different from the Europe-wide one, may prohibit a true international comparison of efficiency.

This leads us to the following conclusions. First, efficiencies based on estimation using a stochastic frontier model in a multicountry setting and including country dummies, are impracticable for comparisons between countries, due to interference between country dummies and average efficiencies. Second, efficiency estimates from stochastic frontier models for single countries can be very misleading, as country-specific frontiers may deviate strongly from a Europe-wide one. For this reason, single-country studies tend to overestimate efficiency. Especially the second conclusion has important implications, since most of the literature on efficiency is based on single-country studies.[39]

The above analysis indicates that the dummy coefficients in the multiproduct cost function, which constitutes the stochastic frontier model, not only measure differences in the cost level of banks in the various countries in producing identical combinations of financial services, but also reflect differences in average X-efficiency levels. This suggests that these dummy coefficient estimates provide a straightforward alternative measure of differences in efficiency between the countries. Straightforward, because this alternative is less sophisticated than the X-inefficiency measure of the stochastic frontier model, and because the closely related concepts of deviations in cost level and X-inefficiency are taken together.

APPENDIX 6.C VARIOUS TABLES

Table 6.C.1 *Sensitivity analysis for the number of German banks or observations: efficiencies and ranks for various samples*

	Original sample		Less German observ.		Less German banks I		Less German banks II	
	Efficiency	*Rank*	*Efficiency*	*Rank*	*Efficiency*	*Rank*	*Efficiency*	*Rank*
Belgium	0.521	14	0.573	14	0.469	13	0.463	13
Denmark	0.597	9	0.616	10	0.519	10	0.515	10
Finland	0.690	5	0.731	5	0.593	7	0.588	7
France	0.568	12	0.593	12	0.509	12	0.501	12
Germany	0.740	2	0.746	4	0.684	3	0.667	4
Greece	0.500	15	0.551	15	0.428	15	0.411	15
Ireland	0.798	1	0.799	1	0.725	2	0.725	2
Italy	0.578	11	0.604	11	0.515	11	0.504	11
Luxembourg	0.738	3	0.754	3	0.743	1	0.744	1
Netherlands	0.641	8	0.646	8	0.611	6	0.609	5
Portugal	0.685	6	0.719	6	0.589	8	0.585	8
Spain	0.548	13	0.577	13	0.465	14	0.463	13
Sweden	0.590	10	0.637	9	0.560	9	0.553	9

(Continued)

Table 6.C.1 *(Concluded)*

	Original sample		Less German observ.		Less German banks I		Less German banks II	
	Efficiency	*Rank*	*Efficiency*	*Rank*	*Efficiency*	*Rank*	*Efficiency*	*Rank*
Switzerland	0.731	4	0.764	2	0.681	4	0.673	3
UK	0.666	7	0.703	7	0.615	5	0.607	6
Averages	*0.690*		*0.699*		*0.596*		*0.586*	
No. of observations	6 350		4 526		4 074		4 215	
Idem, for Germany	2 983		1 159		707		848	
No. of banks	2 558		2 214		1 431		1 431	
Idem, for Germany	1 503		1 159		376		376	
			Correlations over twelve countries [a]					
Original sample			0.987	*0.972*	0.971	*0.965*	0.967	*0.947*
Less German observ.					0.952	*0.951*	0.947	*0.961*
Less German banks I							0.999	*0.983*

[a] Excluding Finland, Ireland and Sweden.

Notes: 'Less German observations' means that, for Germany, only 1 997 observations are included in the sample (and not those of earlier years). 'Less German banks I and II' means that, for Germany, the sample consists of only the first and second quarter of the banks (in other words, the other quarters are left out). Shading refers to countries with a limited number of observations.

Table 6.C.2 *Cost effects in a translog cost model by country and by bank-size class*

	Class 1 (total assets[a] <500)					Class 2 (500-<1 250)					*Weighted effects*
	Dummy coeff.[a]		*Effects*[b]	*Ranking*	*# banks*	*Dummy coeff.*		*Effects*	*Ranking*	*# banks*	
Belgium	-0.590	(5.4)	0.68	1	3	0.537	(2.9)	1.33	14	2	0.95
Denmark	-0.088	(1.3)	1.12	7	6	0.480	(5.8)	1.25	12	8	1.12
Finland	—	—	—	—	—	0.050	(0.3)	0.81	3	2	0.96
France	-0.185	(4.5)	1.02	5	65	0.360	(5.9)	1.11	9	63	1.12
Germany	-0.308	(7.5)	0.90	4	599	0.237	(3.8)	0.98	8	468	0.94
Greece	0.094	(0.9)	1.34	11	4	0.489	(4.3)	1.26	13	7	1.21
Ireland	—	—	—	—	—	0.104	(0.7)	0.86	5	2	0.78
Italy	-0.182	(4.5)	1.02	6	125	0.413	(6.7)	1.17	11	78	1.23
Luxembourg	-0.053	(0.7)	1.15	8	10	0.112	(1.6)	0.87	7	23	0.76
Netherlands	—	—	1.22	10	14	—	—	0.77	2	6	1.02
Portugal	-0.028	(0.2)	1.19	9	2	0.069	(0.7)	0.83	4	5	1.03
Spain	—	—	—	—	—	0.406	(2.6)	1.16	10	2	1.37
Sweden	0.125	(0.5)	1.39	12	1	—	—	—	—	—	1.03
Switzerland	-0.565	(10.6)	0.69	2	65	-0.050	(0.7)	0.74	1	42	0.73
UK	-0.430	(8.4)	0.79	3	21	0.112	(1.5)	0.87	6	17	0.87
σ^2_{ols}	0.046					0.060					
R^2, adjusted	0.889					0.804					

(Continued)

Table 6.C.2 (Concluded)

	Class 3 (1 250-<5 000)					Class 4 (5 000+)					Weighted
	Dummy coeff.		*Effects*	*Ranking*	*# banks*	*Dummy coeff.*		*Effects*	*Ranking*	*# banks*	*ranking*
Belgium	0.723	(5.0)	1.52	15	3	-0.350	(3.7)	0.79	4	10	6
Denmark	0.250	(2.5)	0.95	7	10	0.040	(0.4)	1.16	11	14	12
Finland	0.255	(1.3)	0.95	8	12	-0.132	(1.0)	0.98	5	18	5
France	0.503	(9.9)	1.22	12	20	0.147	(2.7)	1.29	14	30	11
Germany	0.330	(6.6)	1.03	10	33	-0.062	(1.2)	1.05	8	23	7
Greece	0.260	(2.1)	0.96	9	4	0.089	(0.7)	1.22	12	5	14
Ireland	0.124	(1.4)	0.84	6	2	-0.428	(2.5)	0.73	2	6	2
Italy	0.567	(10.9)	1.30	13	375	0.124	(2.3)	1.26	13	104	13
Luxembourg	0.107	(1.6)	0.82	5	93	-0.562	(7.7)	0.64	1	100	3
Netherlands	—	—	0.74	2	6	—	—	1.12	10	3	10
Portugal	0.103	(1.4)	0.82	4	8	-0.007	(0.1)	1.11	9	27	9
Spain	0.635	(8.5)	1.40	14	92	0.177	(2.8)	1.33	15	60	15
Sweden	-0.074	(0.5)	0.69	1	1	-0.078	(0.6)	1.03	7	4	8
Switzerland	0.048	(0.8)	0.78	3	25	-0.377	(5.3)	0.77	3	27	1
UK	0.395	(6.3)	1.10	11	5	-0.128	(1.9)	0.98	6	6	4
σ^2_{ols}	0.069					0.104					
R^2, adjusted	0.843					0.951					

[a] Millions of Deutsche Marks.

Note: Shading refers to countries with a limited number of banks.

Table 6.C.3 *Average cost level by country and by bank category (1990–97)*

	Commercial banks					Cooperative banks				
	Dummy coeff.[a]		*Costs effects*[b]	*Ranking*	*# banks*	*Dummy coeff.*		*Cost effects*	*Ranking*	*# banks*
Belgium	0.211	(2.2)	1.21	13	14	-0.248	(2.2)	0.99	3	1
Denmark	0.189	(2.9)	1.18	12	20	—	—	—	—	—
Finland	-0.074	(0.5)	0.91	5	4	-0.351	(2.6)	0.89	2	1
France	0.160	(3.8)	1.15	11	166	-0.010	(0.1)	1.25	6	68
Germany	-0.032	(0.7)	0.95	7	113	-0.181	(2.1)	1.05	4	799
Greece	0.107	(1.0)	1.09	10	13	—	—	—	—	—
Ireland	-0.324	(2.5)	0.71	1	6	—	—	—	—	—
Italy	0.249	(5.4)	1.25	14	66	0.004	(0.0)	1.27	8	164
Luxembourg	-0.125	(2.3)	0.86	3	67	-0.085	(0.5)	1.16	5	2
Netherlands	—	—	0.98	9	32	—	—	1.26	7	1
Portugal	-0.050	(0.7)	0.93	6	18	0.045	(0.3)	1.32	9	1
Spain	0.287	(3.7)	1.30	15	9	0.074	(0.6)	1.36	10	3
Sweden	-0.005	(0.0)	0.97	8	7	—	—	—	—	—
Switzerland	-0.128	(2.2)	0.86	4	86	-1.355	(11.1)	0.33	1	3
UK	-0.152	(2.9)	0.84	2	52	—	—	—	—	—
σ^2 / R^2, adj.	0.151	0.962				0.023	0.987			

(Continued)

Table 6.C.3 **(*Continued*)**

	Savings banks					Investment banks				
	Dummy coeff.		*Costs effects*	*Ranking*	*# banks*	*Dummy coeff.*		*Cost effects*	*Ranking*	*# banks*
Belgium	2.232	(4.3)	3.56	14	1	—	—	—	—	—
Denmark	0.715	(5.2)	0.78	4	1	—	—	—	—	—
Finland	0.861	(5.4)	0.90	5	1	—	—	—	—	—
France	1.105	(7.9)	1.15	10	21	-0.088	(0.6)	1.70	9	2
Germany	0.864	(6.6)	0.91	6	560	-1.123	(3.3)	0.61	1	1
Ireland	1.010	(6.6)	1.05	9	1	-0.872	(4.7)	0.78	3	1
Italy	1.126	(8.6)	1.18	11	63	-0.378	(2.3)	1.27	7	3
Luxembourg	-0.048	(0.3)	0.36	2	1	-0.256	(1.3)	1.44	8	3
Netherlands	—	—	0.38	3	1	—	—	1.86	10	6
Portugal	0.949	(7.3)	0.99	8	3	-1.085	(7.7)	0.63	2	4
Spain	1.185	(8.8)	1.25	12	19	-0.395	(2.0)	1.25	6	1
Sweden	0.904	(5.4)	0.94	7	1	—	—	—	—	—
Switzerland	-0.079	(0.6)	0.35	1	12	-0.780	(5.7)	0.85	4	33
UK	1.699	(10.2)	2.09	13	1	-0.612	(5.4)	1.01	5	19
σ^2 / R^2, adj.	0.012	0.990				0.071	0.963			

(*Continued*)

Table 6.C.3 *(Concluded)*

	Other categories					Weighted costs eff.	Its ranking	Weighted ranking
	Dummy coeff.		*Costs effects*	*Ranking*	*# banks*			
Belgium	0.953	(0.7)	1.05	9	2	1.31	14	14
Denmark	—	—	—	—	—	1.16	10	12
Finland	3.162	(6.5)	9.53	13	1	2.14	15	6
France	0.422	(2.2)	0.62	4	8	1.16	11	10
Germany	1.129	(7.2)	1.25	11	30	0.99	7	5
Greece	1.179	(3.7)	1.31	12	2	1.12	9	11
Ireland	0.961	(4.4)	1.05	10	2	0.82	2	4
Italy	0.460	(2.7)	0.64	5	15	1.22	12	13
Luxembourg	0.041	(0.1)	0.42	2	1	0.88	3	1
Netherlands	—	—	0.40	1	1	1.09	8	9
Portugal	0.876	(2.4)	0.97	8	1	0.91	5	7
Spain	0.578	(1.8)	0.72	6	2	1.24	13	15
Sweden	—	—	—	—	—	0.97	6	8
Switzerland	0.314	(1.3)	0.55	3	16	0.77	1	3
UK	0.818	(1.8)	0.91	7	2	0.90	4	2
σ^2 / R^2, adj.	0.047	0.980						

[a] *t*-values in parentheses; [b] geometric mean for 'effects'.

Note: Shading refers to countries with a limited number of banks.

Table 6.C.4 Estimates of cost effects in a translog cost model for two sub-periods

	Period 1 (1990–95)					Period 2 (1996–97)				
	Dummy coeff.[a]		*Effects*[b]	*Ranking*	*# banks*[c]	*Dummy coeff.*[a]		*Effects*	*Ranking*	*# banks*
Belgium	0.285	(2.4)	1.16	13	6	-0.235	(3.6)	0.87	2	23
Denmark	0.192	(2.3)	1.06	11	15	0.044	(0.8)	1.15	11	21
Finland	0.100	(0.3)	0.96	7	1	-0.197	(2.3)	0.90	3	7
France	0.195	(4.9)	1.06	12	256	0.096	(2.2)	1.21	13	111
Germany	0.029	(0.6)	0.90	5	399	-0.096	(2.4)	1.00	9	1 490
Greece	0.612	(5.5)	1.61	15	10	0.107	(1.3)	1.22	15	15
Ireland	-0.221	(1.1)	0.70	1	3	-0.146	(1.9)	0.95	8	10
Italy	0.190	(4.4)	1.05	10	267	0.075	(1.8)	1.18	12	306
Luxembourg	0.144	(2.2)	1.01	9	41	-0.150	(3.3)	0.95	7	73
Netherlands	—	—	0.87	4	37	—	—	1.10	10	36
Portugal	0.101	(1.2)	0.96	8	15	-0.177	(3.2)	0.92	4	27
Spain	0.365	(5.7)	1.26	14	22	0.104	(1.9)	1.22	14	33
Sweden	0.089	(0.6)	0.95	6	5	-0.175	(2.0)	0.92	5	7
Switzerland	-0.131	(2.0)	0.76	2	57	-0.404	(8.8)	0.73	1	145
UK	-0.024	(0.4)	0.85	3	49	-0.167	(3.8)	0.93	6	73
σ^2_{ols} / R^2, adj.	0.111	0.963				0.070	0.968			

[a] *t*-values between parenthesis; [b] geometric mean for 'cost effects' is set at 1; [c] number of banks.

Note: Shading refers to countries with a limited number of banks.

NOTES

1. The comparative advantages which domestic banks used to have on the domestic markets for bonds and equity in the field of underwriting and trading activities have diminished since the euro has replaced national currencies. For similar reasons, fund management has ceased be the preserve of local financial institutions.
2. Which is, by the way, difficult to assess empirically, as shown in Chapter 4.
3. Though, efficiency gain is only one among the many incentives for mergers, see for example Dermine (1999).
4. See also Appendix 6.B.
5. See also Appendix 6.B.
6. The few studies dedicated to international comparison of efficiency which include at least the major EU countries are based on quite different methodologies and obtain diverging results in terms of the ranking of countries and the magnitude of inefficiencies (Allen and Rai, 1996; Pastor et al., 1997; Wagenvoort and Schure, 1999; Altunbas et al., 2001). Related studies are Maudos et al. (1999, 2001 and 2002) and Hasan et al. (2000). For an overview see Gehrig and Sheldon (1999).
7. For an overview see Berger and Humphrey (1997).
8. In the rest of this chapter, for the sake of presentation, efficiency and its complement inefficiency will be used alternately, and the prefix X will be dropped where possible.
9. See Coelli et al. (1998) for a more comprehensive discussion of this issue.
10. This expression relies upon the predicted value of the unobservable, u_{it}, which can be calculated from expectations of u_{it}, conditional upon the observed values of v_{it} and u_{it} (see Battese and Coelli, 1992, 1993, 1995).
11. Note that the $E(C_{it} \mid u_{it}, X)$ differs from actual costs, C_{it}, due to v_{it}.
12. Provisions for credit losses are not included in costs. Although they may reflect inadequate credit risk management in the past (which would call for inclusion), the delayed nature of the link between inadequate managment and provisions would disturb the analyses.
13. An alternative would have been to correct the wage rate for national differences in labour productivity and average working time
14. Zero values do not fit into a model of a logarithmic nature.
15. The often used cost income ratio, for instance, is ambiguous. It is common to assume that a high ratio indicates efficiency, strong competition and low profits. An alternative view is that *in*efficiency causes higher cost and hence a higher ratio. Empirical analysis supports the later view. However, the correlation with X-inefficiency is low, lower than most of the other proxies, see Section 1.2.
16. This accepted view is partly based on the (disqualified) simple proxies of efficiency as mentioned above, as, for instance, higher interest rate margins and labour cost shares in Italy and Spain and lower ones in Luxembourg and Switzerland, higher per capita labour intensity in Germany, lower concentration in Germany and Italy (see Table 1.1 in Section 1.2). Elsewhere the expert-view ranking is not in line with these proxies (for example, high interest rate margin in the UK, special positions of Luxembourg and Switzerland).
17. See Group of Ten (2001) for descriptions of the banking markets of the various countries considered.
18. The likelihood per observations is included, because numbers of observations vary (slightly), when the loans-assets ratio is included as an additional variable. Of course, in theory, this distorts a statistically correct comparison, but in this case the difference can practically be disregarded.
19. The correction reduces the proportion between the 5th and 95th percentile of capital prices from 13.1 to 2.4, the latter proportion being much more plausible than the former.
20. The sample reduces by 8 to 6 350 observations and by 5 to 2 558 banks, due to missing observations of variable *L*/*A*.

21. At the 5% significance level, two times the difference in the logarithms of the likehood is larger than the critical value of the chi-square distribution: 2 x 8.6 = 17.2 > 15.5 = $\chi^2_{0.05}(8)$, but at the 2.5% level it is smaller, so that the restrictions can not be rejected ($\chi^2_{0.025}(8)$ =17.5). In fact, the likehood ratio test statistic has a mixed χ^2 distribution, see Lee (1993).
22. In general, the European data are less accurate than those from the USA. Measurement errors should be picked up by the error terms, but may also have contributed to larger inefficiency terms. For this and other reasons, such as model specification errors and sample characteristics, the inefficiency estimates should be interpreted with caution.
23. Denmark takes up an intermediate position according to the standard SCF model. The extended SCF indicates a lower X-efficiency, which may be due to the skew distributions of the banking types (almost all Danish banks in the sample are 'commercial') or to some irregularity.
24. Moreover, international banks may have branches in these countries, particularly in Luxembourg, while costs may mainly weigh down on the parent bank in its home country.
25. A first step, the addition of dummies for the banking categories to the standard model, in order to take into account possible differences in cost levels (to the extent these differences are constant and not related to, for instance, the size of the explanatory variables), affected neither the ranking nor the leading position of Germany, see left columns of Table 6.2.
26. Although some differences occur in the general level of inefficiencies.
27. In general, the number of observations is two or three times larger than the number of banks.
28. It is sometimes difficult to classify a large and complex universal bank into a single category, especially because data on their separate business units are lacking. Relatively many large banks are labelled as commercial banks, see Table 6.4.
29. See Table 6.4.
30. As management problems increase with size, it is relevant to observe that commercial banks and 'other banks' are overrepresented in the (two) large bank size classes.
31. Actually, this is not so clear as regards the cooperative and savings banks, because the numbers of similar banks in the other countries are too low to obtain reliable results, but is is clear for commercial banks and other categories.
32. However, the corrected rankings of these countries are not substantially lower than in Table 6.2. The correction compensates for the shift resulting from the category-specific estimates in Table 6.6 (last column but one).
33. In Bikker (2001), input prices were dropped, which resulted in an abundance of available data (as data on wages and capital prices is a limiting factor), but a rather reduced explanatory model for costs.
34. In the Netherlands, there is only one cooperative bank (Rabobank), but it has a large market share.
35. For Luxembourg, the small size of the population also affects per capita ratios.
36. See for instance Bos (2002), page 119ff.
37. Or, actually, from the Dutch cost level, as in the empirical application $\delta_{Netherlands}$ is omitted to avoid indeterminacy of the country dummies. (If all countries were included, there would be a linear relationship between these countries and the constant).
38. The coefficients of the translog cost function – equation (6.7) with u_{it} assumed to be zero – are estimated with OLS.
39. This problem may be less serious for studies of the USA, given its vast size, but appears to be disastrous for studies of countries the size of Germany and Italy.

7. Cyclical patterns in profits, provisioning and lending of banks

7.1 INTRODUCTION

Regulators worldwide work for the financial soundness of banks, in an increasingly market-oriented fashion. The upcoming new Basel Accord on capital requirements, expected to enter into force at the end of 2006, is a topical case in point (BCBS, 2003). The main purpose of the new accord is to introduce a more risk-sensitive method for determining the minimum capital required to absorb losses, in particular credit losses. The current capital requirements under the Basel Accord are mainly determined by fixed weights attached to categories of borrowers, such as businesses, government or banks, and disregard any variation within categories as to creditworthiness. Categorization into risk classes is crude, so that as reflections of the actual risk, the accompanying risk weights are inadequate to the point of arbitrariness, while improvement or deterioration of creditworthiness with the ups and downs of the business cycle is disregarded in determining capital requirements. In reaction to this, many banks have reshuffled their assets in such a way that the accompanying capital requirements are (too) low in comparison to the actual risks involved.

Under the proposed new capital accord, risk weighting for the purpose of determining capital requirements does take in the creditworthiness of individual firms. In many cases, the Standardized Method will be used, under which banks may use ratings determined by external rating firms – such as S&P and Moody's – to weight risks for loans to businesses. A change in creditworthiness will be expressed in the ratings and hence in capital requirements. Under certain conditions, more sophisticated banks may apply the *internal rating-based* (IRB) method, whereby they attach their own ratings to credits. The most sophisticated banks are allowed to go much further in classifying assets and the collateral that covers them. This development, whereby banks are allowed to classify loans into risk categories according to their own internal rating methods, is a revolutionary and market-oriented innovation in banking supervision.

The new accord thus promotes the financial soundness of individual banks and the financial stability of the banking system. A possible disadvantage, however, is that the novel risk sensitiveness of capital requirements could exert a procyclical influence on the macroeconomy, where banks, as suppliers of credit, play a major role. When during a downward slope of the business cycle the risk of business loans and the related capital requirements increase, there is the danger that banks become less forthcoming in extending loans, thus reinforcing the cyclical slowdown in what is called a *credit crunch*. In order to estimate the procyclical effect of bank behaviour – both under the old and the new accord – one should realize that, in reality, capital and reserves are significantly higher than minimum capital requirements for almost all banks. (Also the first capital accord has only improved the level of capital of the worst capitalized banks, see Jackson (1999).) Apparently, banks typically aim at a considerably higher external credit rating than corresponding with the minimum requirements. For that reason it is actual and not regulatory capital that counts in practice.

At this stage, there is only a limited number of studies estimating the extent to which the new accord will turn out to reinforce the procyclicality of banks' risk management.[1] Even under the present Accord, with capital requirements insensitive to the business cycle, the banking system is in some respects procyclical. In the first place, there is the possibility that loans will be extended less liberally during a cyclical downswing, the argument being that risk premiums are, in fact, assumed to be insufficient cover for the increased risk or inadequate due to adverse selection and moral hazard problems (Stiglitz and Weiss, 1981). Second, there are several channels through which the business cycle impacts a bank's profits, such as decreased demand for credit and stock market transactions; provisions necessitated by the deterioration of existing loans; and in some cases a less favourable interest structure. Thus, less profits are added to capital and reserves, while at the same time it is harder to raise new capital on the stock market.

The concerns about a possible acceleration of the procyclical behaviour of banks after implementation of Basel II has raised interest in the question of how and to what extent banks' characteristics, such as profitability, their business activities, such as lending, and their internal actions, such as making provisions for (future) credit losses, relate to the business cycle. Such an analysis will indicate how procyclical the current arrangement already is. For instance, greater profits imply the possibility to enlarge the capital buffer and increase lending. The present chapter addresses these questions and provides a view on the (possible) procyclicality of banks' behaviour during the last few decades. Such a backward-looking analysis is useful but cannot shed light on the question to what extent Basel II will add to this (alleged) procyclical behaviour.[2]

The structure of this chapter is as follows. The next section provides a bird's eye view of empirical literature on procyclicality in banking. Section 7.3 presents an empirical research into banks' profitability and the way it relates to the business cycle, while Section 7.4 takes a similar approach to the making of provisions for future credit losses. Section 7.5 then provides an empirical study of lending practices, with special focus on demand and supply factors because of their pivotal role in the so-called *bank lending channel* theory.

7.2 PROCYCLICALITY IN BANKING

As already said, banks, as suppliers of credit, can play an important role in the business cycle, if during a cyclical downswing their lending policy becomes less liberal. This will reinforce trends in the real world and therefore be procyclical in effect. However, whether a drop in lending is actually the result of demand or of supply factors is difficult to determine in practice. *Bank lending channel* theory argues that monetary policy influences expenditures via the supply of bank credit (Bernanke and Gertler, 1995; Berk, 1998).[3] Tightening of monetary policy causes a decrease in banks' liabilities, followed by a decrease of bank credit, referred to in its worst form as a *credit crunch* (Kliesen and Tatom, 1992). If the credit supply decreases mainly through a decline in banks' capital, we speak of a *capital crunch*. This is the kind of situation which, some fear, could materialize under the new capital accord during a cyclical downturn: increased risk causes capital requirements to grow so much that the capital available for lending becomes too small. However, the new accord precisely encourages banks to pursue more prudent policies, promoting the financial soundness of the banking system. Thus, in principle, the accord aims at mitigating the risk of the most serious credit crunch, namely a dry-up of lending in a banking crisis.[4]

In *balance sheet channel* theory, fluctuations in lending are explained not from supply but from demand factors (Bernanke and Gertler, 1995). Here the central tenet is that changes in net capital positions of businesses and households caused by the business cycle may be responsible for a decline in credit demand. The economic downturn confronts businesses with declining sales and households with decreasing dwelling and stock prices, taking away the need for new credit. The decline in net capital positions will, in fact, not only push down credit demand but also the willingness to extend loans.

Many analysts have linked the strong decline in lending in the USA over 1989–92 to the 1990–91 recession and regarded it as an exemplary case of credit crunch.[5] It is unclear, however, whether the decline in lending was caused mainly by a decrease in demand or by a decrease in supply (Kliesen and Tatom, 1992; Peek and Rosengren, 1995). Sharpe (1995) juxtaposes a number of macro- and microeconomic analyses of credit crunches as they relate to capital requirements, disequilibrium and supervisory practices. Kliesen and Tatom (1992) used a macroeconomic model to study the relationship between interest and credit, and concluded that demand factors far outweighed supply factors. Such models, however, underrate the transmission channel and the role played by bank capital. Microeconomic models focus directly on the impact of capital requirements. Peek and Rosengren (1995) found a positive effect of bank capital on credit growth during 1990–91, while Bernanke and Lown (1991) also detected a positive, albeit marginal, correlation. Brinkmann and Horvitz (1995) conclude that banks which do not meet capital requirements are, in fact, far less successful in realizing credit growth. Wagster (1999) finds for Canada, the UK and the USA that during 1990–92, due to stricter supervision, less credit was extended towards lower-risk investments such as government bonds. Nevertheless, these authors, and others such as Akhtar (1994) and Berger and Udell (1994), emphasize the role of both demand and supply factors in a lending decline. Lown and Wenninger (1994) perceive different correlations in different periods, the decline in lending during 1990–91 in the USA being mainly caused by a drop in demand, whereas during 1988–89 supply played the larger role.

Summing up, we conclude that empirical research into lending suggests a possible but usually very restricted role for demand; convincing empirical support for *bank lending channel* theory has failed to materialize. A positive effect of capital (requirements) on lending supporting either a credit or a capital crunch is found, but here, too, the evidence is rather weak. Almost invariably, demand factors dominate the picture. Berk (1998) who refers to other empirical studies than those mentioned above, draws the same conclusion. Sharpe (1995) therefore concludes that empirical research has so far failed to come up with sufficient evidence to support the thesis that the decline in lending was caused by changes in capital requirements. Thus, while the procylicality of banks' behaviour and the perceived increased procyclicality caused by the new capital accord are genuine problems, they are unlikely to have a substantial adverse effect on macroeconomic stability.[6] By contrast, the new accord does help to enhance the financial health of the banking system, thereby diminishing the risk of the worst possible credit crunch – that caused by a banking crisis.

7.3 BANKS' PROFITS AND THE BUSINESS CYCLE

Against the backdrop of the concern that has arisen over the procyclical effects of the new capital accord, it is interesting to find out what degree of correlation there is between banks' profitability and the business cycle. In the literature, two types of causality have been investigated for the correlation between the banking system and macroeconomics. Some scholars have studied the influence of the development of the financial system on economic growth, on the one hand, focussing on the long term, finding a positive effect (for example Levine, 1997; Van der Zwet and Swank, 2000; Arestis et al., 2001; Fase, 2001), and on the other hand concentrating on the short term, as discussed in the former section. Others analysed the influence of economic development on banks' profitability. In this line Demirgüç-Kunt and Huizinga (1999) explain banks' profitability and interest margins during 1988–95 and across 80 countries, using macroeconomic as well as banking-specific and institutional factors.[7] Taking into consideration differences in types of banking activity, leverage and macroeconomic developments, they emphasize the explanatory powers of institutional factors, such as differences in financial and legal structure, capitalization and taxation.[8] Cavello and Majnoni (2002) produced a similar study. Although these articles do cover macroeconomic factors, the role of these determinants remains underexposed and the results are not very plausible.[9] Arpa et al.(2001) do focus more on the influence of macroeconomic developments in explaining (components of) bank incomes and provisions for future credit losses over 1990–99. They demonstrate that Austrian banks make more provisions for credit risk as gross domestic product (gdp) growth figures decline (with a procyclical effect) and as net income rises (with a countercyclical effect).

Following Demirgüç-Kunt and Huizinga and Arpa et al., we will focus on the influence of the business cycle (and banking-specific factors) on profits, bringing macroeconomic influences more to the fore than the former studies and considering far more countries than the latter. In order to clarify the influence exerted by the business cycle, we collected data on a period covering several decades. Moreover, we used data from many countries in order to gain an overall view of the banking system in the industrial world, where the new capital accord will be adopted, and also to obtain a large number of observations for our empirical analysis. Thus we arrive at a collection of macroeconomic and banking-specific determinants of banks' profits, which are described in detail in Section 7.3.2.

Following the usual practice in the literature, we use two possible definitions for the dependent variable *profits*: the margin or returns on (all) assets (ROA) and the returns on equity (ROE), both expressed as percentages.[10] These variables make it possible to compare data across countries and through time. Returns are always taken before taxes and therefore undistorted by taxation differences across countries. For subsequent analyses of portions of the returns, it is useful to know that returns before taxes, as referred to in this chapter, is a bookkeeping concept calculated as shown in Table 7.1.

Table 7.1 Breakdown of banks' profits

Interest income
– Interest expenditure
Net interest income
– Non-interest earnings +
Gross profits (operational profits)
– Operational expenditure
Net profits (operational results)
– Provisions
Profits before taxes

7.3.1 Data Used

The macroeconomic data used for the combined time series and cross section analysis were provided by Datastream[11] and the data specific to the banking sector were taken from *Bank profitability: financial statements of banks* published by the OECD (2000). There are no OECD data going back to before 1979, which is why our analyses refer to the years 1979–99. Using longer series increases the accuracy of estimates but goes with the risk of ignoring changes in the underlying processes. In this trade-off we choose for the longer estimation period, also because shorter periods are inadequate to cover a sufficient number of business cycles, but we checked for regime changes by re-estimating each model for two subperiods: the *pre*-Basel I years (1979–90) and the *post*-Basel I years (1991–99).[12]

Of the 29 OECD countries, 26 had sufficient data available to participate in the analyses: Australia, Austria, Belgium, Canada, Denmark, Finland, France, Germany, Greece, Iceland, Ireland, Italy, Japan, Luxembourg, Mexico, the Netherlands, New Zealand, Norway, Portugal, South Korea, Spain, Sweden, Switzerland, Turkey, the UK and the USA.[13] For the sake of comparability across countries and through the years, all data are presented as growth figures, percentages or ratios, so as to avoid scaling difficulties. Data on differences between countries in financial structure, taxation regime, market structure, institutional conditions or management culture were not available for the entire period under review. In order to take country-specific factors into account despite the lack of data, we introduced a dummy variable for each country by way of simple approximation.

7.3.2 A Model of Bank Profits

Cavello and Majnoni (2002) developed the following theoretical model for bank profits:

$$\pi = L((r_B + E(d) + k) - r_D) - BL - (\gamma E(d)\,L - BL) = \text{ either}$$
$$L((r_B + k) - r_D) + (1-\gamma)\,E(d)\,L \quad \text{if } LLR > 0\text{, or}$$
$$L((r_B + k) - r_D) + (E(d)\,L - BL) \quad \text{if } LLR = 0 \qquad (7.1)$$

where π represents bank profits, L loans, r_B the risk free interest rate, $E(d)$ the expected default ratio on loans as an average through the business cycle, k the risk premium, r_D the funding rate, BL bank losses on loans and LLR loan loss reserves. The loan loss provisions $\gamma E(d)\,L - BL$ are set equal to a fraction γ of the expected default ratio $E(d)$ minus the actual losses, as long as the loan loss reserves allow for this reduction. The business cycle feeds into bank profits through bank losses (BL), the demand for loans (L) and, probably, the levels of the interest rates. In principle, the expected default ratio $E(d)$ does not depend on the business cycle, but in reality it may be affected. This theoretic model ignores other bank activities (such as trading and bank services) and bank-specific characteristics such as those related to funding (for example non-bank deposits and capital and reserves). Therefore, we estimate the following more elaborated model equation

$$\textit{profits}_t = \alpha_1\, \textit{gdp}_t + \alpha_2\, \textit{unemployment}_t + \alpha_3\, \textit{inflation}_t + \alpha_4\, \textit{share price}_t + \alpha_5\, \textit{M3}_t + \alpha_6\, \textit{loans}_t + \alpha_7\, \textit{interest differential}_t + \alpha_8\, \textit{non-bank deposits}_t + \alpha_9\, \textit{capital and reserves}_t + \Sigma_{i=1...26}\, \alpha_{9+i}\, d_i + u_t \qquad (7.2)$$

with variables either described summarily or abbreviated. In variant versions of the model, more explanatory variables have been included, while the interest differential may be substituted by its two components, short-term and long-term interest rates. Some variables have been delayed. Bottom index t refers to time (1979–99). The country dummies are referred to as d_i. If all 26 countries have a dummy variable, the intercept becomes superfluous.[14] The error term is referred to as u_i. Equation (7.2) constitutes an unbalanced, fixed-effect panel data model,[15] which is estimated by OLS (Baltagi, 1995). As the variable to be explained, we take returns on assets before taxes. Below the macroeconomic variables and banking sector-specific factors inserted in Equation (7.2) are explained in greater detail.

7.3.2.1 Macroeconomic factors

1. *Real gdp growth (per cent change)* The gdp growth figure is the most general and most direct measure of macroeconomic developments. In our context, it is first and foremost an indicator of the demand for banking services, including the extension of loans, and the supply of funds, such as

deposits, and as such is a direct determinant of profits. As a growth figure, it is the single most useful indicator of the business cycle, while the costs of banks are also expected to be linked to the gdp cycle. The gdp growth figure is made real by deflating it with gdp inflation.

2. *Long-term interest rate (10–year government bonds)* Part of the loans extended by banks to businesses or homeowners are long-term, and therefore carry an interest rate based on the long-term rate.[16] Banks' interest receipts, therefore, depend in large measure on the long-term interest rate. And since the actual credit rate is not available, the long-term rate is used as an approximation. Apart from this direct effect of the long-term rate on banks' profits, there is the indirect interest effect, caused by the (negative) long-term influence of the long-term rate on economic growth. We assume that in the relation under discussion, the direct (positive) short-term effect is more important.

3. *Short-term interest rate (three-month money market)* Moneys banked by businesses and private households, especially in the form of deposits, are usually short-term in nature and therefore carry an interest rate linked to the short-term rate. Thus the short-term rate is a factor in determining funding costs, and a high short-term rate will eat into the bank's profits. And as the actual figure we need, the (average) deposit rate, is not available for every country, the short-term rate is used as an approximation. In addition, the short-term rate is an indicator of monetary policy. The *interest differential* (long-term rate–short-term rate) could perhaps replace the individual long- and short-term rates as an explanatory factor.

4. *Share price index (per cent change)* The share price index impacts banks' profits directly in so far as it indicates the demand for stock exchange-related banking services, such as share issues, transactions and portfolio management. In addition, share prices reflect expectations as to businesses' financial positions and future economic growth (Berk and Bikker, 1995; Arestis et al., 2001). As such, the share price index is also an indicator of (expected) cyclical development.

5. *Unemployment (per cent)* Unemployment does not directly influence profitability, but it is a major cyclical indicator. If short-term unemployment is primarily a reflection of the business cycle, long-term unemployment especially indicates structural disequilibrium in the economy. In addition, unemployment is a measure of the current *phase* in the business cycle, whereas a figure like gdp growth merely indicates the *degree of change* in the business cycle.

6. *Failures (per million inhabitants)* The failures variable is a direct indicator of credit risk and loss on loans outstanding. The number of failures usually increases during a cyclical downturn. If official administration of failures lags behind as a result of time-consuming legal procedures, the failures variable should be included with a proportional *lead* (or negative

lag). Failures are quoted in proportion to population in order to allow comparisons across countries and across time.

7. *Inflation (per cent)* Inflation directly diminishes the real value of net assets. In addition, inflation impacts profitability through various indirect channels: it passes through into business and family spending, into nominal interest rates, into share prices and into the real money supply. Inflation also reflects (an aspect of) the business cycle. Because of its many indirect effects, the inflation coefficient is difficult if not impossible to interpret; inflation is used primarily as a *control* variable.[17]

8. *Real money supply (M3; per cent change)* The money supply is represented by the monetary aggregate M3, defined as the sum of cash and non-cash balances held by the public, short-term deposits, foreign-exchange holdings and short-term savings.[18] Growth of the money supply makes real growth possible, and is primarily an indicator of future growth potential (see Boeschoten et al., 1994; Berk and Bikker, 1995). In the first place, it reflects the availability of money, which is strongly linked to the creation of money by banks through lending. Excessive money growth implies a risk of overheating the economy and its concomitant, rising inflation. The ECB therefore regards excessive M3 growth as a preamble to rising inflation.[19] The impact of money supply on profits is mostly indirect, which is why this variable, too, functions mostly as a *control* variable. Like real gdp, the real money supply is deflated by gdp price increase.

9. *Housing prices (per cent change)* Housing prices are important because they are partly responsible for mortgage loan demand. In addition, they affect the risk run by banks on such loans caused by the collateral value. For the years reviewed, however, housing prices were available for a limited number of countries only, so that this variable in this chapter is used only once.

7.3.2.2 Banking sector specific factors

1. *Loans (as a share of total assets)* This variable represents the (relative) size of lending. Generally speaking, loans have a positive influence on profitability, because, as a bank's core business, they are a major generator of interest income. But lending also entails operational costs and credit losses. If costs and risks are not expressed adequately in the price of credit (that is the interest rate), for instance, as a result of cross subsidization, then lending becomes a loss-making business. In any case, this variable serves to characterize a bank's balance sheet. Like the variables that follow below, the loans variable is divided by total assets in order to standardise it and allow comparisons across countries and years.

2. *Risk-weighted assets ratio (RWAR)* This ratio is composed of the risk-weighted assets on the balance sheet plus the risk-weighted off-balance credit, divided by total assets, and is a measure of banks' risk profile. The risk weights are determined by the Basel capital accord of 1988 and are independent of cyclical influences.[20] As is the case with 'loans', the impact

of RWAR on profits depends on the extent to which risk has been factored into pricing. It should be noted, moreover, that the (old) Basel risk weights are, for most purposes, very crude and imprecise.

3. *Capital and reserves (as a share of balance sheet total)* This includes paid-up capital, reserved funds, retained profits and other capital funds. Generally speaking, capital and reserves constitute the 'own funds' or core capital of a bank and – as an item in the balance sheet total – its solvency. The more risk investments carry, the more capital is needed, so that the coefficient may become negative. While high-risk investments bring in more returns, greater capital could go together with high profits, so that a positive coefficient may be expected as well, depending on the degree to which risk pays off. If profits are defined as *returns on equity*, then a relatively small capital may leverage high profits, and one should expect to see a negative coefficient. If 'profits' is defined as the margin on assets, capital and reserves become a 'free' source of finance, so that, from this perspective, one must expect a positive coefficient. Thus, on account of the many possible ways they may pass through to the results, the capital and reserves variable is primarily a *control* variable.

4. *Non-bank deposits (as a share of balance sheet total)* Non-bank deposits include all deposit liabilities of banks except interbank deposits. This variable characterizes the funding structure of the banking system.

7.3.3 Empirical Results

Table 7.2 presents results for two variants of Equation (7.2): (i) a base model including all explanatory variables examined, regardless of significance, and (ii) a reduced model with significant variables only (columns 1 and 2, respectively).[21] The first variant shows the 'raw' estimation results, whereas the second presents a model 'sparsely' equipped with variables. Also, the second variant is based on more observations because fewer variables were required.[22]

Both contemporaneous and delayed real gdp growth were included, because cyclical effects could conceivably have a delayed impact on profit margins, for instance through delayed adjustments of interest rates or staff size, or by way of delayed customer response. Both the contemporaneous and the delayed coefficient of gdp turn out to be positive, indicating how strong the correlation is between profit margins and the business cycle or, more particularly, real economic growth, presumably owing to demand effects. When gdp growth is over 2 per cent, profits turn out to be almost 2.5 times as high as when gdp growth is under 2 per cent. This result is more plausible than the ones found by Arpa et al. (2001) or Demirgüç-Kunt and Huizinga (1999), neither of which studies found any effects of gdp growth on profits.

The unemployment coefficient carries, as expected, a significantly negative sign. Here, too, the correlation between profit and business cycle is in evidence. Where gdp growth reflects cyclical *change*, unemployment indicates the *phase* of the business cycle, although usually with some delay. A larger structural component of unemployment, moreover, indicates economic unbalance and less favourable economic conditions, which have their own adverse effects on profit margins.

Inflation, as was also found by Arpa et al. (2001), carries consistently positive coefficients. Possibly, nominal interest rates vary with inflation, so that real interest rates are more constant. In principle, this effect ought to be explained by the interest rates, but neither the interest rates themselves[22] nor the interest differential are found to carry a significant coefficient, as also found by Arpa et al. Presumably, long-term and short-term interest rates are inadequate proxies of, respectively, credit and deposit rates. Later on, we will discuss other possible causes of distortion with respect to interest rates.

The significant negative relation between loans and profit margin is puzzling, since a positive relation had been expected a priori (see Section 7.3.2). The premium put on the long-term interest rate, as included in the credit rate, is possibly insufficient cover for processing costs, credit losses and the cost of required capital reserves, which is not uncommon practice.[23] This might be explained in part by heavy and even increased competition in the banking market and by competition from the capital market and other non-bank financial institutions: banks prefer to retain their market shares even where they may run up losses. Another argument is cross-subsidization: banks may lose on loans but make profit on other bank services to the respective obligors. There is no doubt that this argument is valid, but, unfortunately, it does not really explain the unexpected negative sign of loans: subsidization implies that losses on loans are compensated for by higher revenues elsewhere. Possibly some banks follow a 'gamble for resurrection'. As yet, a fully convincing explanation is lacking. Anyhow, the negative coefficient of loans does not imply that lending is not profitable, but suggests that it is less profitable than other assets.

The coefficient of capital and reserves is significantly positive. A possible explanation for this is that capital and reserves contribute to ROA as a 'free' source of finance. Finally, share prices, real money supply and non-bank deposits seem to have no significant effect on profit margins.

In order to obtain meaningful coefficients and *t*-values for the dummy variables, the intercept in the model was maintained while one country dummy (that of Sweden) was left out.[24] The country-specific differences pointed up by the dummies (that is, differences not included in the model) were found to be significant in the case of some countries.[25] In the non-European Anglo-Saxon countries Canada, New Zealand and the USA, profit margins are significantly higher than elsewhere, as could be expected, while the same is true in Turkey, possibly in compensation for the substantial volatility of margins. Owing to various causes, profit margins in Finland, Japan, Luxembourg and South Korea are significantly lower than elsewhere.

Table 7.2 Explanation of profit margin on assets before tax in 26 countries (1979–99)

	All countries				Selected countries				Incl. risk weighted assets ratio			
	All variables		*Sign. variables*		*All variables*		*Sign. variables*		*All variables*		*Sign. variables*	
column:	*1*		*2*		*3*		*4*		*5*		*6*	
Explanatory variables	*Coeffi-cient*	t-*value*	*Coeffi-cient*	t-*value*	*Coeffi-cient*	t-*value*	*Coeffi-cient*	t-*value*	*Coeffi-cient*	t-*value*	*Coeffi-cient*	t-*value*
Real gdp growth [a]	0.06	4.8	0.06	5.4	0.02	0.9	—	—	0.00	-0.2	—	—
Idem, delayed	0.04	2.8	0.04	3.2	0.05	3.2	0.05	3.7	0.04	1.7	—	—
Inflation	0.01	2.0	0.01	4.4	0.00	-0.1	—	—	-0.03	-2.0	—	—
Unemployment	-0.06	-3.0	-0.05	-3.0	-0.07	-3.1	-0.07	-4.0	-0.20	-4.6	-0.19	-5.8
Share price index [a]	0.00	1.3	—	—	0.00	1.3	—	—	0.01	2.6	0.00	2.9
Real money supply [a]	0.00	0.2	—	—	0.01	1.3	—	—	-0.02	-2.0	—	—
Interest differential	-0.01	-0.7	—	—	0.07	2.9	0.06	2.9	-0.04	-2.1	—	—
Loans [b]	-2.17	-2.9	-1.63	-3.1	-1.82	-2.3	-1.45	-2.6	-0.66	-0.4	—	—
Non-bank deposits [b]	0.73	1.5	—	—	0.95	1.6	—	—	3.18	2.9	2.40	2.4
Capital and reserves [b]	3.48	2.7	3.65	3.1	2.42	2.0	—	—	0.01	0.0	—	—
Risk weighted assets ratio	—	—	—	—	—	—	—	—	-0.22	-4.5	-0.22	-5.4
Country dummies:												
Australia	0.36	1.4	0.26	1.2	0.28	1.1	0.48	2.4	0.81	1.9	0.72	2.4
Austria	-0.22	-1.0	-0.33	-1.7	-0.22	-1.1	-0.25	-1.4	-0.30	-0.9	-0.39	-1.3
Belgium	-0.11	-0.4	-0.23	-1.1	-0.03	-0.1	-0.21	-1.0	1.23	2.3	1.12	2.4
Canada	0.75	2.7	0.64	2.8	0.60	2.1	0.63	2.8	—	—	—	—
Denmark	-0.03	-0.2	-0.06	-0.3	-0.06	-0.3	0.03	0.2	—	—	—	—
Finland	-0.51	-2.2	-0.53	-2.8	-0.50	-2.2	-0.41	-2.2	—	—	—	—
France	-0.07	-0.3	-0.27	-1.2	0.03	0.1	-0.23	-1.1	—	—	—	—
Germany	0.17	0.8	0.08	0.4	0.03	0.2	-0.02	-0.1	—	—	—	—
Greece	-0.16	-0.5	0.05	0.2	—	—	—	—	0.16	0.3	0.22	0.5

Iceland	0.26	0.9	-0.16	-0.8	—	—	—	—	-0.46	-1.0	-0.46	-1.5
Ireland	0.21	0.9	0.16	0.5	0.33	0.9	0.58	1.8	0.98	1.8	0.87	2.6
Italy	0.09	0.4	-0.16	-0.8	0.26	1.0	0.21	1.1	0.94	2.3	0.88	2.5
Japan	-0.56	-2.4	-0.39	-2.2	-0.82	-2.9	-0.60	-3.6	-2.13	-4.1	-1.89	-4.3
Luxembourg	-1.26	-4.1	-1.06	-4.9	-1.13	-3.5	-1.02	-4.8	—	—	—	—
Mexico	-0.03	-0.1	-0.06	-0.3	—	—	—	—	-0.62	-1.3	-0.96	-2.7
Netherlands	0.29	1.4	0.16	0.9	0.15	0.7	0.08	0.5	-0.12	-0.3	-0.24	-0.9
New Zealand	0.82	2.5	0.93	3.8	0.64	1.8	0.92	3.9	-0.22	-0.4	-0.12	-0.3
Norway	-0.01	-0.1	-0.04	-0.2	-0.09	-0.4	-0.04	-0.2	-0.98	-1.9	-0.93	-3.1
Portugal	-0.28	-1.0	-0.29	-1.7	-0.34	-1.2	-0.08	-0.5	0.02	0.0	-0.19	-0.3
South Korea	-1.13	-4.9	-1.15	-5.5	—	—	—	—	-0.88	-2.1	-0.85	-2.5
Spain	0.63	1.8	0.54	1.9	0.76	2.0	0.96	3.3	2.70	3.9	2.50	5.0
Sweden	—	—	—	—	—	—	—	—	—	—	—	—
Switzerland	-0.05	-0.2	-0.13	-0.8	-0.11	-0.5	-0.22	-1.3	—	—	—	—
Turkey	0.95	2.6	0.61	2.4	—	—	—	—	3.02	2.8	1.43	4.0
UK	0.24	0.9	0.39	2.0	0.19	0.7	0.46	2.4	1.00	2.1	0.51	1.6
USA	0.57	2.6	0.49	2.6	0.41	1.9	0.48	2.6	0.31	0.9	0.26	1.0
Intercept	1.25	2.5	1 33	4.1	1.14	2.1	1.68	5.0	2.67	2.7	2.59	4.5
No. of observations	343		418		293		337		125		136	
R^2, adjusted	0.51		0 49		0.34		0.33		0.64		0.61	
F-test entire model [c]	11.03		13 92		6.11		8.01		8.56		10.79	
F-test dummy variables [d]	5.94		7 21		4.57		4.53		4.34		7.47	
Durbin–Watson	1.60		1 48		1.70		1.63		1.85		1.88	

[a] Percentual change; [b] divided by total assets; [c] all models are accepted at the 99% level of confidence; [d] in all models, the dummy variables are accepted jointly at the 99% level of confidence.

Note: For the sake of readability, all coefficients were multiplied by 100 (that is, growth figures as ratios, and ratios in percentages of the denominator variable).

The time dimension appears not to play a relevant role in this panel analysis. The coefficient of an added time trend, for instance, is found to be non-significant. In the first column, the Durbin–Watson (D–W) of 1.60 is within the critical limit,[26] so that a positive auto-correlation is absent. The R^2 adjusted for degrees of freedom at 0.51 is satisfactory for a panel analysis.

7.3.3.1 Selection of countries

The non-significance of the interest difference coefficient may be attributable to an inverted interest structure or unreliable interest data for some countries. Greece and Turkey in particular show highly volatile interest rate developments, with short-term rates sometimes far exceeding long-term rates. Iceland and Mexico, too, have seen highly fitful interest rate developments, with extremely high long-term and short-term rates. In order to find out to what extent this effect distorted estimates, therefore, we looked at a variant including a smaller group of selected countries where financial and economic conditions have been stable. For this reason, Greece, Iceland, Mexico, South Korea and Turkey were left out, either on account of unreliable interest rate data or extreme interest rate values, or because of their less developed financial and economic systems.

For this group of selected countries, a positive effect of economic growth on profits was found to be significant (see Columns 3 and 4 in Table 7.2). The effects of unemployment and loans is also significant, as before, while the country dummies display a pattern similar to that of the base variant (see Column 1). This time, interest difference, in contrast to the base variant, appears to have a significantly positive effect on profits, owing, probably, to a more stable development of interest rates in these selected countries, or to more reliable interest data.

7.3.3.2 Risk-weighted assets ratio

In order to find out how strong the effect of banks' risk profile on their profit margin is, we estimated a final variant including a *risk-weighted assets ratio* (RWAR) as an extra explanatory variable. RWAR was left out of the base variant because data were available for far fewer countries, and only for the more recent years: the number of observations is a mere 130, as against 400 in the base variant. Columns 5 and 6 of Table 7.2 show that high-risk credit portfolios carry a significantly lower profit margin. Apparently, the extra profit margin on high-risk loans in no way compensates for the losses suffered from the additional risk.[27] This outcome should be regarded with some caution, because the Basel risk weights – on which the RWAR is based – are very crude and imprecise. In comparison to the earlier estimates, two changes stand out.[28] First, the loans variable has ceased to be significant. This should not surprise us, because this variable also acted as an approximation of the risk profile, a function fulfilled here by RWAR. And second, the share price index now carries a significant coefficient. This too is according to expectations, because the demand for banking services depends in part on developments on the stock exchange.

7.3.3.3 Return on equity

Besides returns on assets (ROA), returns on equity (ROE) are also often used in the literature as a measure of profit. Therefore, the above analyses were repeated with ROE as the variable to be explained. ROE results, by and large, confirm the ROA analysis – that is, no significant differences are found – and are therefore not discussed separately here.

7.3.3.4 Pre- and post-Basel I subperiods

Finally, the estimations have been repeated for two subperiods, respectively before and after the beginning of 1991, when the 1988 Basel capital accord became effective. The estimation results of the later subperiod are similar to those in Table 7.2 with even more significant coefficients, reflecting strong cyclical effects on bank profits. Hence, for those years the same conclusions apply as drawn above. In the former subperiod, the relationship is weaker, nevertheless showing a significant effect of gdp on profits. Differences between the two periods are probably due to changes in bank behaviour or economic and institutional conditions and cannot be attributed to the first Basel accord.

7.4 CREDIT LOSS PROVISIONING AND THE BUSINESS CYCLE

As is shown by Table 7.1, profits are calculated by deducting credit loss provisions from net profits. Even more than profit itself, credit loss provisions embody the relation between credit risk and capital. For provisions made to absorb (expected) credit losses press down profits before they are added to capital and reserves. In this section, we look more closely at the coherence between provisions for credit losses and the business cycle, in order to gain a sharper insight into the possible risks of procyclicality. As was mentioned earlier, credit quality of loans is expected to move up and down with the business cycle. During a cyclical downturn, banks must take larger amounts away from – already low – profits by way of provisions, while in times of favourable cyclical developments the provisions for expected credit losses go down, augmenting profits. The countercyclical behaviour of provisions would thereby reinforce the cyclical nature of profits. Indeed, Cavello and Majnoni (2002) have observed such behaviour for the non-G-10 countries. However, for the G-10 countries, they recorded that banks look further ahead or, as they call it, even out their profits rather than allow them to fluctuate more strongly; thus during a cyclical boom, when net profits are high, they also make large provisions. Arpa et al.(2001) found the same countercyclical behaviour to be true for Austria. In addition to profit stabilization, Kwan and O'Toole (1997) mention the influence of tax legislation and the Basel capital requirements as determinants of provisions for credit losses. Provisions, Kwan and O'Toole note, tend to be larger if credit losses are tax-deductible. In some countries, provisions for credit losses are grouped under Tier 2 capital, so that under Basel capital requirements they count as capital only up to a certain limit, while in other countries, they are not treated as capital at all. Such regulations make this type of provision less attractive. Cavello and Majnoni (2002), also found a clear negative influence of public debt – as an indicator of heavier taxation in the future – on provisioning practices. These analysts, however, focus more on institutional factors, such as legislation, taxation and banking supervision, than on macroeconomic influences.

7.4.1 Determinants for Provisioning

In the theoretical model of Cavello and Majnoni (2002), referred to in Section 7.3.2, additions to provisions for credit losses (*PVL*) are modelled as:

$$PVL = \gamma\, E(d)\, L - BL \tag{7.3}$$

PVL is a certain share γ of the average expected losses $E(d)\ L$ minus the actual losses *BL*. *PVL* is effected by the business cycle through loans *L* and credit losses *BL*. In our empirical model equations we use three macroeconomic variables (real gdp growth, unemployment and inflation) to describe the business cycle and failures to describe credit losses:

$$provisions_t = \alpha_1\, gdp_t + \alpha_2\, unemployment_t + \alpha_3\, inflation_t + \alpha_4\, loans_t + \alpha_5\, net\ interest\ income_t + \alpha_6\, failures_t + \Sigma_{i=1..21}\, \alpha_{7+i}\, d_i + u_t \tag{7.4}$$

In Equation (7.3), the share γ may fluctuate, as according to the income smoothing hypothesis. Therefore we also include net interest income. Similar results are obtained when net interest income is replaced by net profits (see Table 7.1). The dependent variable *provisions* is defined as the net addition to provisions for credit losses in proportion to loans outstanding. Net interest income is scaled in relation to balance sheet total. For Australia, Luxembourg, New Zealand, Switzerland and the UK, provision data are unavailable, so that 21 countries remain.

The first two columns of Table 7.3 clarify the large extent to which provisions for credit losses depend on the business cycle: the coefficients of real gdp growth – both contemporaneous and delayed – and inflation turn out to be significantly negative, while the coefficient of unemployment is significantly positive, implying that provisions increase during cyclical lows. When gdp growth is less than 2 per cent, provisions are larger by two-thirds than in times of higher gdp growth, and when gdp growth is lower than -2 per cent, they are almost 2.5 times larger. Arpa et al., too, found a negative sign for the gdp coefficient. Such countercyclical behaviour acts procyclically on the macroeconomic level.

A second important result is that in years of high net interest income,[29] significantly more is added to provisions for credit losses, in line with what was found for Austria by Arpa et al. (2001), and for the G-10 countries by Cavello and Majoni (2001).[30] Apparently, in (relatively) good years for banks, there is a tendency to reserve more, for instance because as a precaution – more provisions are made in fat years for use in lean ones – or, as is suggested in the literature, for *credibility* (not to say window dressing), that is presenting a fairly constant profit over the years. As a result of such prudent (countercyclical) provisioning policy, banks are significantly less procyclical than would appear to follow from their dependence on the business cycle. Under the new Basel Accord, therefore, such prudent behaviour ought to be encouraged in the context of the Supervisory Review of Pillar II, as is envisioned. Under Pillar II banks are obliged to show how the creditworthiness of their lending portfolio and the value of the corresponding collateral deteriorates when the business cycle goes down. Furthermore, they need to demonstrate that their capital is sufficient to meet the minimum capital requirements under such a downswing in conditions.

Finally, we find only little differences in provisioning from country to country (see country dummies in Column 1).

Provisions for credit losses strongly depend on business failures, or rather, expectations regarding business failures. Therefore, a failures variable was included in a variant on the base model, where it was given a one-year lead, because provisions are made in anticipation of future failures, while failures lag behind the business cycle. For when failure is declared, it is the final moment in the survival process. Failures have not been used before in this chapter, because data are available for five countries only. Yet the number of failures turns out to be a highly significant contributor to the explanation of provisions – see Columns 3 and 4. As the failures variable itself also follows a strongly cyclical pattern, its inclusion contributes to sharp shifts in the coefficients of the other cycle-related variables, net profits among them.[31] Another reason for these sharp shifts is the more limited number of observations. At any rate, the failures variable, in line with expectations, turns out to be an important determinant of credit risk provisions.

Re-estimation of Equation (7.4) for the two distinguished subperiods provides fairly similar results as presented in Table 7.3, somewhat more significant in the latter period, and slightly less significant in the former. In both periods, we find significant impact of gdp as well as net interest income on credit loss provisioning.

Table 7.3 Explanation of credit loss provisioning for 21 countries (1979–99)

	Base model				Including failures			
	All variables		Sign. variables		All variables		Sign. variables	
Explanatory variables *column:*	*1*		*2*		*3*		*4*	
	Coefficient	*t*-value	Coefficient	*t*-value	Coefficient	*t*-value	Coefficient	*t*-value
Real gdp growth [a]	-0.11	-5.0	-0.11	-5.1	-0.07	-1.5	—	—
Id., delayed	-0.06	-2.4	-0.06	-2.4	-0.03	-0.6	—	—
Inflation	-0.02	-2.6	-0.02	-2.7	0.05	1.6	0.09	3.6
Unemployment	0.07	2.0	0.07	2.0	0.08	1.3	0.12	3.4
Loans [b]	0.18	0.1	—	—	-2.11	-0.8	—	—
Net interest income[b]	65.65	7.0	65.62	7.0	0.00	0.0	—	—
Failures [c]	—	—	—	—	28.81	5.1	28.10	8.1
Country dummies:								
Austria	0.05	0.1	0.15	0.4	—	—	—	—
Belgium	-0.66	-0.8	-0.59	-1.0	-1.90	-1.4	-3.34	-5.5
Canada	-0.50	-0.5	-0.36	-0.8	—	—	—	—
Denmark	0.44	0.6	0.53	1.3	—	—	—	—
Finland	0.08	0.1	0.21	0.6	—	—	—	—
France	-0.11	-0.1	-0.03	-0.1	0.07	0.4	-0.86	-1.9
Germany	0.12	-0.1	-0.01	0.0	—	—	—	—
Greece	0.31	0.5	0.38	0.8	—	—	—	—
Iceland	0.74	0.7	0.89	2.8	—	—	—	—

Ireland	0.03	0.0	0.15	0.2	—	—	—	—
Italy	-0.17	-0.2	-0.09	-0.2	—	—	—	—
Japan	0.19	0.2	0.31	1.2	—	—	—	—
Mexico	1.32	1.4	1.44	3.3	—	—	—	—
Netherlands	-0.29	-0.3	-0.17	-0.4	0.20	0.1	-1.71	-4.6
Norway	0.35	0.3	0.49	1.6	0.56	0.3	-1.51	-3.9
Portugal	1.11	1.6	1.19	2.9	—	—	—	—
South Korea	1.69	2.1	1.79	4.7	—	—	—	—
Spain	-0.83	-0.8	-0.72	-0.9	0.44	0.2	-1.83	-2.3
Sweden	0.05	0.1	0.15	0.5	—	—	—	—
Turkey	0.97	1.0	1.07	1.4	—	—	—	—
UK	—	—	—	—	—	—	—	—
USA	-0.28	-0.3	-0.16	-0.4	—	—	—	—
No. of observations	286		286		54		56	
R2, adjusted	0.40		0.41		0.66		0.66	
F-test entire model [d]	8.42		8.79		10.31		16.39	
F-test dummy variables [e]	3.39		3.69		13.95		14.43	
Durbin–Watson	1.09		1.09		1.82		1.73	

[a] Percentage change; [b] divided by total assets; [c] divided by population; [d] all models are accepted at the 99% level of confidence; [e] in all models, the dummy variables are accepted jointly at the 99% level of confidence.

Note: For the sake of readability, all coefficients were multiplied by 100 (that is, growth figures as ratios, and ratios in percentages of the denominator variable).

Bikker and Metzemakers (2002) investigate a model, which is similar to Equation (7.4), but with the equity to total assets ratio as an additional explanatory variable. Their model estimates, based on no less than 8 000 Fitch–IBCA observations of banks from 29 OECD countries over 1991–2001, generate similar results as those found above. Furthermore, they investigate separate countries and the level of loan loss reserves (instead of the annual additions to provisions). The results of Bikker and Metzemakers confirm our conclusions above.

7.5 LENDING AND THE BUSINESS CYCLE

According to *bank lending channel* theory, the central point in the issue of procyclical behaviour of banks is the passing through of lending into the macroeconomic sphere. Therefore, this section briefly discusses the extent to which lending depends on either demand or supply variables. The demand for credit depends on the business cycle and the interest rate on loans and is defined as:

$$Lending^D = \mathrm{f}\,(business\ cycle,\ interest\ rate\ on\ loans) \tag{7.5}$$

Credit supply depends on the interest rate on loans, banking-specific factors (*BSF*) and expected profits:

$$Lending^S = \mathrm{f}\,(capital\ and\ reserves,\ interest\ rate\ on\ loans,\ expected\ profits,\ BSF) \tag{7.6}$$

Most important among the *BSF* are 'capital and reserves', for they are subject to supervision regulations which kick in during a cyclical low when capital and reserves are eaten into by losses, while at the same time risks – and hence capital requirements – have increased.[32] The reduced-form model for lending can be derived by solving Equations (7.5) and (7.6) with the interest rate on loans as equating price. Using the macroeconomic variables as presented in Section 7.3.2 to described the business cycle, our empirical model for lending reads as:

$$lending_t = \alpha_1\, gdp + \alpha_2\, unemployment_t + \alpha_3\, inflation_t + \alpha_4\, share\ price_t + \alpha_5\, M3_t + \alpha_6\, interest\ differential_t + \alpha_7\, non\text{-}bank\ deposits_t + \alpha_8\, capital\ \&\ reserves_t + \alpha_9\, profits_t + \Sigma_{i=1..26}\, \alpha_{10+i}\, d_i + u_t \tag{7.7}$$

Lending is defined as the change in loans divided by total assets. Expected profits is proxied by actual profits.[33] Alternatively, or in addition, the interest differential (long minus short rate) may explain expected profit: the greater the differential, the more attractive lending becomes.

Table 7.4 shows that the influence of the cyclical variables used, such as real gdp growth, inflation and real money supply, are significantly positive, while that of unemployment is significantly negative – all as might be expected. Lending, at over 6 per cent gdp growth, is a good 2.5 times higher than at approximately zero gdp growth. Thus lending is shown to be strongly dependent on demand as indicated by cyclical factors. One might expect that this mechanism would be stronger in continental Europe, where banks dominate credit lending, than in Anglo-Saxon countries where, (also) in this respect, the market plays a leading role. However, re-estimation of Equation (7.7) for banking-based countries, using the classification of Demirgüç-Kunt and Huizinga (2001), did not provide any support for this view: the estimation results are almost identical.

By contrast to the strong demand effect on lending, the preeminent supply variable, capital and reserves, turns out to be completely non-significant. This would indicate that (during a cyclical downturn), there is (almost) no evidence of credit rationing, which in turn qualifies the bank lending channel hypothesis. That supply does yet have some impact is suggested by the significance of the profit margin, especially if delayed. The delay makes sense because the measure of profitability is something, which becomes evident only after some time, that is, literally, on the bottom line. Lending increases by 50 per cent if profits are doubled, indicating that much more credit is extended as a bank's profits increase.[34]

The significantly negative coefficient of non-bank deposits is a bit problematic. A possible explanation could be that private deposits are fairly inert to interest rate pressure, and therefore changes are largely exogenous in nature. Hence additional lending would have to be financed from other sources, that is, on the interbank or capital markets, explaining the negative impact. Lending differs significantly from one country to the next. In some cases there is a simple reason: in countries whose banking systems serve as safe havens for foreign capital, such as Luxembourg and Switzerland, lending is far less dependent on national economic conditions.

In Equation (7.7), the price of housing has also been included as an alternative determinant of lending. Because data were available for only seven countries, the number of observations becomes so low as to severely impair the value of the analysis. And even so, housing prices, as an additional variable, just fail to make a significant contribution.[35]

The results of this section coincide to a large extent with the empirical results in the literature as discussed in Section 7.2: various demand factors contribute significantly to the explanation of lending; the most typical supply factor, capital, is not significant, but the profit margin is. Hence the role of the supply side, though modest, is not negligible so that at least some room remains for the *bank lending channel* of transmission.

Table 7.4 Explanation of lending for 26 countries (1979–99)

	All variables		Significant variables	
Explanatory variables	Coefficient	*t*-values	Coefficient	*t*-values
Real gdp growth [a]	0.48	5.1	0.44	5.3
Idem, delayed	-0.04	-0.4	—	—
Inflation	0.15	6.1	0.25	12.0
Unemployment	-0.67	-5.5	-0.65	-5.8
Share price index [a]	0.00	0.7	—	—
Real money supply [a]	0.15	3.5	0.18	4.3
Interest differential	-0.10	-1.6	—	—
Non-bank deposits [b]	-9.23	-2.9	-9.07	-3.0
Capital and reserves [b]	-5.11	-0.6	—	—
Profits [b]	49.56	1.3	—	—
Idem, delayed	163.74	4.1	174.80	4.7
Country dummies:				
Australia	0.93	0.6	0.67	0.4
Austria	-1.69	-1.2	-1.77	-1.2
Belgium	0.14	0.1	0.12	0.1
Canada	2.15	1.7	2.14	1.6
Denmark	-0.98	-0.8	-1.19	-1.0
Finland	2.61	2.0	2.26	1.7
France	-1.04	-0.6	-0.94	-0.6
Germany	—	—	—	—
Greece	2.41	1.4	2.02	1.2
Iceland	-0.18	-0.1	2.71	2.0
Ireland	3.81	1.6	3.55	1.5
Italy	0.54	0.4	0.38	0.3
Japan	-0.99	-0.6	-1.02	-0.7
Luxembourg	-9.04	-5.9	-8.88	-5.6
Mexico	2.48	1.5	0.29	0.2
Netherlands	1.28	1.1	1.26	1.0
New Zealand	5.44	2.9	5.75	3.0
Norway	2.4	1.8	2.41	1.8
Portugal	1.03	0.6	1.00	0.8
South Korea	-2.51	-1.5	-3.15	-1.9
Spain	8.24	4.2	7.46	4.1
Sweden	-2.63	-2.1	-2.31	-1.9
Switzerland	-3.53	-2.3	-3.51	-2.4
Turkey	-3.26	-1.3	-8.15	-3.7

(Continued)

Table 7.4 (Concluded)

	All variables		Significant variables	
Explanatory variables	Coefficient	*t*-values	Coefficient	*t*-values
UK	3.28	2.1	3.13	2.0
USA	-1.13	-1.0	-1.03	-0.8
Intercept	10.73	5.1	10.00	4.9
No. of observations	333		377	
R^2, adjusted	0.62		0.67	
F test entire model [c]	15.94		25.20	
F test dummy variables [d]	4.51		6.46	
Durbin-Watson	1.76		1.54	

[a] Percentage change; [b] divided by total assets; [c] all models are accepted at the 99% level of confidence; [d] in all models, the dummy variables are accepted jointly at the 99% level of confidence.

Note: For the sake of readability, all coefficients were multiplied by 100 (that is growth figures in perunes en ratios in percentages of the denominator variable).

Re-estimation of Equation (7.7) for the subperiods 1979–90 and 1991–99 produces pretty similar results as in Table 7.4. Actually, a stronger impact of capital on lending after the introduction of the Basel capital accord in 1991 would have been plausible. However, we find such effect neither before nor after 1991, indicating limited support for the capital crunch theory. Over time, the demand effect of gdp on lending declines somewhat, whereas the supply effect of profits on lending was not significant in the first decade.

7.6 SUMMARY AND CONCLUSIONS

According to current proposals for a new Basel capital accord, capital requirements for lending will be determined in greater measure than at present by current credit risk. Many assume that banks during a cyclical downturn are less willing to loan money on account of increased credit risk, thereby reinforcing the cyclical downswing in a so-called *credit crunch*.[36] If banks are forced to maintain larger capital buffers in such circumstances, the presumed procyclical nature of bank lending is liable to become even stronger. Against the backdrop of increasing concerns over procyclical effects caused by the proposed new accord, this chapter investigated, first, to what extent banks' profits, additions to provisions for future credit losses and lending in 26 OECD countries related to the business cycle over the 20-year period 1979–99.

Real gdp growth and other cyclical variables all turn out to have a significant effect on profits or profit margins. Profits, at a gdp growth level of over 2 per cent, turn out to be almost 2.5 times those at gdp growth levels below 2 per cent. This mechanism demonstrates how capital and reserves (augmented by profits after deduction of taxes and dividends) generally accumulate much faster during a multi-year cyclical boom than in adverse cyclical years, while at the same time, additional capital is far easier to come by during an economic boom.

Other determinants of bank profits also carry plausible coefficients. A salient outcome is that lending portfolios carrying high risk profiles yield significantly lower profit margins. Apparently, the extra profit margin on high-risk loans is far from able to make up for the additional costs and losses. Hopefully, the new capital accord will encourage banks to pursue a more rational – that is, risk sensitive – pricing policy, better enabling them to cover credit losses and the costs of capital requirements (and to raise social welfare by improving the allocation of credit). This might prove procyclical if higher interest rates for credit should prevent businesses from taking out loans, but the effect will more probably be countercyclical, as it would prevent banks from credit rationing during downturns. In any case, it would improve the financial soundness of banks.

Enlargement of provisions for (future) credit loss also turns out to depend strongly on the business cycle in the sense that provisions increase in bad times. It appears that the augmentation of provisions in times of less than 2 per cent gdp growth is higher by two-thirds than it is in times of faster gdp growth, while it is almost 2.5 times higher when gdp growth is below -2 per cent. Importantly, banks contribute significantly more to credit loss provisions in years of relatively high net profits. Apparently, banks reserve more in these good years, as a precaution or, possibly, in order to present flattened out profits. Irrespective of the underlying motives, such provisioning policy causes the banking sector to be less procyclical than would, at first sight, seem to follow from the dependency of banks' profits on the business cycle. This prudent provision policy is strongly encouraged under the new Basel accord, where in the context of the Supervisory Review of Pillar II, banks need to show that they have surplus capital and provisions to also meet the minimum capital requirements when the business cycle deteriorates.

Finally, given the direct link between lending and economic activity as perceived by *bank lending channel* theory, we investigated to which extent lending depends on demand or supply. Surprisingly, the preeminent supply variable, capital and reserves, turns out to be non-significant as a determinant of lending. This is an indication that credit rationing during a cyclical downturn is driven in only a minor degree, if at all, by a shortage of capital, as assumed by the *capital crunch* hypothesis. It should be noted that for most banks, actual capital is substantially larger than regulatory capital (as it is also expected to be under the new capital accord), so that the restraining effect of the latter in periods of recession is most probably limited. Lending *is* impacted by supply in so far as this significant determinant correlates positively to the profit margin, but lending is dominated by demand. For instance, lending, at 6 per cent or higher gdp growth, is over 2.5 times the figure at close to zero gdp growth. These outcomes underline findings in the empirical literature that the influence of demand factors dominates the market and that – barring exceptional circumstances such as banking crises – it is fairly difficult to observe demonstrably supply-driven *credit crunch* effects.

APPENDIX 7 DATA SOURCES USED AND DESCRIPTIVE STATISTICS OF THE DATA

Table 7.A.1 Data sources used

	GDP	Short-term rates	Long-term rates	Shares-index	Unemployment	Failures	Money supply
Australia	OECD	IMF	OECD	OECD	OECD	—	Reserve bank of Australia
Austria	OECD	OECD	IMF	IMF	OECD	—	BIS
Belgium	OECD	IMF	IMF	IMF	Inst. Nat. De Statistique	Graydon Belgium	BIS
Canada	OECD	IMF	IMF	IMF	OECD	—	Cansim-statistics Canada
Denmark	OECD	OECD	OECD	OECD	OECD	—	BIS
Finland	OECD	OECD	OECD	OECD	Central Statistical office of Finland	—	Bank of Finland
France	OECD	IMF	IMF	IMF	OECD	INSEE	Banque de France
Germany	OECD	IMF	—	IMF	OECD	—	OECD
Greece	OECD	IMF	OECD	OECD	OECD	—	Bank of Greece
Iceland	OECD	OECD	IMF	OECD	OECD	—	OECD
Ireland	OECD	IMF	OECD	IMF	OECD	—	OECD
Italy	OECD	Banca d'Italia	IMF	IMF	OECD	—	BIS
Japan	OECD	Eurostat	OECD	IMF	OECD	—	Bank of Japan
Luxembourg	OECD	IMF	IMF	IMF	OECD	Statec	BIS

Mexico	OECD	IMF	OECD	OECD	OECD	—	Banco de Mexico
Netherlands	OECD	Eurostat	IMF	OECD	OECD	Statistics Netherlands CBS	De Nederlandsche Bank
New Zealand	OECD	IMF	IMF	IMF	OECD	—	Reserve bank of New Zealand
Norway	OECD	OECD	IMF	IMF	OECD	Statistics Norway	Statistics Norway
Portugal	OECD	IMF	IMF	IMF	OECD	—	IMF
South Korea	OECD	OECD	IMF	IMF	OECD	—	The bank of Korea
Spain	OECD	IMF	IMF	IMF	OECD	Ministerio de ec. y hac.	Ministerio de economía y hacienda
Sweden	OECD	IMF	OECD	IMF	OECD	Statistics Sweden	Bank of Sweden
Switzerland	OECD	IMF	Datastream	OECD	OECD	—	Nat. Bank of Switzerland
Turkey	OECD	OECD	OECD	OECD	OECD	—	Central bank of the Rep. of Turkey
UK	OECD	Datastream	IMF	IMF	OECD	—	Bank of England
USA	OECD	IMF	OECD	IMF	OECD	—	Federal Reserve

Table 7.A.2 Descriptive statistics of the data of the profit margin on assets model for 26 countries (1979–99)

	ROA[a]	Real gdp growth	Inflation	Real money supply	Loans	Capital and reserves	Non-bank deposits	Interest differential	Share price index	Unemploy -ment	RWAR[b]
Base model [c]											
Mean	0.007	2.75	7.78	3.81	0.53	0.058	0.56	0.70	19.21	7.19	
Median	0.007	2.75	3.45	3.42	0.55	0.053	0.55	0.80	12.77	6.91	
Standard deviation	0.007	2.64	16.14	5.39	0.13	0.029	0.15	6.21	38.77	4.26	
No. of observations	361										
Correlation matrix											
ROA[a]	1.00										
Real gdp growth	0.23	1.00									
Inflation	0.45	-0.04	1.00								
Real money supply	0.11	0.32	0.01	1.00							
Loans	-0.06	-0.03	-0.14	0.06	1.00						
Capital reserves	0.18	0.02	0.00	-0.03	0.01	1.00					
Non-bank deposits	0.19	-0.02	0.14	0.11	0.42	0.01	1.00				
Interest differential	-0.12	-0.12	-0.07	0.03	-0.03	0.00	0.01	1.00			
Share price index	0.31	0.13	0.56	0.01	-0.09	-0.02	0.05	0.28	1.00		
Unemployment	-0.01	-0.13	-0.06	-0.12	-0.24	0.11	-0.12	0.04	0.00	1.00	

Model including RWAR [c]											
Mean	0.009	3.04	8.42	4.45	0.55	0.069	0.58	0.37	21.39	8.06	8.72
Median	0.009	3.11	3.03	4.16	0.57	0.067	0.56	1.05	15.58	6.89	8.68
Standard deviation	0.008	2.75	18.07	5.79	0.14	0.040	0.14	4.21	33.91	4.84	1.41
No. of observations	129										
Correlation matrix											
ROA[a]	1.00										
Real gdp growth	0.22	1.00									
Inflation	0.54	-0.01	1.00								
Real money supply	0.13	0.32	0.20	1.00							
Loans	-0.14	0.10	-0.32	0.00	1.00						
Capital & reserves	0.04	0.01	-0.06	-0.08	-0.10	1.00					
Non-bank deposits	0.10	0.01	0.10	0.17	0.40	-0.15	1.00				
Interest differential	-0.42	-0.12	-0.62	-0.21	-0.02	0.11	-0.12	1.00			
Share price index	0.50	0.22	0.64	0.08	-0.25	0.00	0.03	-0.32	1.00		
Unemployment	-0.02	-0.10	-0.06	-0.14	-0.48	0.13	-0.11	0.10	0.00	1.00	
RWAR [b]	-0.22	-0.11	0.02	0.27	0.13	-0.10	0.36	0.03	-0.03	-0.02	1.00

[a] ROA is net interest income before taxes divided by total assets; [b] RWAR is risk weighted assets ratio; [c] for the model, see Section 7.3.2 and Table 7.2.

Table 7.A.3 Descriptive statistics of the data of the credit loss provisioning model for 21 countries (1979–99)

	Credit loss prov.	Real gdp growth	Inflation	Loans	ROA[a]	Unemploy-ment	Failures
Base model[b]							
Mean	0.010	2.75	9.05	0.54	0.007	7.21	
Median	0.008	2.75	3.90	0.54	0.007	6.80	
Standard dev.	0.011	2.68	15.83	0.13	0.008	4.46	
No. of observ.	303						
Correlation matrix							
Credit loss prov.	1.00						
Real gdp growth	-0.15	1.00					
Inflation	0.20	0.04	1.00				
Loans	-0.14	0.04	-0.12	1.00			
ROA[a]	-0.16	0.28	0.51	-0.19	1.00		
Unemployment	0.04	-0.11	-0.11	-0.45	0.01	1.00	
Model including failures[b]							
Mean	0.008	2.58	4.29	0.51	0.006	11.00	0.04
Median	0.006	2.67	2.89	0.45	0.007	11.02	0.02
Standard dev.	0.008	1.63	3.83	0.14	0.006	6.19	0.04
No. of observ.	66						
Correlation matrix							
Credit loss prov.	1.00						
Real gdp growth	-0.28	1.00					
Inflation	0.19	-0.15	1.00				
Loans	0.33	0.17	0.12	1.00			
ROA[a]	-0.71	0.22	0.18	-0.18	1.00		
Unemployment	0.10	-0.09	0.15	-0.58	0.20	1.00	
Failures	0.03	0.05	-0.41	0.29	-0.19	-0.52	1.00

[a] ROA is net interest income before taxes divided by total assets; [b] for the model, see Section 7.4.1 and Table 7.3.

Table 7.A.4 Descriptive statistics of the data of the lending model for 26 countries (1979–99) [c]

	Share price index	Real gdp growth	Real money supply	Inflation	Capital and reserves	Lending	Non-bank deposits	RWAR [b]	ROA [a]	Unemployment
Mean	19.21	2.75	3.81	7.78	0.058	0.064	0.56	0.70	0.007	7.19
Median	12.77	2.75	3.42	3.45	0.053	0.045	0.55	0.80	0.007	6.91
Standard deviation	38.77	2.64	5.39	16.14	0.029	0.087	0.15	6.21	0.007	4.26
No. of observations	361									
Correlation matrix										
Share price index	1.00									
Real gdp growth	0.13	1.00								
Real money supply	0.01	0.32	1.00							
Inflation	0.56	-0.04	0.01	1.00						
Capital and reserves	-0.02	0.02	-0.03	0.00	1.00					
Lending	0.26	0.21	0.24	0.41	-0.01	1.00				
Non-bank deposits	0.05	-0.02	0.11	0.14	0.01	0.11	1.00			
RWAR [b]	0.28	-0.12	0.03	-0.07	0.00	0.01	0.01	1.00		
ROA [a]	0.31	0.23	0.11	0.45	0.18	0.30	0.19	-0.12	1.00	
Unemployment	0.00	-0.13	-0.12	-0.06	0.11	-0.13	-0.12	0.04	-0.01	1.00

[a] ROA is net interest income before taxes divided by total assets; [b] RWAR is risk weighted assets ratio; [c] for the model, see Section 7.5 and Table 7.4.

NOTES

1. Based on the second consultative BIS document of January 2001, Ervin and Wild (2001) show that this swing could amount to 19%. Bangia et al. (2000) find a 25 to 30% higher VaR for credit risk under recession compared to under expansion. For an overview, see Lowe (2002).
2 See Bikker and Metzemakers (2003).
3. A different cause might be that asymmetrical information in credit markets might induce banks to ration credit in order to avoid adverse selection and moral hazard; see Stiglitz and Weiss (1981).
4. For a survey of possible shortcomings and risks of both the old and new Basel Accord, see Tonveronachi (2001).
5. Another example is the situation wherein Japanese banks found themselves after the burst of the speculative bubble in the real estate prices at the beginning of the 1990s.
6. Of course, apart from the fact that credit risk will be incorporated in the minimum capital requirements, the lending channel itself may be affected by the new accord, as the pricing of credit risk will improve substantially. This might work out procyclical, as the interest rate of credit may rise at a downturn, or countercyclical, as it may prevent banks from credit rationing during downturn.
7. Interest margin is the ratio of net interest income and total assets.
8. Their results show, for instance, that well-developed banks realize higher net interest margins and are more profitable. Also, banks in more competitive sectors appear to work for lower margins and to bring less profit. The size of banks and their degree of concentration, by contrast, appear to have positive effects, while institutional and legal indicators such as efficiency of legislation, compliance with contrasts, high taxation and the absence of corruption appear to influence interest margins and profitability in a negative sense. Finally, and surprisingly, neither gdp growth nor gdp per capita appear to have significant influences on interest margin and profitability.
9. Demirgüç-Kunt and Huizinga (1999) used gdp per capita, real gdp growth, gdp inflation and real short-term interest rate as macroeconomic indicators.
10. ROE results, by and large, confirm the ROA analysis – that is, no significant differences are found – and are therefore not discussed separately here.
11. See Appendix 7 for the sources used.
12. The 1988 Basel capital accord became effective at the beginning of 1991.
13. Data for all variables and for all years are not available for every country. In the case of Czech Republic, Hungary and Poland, crucial data are lacking.
14. Identical outcomes are obtained if one keeps the intercept and leaves out one country dummy; see below.
15. 'Unbalanced' as a number of year-country combinations is lacking and 'fixed effects' such as country effects are measured by dummy variables.
16. Interest on (non-mortgage) consumer credit is, in principle, based on short-term rates, marked up for risk and costs.
17. In other words, while inclusion of this variable may reduce the bias in the estimates of the other parameters, it plays no part in achieving the objectives of this chapter.
18. For the Czech Republic, Norway and Poland, M2 was chosen because for the period under review, M3 was unavailable.
19. Bikker and Kennedy (1999), however, think that for most of the countries under review, money supply is an inadequate predictor of inflation.
20. In the proposed new accord, rating-based weights are introduced which move up and down with the business cycle.
21. On the basis of the 95% level of confidence.

22. An alternative method reducing bias as compared to the original would be to use the same data set as in the base variant, with the disadvantage of having the same (lower) number of observations.
22. The estimated results are not shown here.
23. The recent and current introduction of internal rating-based approaches in banks has revealed that the risk on many lending categories has been higher than banks did realize.
24. Sweden is the most 'average' country: in the initial estimate of the base variant, its dummy coefficient came out closest to the arithmetic average of all dummies. This is not necessarily true, however, of the later variants.
25. In this and all subsequent estimates, the country dummies were also found to be jointly significant.
26. This limit is derived from an estimated critical lower limit, Dl, which is downward-distorted as the number of explanatory variables (k) increases. The usual DW tables run to $k=6$ as a maximum with a DW index of 1.57. As this model and subsequent models in this and next tables all contain considerably more than six variables and considerably more observations, we may deduce that the critical Dl is below 1.57. One alternative might be the inclusion in the model of an autoregressive term. While significant, however, this term turns out not to have any sizeable effect on the results. This conclusion holds also for the base model in Table 7.3. An alternative for an autoregressive term would be to add more lagged variables.
27. This conclusion was drawn before, on the basis of the negative effect which loans have on profits.
28. The coefficient of the interest rate differential in Column 5 appears to be negative where it was positive or zero in the earlier variants of the model. This is due to the smaller – so different – sample in Column 5 and not to the inclusion of RWAR.
29. After the level of gdp growth (and other variables) have been taken into account, as is self-evident in multiple regression analyses.
30. The same result is obtained if instead of net interest income operational profits are used, as Arpa et al. do.
31. The coefficient of net interest income in Column 3 appears to be zero where it was positive in the earlier variants of the model. This is due to the smaller – hence different – sample in Column 3 and not to the inclusion of failures.
32. It should be mentioned that in reality, capital and reserves are significantly higher than minimum capital requirements for almost all banks. As banks aim at a higher external rating than corresponding with the minimum requirements, it is actual and not regulatory capital that counts in practice.
33. Expectations of economic conditions may also be described by the included macro-economic variables.
34. Possibly, of course, the third-factor effect might be at play here, the third factor being favourable economic conditions boosting both profits and lending. This effect is, however, 'adjusted for' by the macroeconomic variables, included in model Equation (7.7).
35. That is, at the 95% level of confidence; at the 90% level, it is significant.
36. This assumption essentially argues that risk premiums are insufficient cover for the increased risk, an argument which is, in fact, supported by empirical evidence, see below.

8. Structural changes in the EU banking industry and policy recommendations

8.1 EFFECTS OF FINANCIAL INTEGRATION OBSERVED IN THE EU

This section provides an overview of the effects of economic and financial integration in the EU and the euro area on the structure of their markets and financial institutions, as observed and investigated in this book. It also presents a summary of the analyses and estimation exercises performed on competition and efficiency in the EU countries, regarding both the levels and the changes of these variables during the last decade and distinguishing various bank size groups, bank categories and product markets. The next section discusses possible policy issues raised by the observed developments and policy recommendations addressing these problems.

8.1.1 Structural Changes in the EU Banking Industry

Disintermediation

Apart from information technology and demographic factors, factors which have made particularly strong contributions to the further disintermediation of financial assets in Europe are the liberalization of the banking industry, the international integration of capital markets and the establishment of the euro. The share of financial assets of households and other sectors of the economy held by banks has fallen steadily in recent years. The introduction of the euro has led to a further increase in the diversification of investors' portfolios within and between assets classes. Other developments, plus the internationalization of financial markets, have boosted equity financing and especially bond financing tremendously, contributing to disintermediation of financial liabilities in the EU banking industry. While bank loans may have fallen as a share of total bank assets, they have nevertheless *increased* as a percentage of gross domestic product (gdp), so that banks still remain the predominant players in the euro area financial system. Banks have shifted activities from traditional bank lending towards investment banking style activities such as enhancing financial market intermediation by creating and selling new capital market products, administrating investment funds and advising clients on mergers and acquisitions. This is in turn reflected by a shift in bank revenue flows from interest income to non-interest income such as fees, commission and profit on trading activities. At least for the moment, most euro area enterprises remain by and large dependent on banks for financing.

Internationalization and consolidation

The introduction of the euro has promoted internationalization through the merging of the infrastructures for large-value payments and interbank markets, the increasing integration of capital markets and the intensification of competition. Banks have faced this challenge by working for consolidation and internationalization. Cross-border banking in the EU countries has developed through the direct provision of financial services and through the establishment of foreign branches, acquired either by international take-overs or through investments in new regions. Loans to foreign non-banks and deposits from foreign non-banks have almost doubled in the five years since 1996, whereas the market share of foreign banks has increased only slightly.

Mergers and acquisitions (M&As) have contributed to the further concentration of the EU banking industry and have resulted in a number of institutions of unprecedented size. Only a limited part of M&As has been international (22 per cent), reflecting persistent obstacles in the form of cultural and language differences, which diversification benefits were apparently unable to offset. Only a minority of M&As has been across industries (29 per cent). The volume of M&As was high in 1995 and accelerated sharply up to 1999.

Information technology

Information technology has changed banks' production and products and the size of financial markets. The Internet in particular has the potential to change radically the way banks interact with their customers and to make established markets more vulnerable to new entrants. Many banks are cautious about these developments and are opting for a multi-channel distribution strategy, combining the traditional 'bricks-and-mortar' branch network with remote distribution channels such as telephone banking and Internet banking.

Revenues, costs and competition

The net interest rate margin is not only a measure of bank profitability, but also reflects competitive conditions or efficiency, assuming that competition enforces efficiency and presses the margin down. In the EU we observe a downward trend in margins, and also in the cost-income ratio, both indeed indicating growing competition. Other sources of income, such as fees, commissions and profit on trading, grew over time for banks of all sizes, at the expense of the share of interest income, reflecting, among other things, the process of disintermediation described above.

8.1.2 Effects of Financial Integration on Competition

Panzar-Rosse approach

The ongoing, dramatic structural changes in the banking industry, particularly in Europe, are expected to affect competition, especially on local markets and for banks' retail services. Chapter 4 applies the Panzar–Rosse approach to 23 industrialized countries over a time span of more than ten years in order to obtain measures of competitive conditions (*H*-statistics) over the last decade for the entire EU, as well as for each of the countries considered. Also in Chapter 4, we attempt to take account of the geographical and product dimension of banking operations by defining three submarkets in terms of bank sizes for each country and by estimating the degree of competition for each submarket.

The resulting *H*-statistic provides strong evidence that the banking markets in the entire EU as well as in each of the examined EU countries (and, for that matter, non-EU countries) are characterized by monopolistic competition or certain forms of partial collusion. The absence of variation in the *H*-estimates across countries is remarkable. Competition appears to be stronger among large banks – operating predominantly in international markets – and weaker among small banks – operating mainly in local markets – while medium-sized banks take an intermediate position. In some countries, perfect competition has been found among large banks.

The competitive measure *H* has been modelled as time-dependent. For a number of countries, estimates of the *H*-statistic over time indicate a significant increase in competition. However, these improvements in competition appear to be only slight, that is to say smaller than expected. For most of the other countries, competition did not change over time. Decreasing competition is observed in a few countries only, and could be in part erratic. The growth of competition has been higher in EU countries than in non-EU countries such as the USA, Canada and Japan, for the all-bank sample and for small banks, but lower for large banks. The latter result is remarkable as stronger competition growth in the EU countries was expected for all bank sizes. Presumably, the rise in European competition, which had been expected especially for the years around 1997, has not yet materialized substantially or fully. Absence of a clear rise in competition was also found in the pooled EU model which, in fact, reveals a (slight but significant) fall in competitiveness.

Bresnahan's market power model

Bresnahan and Lau's model of profit-maximizing oligopoly banks enables us to estimate an alternative measure of competition. The data requirements of the model allow testing for and measuring the possible use of market power in submarkets. Chapter 5 investigates the degree of competition on both the deposit and loan markets in nine EU countries, separately as well as jointly. The results indicate a high degree of competition on either the deposit and loan markets in the nine EU countries under consideration, both separately and jointly. A hypothesis of perfect competition can be rejected for the deposit market of the 'entire' EU, for the deposit markets of Germany and Spain and for the lending markets of Germany, Portugal, Spain, Sweden and the UK. Nevertheless, these markets are characterized by high competition, as the use or abuse of market power is very limited. In the other country-market combinations, where we cannot reject perfect competition, we conclude that competition is high, leaving open the question of whether these markets face perfect competition or a kind of oligopoly with competition fairly close to perfection. The data did not contain sufficient information to estimate changes in competition over time. As the estimation results reflect the average market structure and competitive conditions over the last two decades, the general perception is that competition has increased over time. This suggests that – other caveats aside – our estimation results represent the lower limit of the current competitive situation.

This assessment of highly competitive banking markets in EU countries for deposit facilities and loans is in line with the results of the Panzar–Rosse model, which also indicate (at least) the existence of monopolistic competition for almost all European countries and cannot reject perfect competition in some countries. Generally speaking, our findings are in keeping with comparable studies in the literature, which also point to monopolistic competition in most countries. All in all, the limited increase in competition over the last decade in some EU countries and the weak evidence of such an increase in other EU countries does not fully reflect prevailing wisdom, which is that competition in the EU has increased over time. Some effects of liberalization and economic and financial integration in the EU may need more time to wear off completely.

Concentration and competition

Chapter 4 also investigates the impact of the market structure on competition. Therefore, the estimated *H*-values from the Panzar–Rosse model are used as proxies of competition and are related both to the concentration indices considered (that is, various *k* bank concentration ratios and the Herfindahl–Hirschman index) and to the absolute number of banks operating in these markets, acting together as a proxy of the market structure. The impact of both market structure measures on competition appears to be significant. This confirms the view that consolidation might impair competition. This effect is most marked when the *k* bank concentration indices are used. This latter finding corroborates the observation that a few large (cartel) banks can restrict competition and that a multitude of fringe competitors is unable to kindle competition.

8.1.3 Effects of Financial Integration on Efficiency

Chapter 6 assesses cost efficiency of the European banking industry, considering both X-efficiency, which measures managerial competence, and cost level differences across European countries, which reflect institutional and economic conditions. Furthermore, it provides sensitivity analyses with respect to bank size, bank type category and developments over time. This chapter observes that average X-inefficiency in Europe is rather high at 30 per cent, generally higher than the 20 per cent often found in the literature.[1] However, most of the earlier studies analyse only a single country, ignoring foreign best-practice banks and thereby seriously underestimating inefficiency.

Special attention is paid to differences across countries. In terms of X-efficiency, banks in Luxembourg and Switzerland are the most efficient, which however is owing at least in part to their privileged position as tax havens for foreign investors and, by implication, less to managerial ability. Compared to their banking category peers, the efficiency of German banks – dominated in numbers by cooperative and savings banks – is just above the European average. The efficiency of the – generally large – Spanish banks is also close to the European average, compared to their bank size peers. Banks in Denmark, the Netherlands, Portugal and the UK rank among the more efficient ones, whereas banks in Belgium, France, Greece and Italy are typically less efficient.

Apart from X-efficiency, a related but distinct measure of efficiency has been employed, namely the cost level, reflecting mainly institutional and economic conditions. Cost levels in Luxembourg and Switzerland, corrected for input prices and banking activities, are 20 per cent below those in Germany, the Netherlands, Portugal and the UK. Of course, many banks in the former two countries are branches of foreign banks with relatively low costs. Costs in Belgium, Denmark, France and Italy are 15 per cent higher and in Spain and Greece as much as 25 per cent and 35 per cent higher, respectively. This points up the vast spectrum of differences in institutional and economic conditions that exists among European banks. Apparently, economic and financial integration in the EU is far from completed in many areas, including supervisory regimes, government interference, customer preferences and level of development.

Estimated inefficiency appears to be depending on bank size and bank type. On average, large banks are twice as inefficient as small banks. Apparently, shortcomings in managerial ability resulting in inefficiency are manifested earlier in large financial institutions. If mergers aim to reduce inefficiency, this should be seen as a challenge rather than taken for granted. On average, cooperative and savings banks are efficient, whereas commercial banks typically are rather inefficient. Cost levels show different patterns with respect to categories, as savings and investment banks face 10 per cent and 20 per cent higher costs, respectively, than cooperative and commercial banks, whereas some specialized bank types operate 30 per cent more economically.

Differences over time appear to be vast. Inefficiencies were nearly 45 per cent lower in 1997 than in 1990, while cost levels also fell by more than 10 per cent.[2] Apparently, deregulation, liberalization and ongoing financial and monetary integration in the EU have increased competitive pressures and forced European banks to operate more economically. It is remarkable that where we could observe only slight increases in competition, improvements in efficiency have been so overwhelming. Although we have to take into account that the scales on which we measure competition and efficiency are incomparable, these results suggest that improvement of efficiency is driven by more forces than competitive pressure only.

8.2 POLICY IMPLICATIONS AND RECOMMENDATIONS

Differences across EU countries

The average levels of inefficiencies and costs of banks as estimated in Chapter 6 reveal large spreads across the EU countries. This outcome confirms the observation also made in Chapter 2 (Survey on European banking) that is that differences between countries in banking activities and market conditions are large, for instance with respect to bank market concentration, balance sheet and off-balance sheet activities (such as wholesale banking), funding and foreign activities. The international inefficiency and cost differences are due to diverging national economic and institutional conditions, such as supervisory regime, government interference, economic development, market structure, flexibility of the labour market and consumer preferences (for example, regarding type and personal attention of customer-related service), but also to managerial ability and related aspects of the organizational structure of banks. Bank conduct, too, differs across the countries, as is reflected by the varying levels of competition observed in Chapters 4 and 5.

The increased pressure for further harmonization of regulatory regimes across the EU, brought about by the establishment of EMU, has been recognized by the European Commission. The EU Financial Service Action Plan seeks to cut down remaining obstacles to cross-border competition and to finalize the integration of EU financial markets within a few years. Especially regarding the retail markets, more progress in terms of harmonization is needed in order to establish a fully integrated market. Examples of impediments are diverse consumer protection regulations; differences in the implementation of regulatory standards for the banking industry across countries; and the high cost of cross-border payments and asset transactions (EC, 2002).

In various other areas, progress on harmonization is under way. Within a few years new International Financial Reporting Standards (IFRS) will be mandatory within the EU for firms quoted on the stock exchange, levelling out existing large cross-country differences in accounting rules.[3] The new Basel Capital Accord for banks is expected to be released in mid 2004 and to enter into force by end 2006. The translation of this Accord into the EU Capital Adequacy Directive III will be released with some delay, but is also expected to come into effect by end 2006. These new regulatory regimes will provide a comprehensive new risk-sensitive and market-based minimum capital regime, which will also promote transparency and market discipline. However, the new regime will not level out all regulatory differences across countries, as it still includes a number of so-called national discretions, which may lead to (small) regulatory differences. Convergence of regulatory rules and supervisory practice should minimize potential differences between countries in order to ensure a truly level playing field for financial institutions.

Differences in the legal framework relating to taxes, pensions, businesses, bankruptcy, mortgages, shareholders, consumer protection and so on, are major hindrances for cross-border competition. Obviously, further convergence in these areas across the EU would encourage foreign activities by European banks. Differentiation between the characteristics of financial consumer products, sometimes introduced by financial firms in order to attempt to reduce competition (especially in the EU banking market where monopolistic competition prevails) may be another impediment to foreign competition. To improve competition in the pensions sector, and to enable less sophisticated customers to make a choice, authorities in the UK have developed a detailed description of a standard pension, which is now offered by almost all insurance firms. The Financial Services Authority maintains a website listing the current prices (or guaranteed returns) of these standardized pensions for all firms. Such an initiative provides an important contribution to social welfare and hence could serve as an example to several other sectors. Cross-border examples of such services – especially if covering the entire euro area – would boost cross-border activities by financial institutions.

The fact that many banks in the EU, in particular in Germany, France and Spain, are in (local) government hands may affect the overhaul of the EU financial system. Such non-profit institutions are usually established to promote consumer savings and enjoy the advantages of benefits, such as governmental guarantees. Many such banks are safe, which is good for soundness and financial stability, but not very efficient, which is unfavourable for social wealth. In some countries such banks have a dominant position in retail markets, with extended networks of branches which hinder the smooth entry of new, particularly foreign, players. Typically, such (semi-) public banks will not look for incorporated banks as merging partners or as take-over preys when attempting to achieve optimum scale or to reduce inefficiencies, nor are they in the market for takeover bids. This characteristic could limit nonincorporated but also incorporated banks in attaining their most desirable volume or efficiency level in the most cost-effective manner. Many of these banks never reach the scale at which it becomes efficient to invest in information technology – for example for the Internet. Privatization of state-owned banks could improve competition and contribute to an efficient banking system, thereby increasing prosperity, as long as a sufficient supply of retail banking services to local markets is safeguarded.

Consequences of further consolidation

Healthy competition and a sound market structure are important for social welfare, implying as they do low prices, low interest rates and adequate lending to consumers and firms, in particular small and medium-sized enterprises. The observed large spreads in estimated average inefficiency levels across the EU countries indicate that its banking industry is still wasting resources and could contribute more to the wealth of customers and shareholders. Moreover, inefficiency may impair the viability of individual banks or even a country's entire banking industry. The observed high level of competition in most banking markets coexisting with high inefficiencies raises the question whether new policies aimed at boosting banking market competition are sufficient to improve social welfare within a reasonable time span, as the theory suggests. Probably, inefficiency should also be combated more directly, for instance, where possible, through the elimination or the proper adjustment of hindering country-specific institutional conditions, as listed in the sections above.

Furthermore, the observed inefficiencies point to the fact that, apparently, the process of scaling up and rationalization – partly in preparation for increased foreign competition – has, for at least some of the banks, only just begun. Poorly managed and inefficient banks abound and are an easy prey for institutions with better-performing management, hunting for take-over game.[4] Especially in countries where banks are substantially less efficient than elsewhere, large-scale consolidation and rationalization of the banking industry will be inevitable and even necessary for the eventual improvement of both welfare and the survival prospects of banks or even the entire banking system. Meanwhile, large-scale consolidation may impair competitive conditions, as is at least suggested by Figure 2.4 and Section 4.4. Although, on average, current competitive conditions do not seem to be alarming, it should be kept in mind that they do differ sharply across product and geographical markets. As part of the customers only use traditional bank-selling channels such as branches, and small and medium-sized enterprises depend heavily on bank lending, antitrust policies should focus especially on retail markets and rural areas, sparsely populated with banks.

One often-cited motive for mergers is the reduction of interest margins and the focus on shareholder values, which have led to mergers as an instrument to reduce costs or to improve efficiency.[5] Experience with past mergers involving banks on the European continent provides very little evidence of substantial efficiency gains, mainly as a result of strong restraints on the reduction of labour costs. While one does find reductions in labour costs and costs of branches, and benefits of economies of scale, bottom line savings have been limited.[6] Apparently, mergers and acquisitions are not the most obvious ways to achieve higher efficiency. One of the reasons for this is the high cost of job cutting in many euro countries. Another is the integration costs of mergers, which – as the literature explains – are often under-estimated. The major benefits are new revenues from cross-selling products.

In certain areas such as wholesale banking where the optimal scale is huge, consolidation has taken place smoothly. In a number of wholesale business lines, only a handful of global providers has survived. Cross-sector mergers producing large financial conglomerates have also been fairly successful as they helped create new products, opened new selling channels and led to diversification of income (Bikker, 2002b, Bikker and Lelyveld, 2003). A second often-cited reason for mergers ('the formation of financial conglomerates enables firms to provide new integrated financial products and to diversify income and risk') appears to be more valuable than the first. Overall, cross-sector consolidation has been predominantly domestic. Although domestic consolidation does have its economic benefits (reduction of branch networks or strengthening the position on the home market before going abroad), it may also be driven by defensive arguments, such as the need to avoid a hostile takeover, or to strengthen market power. (Increasing market power in order to be able to gain larger margins is another frequently cited merging motive.) Such domestic mergers are often less beneficial for the public interest. Larger market power may reduce incentives to improve efficiency, consolidated banking markets may limit competition on, in particular, the local retail market while large national banks may be considered as 'too big to fail' institutions, raising moral hazard and aggravating the burden for supervisors.

The prevalence of consolidation at the national level rather than across borders could hurt competition, particularly at the retail level. Neven and von Ungern-Sternberg (1997) made clear that the concentration in the Swiss retail market following the UBS-SBC merger would not have been accepted if US antitrust standards had been applied. In Switzerland, the merge was evaluated largely on the basis of the global wholesale components of both institutions, while the effects on the retail market were disregarded. US rules would have called for a full divestiture of one of the two retail networks. This example stresses the importance of an antitrust policy that focuses on the retail market. Cruickshank (2000) found adverse concentration effects in the UK, where the largest four banks, constituting three-fourths of the retail market, showed evidence of collusive behaviour. These examples indicate that the risk of concentration and insufficient competition having unfavourable effects on the retail markets poses a real threat. In many smaller EU countries high concentration is hardly avoidable, given the current viable size for a bank. Consolidation also precludes ruinous competition and inadequate profitability (Belaisch et al., 2001). Orientation of larger banks on more profitable or bigger operations could possibly lead to reductions in bank services to smaller customers. However, Collender and Shaffer (2003) show for the USA that larger banks usually continue to devote resources to small customers, whereas other types of institutions tend to fill the gap when bigger banks abandon the retail market. To prevent collusive practises among the few remaining banks or reductions in services to smaller clients, 'free' entry of new and foreign banks should be ensured in order to keep the retail market contestable.

Stability–competition trade off

Increased competition as observed in Chapters 4 and 5 is welcomed as a major contribution to allocative efficiency and social wealth, although the main blessing of firm competition, namely high efficiency, has so far failed to materialize. The downside of (almost) perfect competition is that in the absence of market power, banks do not benefit from excess margins on prices. This might lead to lower profit rates, which could make banks more vulnerable to shocks (see also Section 2.7). Absence of excess margins on prices is exactly what we observe, although in combination with a waste of resources due to inadequate managerial abilities or unfavourable institutional and economic conditions.

The literature makes clear that concentration, increased competition and lower margins combined may indeed be liable to impair financial stability, although competition in general does not (necessarily) cause instability. It depends on specific cases and circumstances whether a change in levels of competition and concentration is associated with growing or decreasing (in)stability (Group of Ten, 2001). This outcome stresses how important it is to enable antitrust and supervisory authorities to control mergers and takeovers in the banking industry with the help of well-designed rules and powers, and to have constantly watchful supervisory authorities maintain financial stability where competition is rising or already fierce. Of course, this tradeoff should not prevent authorities from encouraging banks to improve their efficiency.

Changes in the regulatory regime

The upcoming new Basel Capital Accord and the new EU Capital Adequacy Directive are another, final factor that may affect consolidation, competition and efficiency in the banking industry. The effects are, however, extremely difficult to predict. In the near future, the – prospect of a – new regulatory regime may contribute to a further increase in scale, as large banks are in a better position to develop sophisticated risk measurement methods, such as the advanced internal rating-based approach for credit risk, have more of the scarce but necessary data on defaults available, for example, and can afford the required but expensive IT systems. (A fourth ground quoted for mergers is that new information technology has pushed up the optimal scale of banking production.)

The Basel II framework will closely parallel banks' perceptions of riskiness. It may thus increase competition in some areas, as banks will be better aware of the risks they engage in and price them more accurately, instead of relying on cross subsidizing in a looser sense, for example. It may also reduce competition, as all banks face similar conditions and need to attain certain minimum profit margins rather than striving for larger market shares. An opposite effect is the reinforcement in Basel II of supervisory discretion which may lead to a deterioration of the level playing field across countries and cripple foreign competition somewhat. Basel II may also affect the position of non-banks, which are exempt from capital requirements, and that of public sector banks which, under Basel II, will be obliged to hold capital more in line with risk levels. Transparency, the third pillar of the new accord, will enforce market discipline and thereby encourage competition and improve efficiency. Market participants will be better informed regarding the real risk of banks and this will affect their funding cost, so that the underlying risks are more adequately priced.

While individual banks may face higher or lower capital requirements, affecting their competitive positions, this may not necessarily affect overall competition, as these effects may cancel each other out. Competitive conditions for smaller banks will be less favourable, as they find it more difficult and expensive to meet the many requirements of the more advanced approaches, such as data collection and storage requirements, model building and organizational requirements. The capital requirements for credit risk under the 'simple' standardized approach are, on average, (slightly) higher than those imposed by the *foundation* internal ratings-based (IRB) approach and much higher that those imposed by the *advanced* IRB approach (although the requirements vary strongly across the type of exposure). Ongoing consolidation is likely, as the most advanced – and most effective capital-saving – techniques are accessible to only the most sophisticated banks.

Procyclicality

Under the new Basel Capital Accord, capital requirements for lending will be determined in greater measure than today by current credit risk. Many assume that during a cyclical downturn banks are less willing to lend money on account of increased credit risk, thereby reinforcing the cyclical downswing into a so-called *credit crunch*. If banks are forced to maintain larger capital buffers in such circumstances, the presumed procyclical nature of bank lending is liable to become even stronger. Analyses in Chapter 7 demonstrate how capital and reserves generally accumulate much faster during a multi-year cyclical boom than in adverse cyclical years, while at the same time, additional capital is far easier to come by during an economic boom. Surprisingly, this typical supply variable, capital and reserves, turns out to be non-significant as a determinant of lending, suggesting that credit rationing during a cyclical downturn is driven in only a minor degree, if at all, by a shortage of capital, as assumed by the *capital crunch* hypothesis. But lending *is* impacted by supply in so far as this significant determinant correlates positively to the profit margin. All in all, lending is dominated by demand.

Provisioning for (future) credit loss also turns out to depend strongly on the business cycle in the sense that provisions increase in bad times. Importantly, banks contribute significantly more to credit loss provisions in years of relatively high net profits. It appears that banks reserve more in such good years, as a precaution or, possibly, in order to present levelled-out profits. Irrespective of the underlying motives, such a provisioning policy causes the banking sector to be less procyclical than would, at first sight, seem to follow from the dependency of banks' profits on the business cycle. Prudent provisioning policies are strongly encouraged under the new Basel accord, where in the context of the Supervisory Review of Pillar II, banks need to show that they have sufficient surplus capital and provisions to continue meeting the minimum capital requirements when the business cycle deteriorates. Supervisors should stress such prudent behaviour in order to limit the risk of procyclicality.

NOTES

1. As is well known, the *level* of cost inefficiency estimates depends in part on the methodology applied, whereas the estimates may also be affected by data inaccuracy. Therefore the results should be interpreted with some caution. We use the stochastic cost frontier approach.
2. This could be almost entirely due to improvement in X-inefficiency, see Chapter 6.
3. EU Member States may make these accounting rules compulsory for all financial institutions.
4. Note that the inefficiency spreads across banks is still much wider than the reported differences across countries.

5. This section is based in part on Belaisch et al. (2001).
6. See for example Berger et al. (1999).

References

Adelman, M.A. (1951), 'The measurement of industrial concentration', *Review of Economics and Statistics* **33**, 269–296.

Adelman, M.A. (1969), 'Comment on the "H" concentration measure as a numbers equivalent', *Review of Economics and Statistics* **51**, 99–101.

Aigner, D.J., C.A.K. Lovell and P. Schmidt (1979), 'Formulation and estimation of stochastic frontier production function models', *Journal of Econometrics* **6**, 21–37.

Akhtar, M.A. (1994), *Causes and Consequences of the 1989–92 Credit Slowdown: Overview and Perspective, Studies on Causes and Consequences of the 1989–92 Credit Slowdown*, Federal Reserve Bank of New York.

Alexander, D.L. (1988), 'The oligopoly solution tested', *Economic Letters* **28**, 361–364.

Allen, F. and D. Gale (2000), *Comparing Financial Systems*, MA: MIT Press, Cambridge.

Allen, L. and A. Rai (1996), 'Operational efficiency in banking: an international comparison', *Journal of Banking & Finance* **20**, 655–672.

Altunbas, Y., P. Molyneux and R. DiSalvo (1994), 'Inefficiency in the Italian credit cooperative bank sector – a stochastic frontier analysis', *Institute of European Finance Discussion Paper.*

Altunbas Y., D. Maude and P. Molyneux (1995), 'Efficiency and mergers in the UK Retail banking market', *Institute of European Finance Working Paper*, 1–40.

Altunbas, Y., E.P.M. Gardener, P. Molyneux and B. Moore (2001), 'Efficiency in European banking', *European Economic Review* **45**, 1931–1955.

Amihud, Y., L. DeLong and A. Saunders (2002), 'The effect of cross-border bank mergers on bank risk and value', *Journal on International Money and Finance* **21**, 857–878.

Arestis, P., P.O. Demtriades and K.B. Luintel (2001), 'Financial development and economic growth: the role of stock markets', *Journal of Money, Credit and Banking* **33**, 16–41.

Arpa, M., I. Giulini, A. Ittner, and F. Pauer (2001), 'The influence of macroeconomic developments on Austrian banks: implications for banking supervision', *BIS Papers* no **1**, 91–116.

Bain, J.S. (1951), 'Relation of profit rate to industry concentration: American manufacturing 1936–40', *Quarterly Journal of Economics* **65**, 293–324.

Baltagi, B.H. (1995), *Econometric Analysis of Panel Data*, John Wiley & Sons, New York.

Baltensperger, E. and J. Dermine (1990), 'European banking: prudential and regulatory issues', in J. Dermine (ed.), *European Banking in the 1990s*, Blackwell, London.

Bangia, A.F., F. Diebold and T. Schuermann (2000), 'Rating migration and the business cycle, with applications to credit portfolio stress testing', *Working Paper*, Wharton Financial Institutions Center.

Barr, R., L.M. Seiford and T. F. Siems (1994), 'Forecasting bank failure: a non-parametric frontier estimation approach', *Recherches Economiques de Louvain* **60**, 417–429.

Battese, G.E. and T.J. Coelli (1992), 'Frontier production functions, technical efficiency and panel data: with applications to paddy farmers in India', *Journal of Productivity Analysis* **3**, 153–169.

Battese, G.E. and T.J. Coelli (1993), 'A stochastic frontier production function incorporating a model for technical inefficiency effects', *Working Papers in Econometrics and Applied Statistics* no. **69**, Department of Econometrics, University of New England, Armidale.

Battese, G.E. and T.J. Coelli (1995), 'A model for technical inefficiency effects in a stochastic frontier production function for panel data', *Empirical Economics* **20**, 325–332.

Battese, G.E. and G.S. Corra (1977), 'Estimation of a production frontier model: with application to the pastoral zone of Eastern Australia', *Australian Journal of Agricultural Economics* **21**, 169–179.

Baumol, W.J. (1977), 'On the proper cost tests for natural monopoly in a multiproduct industry', *American Economic Review* **67**, 809–822.

Baumol, W.J. (1982), 'Contestable markets: an uprising in the theory of industry structure', *American Economic Review* **72**, 1–15.

Baumol, W.J., J.C. Panzar and R.D. Willig (1982), *Contestable Markets and the Theory of Industry Structure*, Harcourt Brace Jovanovich, San Diego.

BCBS (2003), *The New Basel Capital Accord: Consultative Document,* Basel Committee on Banking Supervision, BIS, Basel, April (www.bis.org).

Beck, T., A. Demirgüç-Kunt and R. Levine (2003), 'Bank concentration and crises', *NBER Working Paper Series* **9921**, National Bureau of Economic Research, Cambridge, MA (www.nber.org/papers/w9921).

Belaisch, A., L. Kodres. J. Levy and A. Ubide (2001), 'Euro-area banking at the crossroads', *IMF Working Paper* **01/28**, Washington DC.

Berger, A.N. and D.B. Humphrey (1991), 'The dominance of inefficiencies over scale and product mix economies in banking', *Journal of Monetary Economics* **28**, 117–148.

Berger, A.N., D. Hancock and D.B. Humphrey (1993), 'Bank efficiency derived from the profit function', *Journal of Banking & Finance* **17**, 317–347.

Berger, A.N. and D.B. Humphrey (1997), 'Efficiency of financial institutions: international survey and directions for future research', *European Journal of Operational Research* **98**, 175–212.

Berger, A.N. and R. DeYoung (1997), 'Problem loans and cost efficiency in commercial banks', *Journal of Banking & Finance* **21**, 849–870.

Berger, A.N. and L.J. Mester (1997), 'Inside the black box: what explains differences in the efficiencies of financial institutions', *Journal of Banking & Finance* **21**, 895–947.

Berger, A.N. and G.F. Udell (1994), 'Do risk-based capital allocate bank credit and cause a credit crunch in the United States?', *Journal of Money, Credit and Banking* **26**, 585–628.

Berger, A., R. Demsetz and P. Strahan (1999), 'The consolidation of the financial services industry: causes, consequences and implications for the future', *Journal of Banking & Finance* **23**, 135–194.

Berk, J.M. and J.A. Bikker (1995), 'International interdependence of business cycles in manufacturing industry: the use of leading indicators for analyses and forecasting', *Journal of Forecasting* **14**, 1–23.

Berk, J.M. (1998), 'De interactie tussen financiële structuur en de conjunctuur' ('Interaction between financial structure and the business cycle'; in Dutch), *Maandschrift Economie* **62**, 79–96.

Bernanke, B. S. and C.S. Lown (1991), 'The credit crunch', *Brookings Papers on Economic Activity* **7**, 205–247.

Bernanke, B.S. and M. Gertler (1995), 'Inside the black box: the credit channel of monetary policy transmission', *Journal of Economic Prospects* **9**, 27–48.

Besanko, D. and A.V. Thakor (1993), 'Relationship banking, deposit insurance and bank portfolio', in C. Mayer and X. Vives (eds), *Capital Markets and Financial Intermediation*, Cambridge University Press, Cambridge, UK, pp. 292–318.

Bikker, J.A. (2001), 'Efficiency in the European banking industry: an exploratory analysis to rank countries', *Cahiers Economiques de Bruxelles* **172**, 3–28.

Bikker, J.A. (2002a), 'Efficiency and cost differences across countries in a unified European banking market', *Kredit und Kapital* **35**, 344–380.

Bikker, J.A. (2002b), 'Cross-sector diversification in financial conglomerates: simulations with a fair-value assets and liabilities model', *Banca Nazionale del Lavoro Quarterly Review* **55**, 363–389.

Bikker, J.A. (2003), 'Testing for imperfect competition on the EU deposit and loan markets with Bresnahan's market power model', *Kredit und Kapital* **36**, 167–212.

Bikker, J.A. and N.O. Kennedy (1999), 'Composite leading indicators of underlying inflation for seven EU countries', *Journal of Forecasting* **18**, 225–258.

Bikker, J.A. and J.M. Groeneveld (2000), 'Competition and concentration in the EU banking industry', *Kredit und Kapital* **30**, 62–98.

Bikker, J.A. and H.M. Prast (2001), 'De depositoverzekering tegen het licht' ('A close look at the deposit insurance'; in Dutch), *Economisch-Statistische Berichten* **86**, 820–822.

Bikker, J.A. and K. Haaf (2002a), 'Measures of competition and concentration in the banking industry: a review of the literature', *Economic & Financial Modelling* **9**, 53–98.

Bikker, J.A. and K. Haaf (2002b), 'Competition, concentration and their relationship: an empirical analysis of the banking industry', *Journal of Banking & Finance* **26**, 2191–2214.

Bikker, J.A. and H. Hu (2002), 'Cyclical patterns in profits, provisions and lending of banks and procyclicality of the new Basel capital requirements', *Banca Nazionale del Lavoro Quarterly Review* **55**, 143–175.

Bikker, J.A. and P.A.J. Metzemakers (2002), 'Bank provisioning behaviour and procyclicality', *Research Series Supervision* **50**, De Nederlandsche Bank, Amsterdam (www.dnb.nl).

Bikker, J.A. and P.A.J. Metzemakers (2003), 'Procycliciteit en Bazel II' ('Procyclicality and Basel II'; in Dutch), *Economisch-Statistische Berichten* 88, 396-398.

Bikker, J.A. and I.P.P. van Lelyveld (2003), 'Economic versus regulatory capital for financial conglomerates', in T.G. Kuppens, H.M. Prast and A.A.T. Wesseling (eds), *Supervision on a Cross-road*, Edward Elgar, Cheltenham, UK, and Northampton MA, USA, 169–216.

Bikker, J.A. and A.A.T. Wesseling (2003a), 'Intermediation, integration and internationalisation: a survey on banking in Europe', *Occasional Paper* no. **3**. De Nederlandsche Bank, Amsterdam, 47 pages (www.dnb.nl).

Bikker, J.A. and A.A.T. Wesseling (2003b), 'Intermediatie, integratie en internationalisering: een overzicht van het Europese bankwezen' ('Intermediation, integration and internationalisation: a survey on banking in Europe'; in Dutch), *Maandschrift Economie* **67**, 287–314.

Bisignano, J. (1992), 'Banking in the European Economic Community: structure, competition and public policy', in G.G. Kaufman (ed.), *Banking Structures in Major Countries*, Kluwer Academic Publishers, 155–244.

Blanchard, O.J. (2000), *Macroeconomics*, 2nd edition, Massachusetts Institute of Technology, Prentice Hall Int. Inc.

Boeschoten, W.C., P.J.A. van Els and J.A. Bikker (1994), 'Monetary transmission in a small open economy: the case of the Netherlands', *Research Memorandum WO&E* nr **406**, The Nederlandsche Bank, Amsterdam.

Boot, A. and A.V. Thakor (1993), 'Self-interest bank regulation', *American Economic Review,* **83**, 206–212.

Borio, C., C. Furfine and P. Lowe (2001), 'Procyclicality of the financial systems and financial stability: issues and policy options', *BIS Papers* no. **1**, 1–57.

Bos, J.W.B. (2002), *European Banking: Market Power and Efficiency*, University Press Maastricht (PhD thesis).

Bos, J.W.B. (2003), 'Improving market power tests: does it matter for the Dutch banking market?', *De Economist* (forthcoming).

Bresnahan, T.F. (1982), 'The oligopoly solution concept is identified', *Economic Letters* **10**, 87–92.

Bresnahan, T.F. (1989), 'Empirical studies of industries with market power', in R. Schmalensee and R.D. Willig (eds), *Handbook of Industrial Organisation*, Volume **II**, 1012–1055.

Bresnahan, T.F. and P.C. Reiss (1991), 'Entry and competition in concentrated markets', *Journal of Political Economy* **99**, 977–1009.

Brinkmann, E.J. and P.M. Horvitz (1995), 'Risk-based capital standards and the credit crunch', *Journal of Money, Credit, and Banking* **27**, 848–863.

Büschgen, H.E. (1993), *Bankbetriebslehre*, Gabler, Wiesbaden.

Cabral, I., F. Dierick and J. Vesala (2002), 'Banking integration in the euro area', *Occasional Paper* no. **6**, European Central Bank, Frankfurt am Main.

Calem, P.S. and G.A. Carlino (1991), 'The concentration-conduct relationship in bank deposit markets', *Review of Economics and Statistics* **73**, 268–276.

Caminal, R., J. Gual and X. Vives (1990), 'Competition in Spanish banking', in J. Dermine (ed.), *European Banking in the 1990s*, Blackwell, London.

Caminal, R. and C. Matutes (2002), 'Market power and banking failures', *International Journal of Industrial Organization* **20**, 1341–1361.

Canoy, M., M. van Dijk, J. Lemmen, R. de Mooij and J. Weigand (2001), 'Competition and stability in banking', *CPB Document no.* **15**, Central Planning Bureau (Dutch Bureau for Economic Policy Analysis), The Hague.

Carletti, E., P. Hartmann and G. Spagnolo (2002), 'Bank mergers, competition and financial stability', Mannheim University and European Central Bank, mimeo (http:/www.bis.org/cgfs/hartmann.pdf).

Carletti, E. and P. Hartmann (2002), 'Competition and stability: what is special about banking?', *Working paper* no. **146**, European Central Bank, Frankfurt am Main.

Cavello, M. and G. Majnoni (2002), 'Do banks provision for bad loans in good times? Empirical evidence and policy implications', in R. Levich, G. Majnoni and C. Reinhart (eds), *Ratings, Rating Agencies and the Global Financial System*, Kluwer Academic Publishers, Boston, Dordrecht and London.

Cecchetti, S.G. (1999), 'Legal structure, financial structure, and the monetary policy transmission mechanism', *Economic Policy Review* **5**, Federal Reserve Bank of New York, 9–28.

Cetorelli, N. (1999), 'Competitive analysis in banking: appraisal of the methodologies', *Economic Perspectives* **23**, Federal Reserve Bank of Chicago, 2–15.

Christensen, L.R., D.W. Jorgenson and L.J. Lau (1973), 'Transcendental logarithmic production frontiers', *Review of Economics and Statistics* **55**, 28–45.

Coccorese, P. (1998), 'Assessing the competitive conditions in the Italian banking system: some empirical evidence', *Banca Nazionale del Lavoro Quarterly Review* **51**, 171–191.

Coelli, T.J., D.S. Prasada Rao and G.E. Battese (1998), *An Introduction to Efficiency and Productivity Analysis*, Kluwer Academic Publishers, Boston.

Collender, R. and S. Shaffer (2003), 'Local bank office ownersip, deposit control, market structure and economic growth', *Journal of Banking & Finance* **27**, 27–57.

Cowell, F.A. (1995), *Measuring Inequality*, Phillip Allan, Oxford.

Cowling, K.G. (1976), 'On the theoretical specification of industrial structure-performance relationships', *European Economic Review* **8**, 1–14.

Cowling, K.G. and M. Waterson (1976), 'Price-cost margins and market structure', *Economica* **43**, 267–274.

Cruickshank, D. (2000), *Review of Banking Services in the UK*, UK Government (www.bankreview.org.uk).

Curry, B. and K. George (1983), Industrial concentration: a survey, *Journal of Industrial Economics* **31**, 203–255.

Danthine, J.-P., F. Giavazzi, X. Vives and E.-L. von Thadden (1999), *The Future of European Banking*, Monitoring European Integration no. 9, Centre for Economic Policy Research, London.

Davies, S.W. (1979), 'Choosing between concentration indices: the iso-concentration curve', *Economica* **46**, 67–75.

Davies, S.W. (1980), 'Measuring industrial concentration: an alternative approach', *Review of Economics and Statistics* **62**, 306–309.

DeBandt, O. and E.P. Davis (2000), 'Competition, contestability and market structure in European banking sectors on the eve of EMU', *Journal of Banking & Finance* **24**, 1045–1066.

Demirgüç-Kunt, A. and H. Huizinga (1999), 'Determinants of commercial bank interest margins and profitability: some international evidence', *World Bank Economic Review* **13,** 379–408.

Demirgüç-Kunt, A. and H. Huizinga (2001), 'Financial structure and bank profitability', in: A. Demirgüç-Kunt and R. Levine (eds), *Financial Structure and Economic Growth: A Cross-country Comparison of Banks, Markets, and Development,* MIT Press, Cambridge and London, 243–261.

De Nicolo, G. and M. Kwast (2001), 'Systemic risk and financial consolidation: are they related?', *Finance and Economics Discussion Paper* no. **2001–33**, Board of Governors of the Federal Reserve System.

Deppe, H.-D. (1978), *Bankbetriebliches Lesebuch*, C.E. Poeschel Verlag, Stuttgart.

Demsetz, H. (1973), 'Industry structure, market rivalry and public policy', *Journal of Law and Economics* **16**, 1–10.

Dermine, J. (1999), 'The economics of bank mergers in the European Union: a review of the public policy issues', *INSEAD Working Papers* **99/35**/Fin, 1–35.

Diamond, D.W. (1984), 'Financial intermediation and delegated monitoring', *Review of Economic Studies* **51**, 393–414.

Dickson, V.A. (1981), 'Conjectural variation elasticities and concentration, *Economics Letters* **7**, 281–285.

European Commission (1997), *The Single Market Review: Credit Institutions and Banking*, Subseries II: Impact on Services, volume **4**, European Commission, Brussels.

European Commission (2002), Report on EU financial integration, *Economic Papers* no. **171**, European Commission, Brussels.

European Central Bank (2002), *Report on financial structures*, European Central Bank, Frankfurt am Main.

Edwards, F. and F. Mishkin (1995), 'The decline of traditional banking: implications for financial stability and regulatory policy', *Federal Reserve Bank of New York Economic Policy Review* **1**, 7–45.

Ervin, W. and T. Wild (2001), *Capital Volatility and Pro-cyclicality in the New Accord*, Crédit Suisse First Boston.

Farrell, M.J. (1957), 'The measurement of productive efficiency', *Journal of Royal Statistical Society* **120**, sec A, 253–281.

Fase, M.M.G. (2001), 'Financial intermediation and long-run economic growth in the Netherlands between 1900 and 2000', in Klok, H., T. van Schaik and S. Smulders (eds), *Economologues, Liber Amicorum Prof. dr. Th. van de Klundert*, Katholieke Universiteit Brabant, Tilburg, 85–98.

Garcia, G. (2000), 'Deposit insurance – actual and good practices', *Occasional Paper* no. **197**, IMF, Washington DC.

Gardener, E.P.M. and P. Molyneux (1990), *Changes in Western European Banking*, Allen Unwin, London.

Gehrig, T. and G. Sheldon (1999), *Cost Competitiveness and the Changing Structure of European Banking*, Banque de France (mimeo).
Genesove, D. and W. Mullin (1998), 'Testing static oligopolistic models: conduct and cost in the sugar industry, 1890–1914', *RAND Journal of Economics* **29**, 355–377.
Gilbert, R.A. (1984), 'Bank market structure and competition – a survey', *Journal of Money, Credit, and Banking* **19**, 617–645.
Gilibert, P.L. and A. Steinherr (1989), 'The impact of financial market integration on the European banking industry', *EIB Papers* no. **8**, European Investment Bank.
Gorton, G. and R. Rosen (1994), 'Corporate control, portfolio choice, and the decline of banking', *Journal of Finance* **50**, 1377–1420.
Graddy, K. (1994), 'Testing for imperfect competition at the Fulton Fish Market', *RAND Journal of Economics* **26**, 75–92.
Greene, W.H. (2000), *Econometric Analysis,* Fourth edition, Prentice Hall, London.
Groeneveld, J.M. (1999), 'The forces behind the consolidation trend in the European banking industry', *Kredit und Kapital* **32**, 369–392.
Group of Ten (2001), *Report on Consolidation in the Financial Sector*, Working Party on Financial Sector Consolidation, BIS, IMF and OECD (www.bis.org, www.imf.org and www.oecd.org).
Gual, J. and D. Neven (1992), 'Deregulation of the European banking industry', *CEPR Discussion Paper* no. **703**, Centre for Economic Policy Research, London.
Gual, J. and D. Neven (1993), 'Banking', in 'Social europe – market services and European integration', *European Economy, Report and Study* no. **3**.
Guzman, M.G. (2000), 'The economic impact of bank structure: a review of recent literature', *Economic and Financial Review* (2nd Quarter), Federal Reserve Bank of Dallas, 11–25.
Hall, M. and N. Tideman (1967), 'Measures of concentration', *American Statistical Association Journal* **62**, 162–168.
Hannah, L. and J.A. Kay (1977), *Concentration in Modern Industry*, MacMillan Press, London.
Hart, P.E. (1975), 'Moment distribution in economics: an exposition', *The Journal of the Royal Statistical Society*, series A, **138**, 423–434.
Hasan, I., A. Lozana-Vivas and J.T. Pastor (2000), 'Cross-border performance in European banking', *Bank of Finland Discussion Papers* no. **24/2000**, Helsinki.
Hause, J.C. (1977), 'The measurement of concentrated industrial structure and the size distribution of firms', *Annals of Economic and Social Measurement* **6**, 73–107.
Hondroyiannis, G. S. Lolos and E. Papapetrou (1999), 'Assessing competitive conditions in the Greek banking system', *Journal of International Financial Markets, Institutions & Money* **9**, 377–391.

Horvarth, J. (1970), 'Suggestion for a comprehensive measure of concentration', *Southern Economic Journal* **36**, 446–452.

Hyde, C.E. and J. M. Perloff (1995), 'Can market power be estimated?', *Review of Economic Organisation* **10**, 465–485.

Iwata, G. (1974), 'Measurement of conjectural variations in oligopoly', *Econometrica* **42**, 947–966.

Jackson, P. (1999), 'Capital requirements and bank behaviour: the impact of the Basle Accord', *Basle Committee on Banking Supervision Working Papers* no **1** (www.bis.org).

Jorgenson, D.W. (1986), 'Econometric methods for modeling producer behaviour', in Z. Griliches and M.D. Intriligator (eds), *Handbook of Econometrics*, Volume **III**, Elsevier Science Publishers BV, 1842–1905.

Kashyap, A.K. and J.C. Stein (1997), 'The role of banks in monetary policy: a survey with implications for the Economic Monetary Union', *Economic Perspectives* (September-October), Federal Reserve Bank of Chicago, 2–18.

Kellerer, H. (1960), 'Zur statistischen Messung der Konzentration', in H. Arndt (ed.), 'Die Konzentration in der Wirtschaft', *Schriften des Vereins für Sozialpolitik* (N.S.) **20/I**, 41–68.

Kennedy, P. (1998), *A Guide to Econometrics* (4th ed.), Blackwell Publishers, Oxford.

King, R.G. and R. Levine (1993), 'Finance and growth: Schumpeter might be right', *Quarterly Journal of Economics* **108**, 717–737.

Kliesen, K.L. and A.J. Tatom (1992), 'The recent credit crunch: the neglected dimensions', *Federal Reserve Bank Review* nr. **5**, 18–36.

Kottmann, G. (1974), *Die Bewertung der Konzentration in der Kreditwirtschaft*, Verlag Harri Deutsch, Frankfurt and Zürich.

Kwan, S. and R. O'Toole (1997), 'Recent development in loan loss provisioning at the U.S. commercial banks', *Economic Letter*, Federal Reserve Bank of San Francisco.

Kwoka, J. (1985), 'The Herfindahl index in theory and practice', *Antitrust Bulletin* **30**, 915–947.

Lau, L.J. (1982), 'On identifying the degree of competitiveness from industry price and output data', *Economic Letters* **10**, 93–99.

Lee, L.F. (1993), 'Asymptotic distribution for the maximum likelihood estimator for a stochastic frontier model with a singular information matrix', *Econometric Theory* **9**, 413–430.

Leibenstein, H. (1966), 'Allocative efficiency versus "X-efficiency"', *American Economic Review* **56**, 392–415.

Lensing, R. and E. Sterken (2002), 'Monetary transmission and bank competition in the EMU', *Journal of Banking & Finance* **26**, 2065–2075.

Levine, R. (1997), 'Financial development and economic growth: views and agenda', *Journal of Economic Literature* **XXXV**, 688–726.

Lloyd-Williams, D.M, P. Molyneux and J. Thornton (1994), 'Market structure and performance in Spanish banking', *Journal of Banking & Finance* **18**, 433–443.

Lloyd-Williams, D.M., P. Molyneux and J. Thornton (1996), 'Competition and market contestability in Japanese commercial banking market', *Journal of Economics and Business* **48**, 33–45.

Lowe, P. (2002), *Credit Risk Measurement and Procyclicality*, Monetary and Economic Department, Bank for International Settlements, Basel.

Lown, C. and J. Wenninger (1994), 'The role of the banking system in the credit slowdown', in *Studies on causes and consequences of the 1989–92 credit slowdown*, Federal Reserve Bank of New York, 69–112.

Lozano-Vivas, A. (1998), 'Efficiency and technical changes for Spanish banks', *Applied Financial Economics* **8**, 289–300.

Marfels, C. (1971a), 'Absolute and relative measures of concentration reconsidered, *Kyklos* **24**, 753–766.

Marfels, C. (1971b), 'A guide to the literature on the measurement of industrial concentration in the post-war period', *Zeitschrift für Nationalökonomie* **31**, 483–505.

Martin, S. (1993), *Advanced Industrial Economics*, Blackwell, New York and Oxford.

Matutes, C. and X. Vives (1996), 'Competition for deposits, fragility and insurance', *Journal of Financial Intermediation* **5**, 184–216.

Matutes, C. and X. Vives (2000), 'Imperfect competition, risk taking and regulation in banking', *European Economic Review* **44**, 1–34.

Maudos, J., J.M. Pastor and L. Seranno (1999), 'Economic integration, efficiency and economic growth: the European Union experience', *Applied Economic Letters* **6**, 389–392.

Maudos, J. and J.M. Pastor (2001), 'Cost and profit efficiency in banking: an international comparison of Europe, Japan and the USA', *Applied Economic Letters* **8**, 383–387.

Maudos, J., J.M. Pastor, F. Pérez and J. Quesada (2002), 'Cost and profit efficiency in European banks', *Journal of International Financial Markets, Institutions & Money* **12**, 33–58.

Meeusen, W., and J. van den Broeck (1977), 'Efficiency estimation from Cobb–Douglas production functions with composed error', *International Economic Review* **18**, 435–444.

Mester, L.J. (1996), 'Measuring efficiency at US banks: accounting for heterogeneity is important', *Economic Research Division, Working Paper* no. **96–11**, Federal Reserve Bank of Philadelphia.

Molyneux, P., D.M. Lloyd-Williams and J. Thornton (1994), 'Competitive conditions in European banking', *Journal of Banking & Finance* **18**, 445–459.

Molyneux, P. and W. Forbes (1995), 'Market structure and performance in European banking', *Applied Economics* **27**, 155–159.

Molyneux, P., Y. Altunbas and E.P.M. Gardener (1996), *Efficiency in European Banking*, John Wiley & Sons Ltd, Chichester, England.

Molyneux, P. and E.P.M. Gardener (1997), 'Cost economies in European banking and the implications of EMU', *CEPS Business Policy Report* no. **4**, 1–14.

Nagarajan, S. and C.W. Sealey (1995), 'Forbearance, deposit insurance pricing and incentive compatible bank regulation', *Journal of Banking & Finance* **19**, 1109–1130.

Nathan, A. and E.H. Neave (1989), 'Competition and contestability in Canada's financial system: empirical results', *Canadian Journal of Economics* **22**, 576–594.

Nerlove, M. (1958), *The Dynamics of Supply; Estimation of Farmer's Responses to Price*, John Hopkins Press, Baltimore.

Neven, D. and L.-H. Röller (1995), *Competition in the European Banking Industry*, Wissenschaftszentrum Berlin.

Neven, D. and T. von Ungern-Sternberg (1998), 'The competitive impact of UBS-SBC merger', *Cahiers de Recherches Economiques* no. **9805**, Université de Lausanne.

Niehans, H. (1961), 'Round-Table-Gespräch über Messung der industriellen Konzentration', in F. Neumark (ed.), 'Die Konzentration in der Wirtschaft', *Schriften des Vereins für Sozialpolitik* (N.S) **22**, 367–395.

OECD (1998), *Bank Profitability; Financial Statements of Banks*, OECD, Paris.

OECD (1999), *Bank Profitability; Financial Statements of Banks,* OECD, Paris.

OECD (2000), Bank *Profitability; Financial Statements of Banks, OECD, Paris.*

Panzar, J.C. and J.N. Rosse (1987), 'Testing for "monopoly" equilibrium', *Journal of Industrial Economics* **35**, 443–456.

Pastor, J., F. Perez and J. Quesada (1997), 'Efficiency analysis in banking firms: an international comparison', *European Journal of Operational Research* **98**, 175–212.

Peek, J. and E. Rosengren (1995), 'The capital crunch: neither a borrower nor a lender', *Journal of Money, Credit, and Banking* **27**, 623–638.

Peltzman, S. (1977), 'The gains and losses from industrial concentration', *Journal of Law and Economics* **20**, 229–263.

Reid, G.C. (1987), *Theories of Industrial Organization*, Blackwell, New York and Oxford.

Resti, A. (1997), 'Evaluating the cost-efficiency of the Italian banking system: what can be learnt from the joint application of parametric and non-parametric techniques', *Journal of Banking & Finance* **21**, 221–250.

Ribon, S. and O. Yosha (1999), 'Financial liberalization and competition in banking: an empirical investigation', *Working Paper* no. **23–99**, Tel Aviv University, Tel Aviv.

Rime, B. (1999), 'Mesure de degré de concurrence dans le système bancaire Suisse à l'aide du modèle de Panzar et Rosse', *Revue Suisse d'Economie Politique et de Statistique* **135**, 21–40.

Rhoades, S.A. (1995), 'Market share inequality, the *HHI*, and other measures of the firm composition of a market', *Review of Industrial Organization* **10**, 657–674.

Rosenbluth, G. (1955), 'Measures of concentration', in *Business Concentration and Price Policy*, National Bureau Committee for Economic Research, Princeton, 57–99.

Rosse, J.N. and J.C. Panzar (1977), 'Chamberlin vs Robinson: an empirical study for monopoly rents', *Bell Laboratories Economic Discussion Paper.*

Ruthenberg, D. and R. Elias (1996), 'Cost economies and interest rate margins in a unified European banking market', *Journal of Economics and Business* **48**, 231–249.

Saving, T.R. (1970), 'Concentration ratios and the degree of monopoly', *International Economic Review* **11**, 139–146.

Scherer, F.M. and D. Ross (1990), *Industrial Market Structure and Economic Performance*, Houghton Mifflin, Boston.

Schmidt, P. and C.A.K. Lovell (1979), 'Estimation technique and allocative inefficiency relative to stochastic production and cost functions', *Journal of Econometrics* **9**, 343–366.

Shaffer, S. (1982), 'A non–structural test for competition in financial markets. Proceedings of a Conference on Bank Structure and Competition', *Federal Reserve Bank of Chicago*, 225–243.

Shaffer, S. (1983), 'Non–structural measures of competition', *Economic Letters* **12**, 349–353.

Shaffer, S. (1989), 'Competition in the US banking industry', *Economic Letters* **29**, 321–323.

Shaffer, S. (1992), 'Competitiveness in banking', *The New Palgrave Dictionary of Money and Finance*, Macmillan Press, London, 414–416.

Shaffer, S. (1993), 'A test of competition in Canadian banking', *Journal of Money, Credit, and Banking* **25**, 49–61.

Shaffer, S. and J. DiSalvo (1994), 'Conduct in a banking duopoly', *Journal of Banking & Finance* **18**, 1063–1082.

Shaffer, S. (2002), 'Conduct in bank monopoly', *Review of Economic Organisation* **20**, 221–238.

Sharpe, S.A. (1995), 'Bank capitalisation, regulation, and the credit crunch: a critical review of the research findings', *Finance and Economic Discussion Series* **95/20**, Board of Governors of the Federal Reserve Board, 1–23.

Smith, B.D. (1984), 'Private information, deposit interest rates and the "stability" of the banking system', *Journal of Monetary Economics* **14**, 293–317.

Spillar, P. and E. Favaro (1984), 'The effects of entry regulation on oligopolistic interaction: the Uruguayan banking sector', *RAND Journal of Economics* **15**, 244–254.

Steen, F. and K.G. Salvanes (1999), 'Testing for market power using a dynamic oligopoly model', *International Journal of Industrial Organisation* **17**, 147–177.

Stigler, G.J. (1964), 'A theory of oligopoly', *Journal of Political Economy* **72**, 44–61.

Stiglitz, J.E. and A. Weiss (1981), 'Credit rationing in markets with perfect information', *American Economic Review* **71**, 393–410.

Suominen, M. (1994), 'Measuring competition in banking: a two–product model', *Scandinavian Journal of Economics* **96**, 95–110.

Swank, J. (1994), *Bank Behaviour and Monetary Policy in the Netherlands: Theory and Evidence*, PhD thesis, Free University, Amsterdam.

Swank, J. (1995), 'Oligopoly in loan and deposit markets: an econometric application to the Netherlands', *De Economist* **143**, 353–366.

Swank, J. (1996), 'How stable is the multiproduct translog cost function? Evidence from the Dutch banking industry', *Kredit und Kapital* **29**, 153–172.

Theil, H. (1967), 'Economics and Information Theory', *Studies in Mathematical and Managerial Economics* **7**, Noord–Holland Publishing Company.

Theil, H. (1971), *Principles of Econometrics*, John Wiley & Sons, Inc., New York and London.

Tonveronachi, M. (2001), 'Structural biases in prudential regulation of banks', *Banca Nazionale del Lavoro Quarterly Review* **54**, 341–353.

Toolsema, L.A. (2002), 'Competition in the Dutch Consumer Credit Market', *Journal of Banking & Finance* **26**, 2215–2229.

Vander Vennet, R. (1997), 'EMU and Bank Consolidation', *CEPS Business Policy Report* no. **4**, 15–30.

Van der Zwet, A.M.C. (2003), 'The blurring of distinctions between different financial sectors: fact or fiction?', *Occasionnal Studies* no. **2**, De Nederlandsche Bank, Amsterdam (www.dnb.nl).

Van der Zwet, A.M.C. and J. Swank (2000), 'Financial fragility and macroeconomic performance. A comparison of emerging and highly developed countries', *DNB Staff Reports* no. **52**, De Nederlandsche Bank, Amsterdam (www.dnb.nl).

Vanthoor, W.M.F. (2002), *A Chronological History of the European Union: 1946–2001*, Edward Elgar, Cheltenham, UK.

Vesala, J. (1995), 'Testing for competition in banking: behavioral evidence from Finland', *Bank of Finland Studies,* E:1.

Vives, X. (1991), 'Banking competition and European integration', in A. Giovanni and C. Mayer (eds), *European Financial Integration*, Cambridge University Press, Cambridge.

Wagenvoort, R. and P. Schure (1999), *Economies of Scale and Efficiency in European Banking: New Evidence*, Report 99/01, European Investment Bank, 105–126.

Wagster, J. D. (1999), 'The Basle accord of 1988 and the international credit crunch of 1982–92', *Journal of Financial Services Research* **15**, 123–143.

Weiss, L.W. (1989), *Concentration and Price*, MIT Press, Cambridge MA and London.

White, A.P. (1982), 'A note on market structure measures and the characteristics of the markets that they "measure"', *Southern Economic Journal* **49**, 542–549.

Wolfram, C., 1998, *Measuring duopoly power in the British electricity spot market*, Harvard University (mimeo).

Zardkoohi, A. and D.R. Fraser (1998), 'Geographical deregulation and competition is US banking markets', *The Financial Review* **33**, 85–98.

Name index

Subject index